D0500755

FUGITIVES

FUGITIVES

A History of Nazi Mercenaries During the Cold War

• • •

DANNY ORBACH

PEGASUS BOOKS

NEW YORK LONDON

FUGITIVES

Pegasus Books, Ltd.
148 West 37th Street, 13th Floor
New York, NY 10018

Copyright © 2022 by Danny Orbach

First Pegasus Books cloth edition March 2022

Interior design by Maria Torres

ISBN: 978-1-64313-895-4

10 9 8 7 6 5 4 3 2 1

Printed in the United States of America
Distributed by Simon & Schuster
www.pegasusbooks.com

To Adi

CONTENTS

PART III: AFTERSHOCKS AND SHADOWS • 135

INTRODUCTION

There is no present, or future—only the past,
happening over and over again.

—LEON URIS, *TRINITY*

⌐⌐

THE DOWNFALL OF the Third Reich left millions of Germans habituated to serving Hitler's machine of conquest and genocide bereft of employment and of a cause to embrace. Some were professional soldiers, civil servants, and intelligence experts tainted by their association with Nazism. Others were "true believers" in Nazi ideology, members of Nazi security organizations such as the SS and the SD, or direct perpetrators of genocide and other war crimes.

Supposedly, the latter at least would face unremitting justice for their crimes, for the victorious allies had vowed to hunt them down "to the ends of the earth." In practice, no more than a handful of Nazi leaders were tried before the international tribunal at Nuremberg. Plans for thorough denazification of West German society died with a whimper as it became clear that purging West Germany of Hitler's professional soldiers and civil servants, or even Nazi party members, would make its administration prohibitively expensive.

Accordingly, the Federal Republic that rose from the ruins of the Third Reich, while vowing a clean break with Germany's Nazi past, was filled with individuals hiding awkward Nazi skeletons in their closets. Nowhere was this truer than in its intelligence services, which saw former Nazis as uniquely reliable agents in the struggle against communism—and uniquely useful, and deniable, agents of influence in the countries of the Third World.

There was no shortage of such supposedly reliable Nazi agents, as thousands of war criminals had slipped away to the four corners of the world and many others made their own arrangements with the Western allies. Contrary to the perception of former Nazis as solid anti-communists, however, many of them developed similar arrangements, and even ideological attachments, to the Soviet Union and its satellites. Others became freelance arms traffickers, spies, and covert operators, interested in nothing but financial compensation for the skills they developed under the Third Reich. Finally, some retained fantasies of future National Socialist resurgence. In fact, as will become apparent, the dividing line between pro-Western, pro-Soviet, freelance mercenaries and Nazi revanchists was often blurred, with individuals frequently working more than one angle at once, changing sides, and acting as double or even triple agents.

Ultimately, however, it was the Soviet Union that profited most from these morally compromised individuals. This was partially because they offered an opening into the inner working of the Federal Republic's innards, and partially because association with Nazi criminals posed a serious political liability for the West Germans, widely perceived as the heirs of the Third Reich. Indeed, the eventual and inevitable exposure of the extent of this association, and the extent to which it had been exploited by the Soviet Union, crippled the intelligence capabilities of West Germany against East Germany and the Soviets for decades—precisely as Moscow planned.

The hubris and self-delusion that led West Germany's political and intelligence leadership to sanction reliance on Nazi criminals echoed in many respects the fantastic self-delusions of these supposed agents of influence who dreamt of playing an independent role between the Western and Eastern Blocs. From posh German restaurants, smuggler-infested Yugoslav ports, Damascene safehouses, and fascist holdouts in Franco's Spain, Nazi die-hards created a chaotic network of influence and information. Indeed, the OTRACO Firm even fantasized of becoming the indispensable patrons of Arab revolutionaries and nationalists, funding neo-Nazi movements throughout Europe, and establishing a base for a German "national" resurgence.

To be sure, Nazi refugees and the Federal Republic officials who relied on them were not the only deluded actors. False perceptions of the reliability and influence of Nazi agents led the CIA to rely on them to create anti-communist "stay-behind" guerillas in the Soviet Union's satellite states, to be triggered when the "inevitable" WWIII broke out. And, in a very different way, the long shadows cast by the memories of WWII and the Holocaust, memories inflamed by the antics of Nazi loose cannons in the Middle East, led France and Israel to massively overreact to the involvement of German arms smugglers in Algeria and German rocket scientists in Egypt. These overreactions endangered core national interests as well as the common front against the very real, and very present, Soviet menace.

My goal in this book is to tell the story of the Nazi mercenaries in the decades following WWII, then explain the significance of the phenomenon and the ways it converged with the larger picture of the Cold War, the drama of the intra-German struggle, the Israeli-Arab conflict, and the clandestine wars of secret services. In the first part, "Downfall and Resurgence," we will follow the West German secret service from its inception as a group of mercenaries working for the United States until its heyday as the Federal Republic's sole foreign intelligence agency. We will trace the delusions of its founder, General Reinhard Gehlen, that Nazi security experts would serve him best in fighting communism and enhance his own personal career. However, by employing Nazi mercenaries and sharing their fantasies, Gehlen exposed himself to Soviet penetration and planted the seeds of his own destruction.

In the second part, "Fallout and Consequences," we will zoom out to explore worldwide covert operations. We will see how Nazi arms traffickers and free-lance spies created a worldwide gunrunning scheme, intending to exploit its earnings for political buildup and personal enrichment. Mired in fantasies of easy money and eventual National Socialist resurgence, they evoked parallel fears and illusions in France and West Germany, pushing the BND and its French counterpart, SDECE, to undermine the strategies of their own governments with reckless covert operations. The Mossad, Israel's famed intelligence agency, also joined the fray, hunting some Nazi mercenaries while utilizing others in the Israeli-Arab conflict. In the third and final part, "Aftershocks and Shadows," we will see how the Mossad, driven by irrational existential anxieties, launched a covert campaign of terror and intimidation against German rocket scientists in Egypt, thus giving rise to a near-terminal crisis between the Jewish state and West Germany. Nonetheless, the Mossad also used covert operations to resolve this conflict, with unexpected ramifications on Israel's own campaign against fugitive Nazi criminals.

• • •

THIS BOOK EXPLORES three main themes. The first is the coping and adjustment strategies of those who served the Third Reich following its downfall. Given Cold War realities, it was not possible for any but a tiny core of deluded fanatics to cling to Nazi ideology and practice *in toto*. Yet at the same time, few were able to discard Hitler's rubbish heap, and with it a dozen years or more of their life. Instead, they clung to those elements most conducive to their inclinations and sought opportunities to integrate them into the postwar world. Some chose anti-communism and sought to align themselves with the West, others chose aversion to Western democracy and aligned themselves with the East, and others focused on anti-Semitism and vowed to carry on the struggle against the Jews from foreign shores. Such choices almost always demanded compromise. Former Nazis for whom the struggle against communism was the most important goal, for example, had to embrace Western democracy. Those who wanted to continue "fighting the Jews" ended up tilting toward the Soviet Union, Hitler's most hated enemy. Many vowed to become "neutralists," playing all Cold War actors—Americans, Germans, Russians, Arabs, even Israelis—against each other to enrich themselves without committing to any. This ideological flexibility explains the presence of Nazi mercenaries in every nook and cranny of the world stage during the superpower struggle of the 1950s and 1960s.

The second theme explored in this book is the power of illusion and self-deceit. There are the delusions of the old Nazis, neo-Nazis, and admirers of the Third Reich who believed that they were in fact an independent force capable of manipulating states and the superpowers themselves in the Cold War. But the book also addresses the hobgoblins and existential terrors evoked in those facing even the mere hint of Nazi actors in their respective backyards. In the decades after 1945, the word "Nazi" had a strong influence on Cold War audiences, whether journalists, political leaders, or intelligence operatives. Due to the trauma of war and genocide, policymakers tended to assign exaggerated importance to Nazi mercenaries, thus endowing them with more power than they would have otherwise had. More than the Nazi mercenaries themselves, it was the responses they evoked from governments and secret services that truly influenced the course of the Cold War, the history of Germany, and that of the conflict between Israel and its Arab neighbors.

Finally, this book explores the inner workings of intelligence agencies and the frequent incongruence between covert operations and national policy. In the Cold War, covert action often replaced coherent political thinking and led states to international collusions and crises. We will see how German, French, and Israeli secret services undermined the policy of their own governments by colluding, dealing, and fighting with Nazi mercenaries, preventing policy makers from rationally considering their means and ends. Only when clandestine activities were closely linked with realistic and achievable political goals was their outcome ultimately fruitful.

・ ・ ・

WHEN DEALING WITH a history of intelligence operations, authors must contend with prohibitive difficulties. Most intelligence agencies' archives are classified and closed to researchers, and much of the information that is available is unreliable, based on leaks, sensational press articles, and tendentious memoirs. Until recently, researchers could reconstruct only a partial picture at best, and an inaccurate one at worst. Fortunately, in recent years many secret services have partially opened their archives. This book therefore primarily relies on documents of the American, German, and Israeli intelligence agencies, many of them newly declassified, in addition to diplomatic, political, judicial, police, and military records. In some cases, as with certain of the Mossad documents, they are published here for the first time. Writing this book would have been a much more difficult task than it had been absent the unexpected openness of the Mossad History Department, which gave me unparalleled access to hitherto classified materials. I was also pleasantly surprised by the cooperation I received from German intelligence agencies, such as the Office for the Protection of the Constitution (BfV) and the Federal Intelligence Service (BND). By contrast, the archives of Arab and Soviet secret services remain closed, and the archives of the French Intelligence Agency, SDECE, almost completely so. In such cases, I had to rely on leaked secrets, indirect testimonies, private communications, memoirs, and previous studies based on inside information, which I have assessed with the utmost caution. In the French case, a small number of documents were available. Fortunately, the Mitrokhin Archives in Cambridge also offered important, though very partial, glances into the shadowy world of Soviet intelligence. My preference has always been for primary documents over secondary descriptions in order to try and hear the voices of the actors themselves and distinguish between truth, distortion, and falsehood. When I had to choose between conflicting accounts, I preferred those testimonies that were in relative harmony with other available evidence, avoiding uncorroborated, sensational descriptions, even those that have circulated in the historical literature for decades.

I have also relied on excellent works by previous authors, among them the independent committee of historians of the BND, which published in recent years numerous books on the history of this service between 1945 and 1968, as well as experts on the history of the Mossad, the SDECE, and the KGB. I was also able to interview a handful of participants, including Rafi Eitan, the celebrated Mossad spy, a few months before his passing. Last but not least, I was fortunate to receive advice from numerous experts, historians, and investigative journalists, sometimes through long conversations that lasted deep into the night. This book could not have been written without them. The responsibility for mistakes, however, is exclusively my own.

· PART I ·

DOWNFALL AND RESURGENCE

·1·

Misery Meadows

I don't know if he is a rascal. There are few archbishops in espionage.
He's on our side and that's all that matters.

—ALLAN W. DULLES, US DIRECTOR OF CENTRAL INTELLIGENCE, 1953–1961

IT WAS APRIL 1945, and the global conflict triggered by Nazi Germany's invasion of Poland in 1939 was grinding to a halt. At one point, Hitler seemed to be on the verge of subjecting all of Europe to his murderous rule, realizing the Nazi obsession with "living space" by transforming Poland and the Soviet Union into a vast colony. His "General Plan—East" casually slated 80% of the prewar Polish population, roughly two thirds of the USSR's Slavic population, and, of course, all Jews for deportation or outright extermination. The few remaining Slavs would labor under the supervision of German colonists, providing Greater Germany with the resource base, labor force, and geographic depth required to compete with the Anglo-Saxon powers. Eastern Europe would be Germany's British Raj and America's Wild West rolled into one.[1] Instead, the cataclysmic conflict Hitler unleashed on September 1939 dragged in almost every nation on earth, killed over 50 million human beings, and transformed much of Europe into a devastated wasteland. While battle plans rarely survive contact with the enemy, the extent to which Nazi strategy had resulted in an outcome so contradictory to their aims is hard to overstate.

Rather than extinguishing the communist menace, the Second World War would lead to its explosive expansion into the power vacuum generated by the Third Reich's rise and fall. In the next five years, communist governments would come to power from the South China Sea to the Adriatic, and over the next two decades communism would make inroads in the decolonized nations of Africa, Southeast Asia, and even the Western Hemisphere. The struggle between the resurgent revolutionary ideology backed by the Soviet Union and the free-market, free-society ideology promoted by the United States would define the shape of the world to come for the next generation and a half, relegating the former established Great Powers of Western and Central Europe to the sidelines.

Rather than securing Europe to the Urals and expelling the "inferior" Slavs to Siberia, the genocidal policies of Nazi Germany had provoked the Soviets, as well as Poles, Czechs, Balts, Yugoslavs, and Hungarians, to expel over 12 million ethnic Germans from lands they had inhabited and ruled since the 13th century, pushing Germany's ethnic frontiers back to the Oder. Rather than safeguarding the imaginary "racial purity" of the German Nation, German women east of the Elbe would be subjected to repeated gang rapes, followed by mass suicide, mental and physical trauma, and many unwanted pregnancies.[2] Instead of acquiring the geographic base Hitler saw as necessary for existence as a world power, the very survival of Germany would soon depend on the largesse and commitment of the Anglo-Saxon powers, and particularly the United States.

In fact, the Soviet Union was already undertaking the first steps to install puppet governments in Poland and the Balkans—and was poised to do the same in Germany itself. A shadow government of German communists was prepared to assume power on behalf of their Soviet masters the day Berlin fell to the Red Army.

By April 1945, that day was imminent. Over two million Soviet soldiers surrounded Berlin. Between them and the Reich Chancellery stood less than 45,000 regular German soldiers collected from depleted and fragmented units, supplemented by an equal number of untrained and gray-haired Volkssturm, smooth-cheeked Hitler Youth battalions, and SS formations raised, ironically, from Baltic, Croat, and Russian volunteers who would have faced certain death at the hands of the Soviets.[3] And yet, even from the shattered ruins of his capital, Hitler continued to dream of creating an Alpine Fortress in Southern Germany and Austria where Nazi loyalists would endure, and from which they would reclaim a National Socialist Germany when the inevitable conflict between the USSR and the Western allies broke out.[4]

General Reinhard Gehlen, a senior intelligence analyst tasked with preparing this "Alpine Redoubt," had other plans in mind. The slim, steely-eyed officer was also concerned with survival—not of National Socialism, but the survival of his person, personal power, and nation, in that order. The son of a publisher, hardly the stereotypical monocle-twirling Prussian general staff material, Gehlen had clawed his way into the shrunken post-Versailles army in 1920. In the aftermath of Hitler's rise to power and the rapid expansion of the Wehrmacht, he was able to secure an appointment in the general staff, where his career rapidly took off.[5] Gehlen had no intention of jettisoning his hard-won gains just because the regime he had served and his very nation were facing extinction.

To that purpose, Gehlen gathered a group of like-minded officers in an isolated hideaway near the border between Bavaria and Austria, both part of the Great German Reich. A mountainous road twisted amidst the Bavarian Alps into an isolated green field adorned with scattered wild alpine flowers. Misery Meadows (Elendalm), an adjoining wooden chalet, was frequented only by a few gamekeepers and vacationers. There, Gehlen and his confederates prepared for the downfall and its aftermath. Gehlen remembered that modest hut with fondness. "Life in the free nature," he wrote, "was truly enchanting."[6] Indeed, Misery Meadows was a charming place. Outside the window, a waterfall cascaded into a clear brook and the snowcapped peaks of the Alps offered breathtaking vistas from beyond the trees.

Inside the wooden confines of his chalet, Gehlen must have reflected on the grim fortune of the country that he had loyally served over the past six years, and perhaps also on his own role in the looming disaster. Around him, the formerly formidable German Reich was crumbling, its armies beaten, its cities smoking ruins, and its leaders seeking refuge underground. Yet the idyllic surroundings offered the opportunity for redemption of a sort, a chance to conveniently forget the sins of the past and dream of a new life. And Gehlen, former commander of Fremde Heere Ost (Foreign Armies East), an agency responsible for intelligence analysis on the Eastern Front, had much he no doubt wished to forget, and wished even more for others, particularly the Western allies, to overlook.

Gehlen's agency had played a central role in analyzing the ethnic, political, and military vulnerabilities of the USSR prior to the launch of Operation Barbarossa, the German invasion into the Soviet Union, and thereby in setting the stage for the deaths of tens of millions of civilians in the ensuing genocidal conflict, as well as the far more extreme aims of Generalplan Ost (General Plan—East). Nonetheless, he was no Nazi ideologue. As head of the Fremde Heere Ost, he disregarded Nazi racial theories and supported the recruitment of intelligence assets and collaborators from amongst the USSR's many disgruntled nations and ethnicities, assets that he fully intended to exploit even now, though not in the manner his Nazi political masters had intended. Gehlen had foreseen the fall of the Third Reich years earlier and prepared for the occasion, yet he had not taken any risks to advance its fall and save his nation from its consequences. True, he had turned a blind eye to the July 1944 plot to assassinate Hitler and infuriated the Führer with pessimistic military reports, but he had avoided sticking his neck out sufficiently to be garroted by a piano wire, as the handful of brave plotters were.[7] Gehlen, though he viewed himself as a German patriot, was above all else a survivor and a careerist, and he had every intention of surviving, and even thriving, amongst the downfall. Rather than keep low and hide from the victorious allies, Gehlen and his closest aides intended to exploit the Western allies to rebuild their own private intelligence empire from the ashes of the Third Reich. This plot would have ramifications far beyond what any of the conspirators could foresee.

Gehlen's timing was fortunate. Hitler shot himself one day after Gehlen reached Misery Meadows. With the Führer's death, the Nazi plan to make a "last stand" in the Bavarian Alps all but evaporated. Gehlen, whom Hitler had tasked with assuming a position in the command structure of the Alpine Redoubt, cared little for fantasies of National Socialist resurgence. Looking ahead, he plotted to ally with the Americans and amass political power in the "new Germany" that would inevitably rise from the Third Reich's ashes. In order to do so, he carefully prepared a valuable bargaining chip. His top-secret archive on the Red Army was photocopied into microfilms and carefully stored in water-resistant crates. These were cached around Misery Meadows and several other locations. Gehlen hoped to offer his would-be American captors a deal: invaluable intelligence on the Soviet Union and partly extant networks of agents in return for his freedom, the freedom of his closest coworkers, and a revival of his career as an intelligence specialist under the supervision of Washington.[8]

Gehlen's bold scheme was based on assumptions not unlike those of the National Socialist leadership that had sent him to the fantastical Alpine Redoubt. Dreaming in the gloom of Hitler's bunker, even as the Red Army prepared for the storming of Festung Berlin (Berlin Fortress), the Führer, Propaganda Minister Joseph Goebbels, and others gleefully reflected on the growing chasm between the Soviets and the Western powers. They had hoped, right up to the suicide of Hitler and his closest confederates, that at the last moment the Americans would turn their guns on the Soviets and the Reich would be saved.

Such fantasies were reinforced by Gehlen himself in his capacity as an intelligence analyst. "It is clear for the political leadership [in Moscow] that only the German Reich can offer military and political resistance to the Soviet claim to Europe. [The Reich] can be militarily valuable for the British and the Americans in keeping Bolshevik imperialism away from Europe."[9] With such words, Gehlen only fed the pipe dreams of his superiors with soothing opium as the Soviets, the British, and the Americans remained united in their original goal of crushing Nazi Germany. As a state, the Reich was doomed. So, too, were its leaders.

Nevertheless, what Gehlen *did* understand were the implications of the growing discord between the allies on the future of individual German officers, especially himself. Nobody could guarantee that the suspicions between the Soviets and the Americans would lead to a new war, cold or otherwise. But what was almost certain, and here Gehlen foresaw the future with impressive accuracy, was that the Americans would need information on the Soviets. And as a former intelligence chief at the Eastern Front, this was precisely the commodity he was poised to deliver.

But in the chaotic days of spring 1945, the plan was a dangerous gamble at best. Gehlen surely knew that to Nazi eyes, his scheme was nothing but high treason, and the way to Misery Meadows was fraught with peril. SS teams patrolled the roads, arresting and executing deserters on the slightest suspicion. Such trigger-happy zealots could easily condemn him and his officers to an untimely death.[10] Furthermore, he could not be certain that the Americans would value his "treasure" or give him anything in return. Indeed, he and his associates might well end up in an anonymous POW camp or, even worse, be handed over to the Soviets.

In the days following Germany's surrender, Gehlen and his companions expected American GIs to appear at their doorstep. Instead, they were surprised to find themselves ignored. Confounded, they left their mountain hideout to celebrate Pentecost with the parents of a war comrade near Lake Schliersee. After two days of joyful festivities in the country, they gave themselves up to the nearest US command post in Fischhausen. Gehlen was naïvely certain his importance was so great that the Americans would treat him with great respect, even reverence. Gerhard Wessel, his wartime deputy who accompanied him to the Bavarian Mountains following Germany's surrender, assured him that the U.S. Army treated enemy generals well. Instead, Gehlen was arrested and immediately placed in a POW "cage" in Miesbach, Bavaria, overcrowded with captive German officers. He and his companions could not speak English and found it difficult to communicate with their captors, who likewise did not speak a word of German.

Overblown with self-importance and frustration, Gehlen declared to his first interrogator, a junior CIC (Counterintelligence Corps) officer, that "I am a general and the chief of the Intelligence Department of the High Command of the German Army. I have information of the highest importance for your supreme commander and the American government, and I must be taken immediately to a senior commander." The young officer's answer was sobering. "You *were* a general—you *were*, sir. And please don't tell me what I have to do."[11] Indeed, the hands of the CIC were full with many captive German officers who lied about their past to overblow their importance, conceal their crimes, or save their skins. Accordingly, the young officer interrogated Gehlen only on conditions in Nazi Germany without displaying much interest in his knowledge of the Soviet Union. After a brief talk, he ordered him back into the cage.

Subsequently, Gehlen was transferred between several POW camps. Unbeknownst to him, reports on his capture percolated up the hierarchy of US intelligence throughout July 1945, and he was eventually transferred to a villa in Wiesbaden appropriated for interrogation of high-profile German prisoners. There, Gehlen's fortune immediately turned upon meeting Captain John Boker from G-2, the Intelligence Department of the U.S. Army. In contrast to previous interrogators, Boker displayed a friendly demeanor toward Gehlen and invited him for an informal chat on a garden bench next to the villa.[12]

Captain Boker was fluent in German and had some knowledge of the Soviet Union, so he immediately understood he had landed a prime catch. His superior, General Edwin L. Sibert, the G-2 commander of the 12th Army Group, differed from the majority of American officers who still saw the Soviets as allies. Just like the famed George Patton, he perceived the Soviets as a clear and present threat. In the two years that followed the capitulation of Germany, the conflicts between the Americans and the Soviets, the erstwhile victors of WWII, escalated in both scope and nature. Soviet measures to install communist puppet governments in the East European states they had occupied during the war, as well as Stalin's aspirations in Iran, Turkey, and Greece, pushed the two powers apart with alarming speed. The Americans had intelligence on the Red Army but felt they needed more, and Gehlen's secret archive was a welcome addition.[13]

Notwithstanding his original intentions, Gehlen could not force any "deal" on the Americans. As a prisoner of war, he was fully at their mercy. Fully cognizant of his precarious situation, Gehlen provided Sibert with the location of the secret archive without asking for anything in return. Sibert, in turn, brought some of Gehlen's wartime colleagues to Wiesbaden from various POW camps and allowed them to write reports on the history of their intelligence service.[14]

On August 21, 1945, the Pentagon accepted Boker's and Sibert's suggestion to evacuate Gehlen's secret archive to Washington for careful evaluation and analysis. Furthermore, after some persuasion, Boker was able to obtain permission for Gehlen and six of his closest advisers to fly along with the documents, with himself as their guard and companion. The Germans received a hiatus of three days to purchase civilian clothes and collect their personal effects. One of them who could not find a suitcase carried his belongings in a big violin case, imbuing the assembled Wehrmacht officers with the appearance of an entertainment troupe. General Walter Bedell Smith, the 12th Army Group chief of staff and future CIA director, allowed them to use his personal airplane.

Gehlen and his colleagues, still fully convinced of their own importance, expected a friendly reception, if not a red carpet, in the capital of the United States. During the journey, their American guards did everything to remind them they were still prisoners of war. They were not permitted to leave the plane during stopovers to avoid drawing unwanted attention. When they finally arrived in Washington, D.C., no senior officer received them at the airport. Instead, they had to undergo a medical inspection and were hauled to a windowless prison vehicle that waited nearby. To his grave disappointment, Boker could not help them or ease their terms of imprisonment. To the Pentagon officials in Washington, Boker was no more than an anonymous intelligence officer from Europe.[15]

For the next two months, Gehlen and his advisers were locked in isolated cells in Fort Hunt, Virginia. The conditions were relatively comfortable, but still prison-like. According to Gehlen, the "unfriendly" commandant did everything possible to prevent them from contacting the Pentagon until an unlikely ally came to the rescue. Captain Eric Waldman, an American Jew of Viennese descent, was the intelligence officer tasked by the Pentagon to work with Gehlen and his team. Though he had lost family members in the Holocaust, Waldman regarded the Soviets as the enemy of the future and was more than willing to collaborate with Wehrmacht officers. Gehlen, who was never an anti-Semite, remembered Waldman as "reliable and warmhearted," and instinctively understood that he had to cultivate the latter's trust. Suspecting, for example, that their cells were bugged, Gehlen warned his colleagues that anti-Semitic utterances were out of bounds. When one of them called Waldman "a Jewish swine" in private conversation, Gehlen expelled him from the group. For his part, Waldman took care to help Gehlen's family in Germany and was later one of the strongest American advocates of cooperation with the former Wehrmacht general and his team.[16]

Notwithstanding the harsh conditions, Gehlen and his men worked diligently, and by mid-November 1945 had produced a tome of 716 pages on their operations in the Eastern Front and on the Red Army. Grateful for their contribution, Waldman was able to secure better lodging conditions in secluded forest cabins and even arranged shopping and sightseeing trips in Washington for his prisoners.[17]

For a while, Gehlen and some of his associates considered applying for US citizenship and fighting communism from Washington, much like German scientists such as Wernher von Braun. Only after the Americans decided that their new collaborators would be more useful in Europe did the idea of an independent German secret service under American tutelage take shape. In June 1946, Gehlen and his companions returned to Germany along with Waldman and established, under various aliases, the group eventually known as the "Gehlen Org," first in Camp King in Oberursel, near Frankfurt, then in the Kransberg Castle, a picturesque fort in the Taunus Mountains, and finally in Pullach, a village near Munich.[18] But much to Gehlen's annoyance, his American superiors were also working with a competing espionage racket led by one of his rivals, Hermann Baun.

A former military field intelligence expert, the Americans recognized Baun as a brilliant intelligence gatherer and a well-known expert on the Red Army. His life was admittedly tragic. In the final days of the war he lost his entire family in an air raid and became a workaholic chain-smoker with a short temper and a fervent anti-communist obsession.[19] In 1946 and 1947, the Americans divided the work between Gehlen and Baun, their two protégées. High in the mountains in a lodge known as the "Blue House," Baun weaved networks of espionage in the Soviet zone of occupation and oversaw the establishment of SIGINT (Signal Intelligence) facilities designed to eavesdrop on the Red Army. Concurrently, Gehlen was tasked with analysis of the raw intelligence obtained by Baun.[20]

However, Gehlen's relations with Baun soon soured as each man tried to grab power from the other. The officers of G-2 (U.S. military intelligence) were initially undecided, but finally understood they had to choose between their protégées. Gehlen and his right-hand man, Gerhard Wessel, did all they could to portray Baun to the Americans as an anti-Semitic eccentric, an accusation they intuited would be ruinous, perhaps based on vestigial Nazi fantasies regarding the influence of "Jewish power" on their former foes. Baun was a competent professional but "did not trust Jews" and had a narrow education. He was, they charged, subject to the unhealthy influence of his new young wife, and was mentally unstable, an image that Baun's behavior gradually justified.[21]

Baun had stupefied the Americans with his eccentric behavior, stashing a suitcase stuffed with US dollars under his bed and threatening another officer with whom he had a romantic dispute. Even worse, oblivious to the limits of his power, Baun drafted a plan for an international network of espionage all over communist Eastern Europe, the Balkans, and the Middle East. G-2, however, needed limited intelligence on the Red Army in Germany and had no interest in elevating their former German enemies to global importance or preserving their Nazi-era networks of influence.[22] Eventually, the Americans preferred the more down-to-earth Gehlen over the presumptuous Baun, who was pushed aside to positions of secondary importance. With Waldman's blessing, Gehlen took over Baun's espionage networks and SIGINT stations. Baun would assume an important role later, however, as he would lead the Org's penetration into dangerous foreign arenas such as the Middle East.[23]

Over the next nine years, the Gehlen Org would contend with yet other German intelligence organizations and slowly evolve into the secret service of the nascent Federal Republic of Germany. Though many US intelligence officers had misgivings, Gehlen became a major partner of the American intelligence community in Central Europe. So were the seeds of the entry of former Nazi intelligence operatives into the superpower struggle sown. But to understand how this additional shadow layer of Cold War espionage shaped the struggle, it is necessary to introduce several additional players.

Out of the Rubbish Heap—
Nazi Mercenaries After the Downfall

For those in combat gear, and we who impinge,
whether by action or agreement subliminal,
are thrust, muttering "necessity" . . .
into the realm of the war criminal.

—NATHAN ALTERMAN, "ABOUT THIS"[1]

IN LATE APRIL 1945, as Gehlen and his associates buried their treasure in Misery Meadows, a junior American officer drove through the same mountainous roads with a small detachment of infantry troops. At 28, James H. Critchfield was one of the youngest colonels in the U.S. Army, tasked with leading a forward force toward the Alpine Redoubt. On the 29th, he and his men suddenly stumbled upon a German cargo train near the village of Hurlach. They stopped it with some warning shots, and a handful of SS guards jumped down and disappeared in the woods. "Infantrymen riding atop the lead tanks broke open the doors of the boxcars," Critchfield recalled, "and a ghastly cargo of emaciated human beings wearing soiled black and white . . . spilled out into the arms of the stunned American soldiers. At first glance the prisoners seemed more dead than alive. Virtually all of them simply collapsed to the ground."[2] In his memoirs, Critchfield described with genuine horror this first encounter with the National Socialist system of terror and murder. Later, as a senior CIA officer, he saw himself as a devoted enemy of totalitarian dictatorship and a fighter for his country's values of democracy, with considerable sympathy to the plight of the Jews and other victims of the Third Reich.[3] And yet, it was the same Critchfield who played a crucial role in cementing the American collaboration with the Gehlen Org as well as notorious Nazi criminals.

Reinhard Gehlen and his friends were far from the only Nazi officials employed by the US intelligence community. Nor were they the worst. Like many German officers on the Eastern Front, they were implicated in war crimes because they supplied the SS murderers with intelligence that eased their task, but they weren't initiators or direct perpetrators. However, as later investigations revealed, much more nefarious culprits were on the American payroll and their employment involved a great deal of cynicism.

Klaus Barbie is a case in point. A former Gestapo chief in Lyon, he was one of the most notorious secret policemen of occupied France, directly responsible for the execution and sadistic torture of thousands of men, women, and children. In the immediate postwar period, the so-called "Butcher of Lyon" was not only left unpunished, he was employed as a spy by the U.S. Army Counterintelligence Corps (CIC)—the very same authority responsible for hunting Nazi criminals. When Barbie's position finally became untenable, he was whisked away by US intelligence to South America where he returned to his old habits, this time as a security adviser to local dictators.[4]

Barbie was not alone. The CIC employed a dozen SS and Gestapo officials, some of them responsible for large massacres.[5] At the same time, the Truman administration imported German scientists, among them beneficiaries of Nazi slave labor, to the United States. Money counterfeiters who forged currency for SS intelligence were eagerly sought by the Americans as well as all other Cold War powers to work in similar pursuits for their secret services. The CIA, established in 1947, quickly joined the fray. It hired Nazis and other Holocaust perpetrators—Germans, Russians, and Ukrainians—as spies and covert operators in frontier zones as well as within the territory of the USSR and its satellite states. Others were asked to form "stay behind networks" charged with organizing guerilla warfare in case of a Soviet offensive.[6]

It all began on a relatively small scale. On May 10, 1945, the Joint Chiefs of Staff ordered General Eisenhower, commander of the US Forces in the

European Theater, to arrest all Nazi war criminals with the exception of those who could be used for intelligence or other military purposes. "Exception" was the keyword here. According to standing orders, the CIC should prefer German agents "whose ideals conformed to those of the United States" and eschew those still engaged in criminality or with stained pasts that could be discovered and embarrass Washington.[7] American intelligence officials responsible for the recruitment of war crime suspects fully recognized that such a practice was shameful and could be embarrassing (and fodder for Soviet propaganda) if discovered. The more prominent a Nazi was, the graver his crimes, and the risk of exposure and public humiliation was heightened. It was also dangerous to employ veterans of Nazi security organizations such as the SS, SD, or Gestapo, who were themselves a threat to the American occupation regime or to the newly established democracy in West Germany. As a result, employment of such people was always deemed problematic, an exception to be allowed only if absolutely necessary.[8]

As a result of such conflicting pressures, war crime suspects remained a tiny percentage of the thousands of Germans employed by US intelligence agencies (in the CIC's case, later investigations named twenty-four such individuals), and they were subject to a complicated vetting system before being hired. This system, however, did not always work well, and local commanders were often free to choose which SS, Gestapo, or SD agent qualified as an "exception."[9]

Nevertheless, the scope of such exceptions expanded gradually according to changing threat perceptions. Indeed, the security of the occupation remained the biggest worry for the allies. In 1945 and early 1946, the US occupation army in Germany still saw Nazis and neo-Nazis, especially the fabled guerillas known as Werewolves, as the main threat in the occupied zone.[10] In the seven months after Germany's surrender, the CIC arrested 120,000 Germans for war crimes and Nazi or neo-Nazi activity. Some of those were in the "automatic arrest" categories, including senior army officers and members of Reich security organizations such as the SS, SD, or Gestapo. Many were suspected of war crimes, but others were merely dejected youngsters who organized impromptu gangs, minor officials in Nazi organizations, or citizens apprehended due to hearsay, rumors, and false accusations. During these early months, the CIC employed a large number of German communist informers and, in one case, even shared office space with a local communist party.[11]

There were significant restrictions on the employment of Nazis, mainly because they were seen as the biggest danger for the Allied occupation. A counterintelligence officer in Munich complained in late August that "the proscribed list of persons had grown so large that no former member of the Nazi party or Army officer, to say nothing of GIS [German Intelligence Service] personnel, can be hired." He warned that such a policy threatened to drive army veterans into neo-Nazi organizations.[12]

Things were already changing in autumn 1945 as communists gradually replaced Nazis as the major threat in Germany and throughout the European theater.[13] In the winter and spring of 1946, relations between the United States and the Soviet Union began to sour due to conflicts on the postwar fate of Germany, Poland, and other countries. Speaking before Congress in March 1947, President Harry Truman pledged assistance to all free nations threatened by totalitarian encroachment. Truman's military chiefs, greatly overestimating the battle readiness of the Soviet Union, feared an imminent all-out attack on Western Europe. Such fears grew significantly with every instance of communist aggression: The Soviet takeover of Czechoslovakia and blockade of Berlin in 1948, Moscow's first nuclear experiment in 1949, and the North Korean invasion of South Korea in 1950. In order to be able to contain a Soviet military offensive, the commanders of the U.S. Army needed not only military force—and they believed theirs was terribly inadequate—but also intelligence on Soviet intentions, capabilities, and the Red Army's order of battle.[14]

Though the US had intelligence on the Soviet Union, what it lacked was a glimpse into the depths of Russia and its satellite states, which would be required in order to obtain early warnings of an invasion. With a limited ability to collect information through SIGINT (Signal Intelligence—intercepting conversations and reading cyphered messages) at least until the mid-1950s, the Americans had to rely on human sources, including spies, but closed societies such as the Soviet Union are much less vulnerable to espionage than democracies.[15] In order to gather adequate information, it was reasonable to employ agents with the right experience and linguistic capabilities. Many suitable candidates belonged to specific categories implicated in war crimes: Soviet citizens who collaborated with Germany, or Nazi intelligence experts who fought the Soviets in the recent past. In other words, hiring at least some war criminals was seen as a defensive response to an urgent military threat.[16]

Gradually, the problem of trying Nazi criminals was deemed an issue of the past, not of the present, and partly given over to lenient German courts in March 1946. Some CIC officials still hunted suspected Nazi war criminals for a few more years, but starting in 1948, the Americans began to treat their prisoners with greater caution, and even amended harsh sentences given in previous war crime trials.[17] The need to placate the West German population and the Wehrmacht Officer Corps, necessary allies in the fight against communism, was seen as more important than settling past accounts or doing justice to victims of the Third Reich.[18] At the same time, an increasing number of CIC teams hunted communists instead of Nazis. In this task, Hitler's former security officials could also be useful. After all, they knew a lot about the "Reds" and were vehemently anti-communist, weren't they? At the same time, the CIC feared embittered Nazis would find their way into the communist underground.[19]

Terrible as it sounds, this American perception was not completely devoid of merit. Compared with the threat of a Soviet invasion to West Germany, assisted by a communist fifth column from within, the chances of a Nazi resurgence were slim to nonexistent. The defeat of Nazi Germany was so shattering that for most of Hitler's fellow travelers, and even for many ideological Nazis, it was clear that in order to preserve Germany they had to change their worldview, strategy, and politics in substantial ways. Even a convinced Nazi such as Grand Admiral Karl Dönitz, Hitler's loyal lieutenant and successor as leader of the Third Reich, admitted that only certain aspects of National Socialism could be preserved.[20] For more realistic people, it was clear that most elements of the previous regime's ideology would have to be discarded. Every former Nazi who wanted to preserve something from the heap of rubbish left by Hitler had to choose carefully and with great discretion.

Conforming to American expectations, many former Nazi officials picked anti-communism out of the rubbish heap and were fully ready to discard the rest. In order to protect Germany from the hated Bolshevik enemy, they agreed to do away with Hitler's anti-Westernism and his aversion to democracy, as well as with anti-Semitism and racial theory as organizing principles of the state. For them, serving an anti-communist, democratic, and pro-Western country was the best choice, or at least the lesser evil in postwar circumstances.[21] This choice, made by millions of low- and medium-level former Nazis, gave the nascent West German state, the Federal Republic of Germany, much required vitality and stability. For precisely that reason, countless former Nazis who staffed the West German bureaucracy did not try to undermine the state or to pursue a Nazi policy, with the important exception of protecting war criminals from legal persecution.

However, the Americans made a crucial mistake in believing that all former Nazi collaborators picked anti-communism out of the rubbish heap. Some made different choices, or at least defined "anti-communism" more broadly than the Americans. In the early 1950s, US authorities discovered, to their horror, that one of their "stay behind networks," a group known as the League of Young Germans, plotted the murder of Social-Democratic politicians in West Germany.[22] For others, anti-communism was less attractive than other ideas of the old regime. Some hated Western democracies far more than the Soviet Union and were therefore ready to serve as Russian agents. Certain SS veterans believed German independence from both East and West, a popular idea in some Third Reich circles, was the element to keep. Such people, known at the time as "neutralists," were often attracted to the emerging countries of the Third World. Yet others valued anti-Semitism more than anything else and directed their hatred to the Jewish State of Israel, established in 1948. Naturally, they too became anti-Western, pro-Arab, and gradually pro-Soviet.

In other cases, US intelligence officials learned that many of their German partners did not care about anti-communism at all. Some former Nazis, indeed, chose to pick nothing out of Hitler's rubbish heap. Cynical, war-shocked, and alienated from both East and West, they became greedy adventurers and professional con men. German and Austrian cities, most notably Berlin and Vienna, were filled to the brim with such intelligence peddlers who sold their services for cash and other benefits.[23]

The best known of these is probably Wilhelm Höttl, a former SD officer hired as an intelligence contractor by the Americans in Austria. Höttl, a charming and sophisticated agent, had much blood on his hands. As the senior representative of SS intelligence in Hungary, he was deeply implicated, along with the notorious Adolf Eichmann, in the extermination of that country's Jewry. In the Nuremberg trials, however, he testified against Eichmann, and was probably the first to estimate that six million Jews were murdered by the Nazis. He also served as an informant to the Jewish Nazi hunter Simon Wiesenthal.[24]

Höttl offered the Americans two ready-made intelligence networks, code-named Montgomery and Mt. Vernon. In fact, as the Austrian police noted, he was an intelligence peddler eager to work for anyone who paid. He worked for every conceivable intelligence service, including the Yugoslavian UDBA, French SDECE, the Soviet MGB (Ministry of State Security, predecessor of the more famous KGB), Arab agencies, and Jewish organizations. Höttl's agents were former security officials of the Third Reich, Hitler Youth veterans, and Hungarian fascists. They supplied intelligence on communist installations in Austria and Hungary and formed stay-behind networks to prepare for a Soviet invasion. In September 1949, the CIC dropped him because his continued involvement in neo-Nazi activity embarrassed the United States and created political difficulties in Austria.[25] Höttl's intelligence might not have been complete trash, as assumed by some scholars, but it was certainly low-grade. People such as Höttl, whether SS veterans or pro-Nazi Slavic émigrés, had a vested interest to produce alarmist intelligence, emphasizing hostile Soviet intentions and the imminent danger of war in order to justify their existence and earn more money for their efforts. At least some of their information, for example, a detailed report by a Russian activist on an impending Soviet invasion of Iran, was invented out of thin air.[26]

The American intelligence community was a hodgepodge of many autonomous agencies that often jealously guarded their secrets and refused to share them with rival organizations. That created compartmentalization, which somewhat improved security but also gave rise to problems in intelligence assessment. American operators, many of them inexperienced amateurs and autodidacts, lacked the necessary background in German, Eastern European, and Soviet affairs. More often than not, they did not know the relevant languages and could not always juxtapose their information with that of rival agencies. Hence, they became dependent on the translation and evaluation of their unreliable assets. Even when exposed and removed, intelligence peddlers such as Höttl could offer their services to another agency in the heterogenous US intelligence community. Others maneuvered between American, British, French, West German, East German, Soviet, and, later, Arab and Israeli secret services and sold dubious information at inflated prices.[27]

Even the Gehlen Org, whose leaders were ideal "anti-communists" as far as the Americans were concerned, was not immune to these problems. The Org rapidly grew into an unwieldly monster, hardly controlled by Gehlen himself, let alone by the Americans. Recruiting its personnel through wartime networks of military, security, and intelligence organizations, it employed numerous agents and sub-agents of all problematic stripes, not only war criminals, but also Soviet moles, adventurers, and charlatans.[28] This chaotic recruitment policy had sown the seeds for future disaster, but that would not be clear until much later.

· 3 ·

Beggars and Choosers— Gehlen and the CIA

The deadliest venom to a man's morality is confined within the following words: "here it's permitted."

—ZE'EV JABOTINSKY

ON NOVEMBER 18, 1948, three years after his firsthand encounter with concentration camp survivors in the Bavarian countryside, Colonel James H. Critchfield drove his black Chevrolet into the tranquil village of Pullach, south of Munich. He was no longer in uniform and led no troops, having recently retired from the army and joined the newly established Central Intelligence Agency. The young officer who had rescued the ghastly victims of the Nazi regime in the final stage of the Second World War was now headed, on that cloudy autumn day, to a top-secret mission at a heavily guarded compound in the outskirts of the village where he would meet with the former servants of the Nazi regime. This cluster of buildings, now called Camp Nikolaus, had once been a retreat for Nazi officials, with villas and gardens protected by security facilities and surrounding walls. Within the perimeter, an elegant residence known as the White House overlooked a fountain and several additional staff buildings. Critchfield parked his old car in front of the house, taking note of the stars and stripes banner fluttering over the green lawn.

On the steps of the White House, the CIA agent was greeted by a German in a dark gray suit who presented himself as "Dr. Schneider." Years later, Critchfield recalled that his interlocutor was "a man of average stature, lean and trim in appearance, with a small, neatly trimmed mustache and closely cut brown hair." Over coffee and cigars, Critchfield introduced himself as Kent James Marshall.[1] He knew well that Dr. Schneider, or the Doctor, as he was often called by his men, was in fact Reinhard Gehlen, and that Camp Nikolaus now served as the headquarters of his secret service. Munich, the nearby metropolis, was a junction for the flood of refugees from Soviet-occupied Central and Eastern Europe, its ruined streets a playground for spies, mercenaries, and freelance intelligence peddlers working for contending powers. A CIA historian later described the town as "a place of mystery, confusion and intrigue, a war played in the shadows."[2]

Friedrich Schwend, the commander of Operation Bernhard, an SS counterfeiting scheme, worked for the Americans in Munich helping ferret out hidden Nazi assets throughout Austria and Italy.[3] An even more dubious recruit was Dr. Wilhelm Höttl, a former SD spy and a collaborator of Eichmann who sold prepackaged intelligence networks to the Americans while also working for the Soviet Union, communist Yugoslavia, and many other countries. Dr. Schneider and his men were only one more group amongst the motley crowd of intelligence veterans and agents for hire who had made Munich their home. Gehlen, however, was more ambitious than most of his peers. He intended not only to earn money, but to exploit the protection of his American patrons to transform his organization into West Germany's sole intelligence agency.

Gehlen's intelligence enterprise was unofficially established two years earlier under the sponsorship of General Edwin Sibert, then the commander of G-2 in Germany. Sibert admitted this German group as an affiliate of the US intelligence community on his own, without asking for the permission of his superiors.[4] Now he was long gone from Germany, busy with other tasks, and the Americans were at odds as to what to do with his bastard child. The Army wanted to transfer it to the CIA. Admiral Roscoe H. Hillenkoetter, the first director of the agency, was reluctant to accept the "gift" and believed the Org was a deeply flawed intelligence organization marred by loose security procedures, rendering it vulnerable to Soviet penetration. Worse, he believed it might serve as a base for a future resurgence of Nazism and German militarism. Others disagreed, and as a compromise, the young, inexperienced Critchfield was sent on an inspection tour. His mandate was to decide whether the Org should be adopted by the CIA, preserved under the US Army, or liquidated altogether.[5]

In his first meeting with Gehlen, Critchfield had several burning questions. The CIA wanted to ensure the intelligence produced by the Org was worth the cost. In addition, Critchfield was adamant that should the CIA take the Org under its wing, it would have to control its operations from top to bottom. Accordingly, Gehlen would have to submit the real names and aliases of all his agents and employees. He then asked Gehlen whether there were any "Nazis" on his payroll. While CIA standards did not outright forbid the employment of war criminals, Critchfield strongly believed this should be avoided. Gehlen, he insisted, should stay away from veterans of the SS, Gestapo, and senior Wehrmacht officers condemned by the Nuremberg Tribunal unless absolutely necessary. Germans might be the enemies of yesterday, but they were still intensely disliked by many American officers. The CIA was a young struggling agency and weary of suffering embarrassment by the exposure of war criminals in its ranks. Nonetheless, Critchfield implied that the employment of mid-level Wehrmacht officers, such as Gehlen and his peers, was acceptable as far as the CIA was concerned.

Gehlen reacted cautiously. He assured Critchfield that it was his policy "not to employ war criminals" and indeed, the CIA official did not find "immediately definable Nazis" in the Pullach headquarters. However, Gehlen adamantly refused to hand over the roster of his agents or reins of control to any American. Critchfield recalled that "after an obvious pause, during which he puffed on his cigar and emptied his cup, [Gehlen] leaned back and explained to me his basic philosophy in maintaining the integrity and German character of his organization."[6] Critchfield did not agree, and the matter remained disputed. After a few weeks of inspection, he nevertheless advised the CIA to adopt the Org. At the end of the day, beggars could not be choosers. The Americans, and especially the newly established CIA, desperately needed agents versus the Soviets, a new foe against whom they had no human intelligence infrastructure. And former Nazis needed jobs and a new focus to their loyalties, however inimical their new employers were to their old loyalties and attachments. Subsequently, Critchfield was appointed by Admiral Hillenkoetter as the CIA supervisor of Gehlen's enterprise and took permanent residence in Pullach.[7]

From the outset, Critchfield had good reasons to be happy with Gehlen and his work. Though the Org never excelled in political and strategic intelligence and failed to acquire major assets in the Red Army, it did recruit low-level agents and collected ample tactical and operational intelligence on the Soviet order of battle. True, most of these agents were not "insiders"; they consisted mainly of East German citizens who happened to live near Soviet installations, but they were still capable of providing useful intelligence. Most important, Gehlen's spies and SIGINT stations monitored the activity of the Soviet Air Force, essential for Allied pilots running the Soviet blockade of Berlin in 1948.[8] Politically speaking, Gehlen seemed reliable enough. Notwithstanding his ongoing differences with Critchfield on the independence of the Org, he was unquestionably loyal to the Americans. He and his close advisers, or so it seemed, were ideal Germans as far as the CIA was concerned, former Nazis who picked anti-communism from Hitler's ideological rubbish heap and were prepared to discard the rest.

Indeed, for Gehlen's immediate circle, the most important aspect of the old regime was its opposition to communism. In their view, Germany was a protective shield guarding "Western culture" from the eastern hordes. This corresponded with much older German fears, a mixture of racism against "Asiatic Russians" dating back to pre-WWI Wilhelmine Germany and ideological opposition to the Bolshevik order. Even the German national interest was subordinated to the ideological crusade against Moscow. Gehlen declared that if Germany should unite under the banner of communism, he and his men would go into exile and fight their former homeland.[9]

To continue fighting against communism, Gehlen and his associates were prepared to submit to the United States in matters of foreign policy, a concession unthinkable in Nazi times.[10] They were also ready to do away with racial theory and anti-Semitism, crucial principles of the Nazi state. As aforementioned, when one of Gehlen's men called Eric Waldman "a Jewish swine," the general expelled him from the service in order to maintain their relationship with the Americans. As we will see, Gehlen would later lead an intelligence alliance with the Jewish State of Israel, which he considered to be another anti-communist bulwark. "The Israeli soldiers," he later wrote in admiration to a Jewish childhood friend, "are the Prussians of the Middle East." Among other things, Gehlen helped the Mossad smuggle agents into Eastern Europe, and assisted Jewish refugees escaping communist countries to reach Israel. Notably, he supplied cover for Wolfgang Lotz, Israel's top spy in Egypt in the early 1960s.[11]

The problem was that Gehlen had little control over his agents, many of whom did not share his ideological priorities. The Org was a convoluted, loose coalition of semi-autonomous cells, contractors, and external organizations that Gehlen rarely visited, let alone efficiently supervised. During the late 1940s and early 1950s, he was occupied with political machinations in Bonn, trying to convince the new government of West Germany to adopt his organization as the national intelligence agency once the American occupation ended. When Critchfield arrived at Pullach, Gehlen had imperfect control of operations and espionage. That was the fiefdom of his rival and competitor, the former Abwehr officer Hermann Baun. Only in May 1948, half a year before Critchfield's arrival, was Gehlen finally able to expel Baun to a post in the Middle East, but he still found it hard to exercise oversight on the latter's loyalists as well as to fund, support, and evaluate the work of agents throughout Germany.[12]

This persistent problem of control was intermingled with the Org's systemic corruption. In its first few years, it secured neither legal status nor steady governmental financial support, and it was unclear who exactly was responsible for it within the unwieldy American apparatus. Obviously, nobody was enthusiastic to handle the paycheck, and Pullach had to subsist on a tiny monthly budget of 132,000 USD on average. Until the currency reform of June 1948, the ruined German economy was dominated by a thriving black market in which Allied military surplus goods were the "hottest" commodities, especially if you could eat, drink, or smoke them. To keep Gehlen's head above water, the U.S. Army supplied him with coffee and cigarettes and encouraged him to fund his operations by selling them on the black market.[13] Indeed, it is often recounted that German intelligence agents in West Germany identified the occupying power their peers worked for (the United States, Britain, or France) according to the brand of cigarettes they smoked. Germans and Americans alike saw the ruined country as a chaotic place where cunning and deviousness were preconditions to survival. "Here it's permitted" was the unofficial motto of many. Many American officers, including Colonel William Liebel, the first G-2 supervisor of the Gehlen Org in Pullach, were mired in corruption and encouraged their German protégés to do the same.[14]

Such shady financial operations persisted well into the 1950s as Gehlen continued to encounter enormous financial difficulties. He received his allotment in US dollars, devalued since the introduction of the new German currency in 1948, and monthly American support remained both meagre and unreliable.[15] The Pullach Headquarters expected its regional and external organizations to support themselves at least in part via black market operations and independent economic enterprises. The external organization in Karlsruhe, for example, produced Venetian blinds on a small scale, while its counterpart in Bremen ran a petroleum distribution company. Other offices were hidden behind publishing firms or printing presses. Some of the branch offices and external organizations, especially in Berlin, were busy spying on Soviet forces or recruiting assets in East Germany but as their ability was limited, they often purchased information from private intelligence peddlers. As the realms of intelligence and business bled into one another, it was sometimes difficult to distinguish between a "genuine" Org employee and a private intelligence peddler, and sometimes they were one and the same. Many of these people used the Org to make money on the side, embezzled funds, and turned the entire operation into a bubbling swamp of dark business.[16]

Gehlen himself stuck a finger in this pie by employing numerous friends, former comrades-in-arms, and family members as agents, staff officers, or administrative personnel. His half-brother, Johannes, was sent at the Org's expense to Rome where he, at best, collected intelligence on the drink menus in local bars and clubs. A teenaged friend of Gehlen's daughter was employed as a typist when the kindly father heard she was looking for a job. This nepotism overlapped with genuine feelings of military camaraderie. Many former Wehrmacht officers suffered grinding poverty after the war and viewed the Org as a convenient job arrangement, even if they were not really interested in intelligence. Gehlen did not disappoint. Following their chief's example, numerous Org officials staffed regional and local branches with corrupt and incompetent relatives, friends, and friends of friends.[17] The Americans were worried. In a letter to headquarters, Critchfield wrote that "American intelligence is a rich blind man using [the Gehlen Org] as a seeing-eye dog. The only trouble is—the leash is much too long."[18]

In his very first conversation with Critchfield, Gehlen turned this chaos, born out of a mix of necessity, corruption, and incompetence, into a virtue.

When Critchfield, as well as other CIA officers, tried to supervise recruiting and tighten operations and security procedures, Gehlen had a ready answer. He lectured his American counterparts that there was a special "German way" of overseeing intelligence operations the Americans were simply incapable of understanding. Exploiting a trademark concept of the Wehrmacht, Gehlen said that Germans wage wars, overt or covert, with Mission Command (*Auftrag-staktik*, literally: mission tactics): the superior gives a general assignment and does not interfere in its implementation. It is the duty of the subordinate, who knows best the situation on the ground, to decide how to carry the mission out. Therefore, he, Gehlen, tended to give considerable leeway to his agents and avoid meddling in their affairs, economic arrangements, or recruiting practices.[19]

Such loose operational oversight had obvious repercussions on the sensitive issue of employment of former Nazi security officials, SS, and Gestapo veterans, and other war crime suspects. Though he abandoned most aspects of National Socialism except for anti-communism, Gehlen trivialized Nazi Germany's crimes as regrettable events of the past that should not interfere in any way with contemporary intelligence and military objectives.[20] As former members of Nazi security organizations, including the Gestapo, had indispensable experience and knowledge in fighting communism, they simply had to be employed. General Adolf Heusinger, Gehlen's former Wehrmacht superior and now his subordinate in the Org, laughed away reservations against the employment of former SS officers as "nonsense of collective guilt." In a letter to G-2, Gehlen justified recruitment of "nationalists" as long as they were "good Germans" who wholeheartedly supported the West. Later, he added that employment of "good elements" in the SS would marginalize the few embittered radicals in these circles and prevent Soviet penetration of the brotherhoods of SS veterans. Only one of Gehlen's advisers, Heinz Denko-Herre, who served as a liaison to the Americans, opposed altogether the employment of former SS men, believing the political dangers exceeded the benefits.[21]

Gehlen disagreed with Herre but did recognize that employment of SS, SD, and Gestapo veterans could discredit the Org in American eyes. Therefore, he instructed exercising the utmost discretion in the recruitment of such tainted people. Their numbers should not be too high. They should be recruited only when necessary, and then, if possible, far away from Pullach in the external organizations. Of course, the Org should hide from the Americans, as much as possible, the details on the criminal past of such recruits. Interventions and attempts to clean the record of former Nazi criminals should be made only if they proved exceptionally useful. Initially, Gehlen's recruitment policy was cautious. In 1950, the veterans of National Socialist security agencies (SD, Gestapo, and police) in the Org numbered no more than 4 percent of its total manpower.[22]

From time to time, the CIA asked Gehlen to minimize the number of SS veterans in his ranks, although they themselves employed Nazis both indirectly and directly. One director proposed that "unless it can be demonstrated that individuals with political tarnish (former Nazis, SS Men etc.) are vital to the conduct of operations, they should be eliminated from the organization."[23] Critchfield as well as other CIA officers in touch with the Org were concerned about the reliability of former Nazis. Specifically, Critchfield believed that veterans of the SD and the Gestapo were more vulnerable than their untainted counterparts to Soviet recruitment efforts.[24] Ironically, in order to get more information on possible Soviet penetration to the Org, he himself decided to employ an SD officer who had left Gehlen's service. This man, Otto von Bolschwing, was a mass murderer and a direct Holocaust perpetrator in Romania. As part of his CIA role, he developed a network of spies for Critchfield in Romania, Austria, Czechoslovakia, and the Balkans.[25] Critchfield too, it seems, had his own "exceptions." The Soviets, British, French, and Gehlen's West German rivals were no better. They protested against the employment of war crime suspects in the Org but did the same themselves. In the Cold War, one man's moral sin was another's necessity.[26]

Gehlen sought to improve his position by instigating a Red Scare. He cautioned the Americans that a war with the Soviets, though perhaps not imminent, was eventually inevitable. The Federal Republic must not only be part of a newly established union of Western European countries, but a front outpost and bulwark against communist aggression.[27] Gehlen warned that his homeland unfortunately was unprepared to play such a role. In a stream of alarmist yet nebulous reports, he warned that the German authorities, especially the police, were infested with communist spies. Without giving specific verifiable details, he even argued that Soviets were providing specialized training to beautiful girls in the forests of Thuringia, planning to dispatch these "Red Sex bombs" across the border to spy on NATO troops. Another report cautioned that the Stasi established a sabotage school on an island on a lake, which in fact was a periodically flooded isle unsuitable for any sort of construction. Notwithstanding the sensational and even fictional character of his reports, Gehlen successfully hammered into his elite audience that in order to cope with a Russian offensive, they had to eliminate the communist fifth column from within by all means necessary, including by utilizing former Nazi security officials.[28]

When Gehlen's Red Scare line, spreading from the center of the organization, meshed with the fantasies of former Gestapo operatives in the counterintelligence group of the Org, the result was explosive. Ironically, it was precisely this witch hunt against communists, real and imagined, that provided Soviet intelligence with the opening it needed to worm its way into the very heart of the Gehlen Organization.

· 4 ·

Venetian Blindfolds and Red Scares

The point is that we are all capable of believing things which we know to
be untrue, and then, when we are finally proved wrong, impudently
twisting the facts so as to show that we were right.
Intellectually, it is possible to carry on this process for an indefinite time:
the only check on it is that sooner or later a false belief
bumps up against solid reality, usually on a battlefield.

—GEORGE ORWELL, *IN FRONT OF YOUR NOSE*

WE DON'T KNOW who took the photo of house no. 36 on Gerwigstrasse. His name and trade remain unknown. Perhaps he was a sweeper or a policeman, a businessman or a tram conductor. Regardless, on that fine day in 1954, he was but one of many innocent pedestrians strolling down that street, a busy thoroughfare in the industrial zone of Karlsruhe. At one point he paused and took a photo of house no. 36. The picture, still intact in the archives of the Stasi, East Germany's secret service, shows a red-bricked five-story building with chimneys on top; hints of train tracks, a few parked cars.

The anonymous Stasi agent might have known what was hiding behind that drab façade. A more innocent passerby would certainly fail to notice any peculiarity, even if he should cross the archway into the building's inner courtyard. There, a door sported a small sign: Zimmerle & Co. That small company manufactured Venetian blinds. The daughter of the owners lived on the ground floor with her partner, a former sergeant in the Abwehr, Nazi Germany's military intelligence. This man, Alfred Bentzinger, managed the office space on the first floor where dozens of employees came and went, the vast majority of whom had nothing to do with Venetian blinds. Under the convenient cover of Zimmerle & Co., Bentzinger managed one of the most powerful offshoots of the Gehlen Organization, *Generalvertretung L,* or in short, GV-L—the external organization responsible for hunting communist spies in West Germany.[1] Bentzinger was oblivious to the fact that he, the hunter, was about to be cornered by his prey. And even worse, that his negligence, fantasies, and ideological biases would trigger a bomb destined to undermine Western spy agencies for years to come.

· · ·

DURING THE WAR, Alfred Bentzinger served as a sergeant in the Secret Field Police, an Abwehr affiliate charged with cleansing the Wehrmacht's rear of traitors, partisans, and other dangerous elements. Though the Abwehr acquired a reputation as a sanctuary for anti-Nazi resistance fighters, that was never true for most of its departments, and certainly not for the Secret Field Police. As Nazi Germany defined Jews as enemies, saboteurs, and Bolsheviks by nature, they quickly became a target of the Secret Field Police, which practically functioned as a mobile killing squad.[2] It is unknown whether Bentzinger was a direct Holocaust perpetrator, but he was certainly a staunch Nazi and an outspoken anti-Semite.

In 1946, Hermann Baun recruited Bentzinger to the Org as a counterintelligence expert, but he never felt at home there—neither under Baun nor under Gehlen. As a sergeant in an intelligence organization packed with haughty majors, colonels, and generals, he had few friends and was bitter and frustrated. Bad-tempered and overweight, he was known to everyone as "the fat one" (*der Dicke*). Bentzinger, however, possessed a talent for amassing power, and in 1949 already led one of the strongest external branches of the Org with 452 employees, spies, case officers, and couriers, including Germans and immigrant Russians. Most worked in Karlsruhe, but many were scattered in other cities of the American Occupation Zone such as Frankfurt, Heidelberg,

Bremen, and Munich, and also in West Berlin. A select few spied for the Org in East Germany and nearby countries.[3]

In the Org's Pullach headquarters, Bentzinger's sponsor was Dr. Kurt Kohler, the director of Group III (counterintelligence), yet another Abwehr veteran with an unreconstructed Nazi worldview. Both Kohler and Bentzinger surrounded themselves with lieutenants sporting similar convictions. "At the time," Kohler recalled, "we were all Nazis and said so quite openly."[4] With Kohler's blessing, Bentzinger employed the largest number of SS, SD, and Gestapo veterans in the Org. One Gestapo agent recruited another, and the redbrick building in Gerwigstrasse was filled with Nazis and sympathizers. Typically, each referee whitewashed the wartime record of his friends. Executioners became "executives," torturers were transformed into "translators." In one case, the Org sheltered a rapist and former Gestapo informer with the active assistance of the Americans. "He was not one of these pompous and intolerant Gestapo officials, but rather hardworking, diligent and modest," wrote a referee for Heinrich Reiser, a brute responsible for anti-Semitic pogroms, torture, and murder of numerous victims. Reiser, in turn, recommended and recruited other Gestapo veterans to GV-L.[5]

As a result, the initially small number of former Nazi intelligence and security officials in the Org grew significantly with every passing year. From only 4 percent of the personnel roster in 1950, it climbed to 6.1 percent in 1951. The percentage of these veterans remained stable thereafter, but only because numerous agents without Nazi security connections were recruited in the 1950s. In absolute numbers, the number of SD, Gestapo, and Nazi police veterans in the Org almost doubled between 1952 and 1955, from 15 to 30 at a minimum. In July 1963, Gehlen disclosed to Chancellor Adenauer that 32 BND officials had served in the Reich Main Security Office (including SD and Gestapo) and seven more in the Secret Field Police; all in all, 0.85 percent of the force, reflecting the massive influx of new young recruits. Many of these people, including culprits of the Holocaust and other crimes against humanity, began their postwar career in GV-L.[6]

Bentzinger's Nazi agents were tasked with finding East German and Soviet spies in the Federal Republic. They sniffed around political parties, trade unions, and civil society organizations. They also spied on neo-Nazis, especially those that chose to retain the wrong components of Hitler's rubbish heap, including maintaining Nazi animosity to the West instead of anti-communism, holding neutralist positions, or having suspicious ties with East Germany. Finally, some GV-L agents scanned the newspapers for articles critical of the Gehlen Org, and monitored competing West German intelligence organizations. Both in Pullach and Karlsruhe, there was no real difference between enemies of the organization and enemies of the state. All could be defined as communists, especially if they became troublesome.[7]

Gehlen, as usual, was not interested in the details. Rarely did he interfere in counterintelligence work, and certainly not in the affairs of GV-L. Bentzinger and Kohler, however, served his ceaseless attempt to expand the Org's power and authority.[8] If communist infiltration was the biggest threat in the late 1940s and early 1950s, then hunting such spies was a role Gehlen strongly coveted: a solid path to glory, power, and importance—and for eliminating rivals, peddling influence, and becoming politically untouchable.

Critchfield, however, was very unhappy with the work of Kohler and Bentzinger. He believed Karlsruhe had become a sanctuary for unsavory SS veterans with very poor security precautions, and hence highly exposed to penetration by the Stasi and the MGB. In addition, he strongly criticized the intelligence supplied by both Department III and GV-L, defining it as amateurish, even worthless. Critchfield, however, did nothing to halt the counterintelligence operations of Kohler and Bentzinger, a mistake he later came to regret.[9]

To bypass the Americans, Gehlen tried to convince the fledgling German government to adopt his counterintelligence operations. In 1949, he pressured Chancellor Adenauer to accept the Org not only as an agency for external espionage, but also as a guardian of domestic security. Always hungry for more power, he tried to take over the Federal Office for Constitutional Protection (BfV), West Germany's nascent internal security service. Thus, he hoped to create a unified agency that might also include the police, a mammoth complex that resembled, on paper, the all-pervading power of Hitler's Reich Main Security Office. The plan failed in the end due to stubborn British resistance. London feared the political influence of such a clandestine security machine. The CIA, initially on the fence, eventually joined the British, and Gehlen was forced to give up.[10] He installed his own spies inside the BfV, though, and also used his Counterintelligence Group as an informal domestic security service.

Gordon Stewart, the head of the CIA mission in Germany, warned that Gehlen had not given up on his ambitions to control West Germany's internal security. He suffered from "a moral and political inability to see anything wrong in a union of external, internal and even executive (police) security functions."[11] The Counterintelligence Group and GV-L served as springboards for his fantasies of grandeur.

The outbreak of the Korean War in June 1950 reinforced, yet again, the fear of an impending Soviet invasion. Chancellor Konrad Adenauer worried that a communist fifth column would abet the invading army through terror attacks and sabotage operations.[12] Playing on the tunes composed by Kohler and Bentzinger, Gehlen warned that not only open communists but also moderate leftists and anti-Soviet liberals, old and neo-Nazis, or almost anybody could be an enemy agent or at least a "useful idiot" to be manipulated by the Soviets.[13] In July 1950, shortly after the outbreak of the war in Korea, Chancellor Adenauer informally authorized Gehlen to use his Counterintelligence Group to track communist spies in West Germany. A year later, Gehlen also received similar authorization from the Allied High Commissioners, still the highest authority in the occupied country.[14]

• • •

WITH GEHLEN'S BLESSING, Kohler, Bentzinger, and their men gave their counterespionage campaign the character of an anti-communist witch hunt, later known as Operation Crosshairs (*Fadenkreuz*). In their zeal, they revived the phantom of the "Red Orchestra," a wartime invention of the Gestapo and other Nazi security services. Following a wave of arrests of anti-Nazi German officials who gave secret intelligence to the Soviets as well as leftist resistance fighters throughout the Nazi Empire, the Gestapo coined the term Red Orchestra to project the false image of a unified plot of Soviet espionage.

After the war, Gestapo officials involved with the persecution of these anti-Nazi resistance fighters tried to contact both the British MI5 and the American CIC in order to sell the idea that the Red Orchestra was still intact and engaged in anti-Western espionage all over Europe. It took a while, but by 1948 at the latest, both the British and the Americans rejected this conspiracy theory as irrelevant to current Soviet espionage in Europe. The CIC, however, protected these Gestapo officials from trial and extradition in order to conceal their involvement with American intelligence.[15] Some subsequently reached out to Kohler and Bentzinger and sold their recycled merchandise to the Gehlen Organization.

GV-L avidly bought the goods and assumed the exposure of the new Red Orchestra as one of its main tasks. Initially, Ludwig Albert, a former operative of the Secret Field Police who led Bentzinger's Frankfurt office, warned that leftist intellectuals who lived on the shores of Lake Bodensee near Switzerland were in fact cogs in a communist espionage network. The reports of Albert and other agents were based on vague rumors, insinuations, anonymous denunciations, and circular rhetoric, cleverly designed to hide the fact that there was no solid evidence behind them. He and his superiors imagined a vast espionage network and multiple Trojan horses, an all-pervading "conspiracy against the West."[16]

Thus, in spring 1950, GV-L agent Heinrich Reiser wrote a bulky report on the Red Orchestra, portraying it as a multi-headed hydra that controlled all German anti-Nazi resistance groups (including the conservative and military resistance), Yugoslavian partisans, and Western communist spies like Alger Hiss and Klaus Fuchs. And, he warned darkly, these networks were still at large. They were even passed on from one generation to the next. In one particularly bizarre case, a young woman was fingered as a suspect involved with the Red Orchestra merely because someone who might be her mother was once arrested by the Paris Gestapo station as a communist. Family members and friends of resistance fighters executed by the Nazis and, of course, survivors of the resistance were all high on the list, and even people who were acquitted by the Gestapo or the Nazi People's Court became automatic targets for surveillance.

By the end of 1951, GV-L held a card index of at least 900 pages filled with names. Unlike in the Third Reich, they did not have the authority to arrest let alone torture and execute suspects. The only thing they could do was to pass the information through informal channels to West German authorities and to the Americans. Fortunately, the consequences to the people involved were usually minor.[17] But ironically, while the men of GV-L and the Counterintelligence Group were hunting for the nonexistent Red Orchestra, defaming former resistance fighters, and pointing fingers at innocent people, *real* enemy agents were lurking in their midst.

• • •

THE EARLY MISGIVING of Critchfield and other Americans came to pass: compromised agents infested GV-L like maggots in spoiled meat. The problem began with the loose structure of Gehlen's service and the far-reaching autonomy of the external organizations, part and parcel of the chief's ideology of "mission command." The security officers appointed by Pullach, for example, had no executive authority over the external organizations and could not investigate members or examine documents without the authorization of these local leaders, the so-called "intelligence barons." They, in turn, jealously kept their autonomy and resented any interference in their internal affairs.[18]

The distinction Gehlen had drawn between "good" anti-communist Nazis and "bad Nazis" who held pro-Soviet or neutralist views was in fact quite nebulous. In the late 1940s and early 1950s, at least, former Gestapo and SD officials were tied to one another in close ties of friendship and influenced one another, even if some believed Germany should support the West and others preferred a pro-Soviet or neutralist position. In the lower levels of Gehlen's Organization, and especially in GV-L, many of them mixed comfortably, and it was not always easy to tell one from the other.

One such problematic Nazi force that extended its tentacles deep into the Gehlen Organization was the Socialist Reich Party (SRP). Its leaders were Dr. Fritz Dorls and General Otto Ernst Remer. The latter, a former infantry officer, enjoyed enormous popularity in neo-Nazi circles, as he was the officer who quashed the coup d'état of the anti-Nazi military resistance movement on July 20, 1944.[19] Dorls and Remer openly supported a Nazi resurgence, denounced former resistance fighters as foreign dupes, and generally functioned as noisy opposition to the government in Bonn. They railed against Adenauer's pro-Western policy and advocated a neutralist position. Like other "neutralists," Bonn deeply suspected them of being secretly pro-Soviet, and they were therefore considered a target for surveillance by the Gehlen Org. In April 1952, after the SRP scored surprising success in local state elections, it was banned altogether as a threat to West German democracy.[20]

It should have been little surprise, however, that some of the "good" anti-communist Nazis in GL-V actually sympathized with Dorls, Remer, and the SRP. Walter Klein, for example, was a minor Gestapo agent in occupied France who used the war to enrich himself with corrupt private dealings. After the war, he became an SRP activist. In 1951, Reiser recruited him to GV-L through the old boys' network of the Gestapo. Klein played a sophisticated double and triple game. Obeying the orders of Dorls, the SRP leader, he secretly worked for both GV-L and French intelligence, giving both services tendentious information. The goal behind this double dealing was to empower Nazis in the Gehlen Org and Fascists in the French police while milking them for intelligence useful for the neo-Nazi movement. Like other veterans of the Nazi security apparatus, Klein held a "secret dossier" of documents incriminating politicians in communist ties and sinister networks of more than 10,000 "Reds" he claimed pervaded all walks of German life and administration, even Chancellor Adenauer's bureau. These documents were never exposed but rather were used by Klein and his SRP friends to extort money from public figures in West Germany. By employing Klein, the Org became complicit in a Mafia-style blackmail racket.[21]

Soviet intelligence and its junior partners from the Stasi also identified veterans of former Nazi security organizations as potential recruits. A CIA study rightly concluded that the Soviet thesis was simple: "old intelligence hands will flock together, will seek to return to the work they know best. Some of these people might be susceptible to a Soviet approach because of their general sympathies. Others, such as former Elite Guard (SS) and Security Service (SD), many of whom were now war criminals able to make their way only by hiding a past . . . would be vulnerable to blackmail."[22]

One case in late summer 1951 was a harbinger of things to come. Hans Sommer, an SD war criminal responsible for the burning of synagogues and atrocities against the resistance in France, was employed by GV-L. Henrich Reiser vouched for him, as he did for so many others, and ensured the Org he was politically reliable with a "100 percent positive attitude toward the West." His job was to spy upon neo-Nazi and extreme right-wing groups in order to spot former Nazis who worked for the Soviets or the East Germans.[23]

Sommer was then approached by another SS veteran with a tempting offer to work for the Stasi. He reported back to the Org, and they told him to pretend he was a disaffected former Nazi who wanted to spy for East Germany in order to expose the enemy's recruiting network. Composed almost entirely of former SS officers, this network was indeed snuffed out by the Gehlen Org. Ironically, Sommer was a triple agent who worked for the Soviet Bloc and fooled his handlers until 1953 when he was fired due to American pressure. He subsequently moved to arms trafficking, working for the Stasi and collecting information on former SS officers in Gehlen's service.[24]

Some former Nazis served as long-term spies of the Soviet Union. These people who picked the Soviet side in the Cold War with remarkable consistency proved to be the most dangerous, not only because of the secrets they leaked, but as a result of the fallout once they were finally discovered and exposed. Each one of them can be compared to a leaking chemical barrel buried in the foundation of a building, slowly eroding its surroundings, only to explode with great power when finally exposed to air. Armed with unusual cunning, one man would worm his way into Pullach, deal a mighty blow to the CIA, and threaten the very existence of the Gehlen Org.

· 5 ·

The Moscow Gambit— Operation Fireworks

Only the most sensitive and alert person can get the truth out of spies.

—SUN TZU, *THE ART OF WARFARE.*[1]

IN 1951, THE once-elegant city of Dresden was a but a shadow of its former self. Only a few months before Germany's surrender, the Royal and U.S. Air Forces firebombed it into a pyre of smoking ruins and charred bodies in one of the most devastating air raids of the Second World War. At least 25,000 men, women, and children were cremated outright, perished in the firestorms, or suffocated under the rubble.[2] For many local Germans, the story of Dresden was one of survival against all odds under privation and bombing and then under the yoke of the Soviets and their East German puppets. Among SS officers who hailed from this city, the incineration of Dresden sealed a particularly unique bond. These men who took active part in Nazi Germany's atrocities were united not only in memories of their criminal past and fear of legal persecution, but also a reinforced victim mentality. Feeling powerless, destitute, and discriminated against, they yearned for revenge against the Americans and British incinerators. These memories weighed heavily on their choice of what they would pick from Hitler's rubbish heap and which side to align themselves with in the secret struggles of the Cold War.[3]

On a chilly autumn day in early November 1951, one such SD veteran, Heinz Felfe, traveled through the ruined city accompanied by an elegant Soviet officer known to him only as "Max." The Russian, who spoke perfect German, took him around the city, which was now part of the Soviet zone of occupation. It was a rare visit for Felfe, a resident of West Germany, who could not return to his hometown for fear of arrest.[4] Max, recognizing the sensitivities of his companion, took him to his hometown for a reason. He saw Felfe was overcome with emotion, surrounded as he was by the ruins of his former world. Did he really owe anything to the Western democracies that had brought about such wanton destruction? Soon, Max would use Felfe as a pawn in a prolonged chess game against the West.

A well-groomed, balding counterintelligence expert "with large, flappy ears," Heinz Felfe was born in 1918. During the war he served as an official in the Swiss and Dutch departments of the SD Spy Agency (Department VI). Throughout the years he volunteered to serve in an Einsatzgruppe, one of the mobile killing squads in the East, but was constantly rebuffed.[5] His acquaintances later described him as "a highly intelligent man with very little personal warmth . . . with high regard for efficiency, and for authority, but susceptible to flattery; and capable of almost childish displays of vindictiveness." Arrogant and cruel to almost anyone not in a position of power, he was strongly disliked by many colleagues and subordinates.[6]

Felfe walked a long and winding path before becoming Moscow's master spy in West Germany. After the war, like many other veterans of Hitler's security apparatus, he was arrested and, according to his testimony, mishandled, tortured, and robbed by Canadian soldiers.[7] Following his release, he found himself destitute and desperately looking for a job, and wanted to continue his career, even under the Western allies. However, he could not find a job in the newly established German police. Later, Felfe would make much fuss over his hatred of the British who incinerated his beloved Dresden, including his childhood home.[8] He might have hated them, yet nonetheless sought employment with MI6. The British, who interrogated him thoroughly during his POW internment, knew well that he was an SD officer with a stained past. Still, they employed him in July 1947 as an expert in fighting communism. Then they helped him whitewash his record and get through the denazification process, a routine in postwar Germany. Two years later, after the establishment of the Federal Republic, Felfe also worked for a short period in Bonn's domestic security service as—yet again—an expert in smoking out communist agents. He was fired when his employers discovered he tried to sell reports to the East German Communist Party and to local news agencies.[9]

An opportunity for better employment presented itself in March 1950, when Felfe met two SS veterans and fellow Dresdeners, Erwin Tiebel and Hans Clemens. In Nazi times, all three were part of a drinking group that used to meet for weekly merrymaking in an old city beer garden. Clemens, a former piano player, became notorious as a brutal agent of the local Gestapo. The diarist Victor Klemperer, one of Clemens's victims, referred to him as "the boxer," a "big blond fellow" who beat and threatened to kill him simply "because you're a Jew."[10]

Later, as an SD officer in Rome, Clemens took part in an infamous massacre of Italian civilians in the Ardeatine Caves. Clemens later recalled that his wife, who remained in Dresden, gave him a tempting proposal to work for Soviet intelligence. For a while he thought to emigrate to the Middle East and serve, like other SS veterans, as a military adviser in Syria or Egypt, but then decided to accept the Soviet proposal. At the time he "hated the Americans like the pest" and wanted to take "double and triple" revenge for his mistreatment as a POW as well as for the burning of Dresden, in which several of his relatives perished. In addition, he needed money and yearned for adventure. Finally, Clemens believed that in the coming war the Eastern Bloc would inevitably triumph. In the First and Second World War he had been on the losing side. In the Third, he intended to be with the winners.[11]

The Soviets ordered Clemens to recruit more agents among Nazi security veterans. Accordingly, he won Tiebel over, then moved on to Felfe whom, he was certain, would share his adventurism and anti-Western sentiments. That was a dangerous move. Felfe offered his friend as a "double agent" to the British MI6 and the Gehlen Org, an offer that could lead to Clemens's recruitment—or to his arrest. Fortunately for Clemens, both organizations rejected the overture.[12]

On April 15, 1950, the British finally got rid of Felfe due to his unreliability and numerous indiscretions, but ironically, also because of his attempt to "double" Clemens. The British saw the latter, as well as other SD veterans, as desperados with fishy ties. The MI6 understood very early on what would take the Gehlen Org and the CIA much blood and tears to learn: Veterans of the National Socialist security apparatus often mixed in the same social circles. When one of them worked for the East, he could easily recruit others, like a computer virus infecting a densely networked data system.[13] This tendency was particularly strong when veterans shared a common background, such as in this case, an origin in bombed-out Dresden.

After Felfe's dismissal from British service, he gladly accepted Clemens's offer to work alongside him as a Soviet spy. It was not only the money that moved him, but also the thrill of adventure and, as a CIA officer recalled, "the satisfaction of manipulating two powerful political forces."[14] From the Russian side, "Max" (Ivan I. Sumin) initially directed the operation from the Dresden MGB station. A skilled recruiter, he treated his agents to private piano recitals and occasionally wined and dined them with rare delicacies such as lobster, Clemens's favorite dish ("I'll give my life for lobsters," he later said). Then Max handed his two recruits over to another young and refined man, only twenty-three years old. This handsome blond, blue-eyed agent introduced himself in perfect German as "Alfred" (real name Vitali V. Korotkov). He gave Clemens and Felfe the aliases "Peter" and "Paul."[15]

For their first mission, Alfred instructed Clemens and Felfe to penetrate the Gehlen Org. Clemens decided to utilize his Third Reich connections to strike at the weakest point: The external organization GV-L in Karlsruhe. As we have seen in the previous chapter, Bentzinger recruited from his old-boy networks in the Gestapo, the SD, and the Secret Field Police. Wilhelm "Willy" Krichbaum, another native of Dresden, the former commandant of the Field Police and a notorious mass murderer, also worked for Bentzinger. His mission was to comb the pool of former Nazi security officials for potential Org recruits, a mirror image of Clemens's task. The former Nazis were sought by both sides and due to their connections served as a medium through which information flowed from West to East. Krichbaum told Clemens he was back "with the old gang" and invited him to the Gehlen Organization. Subsequently, he recruited both Clemens and Felfe to the GV-L.[16]

On November 1, 1951, only two months after his recruitment to Soviet intelligence, Felfe also started working for the Gehlen Org. He passed reports to Clemens who dispatched them to his wife and to the MGB in Dresden hidden in baby-food cans. Later, the two applied for a more direct mode of communication and met with Alfred in aquariums, cinemas, cathedrals, and other public places in West Berlin, Vienna, and Brussels. Sometimes they simply exchanged material in the forest or on the side of the Berlin autobahn. For more extended meetings, Alfred invited the pair to MGB safehouses in East Berlin.[17]

In his day job, Felfe portrayed himself as an anti-communist firebrand. He participated in the investigation of the fictional Red Orchestra and slowly built his reputation as a dedicated counterintelligence officer. Clemens, by contrast, felt discriminated against in the Gehlen Org. "SD and Gestapo officers," he recalled, "were condemned to dirty jobs in the lower levels," always looked down upon by "army veterans and resistance fighters."[18] Clemens overstated his point, as there were few former resistance fighters in the Gehlen Org and quite a few Gestapo and SD veterans. But it was true that for political reasons, Gehlen initially tried to confine the latter to the lower levels, mostly in external organizations. The Org leader therefore had the worst of both worlds: By employing dubious Nazi intelligence agents, he exposed his ranks to Soviet blackmail and penetration while marginalizing them, keeping them frustrated and even more vulnerable to hostile recruitment.

Gehlen was almost completely blind to such dangers. Indeed, when considering the evidence, it is amazing Clemens and Felfe were not arrested very early on. Both were vain and overestimated their own cunning. They insisted, for example, on meeting Alfred and other senior MGB officers in person and refused security measures such as communication through intermediaries and dead drops.[19] Felfe's behavior was so strange, his curiosity about matters exceeding his purview so intense, that quite a few colleagues suspected something was not right. He had the habit, for example, of making his appearance "in various offices, each time asking for something or other, obviously with the intent of engaging in conversation, only to retract then, saying that he was in the wrong office." Indeed, Felfe lied, falsified, or omitted many details of his SD past, a fact noticed even by some of his Org superiors. Once, he even "disappeared" for a few hours during a trip to Berlin with a CIA colleague, presumably to meet his Soviet handler.[20] Simple background checks with the MI6 or BfV, West Germany's domestic security service, would have revealed he had been rejected due to his dubious ties, corruption, and illegal behavior. But as matters stood, the suspicions against Felfe failed to crystalize into a clear case.

The first serious investigation against Felfe was launched by the 66th CIC Group of the U.S. Army in Heidelberg. Believing that hiring Gehlen was a mistake from day one, these officers deplored the Org's poor security measures and strongly suspected it was penetrated by communist agents. In the early 1950s, they ran a clandestine operation codenamed "Campus" to identify traitors inside the Gehlen Organization and other West German intelligence agencies.[21] Illegally and without consulting the CIA, they installed their own spies inside the Org, and especially in GV-L, in order to find evidence of hostile infiltration, recruiting the director of GV-L, Alfred Bentzinger, the head of his Frankfurt office, Ludwig Albert, and another official.[22] But Operation Campus dragged on without reaching definitive results, and the CIC in any event had no executive authority over the Gehlen Org. Disastrously, they withheld information from the only institution that had such authority, the CIA. James Critchfield and his associates, oblivious to the suspicions against Felfe, believed that he had tied "his personal future to the West and has made the decision to fight communist ideologies and practice."[23] The matter was put to rest, and the time bomb of Felfe and Clemens kept on ticking.

· · ·

ON OCTOBER 1, 1953, the Org transferred Felfe to the center in Pullach, far from GV-L. He was now a senior case officer in the Soviet Section of the Counterintelligence Group under Dr. Kurt Kohler.[24] With Felfe out of the doomed external organization, the Soviet chess masters decided it was time to use their Stasi protégés to eliminate GV-L and other Gehlen agencies once and for all. Operation Fireworks, as it was called, was a concentrated wave of arrests in the Democratic Republic of Germany focusing on Org agents and their local collaborators. Until the end of 1953, at least ninety-four spies, about twenty percent of Gehlen's manpower in East Germany, were behind bars. Many more had their cover blown and had to leave their positions and flee to the West.[25]

GV-L was one of the primary targets of the operation. On November 26, Wolfgang Höher, one of Bentzinger's employees and yet another former SS officer, crossed the lines to East Berlin. Only then did the horrified Bentzinger discover his trusted Nazi lieutenant was in fact an East German agent. That might have been a calculated step to cover for Felfe and Clemens, who had already briefed the Soviets about GV-L and its field operations. Now, as their Soviet handler hinted in a conspiratorial meeting, Höher's defection could easily explain why the Soviets and East Germans knew so much about GV-L.[26] As the spies of the Org disappeared into communist jails, the East German propaganda machine began to rail against the Gehlen Org and GV-L, and the presence of so many heinous Nazis in the latter office provided especially effective fodder for the press. At the same time, the East Germans exposed everything they knew about GV-L: names of agents, addresses of officers, and many other compromising details. CIC estimated that at least 70 percent of this information came from the "SD group" in the external organization.[27]

The result was devastating for Bentzinger, as Gehlen was forced to reorganize and effectively marginalize GV-L, but even more so for the entire Org. Felfe, by contrast, prospered. As he was no longer positioned in the GV-L, he was not tainted by the debacle of the external organization. Moreover, as he had just joined the Counterintelligence Group, he was likewise not held responsible for the Org-wide security failure. The disaster heightened the need to reinforce counterintelligence, Felfe's field of expertise, and he was never seriously examined. When Gehlen's security advisers tried to hunt down double agents, they targeted people with communist ties and veterans of the German resistance, not former Nazi security officials.[28] But while Gehlen was oblivious to the dangers around him, another Org officer began his own investigations. The noose was tightening. The only question was—around whose neck?

· 6 ·

Chess and Double Agents—
The Strange Case of Ludwig Albert

It's always better to sacrifice your opponents' men.

—SAVIELLY TARTAKOWER, CHESS GRANDMASTER

⌒

WE PREVIOUSLY ENCOUNTERED Ludwig Albert when he was one of the officials in charge of the Red Orchestra investigation. Like so many others in GV-L, his record was far from clean. Albert served in the Secret Field Police, a detachment responsible for the mass shooting of Soviet Jews, but as the files of the Secret Field Police were almost entirely destroyed at the end of the war, we know very little about the extent of his personal involvement. Following Germany's defeat, Albert found his way to the GV-L where he was put in charge of its important Frankfurt office and later served as counterintelligence director and deputy chief of the external organization. His job was to collect intelligence on the German Communist Party (KPD) and monitor its communications with East Germany. In order to pinpoint communist infiltration, he led a network of spies in several West German ministries and security agencies as well as some trusted men deep inside East German territory.[1]

Following the blow of Operation Fireworks, Albert was put in charge of internal investigations of Pullach and the external organizations in an attempt to find Soviet and East German moles. Though Gehlen himself ordered this internal investigation, Albert received little cooperation either from the Org's leader or from the directors of the external organizations. His relations with Gehlen's office became especially fraught when Albert warned time and again that the rot extended beyond the external organizations into the center itself. He set a suspicious eye on Heinz Felfe, who climbed from the beaten GV-L to Pullach. Albert noted that the information published by the East Germans could not have come merely from Höher because some of it was known only to high officials in GV-L. Cases on which Felfe worked, he noted, "were fizzled out." Over a period of months, he "interested himself in other matters which were none of his business" and a dossier containing information on his old ties to the East had "mysteriously disappeared."[2]

Though Albert himself was a veteran of the Secret Field Police, a National Socialist genocidal organization, he correctly surmised that SD men with checkered pasts could be vulnerable to Soviet recruitment efforts. But Gehlen did not only turn a deaf ear to any denunciation of Felfe, he refused to improve security procedures or tighten the center's control over external organizations. "A secret service should not be streamlined like an army," he and his advisers retorted. The frustrated Albert reported his suspicions against Felfe to the American CIC as well. Although U.S. Army counterintelligence experts considered Albert to be reliable, they nonetheless did not bother to inform the Org's sponsors at the CIA.[3]

Albert's suspicions were corroborated by other sources. In 1954, a Soviet defector named Piotr S. Deryabin, a counterespionage expert at the KGB Vienna Station, told the CIA that the Soviets had planted two spies inside the Gehlen Org, codenamed "Peter" and "Paul."[4] The CIA now knew the aliases of Clemens and Felfe, though not their real names.

The shrewd Felfe realized very quickly that Albert was after him. The Soviets, who sensed the looming danger, must have understood that it was time to get rid of Albert and his meddlesome investigations. In order to do so, they launched a deception operation known as Lili Marleen. They asked one of their agents to deposit a secret document in a dead drop under a lamppost in the West German city of Ludwigsburg. Then a second agent reported to the police that he saw suspicious activity near the dead drop, and a third was sent to empty the box only to be arrested by the police. Inside the dead drop, law enforcement found a memorandum with thorough information on the organization, structure, and operations of GV-L. It was now clear that a high-level Soviet spy operated inside the external organization. Examining the document, Gehlen and his advisers realized that only Bentzinger or his deputy, Ludwig Albert, were capable of presenting such a detailed and full picture to the MGB. Felfe was no longer suspect, as he had left GV-L in the wake of the Fireworks disaster and was reassigned to headquarters. In order to protect Felfe, the East German denounced him publicly as a Gehlen agent and former SD officer.[5]

The Soviet spy agency, now renamed the KGB, dealt Albert the final blow on June 30, 1955. A Stasi courier was arrested in West Germany on charges unrelated to espionage and offered to reveal all his knowledge in return for legal immunity. He denounced several minor Stasi agents and one big fish— Ludwig Albert. The courier gave a precise description of Albert, his house, and his car, and testified he saw him exchanging money with a Stasi case officer in the woods. Later, the courier was caught in multiple lies, including attempts to frame specific people. As the Americans assumed, he was almost certainly dispatched by the KGB.[6]

Albert heard about the impending police roundup, but did not believe he was a suspect and never tried to escape. To his surprise he was indeed arrested. The police subsequently raided his luxurious home stuffed with Persian rugs far too expensive for the salary of a West German intelligence official. They also found numerous secret documents stashed in three separate piles, requests for information composed on an American typewriter, a microfilm reader produced in East Germany, and 9,000 marks in cash. According to police interpretation of the evidence, Albert was guilty of espionage for both the CIC and the Stasi. His wife ominously told the detectives that if her husband failed to provide an adequate explanation, he might as well hang himself.[7]

Albert denied all allegations and continued to insist that the real mole was roaming free in Pullach. For a while, his chief Bentzinger even tried to protect him, perhaps concerned that Albert would disclose Bentzinger's own cooperation with the CIC. But to no avail: Kohler, the chief of the Counterintelligence Group, hinted to Bentzinger that he had best take a vacation.[8] While Albert languished in jail, the commander of U.S. Army Intelligence, General Arthur G. Trudeau, made a last-ditch attempt to turn the doomed CIC agent's revelations into action. He accosted the West German leader, Chancellor Konrad

Adenauer, during his visit to Washington and warned him that the Gehlen Org was full of Soviet spies. Adenauer did little with this information, except informing the CIA. Allen W. Dulles, the director of central intelligence, felt humiliated by this awkward meddling in his affairs and pressed for Trudeau's dismissal. That was the end of Operation Campus. From that moment on, the CIC washed its hands of the Gehlen Org.[9]

One month later, on July 13, Ludwig Albert's jailers reported that he was on the verge of breaking down and confessing. Accordingly, they recommended tightening the supervision of his cell and person. But the next day at 8:00 A.M., Albert used a moment in which he was unwatched and hanged himself with his pajama cord. He left behind a suicide note in which he confessed misuse of operational funds but denied any connection with the Stasi. Gehlen argued later there was evidence for his guilt but refused to share it even with the CIA. The police, he said, forbade him to disclose this sensitive intelligence.[10]

The question of whether Ludwig Albert was *really* a communist spy is one of the unsolved riddles of Cold War espionage. If he indeed spied for the East, then the Soviets sacrificed one of their agents in order to solidify the position of their more important spies, Felfe and Clemens. As he had accused Felfe of spying for the KGB, Albert's fall would discredit anyone who might voice similar suspicions in the future. James Critchfield, as well as many later historians, believe precisely this version of events.[11] And yet, it leaves many questions unanswered. Unless Albert's Soviet handlers exposed him to their entire plan, which was risky, unprofessional, and unlikely, why did he try to pinpoint Felfe so actively and desperately? In addition, Albert heard about impending arrests of communist spies but did not try to escape. In all likelihood, he did not see himself as a suspect.[12]

Indeed, when we look at the evidence for Albert's treason, it is far from airtight. Certainly Albert lied about his finances and illegally collected secret documents, but this constitutes insufficient proof that he spied for the Stasi or the KGB. He might have financed his luxurious lifestyle by siphoning operational funds, as he confessed before his suicide, and the documents might have been stolen exclusively for the CIC. The police found in his home American, not Soviet or East German, requests for information.

There are two additional pieces of evidence that, according to the police, implicated Albert in communist espionage: the fact that he organized the stolen documents in three piles (presumably, one for the Gehlen Org, one for the CIC, and one for the KGB), and that he possessed a microfilm reader produced in East Germany. While suspicious, it was overwhelming evidence only for people who had already arranged the findings according to a preconceived picture. An intelligence officer may organize his material in any number of piles for many reasons, and prior to the establishment of the Berlin Wall, products from East Germany were regularly sold in the West. Perhaps Albert possessed the machine in order to read and analyze East German documents for the Gehlen Org. Alfred, the Soviet case officer, also advised his agent Hans Clemens that Ludwig Albert did not work for the Stasi or the KGB, though this denial should not be trusted on its own.[13]

Following Albert's demise, there was nobody left to stop the mole Felfe, who quickly rose in the ladders of rank and responsibility. Occasionally, he launched sophisticated counterespionage operations, all based on fodder supplied by his Soviet handlers. In Operation Lena, for example, Felfe recruited an East German journalist who fed the Org information on the KGB. Purportedly, "Lena" was a bright and diligent recruit with a phenomenal memory. He provided the Gehlen Org accurate information on phone numbers, addresses, and license plates of talkative KGB officials, a detailed map of KGB headquarters in Karlhorst, East Berlin, and the true identities of minor East German and Soviet agents in West Germany. This was a sufficient sacrifice to reinforce Felfe's status in the Counterintelligence Group.

Whenever Felfe sought access to the records of the Foreign Ministry, the BfV, the Criminal Police, or the chancellor's office, the KGB only had to ask "Lena" to report on possible KGB recruits in these places. Then, Felfe had to perform "background checks" to rule out hostile penetration. With an amazing amount of chutzpah, he also used Operation Lena to pass information to the KGB through legal channels. At times, Lena reported that certain Org secrets were already leaked to the Soviets. In response, Felfe convinced the attorney general in Bonn to declassify such information, known to the enemy in any case. Then, he provided this useful intelligence to the Soviets through Lena, allegedly in order to "build up" the reputation of his agent. Reinhard Gehlen was exhilarated by the "Lena" materials and used them to promote his status among decision makers in Bonn. Felfe, of course, became one of his favorite agents.[14]

LEFT: "An isolated green field adorned with scattered wild alpine flowers." Here, in Misery Meadows, Reinhard Gehlen buried his treasure trove of Soviet documents, the stepping stone for his clandestine career in the postwar years. *Photo by Danny Orbach.*

RIGHT: Reinhard Gehlen, a former Wehrmacht intelligence analyst and the founding father of West Germany's secret service, made use of Nazi mercenaries during the early years of the Cold War. Here in a Wehrmacht uniform, 1942. *Photo © Ullstein Bild via Getty Images, image no. 537135205.*

BELOW: Heinz Felfe, a former SD officer (center), was Moscow's most dangerous mole in the heart of West German intelligence. *Photo © Mehner/Ullstein Bild via Getty Images, image no. 550250591.*

LEFT: "Eichmann's best man": Alois Brunner, circa 1940. *Photo © AFP via Getty Images, image no.106780796.* CENTER: A fugitive criminal: Alois Brunner (with dark glasses, far right) posing in Damascus along with his business partner Karl-Heinz Späth (second from the right), Späth's wife and Brunner's disgruntled flatmate, Curt Witzke (far left). Brunner and Späth were among the founders of OTRACO, the Nazi arms trading racket. This picture was stolen from Syria in 1960 by the intelligence peddler Hermann Schaefer. *Photographer unknown.* BOTTOM: FLN fighters, 1955. The Algerian Underground, FLN, was starved for weapons during the early phase of its uprising against the French. Many arms merchants hastened to supply their needs, among them the Nazi mercenaries of OTRACO. *Photo © AFP via Getty Images, image no. 1234635007.*

ABOVE: Blown Away: French vengeance against the Nazi arms merchant Wilhelm Beisner was cruel and swift. Beisner's car after the assassination attempt, October 14, 1960. *Photo by Ullstein Bild via Getty Images, image no. 542427651.* RIGHT: "A punitive attack": part of the handwritten report of Ner, the Mossad assassin sent to kill Alois Brunner in Damascus, September 1961. Facsimile copy. *Citation: Yossi Chen*, Ha-mirdaf aharei poshe'i milhama Nazim *(internal Mossad study, declassified in 2014, Yad Vashem Archives), vol. 2, p. 126.* BELOW: Hans Clemens ("the boxer") brought to court with his head covered. The arrest of the Soviet agents, former Nazis Felfe, Clemens, and Tiebel, threatened to undo West German intelligence. *Photo © Fritz Fischer/Picture Alliance via Getty Images, image no. 1063537718.*

"His Nazi past came to haunt him from multiple quarters": State Secretary Hans Globke, West Germany's Chancellor's Chief of Staff (1953–1963, right), here with Chancellor Dr. Konrad Adenauer (left) in Rome, August 1963. Globke was a close ally of Reinhard Gehlen's intelligence service. In the early 1960s, he was dragged into several scandals involving former Nazis. *Photo © DPA/Zumapress.com.*

The Nazi fugitive Franz Rademacher was directly responsible for the extermination of Yugoslavian Jews. In the early 1960s, he was trapped between the Syrian security service, West Germany's spy agency, and greedy Nazi businessmen. Here facing trial in Bamberg, Germany, 1968. *Photo © DPA/Zumapress.com.*

LEFT: Eli Cohen, the Mossad top spy in Damascus, met Franz Rademacher and asked headquarters in Tel Aviv for permission to kill him. The Mossad declined. *Photo © Israeli Government Press Office (GPO).* BELOW: Gamal Abdel Nasser, the president of Egypt (1954–1970). An unrelenting enemy of Israel, Nasser enjoyed enormous popularity in his country and throughout the Arab world. His attempt to hire German rocket scientists raised existential fears in the Jewish State. BELOW: Here with crowds after the nationalization of the Suez Canal, July 1956. *Photo © Hulton-Deutsch Collection/Corbis/corbis via Getty Images, image no. 613468378.*

ABOVE: "It was as if the sky were falling on our heads." Egyptian crowds celebrating new rockets in the Revolution Day parade in Cairo, July 1965. Fears moved Israeli decision makers, especially Mossad chief Isser Harel, to launch a campaign of terror and intimidation against the German scientists in Egypt. *Photo © Keystone-France/Gamma-Rapho via Getty Images, image no. 558632541.* RIGHT: "It was something much more profound than an obsession. You couldn't have a rational conversation about it with him." Isser Harel, head of the Mossad (1952–1963) was the architect of "Operation Damocles," a terror campaign against the German scientists in Egypt. *Photo by Moshe Milner, © Israeli Government Press Office (GPO).*

"The Champagne Spy": Wolfgang Lotz, Israel's flamboyant spy in Egypt, took part in Operation Damocles. Here celebrating the publication of his autobiography with Waltraud Lotz, his wife and partner in espionage, 1972. *Photo © Wildes/ Keystone/Hulton Archive via Getty Images, image no. 914883612.*

Israel's Nazi Agent: SS Commando leader Otto Skorzeny in Spain, 1959. *Photo © Keystone Features/ Hulton Archive via Getty Images, image no. 954630452.*

RIGHT: An astute spy chief who knew how to integrate covert operations into coherent political strategies. Gen. Meir Amit, head of the Mossad, 1963–1968. *Photo by Saar Yaakov, © Israeli Government Press Office (GPO).*

BELOW: In July 1980, the Mossad tried to kill Alois Brunner for the second and last time. Here is the floor plan of his apartment in Damascus, George Haddad St. no. 22, prepared by the agent "Stiff" as part of the operation's intelligence file. *Citation: Yossi Chen,* Ha-mirdaf aharei poshe'i milhama Nazim *(internal Mossad study, declassified in 2014, Yad Vashem Archives), vol. 2, p. 323.*

Though many in the Org detested Felfe as arrogant, "shamelessly curious," and suspiciously eager, this did nothing to halt his rise. Every afternoon he photographed documents he had smuggled under his clothing and developed the negatives in his vacation home built in a discreet location on the Austrian-German border. Throughout his long service to the Eastern Bloc, Felfe gave his handlers over 15,000 secret documents and twenty microtape recording spools and compromised at least 100 CIA agents behind the Iron Curtain. He also curtailed and manipulated operations and provided his Soviet employers with thorough knowledge on the structure and clandestine methods of the Gehlen Org, BfV, and CIA stations in Germany, including cover names and addresses of agents, operation reports, and monthly counterespionage digests. His tips on Bundeswehr armaments proved particularly useful. In addition, he regularly warned Soviet agents of impending arrests so they could safely escape to the East. And to add insult to injury, he, Clemens, and Tiebel embezzled Org funds. CIA analysts wrote later that as a result, Gehlen's counterintelligence "never had a single success worthy of mention." It was a combination of incompetence, fantasies of Gestapists who persecuted nonexistent communist agents while ignoring real ones, and the vulnerability of Nazi security veterans to Soviet recruitment.[15]

On April 1, 1956, nine months after Ludwig Albert's death, the CIA handed over the reins of the Gehlen Org to the government of the Federal Republic, which had achieved full sovereignty and independence with the end of the occupation. Gehlen's organization now became a federal agency, the only external espionage organization in West Germany. The Stars and Stripes were quietly lowered and removed from the mast in Pullach, Critchfield left his office without fanfare, and now only the black-red-gold German flag fluttered over the green lawns in Camp Nikolaus. And yet, Gehlen and his advisers did nothing to reform the compromised operational and communication methods adopted in part to preserve autonomy and avoid American scrutiny. These methods were by now well-known and readily exploited by the Stasi and the KGB.[16]

Heinz Felfe remained in Pullach, reaching a high position in the Counterintelligence Group. Though some in the CIA still suspected him of being a traitor, Critchfield personally told Felfe that the CIA had no suspicions against him, rendering Albert's investigation null and void. Felfe visited the United

States as part of a formal delegation and was cleared without difficulties by the CIC, which remained suspicious yet silent. Possibly, they were paralyzed by the Albert and Trudeau debacles, and were also afraid to expose their illegal espionage activity inside the West German government.[17] When, in spring 1956, the Gehlen Org was officially rechristened the "Federal Intelligence Service" (German: *Bundesnachrichtendienst*, or in short, BND), very few had noticed the irony of the date. It was April Fool's Day.

·PART II·

FALLOUT AND CONSEQUENCES

In 1956, Gehlen had finally realized his ambitions. Within a decade he had transformed himself, utilizing the patronage of American spymasters and selected West German politicians, from a ragtag POW into the undisputed master of an independent West German intelligence service.

In 1962, only six years later, Gehlen was a broken man professionally and personally. Though still formally hanging on to his position, he and the BND itself were discredited in the eyes of West Germany's allies, the West German government, and the West German public. His failures would lead to estrangement from his old patron, Konrad Adenauer, and his bureau chief, Hans Globke. By 1968, six further years down the line, pressure from the government drove him into retirement.

How had matters come to this? Felfe's eventual exposure as a Soviet double agent in November 1961 was certainly the immediate trigger for Gehlen's fall and for the gutting of the BND's effectiveness against East Germany and the Soviet Union. But it could not have had the effect it did were it not for the propensity of Gehlen's BND to fish in troubled waters, foreign and domestic, all too often using Nazi mercenaries as fishing rods.

The exposure risked by such practices might have proved manageable had these waters not been haunted by far bigger and nastier fish than the middling power of the West German Federal Republic, and had the Federal Republic not been so dependent on the goodwill of the US, France, and even tiny Israel to maintain its international position and independence

versus the Soviet juggernaut. Gehlen's fall was ultimately
caused by his unconscious choice of keeping, in addition to
anti-communism, other toxic components of Hitler's rubbish
heap: hubris and willful self-delusion.

Hubris led Gehlen and the BND to profligately make use of the
"diaspora" of Nazi mercenaries in the Middle East and beyond
as agents of influence. Willful self-deception led him to dis-
regard the perils inherent in the exposure of the connections
that "New Germany" maintained with the bloody specters of the
Third Reich—or in the susceptibility of these supposed free
agents to Soviet exploitation and manipulation. Delusions of
a global power role for West Germany led the BND to become
entangled in the Algerian War of Independence through a Nazi
arms trafficking ring, endangering Franco-German rapprochement. Muleheaded repression of the liabilities inherent in
the association of the inheritors of the Third Reich's legacy
with Nazi war criminals exposed the BND and Bonn in general
to the fallout of the Eichmann trial and Mossad's Nazi-hunting
activities. Ultimately, this would endanger Jewish-German
reconciliation and West German international rehabilitation.

In a near-perfect storm, the public scandals of Felfe's
exposure, BND involvement with Nazi mercenaries, the Algerian
War, and the Eichmann trial erupted nearly simultaneously—
thanks in no small part to Soviet manipulation and exacerbated
by the panicked response of Gehlen and other West German
leaders.

Gehlen stands at the center of this account of hubris,
self-deception, and the near-destruction of West German
intelligence. It is the odyssey of the nefarious Alois
Bruner, however, that binds together the disparate threads
of Nazi arms trafficking rings, Mossad Nazi hunters, and
BND's Nazi skeletons. This thoroughly evil man would suffer a
thoroughly evil end in the dungeons of Syria's Assad regime.
But between his flight to Syria and the torture cell where
he would perish, his blood-drenched hands would be on every
sauerkraut jar, ultimately contributing to Gehlen's exposure
and downfall.

· 7 ·

Fishing in Troubled Waters

And it is worthy of remark, that although each person present disliked the
other mainly because he or she did belong to the family, they one and all
concurred in hating Mr. Tigg because he didn't.

—CHARLES DICKENS, *THE LIFE AND ADVENTURES OF MARTIN CHUZZLEWIT*

WEST GERMANY IN the immediate postwar years seemingly had no business engaging in covert intelligence operations overseas. Its independence was not yet fully secured, its representation of the German People challenged by a rival communist government in East Germany, and its security from Soviet expansionism dependent on the commitment of American, British, French, and other European nations, most of them former enemies and victims of the Third Reich. Given this perilous situation, fishing in troubled waters where the substantial interests of West Germany's guarantors collided with that of their Soviet nemesis would seem to be fraught with many risks while promising paltry rewards. Nonetheless, a combination of economic concerns, a residual desire to play a role on the world stage, and private empire building by Gehlen Org operatives resulted in considerable West German involvement in the newly established nations of the Middle East.

Nazi mercenaries would play a key role in this involvement, because both the CIA and its clients from the Gehlen Org believed that the purported anti-communism of these Nazis would make them useful recruits in the ideological struggle between East and West. This assumption had proven a disastrous miscalculation in Europe, as in the case of Heinz Felfe, the communist mole, and other former Nazis who were prepared to work for any paymaster. It would prove to be no less erroneous in the Middle East where Nazi intelligence peddlers served all too frequently as the option of first resort for Bonn's chaotic intelligence efforts.

The efforts of the embryonic West German intelligence agencies to gain a foothold in the Middle East in the late 1940s and the early 1950s did not develop ex nihilo. The Arab world, Turkey, and Iran were replete with strategic value, oil, and other natural resources that attracted the attention of German policy makers even in the pre-WWI era.[1] During the Second World War, many Arabs sympathized with Nazi Germany, the enemy of their British and French colonial overlords, though these feelings were far from being universal. Iraq, for example, erupted in a pro-Axis rebellion that pinned down British forces during the British-German struggle in Egypt's Western Desert. Egyptian officers, including future Egyptian president Anwar Sadat, sought German and Italian aid against the British. The Fascist Young Egypt Party and its Green Shirts openly clashed in the street with adherents of the mainstream national liberal Wafd party and other Egyptian allies of Great Britain. At one point, the British resorted to placing the palace of their client King Farouk under siege in order to force him to expel pro-German advisers and install a government friendly to London. Syria and Lebanon witnessed vibrant Nazi and Fascist movements with considerable popularity, at least until Germany began to suffer defeats in the Levant following the Anglo-French occupation of Syria in July 1941. In Persia, too, Britain and the Soviet Union co-occupied the country following the Shah's refusal to expel German advisers and his insistence on adapting a neutralist position. Turkey signed a treaty of friendship with Nazi Germany and factions within the governing circles, influenced and subsidized by Nazi agents, pushed toward joining Germany's anti-Soviet crusade.[2]

Quite a few Arabs, Iranians, and Turks worked with Nazi intelligence agencies between 1939 and 1945, so it seemed relatively easy to reactivate these networks for the benefit of the emerging West German state. German intelligence leaders also hoped to secure profitable arm deals for German companies, penetrate Arab intelligence services, and crowd out Soviet and East German influence in this strategic region. At the time, it was unclear whether Egypt and Syria would join the capitalist or the communist side of the Cold War, so West Germany's American protectors were not intrinsically opposed to reactivation of these networks, or to exploiting Nazi agents in order to increase their leverage over Cairo and Damascus.[3]

Inside West Germany, the Gehlen Org vied for Middle Eastern influence with a rival intelligence agency, the Friedrich-Wilhelm-Heinz-Dienst (FWHD). This organization operated under the new unofficial Ministry of Defense. Unlike the Gehlen Org, it was independent from the Americans, and therefore initially more attractive to the West German government.[4] Its leader, Friedrich Wilhelm Heinz, was a colorful figure. As a right-wing terrorist, he took part in political assassinations in the Weimar Republic. Later, he turned against the Nazi regime and conspired with the anti-Nazi underground to assassinate Hitler. Heinz and Gehlen competed for influence in the nascent West German government as each one sought to become the single intelligence leader of the new country. A foothold in the Middle East could be an important source of prestige and influence in this domestic struggle. In these turf wars, neither service hesitated to employ former Nazi intelligence hands, including fugitive criminals.

West Germany's feuding spymasters knew, however, that they had to tread cautiously. Until 1955, Germany was formally an occupied country, and its intelligence agencies worked under the auspices of the Allied powers. France, Britain, and, increasingly, the United States and the Soviet Union, competed for influence in the Middle East and could potentially foil German activity in this region.[5] Therefore, it made sense for Gehlen and his archrival Heinz to delegate authority to various intelligence peddlers, mostly former Nazis and their Arab collaborators, and to recruit German officers who worked in Egypt and Syria as military advisers. Gehlen and Heinz believed that by using the service of such third parties, they could maintain plausible deniability in case of trouble with the allies.

On May 14, 1948, Gehlen dispatched his assistant and erstwhile competitor, Hermann Baun, to Tehran as the head of the so-called "Tigris Group." Baun began his postwar career as a leader of yet another competing secret service. Unlike Heinz's operation, however, Baun worked under American tutelage that enabled the Org to leverage its influence with the CIA and swallow Baun's espionage racket. Brilliant but unstable, Baun envisioned a network of spies with deep penetration of trade unions, communist parties, governments, and other organizations throughout the world. In the Middle East, he hoped to capitalize on Arabs who supported Germany during the Second World War. Some of his contacts were Circassians in Syria with ties to Moscow. Others were Moroccan nationalists and exiled Palestinians. The private secretary of the Mufti of Jerusalem, Baun said, could help him penetrate the Muslim republics of the Soviet Union. At the same time, Baun boasted of contacts in the Israeli government and in Jewish international organizations. He claimed he had a Jewish spy who worked for Germany already during the First World War and was now ready to resume contact.[6] Gehlen ordered Baun to focus on Syria and recruit as many German advisers, both Wehrmacht and SS veterans, as possible. The idea was to use these advisers as agents of influence and counter-communist penetration in Damascus.

Walter Rauff, a fugitive criminal leading the western "wanted" list, was one of the informants of the Gehlen Org in Damascus. Far from being an average SS officer, he had a ghastly reputation as a central Holocaust perpetrator. Among other things, Rauff invented the mobile extermination facilities known as the gas vans, in which 700,000 men, women, and children were asphyxiated to death. In 1942, Rauff and his subordinate, Wilhelm Beisner, were tasked with the establishment of Einsatzgruppe Egypt, formed to exterminate the Jewish population of Palestine. Their plan to extend the Holocaust to the Levant was rendered moot, however, after Rommel's defeat in El Alamein. Until the final expulsion of the Wehrmacht from North Africa in 1943, Beisner and Rauff were based in Tunisia, then Greece and Italy. There they persecuted and tortured local Jews and resistance fighters.[7]

After the war, Rauff was neither tried nor punished. Constantly on the run, he joined the small cohort of German military advisers in Syria and became especially close to the military dictator Husni Za'im. Rauff helped to train Za'im's intelligence service "along Gestapo lines." Among other things, he designed torture devices to interrogate and terrorize Syrian Jews. He may have secretly been in the employ of the British MI6 as well.

Following Za'im's overthrow in summer 1949, Rauff fell from grace. His association with Za'im's regime probably made him suspect in the eyes of the new president, General Sami Hinnawi. Rauf was arrested and accused of terrorism, aid to communists, espionage for the Soviet Union, and torture of Jews.

According to his accusers he was professionally ignorant and drunk most of the time. Along with many other German advisers, he was forced to leave Syria for South America. As we shall later see, he found new employment, surprising as it may seem, with the Israeli intelligence services.[8] Baun's plans for Syria, too, became irrelevant with the fall of Za'im. Soon, Gehlen called him back to Germany, where he ended his career and died soon afterward.

The weakening of Gehlen's position in Syria cleared the way for FWHD, the rival intelligence agency led by Friedrich Wilhelm Heinz. Heinz and his right-hand man, Gerhard Schacht, delegated intelligence gathering in the Middle East to a semi-independent network led by Dr. Wilhelm Höttl, a former SD officer implicated in the extermination of Hungarian Jewry. Höttl, a notorious intelligence peddler, worked with Heinrich Mast, aka "Baron Heinrich von Mast." Mast was an old intelligence hand who served in the First World War and later fought in the Baltics for the German right-wing militias knowns as "Freikorps." From there he seems to have returned to Germany with a fake nobility title, calling himself "Baron."[9] In the 1930s, he spied for the outlawed Nazi party in Austria, then served in the Abwehr. Contrary to the way he sometimes tried to portray himself, Mast was a convinced Nazi who saw all resistance fighters as traitors and sympathized with extreme right-wing circles throughout his life. After 1945, he developed a career as an intelligence peddler, sold dubious intelligence to both the Americans and the Gehlen Org, and was finally employed by Höttl as his chief of staff.[10]

Anti-Semitic as they were, Mast and Höttl did not mind working with Jews. Both, for example, sold the Nazi hunter Simon Wiesenthal information on fugitive war criminals. Much of it was spurious, but some was perfectly accurate. In a conversation with Wiesenthal in 1953, Mast introduced himself as an anti-Nazi and gave the first tip on the Argentinian hiding place of Adolf Eichmann, whom he dismissively called "that filthy swine who dealt with the Jews." Some indications show that Mast and Höttl's tip was intended to curry favor with the Israeli intelligence services, with whom Wiesenthal was in close touch. Wiesenthal reported Eichmann's whereabouts, somewhat belatedly, to the Israeli consulate in Vienna and to the World Jewish Congress (which briefed the CIA), but tragically, this crucial piece of information was ignored. Eichmann would only be captured by the Mossad six years later, based on altogether different leads.[11]

Höttl and Mast's network, alternately codenamed L606 and XG, operated from Austria and Italy under the cover of a publishing house called Nibelungen Verlag. They spied on Soviet troops and monitored suspected communists in political parties, companies, trade unions, and other organizations. In addition, they employed attractive women who flirted with Soviet officers to elicit classified information. Using Höttl's excellent connections with the Italian Secret Service and the Vatican, L606/XG cooperated with underground networks that smuggled fugitive war criminals, arms, and contraband goods to Italy, the Middle East, North Africa, and South America.

Department B5 of the network, headquartered in Italy, was responsible for espionage in Middle Eastern countries such as Syria, Lebanon, Egypt, Saudi Arabia, and Tunisia.[12] Heinz, Schacht, and their Austrian contractors actively looked for former Nazi intelligence agents, officers, and experts. They hoped to recruit some of the German advisers in Syria to their espionage venture, which they presented as an anti-communist crusade. With the help of these advisers, they hoped to win support in the new Syrian government, block communist influence, and, according to Schacht's testimony, prevent another war between Israel and the Arabs. In the long term, they wanted to form a basis for espionage in the Soviet Union itself, especially in the Muslim republics of the Caucasus and Central Asia. Schacht insisted that the recruited German advisers must not wear Syrian uniforms, carry arms, or participate in any hostilities against Israel. He also presented himself as a loyal ally of the United States. His agents, he promised, would do their best to safeguard Syrian airports and landing sites for the U.S. Air Force in case of a new World War.[13]

In fact, much of the intelligence supplied by Mast and Höttl was low-grade or outright false, and at least some of the "agents" were products of their fertile imaginations. Even worse, their network was penetrated by the Soviets. At least one of the senior employees, an SS officer named Alois Edder, was a double agent, and the same could probably be said about Höttl himself, who was ready to sell anything to anyone for the right amount of cash. In November 1952, Heinz and Schacht sacked Höttl. He had conned the Americans in the past and now they, along with the French and the British, told Heinz in no uncertain terms what they had already told the Gehlen Org in 1949: that Höttl was a charlatan and a suspected double agent. The sacked intelligence peddler blamed Heinz and other resistance fighters, "traitors to their fatherland," for his misfortune. Heinrich Mast lingered for another year, charged with the gradual liquidation of the operation. On the verge of bankruptcy, he finally found a job as an informer of the French Intelligence Service.[14]

• • •

THE FAILED NETWORK of Höttl and Mast was a prototype for many such future groups. Even after its demise, both Gehlen and Heinz continued to use gangs of former Nazis to expand their foothold in the Middle East and North Africa. Cairo, like Damascus, had its own share of German advisers, including intelligence peddlers, and therefore served as an additional playground for feuding German agencies. Egyptian leaders began to recruit technicians from the former Reich soon after their country's defeat in the Israel-Arab war of 1948. The British left Egypt ample amounts of captured German arms, and Cairo needed German technicians and instructors in order to use them correctly. The defeat in the war with Israel left Egypt licking its wounds and hungry for revenge, and the army needed foreign experts to rebuild its capacities. Many elite Egyptians, especially in the army, admired Nazi Germany and its military leaders, the enemies of their hated British occupiers.[15]

On the German side, there was increased demand for jobs in Egypt. The ruins of the former Nazi Empire were full of people who wanted out. Suspected war criminals were eager to escape German justice, slow and feeble as it might have been. Military experts, technicians, and scientists found no market for their expertise at home. As a result, Germans were tempted to emigrate to the land of the pyramids. Advisers began to arrive in a trickle in the late 1940s under the Egyptian monarchy, and continued to emigrate in greater numbers after the revolution of 1952 to serve the newly established Free Officer Regime. A military cohort led by General Wilhelm Fahrmbacher advised the Egyptian Army and devised its defense plans. The paratrooper Gerhard Mertins trained Egyptian guerillas to fight British occupation soldiers in the Suez Canal Zone. Economic advisers, led by Goering's former assistant Dr. Wilhelm Voss, focused on local industry. Though inflated in many sensational accounts, the number of German advisers in Egypt was in fact quite modest—no more than a hundred at most.[16]

On the periphery of the German advisory community there were also some SS officers, fugitive criminals, and neo-Nazis in exile, including: the Gestapo and Einsatzgruppe officer Joachim Deumling, a double agent who served as an adviser to the Egyptian security services and as a BND spy; the venomous anti-Semitic propagandist Johann von Leers; and Otto Remer, Fritz Dorls, and Ernst-Wilhelm Springer, the leaders of the Social Reich Party, a neo-Nazi organization banned in West Germany.[17] One of the most shady among the Cairo Nazis, who will play a crucial role in our story, was Wilhelm Beisner, Rauff's minion in Einsatzgruppe Egypt and a murderer complicit in numerous pogroms and persecutions of Jews in the Balkans and North Africa. As the head of the Arab Section in the foreign intelligence service of the SS, he was in close touch with Arab nationalists in the Middle East, including Haj Amin Al Husseini, the Mufti of Jerusalem and a staunch ally of the Nazi Germany. These connections would serve Beisner well in his postwar career.[18]

Beisner, an intimidating ruffian of towering height, moved to Egypt in 1951 as a representative of Terramar Hamburg, an arms company that worked with the Gehlen Org. Soon he became one of the more questionable characters in the local German community. Along with his job with Terramar, he worked as an arms dealer for a company known as Egyptian Continental Trading, which was shunned even by the West German Embassy. According to a CIA source, he had "plenty of money, never seems to do any work and is in contact with a number of questionable characters in Egypt." Another source described him as "primitive, rude and ill-mannered."[19] He was also dangerous to deal with: After he broke off with his former business partner, the arms dealer Joachim Hertslet, he provided the West German authorities incriminating evidence on the latter's involvement in foreign espionage.[20] Beisner's wife, known in the arms merchants' milieu as "Blond Alice," remained in Germany. She continued to cooperate in her husband's business, but the relations between them were tense. In the 1950s, Beisner became increasingly violent, and often beat their only child.[21]

Beisner also worked for the Egyptians. Officially, he was the secretary of Abbas Halim, the brother-in-law of deposed King Farouk. After the Free Officers Revolution, he was hired as a sabotage instructor for Egyptian intelligence, and advised Cairo's security services "in the field of personnel and organizational matters."[22] During the early 1950s, Beisner was busy selling military hardware to the Egyptian government, mostly machine guns exported by Alfa, a Madrid firm belonging to Otto Skorzeny, Hitler's most famous commando leader and now a celebrity in the Nazi mercenary community. The transactions failed, though, and Skorzeny's proposal to train Egyptian commandos and replace the existing cadre of German advisers with more militant experts was also turned down. Skorzeny's demands were "astronomical" and unacceptable to the Egyptian government.[23] And yet, Beisner slowly built his reputation as an international arms dealer. He also represented various German firms who wanted a finger in the lucrative pie of the Middle Eastern arms trade.[24]

Installed in Cairo, Beisner became an intelligence peddler. Even though an Org front company helped get him to Egypt, he was initially associated with the Institute for Contemporary Research, the front organization of Gehlen's rivals from Heinz's FWHD.[25] Beisner's wartime role did not deter Heinz, the former anti-Nazi resistance fighter, from working with him, but this cooperation did not last long. In 1953, Gehlen managed to convince the West German government to dissolve Heinz's fledgling service, leaving Gehlen as the one and only foreign intelligence leader of the Federal Republic.[26]

Beisner was quick to switch sides. He began working for Gehlen and the BND, first informally, and then in 1957 as an official agent under the alias "Bertram." Gehlen tried to use him as well as other German mercenaries in Cairo and Damascus to create a bridgehead in the Middle East, fight Soviet influence in the Arab world, and inform Pullach on local affairs. A West German intelligence network based on Nazi intelligence peddlers was slowly taking shape, with the full knowledge and agreement of the Americans, who hoped to receive intelligence and access to agents of influence in the Middle East.[27] However, even as the BND was energetically weaving Nazi exiles into its espionage web, other fugitives, some too toxic for even the BND to employ, were busy securing their own individual positions and building up their own dark networks.

· 8 ·

The House on Rue Haddad

Damascus is simply an Oasis, that is what it is . . . so long as its waters
remain to it away out there in the midst of that howling desert, so long
will Damascus live to bless the sight of the tired and thirsty wayfarer.

—MARK TWAIN, *THE INNOCENTS ABROAD*

THE MOST INFAMOUS of fugitives was supposedly executed by the Soviets in May 1946, following a guilty verdict in the People's Court of Vienna. The defendant, denounced by the newspapers as the "butcher of Jews from Vienna," was a man named Anton Brunner, a former Gestapo employee. He was accused of sending 49,000 Jews to their death. Witness after witness took the stand, and all of them reported how Brunner mistreated, berated, and physically assaulted Jewish prisoners in Vienna. The defendant was indeed guilty of these charges, at least in part. As a former employee of Adolf Eichmann's "Central Agency for the Immigration of Jews," he was part of the genocidal machine. During the trial, however, Brunner insisted he was only a small fry. He claimed that his employee, Alois Brunner, Eichmann's second-in-command, was the real culprit. Some witnesses confirmed the existence of an even more notorious criminal with the same surname. In the Gestapo, they were known as "Brunner I" and "Brunner II."[1]

The judges, however, did not believe the defendant. As far as they were concerned, they had the real culprit in their hands. Anton Brunner was executed on May 24, 1946, giving Alois the opportunity of a lifetime. For years, the similarity between Anton and Alois baffled judicial and police authorities in Austria and other countries. Even some analysts in the CIA believed, as late as 1961, that Alois Brunner was already executed.[2]

Meanwhile, Alois Brunner remained under the radar. As Eichmann's personal assistant, he was responsible for numerous genocidal crimes. In Eichmann's department, Brunner served as a troubleshooter for deportations and was in charge of a systematic machine of manhunt, pillage, and transport of Jews to extermination camps in the East. Brunner's system was designed so the victims would facilitate their own destruction. Jews informed on their brethren to save themselves, only to be murdered shortly afterward. Jewish property was used to finance the deportation machine, and even to remunerate non-Jewish informers and hunters. Far from being only a "desk murderer," Alois Brunner participated in beatings and torture along with his subordinates. He was a true believer.[3]

After the war, like many other Nazi fugitives, Brunner I assumed a false name (Alois Schmaldienst) and spent several short stints in various POW camps. He worked in a variety of menial jobs, including as a café waiter and a driver in an American base. The fugitive had another important advantage. Unlike most SS men, he lacked the infamous blood type tattoo under his arm—the mark of Cain that made one liable to automatic arrest by the occupation authorities.[4] And yet, Alois Brunner could not sleep easy. His name appeared on too many wanted war criminals lists.

The Americans, the Soviets, and other Allied powers were ready to make exceptions for useful Nazis, especially scientists and intelligence specialists, but Brunner was of no use to anybody. Worse, he was unpopular even among many former Nazis. Otto Skorzeny, the famed commando fighter who lived in Spain and was honored as a dignitary in the postwar neo-Nazi community, reportedly said of him, "for a swine I won't lift a finger."[5] And time was pressing. In 1953, trials of Nazi criminals began in West Germany as well.

To be sure, they were feeble and slow, almost deliberately so. Few in Bonn's leadership wanted to engage in a Nazi manhunt or shine a light on Germany's dark past. Most members of the ruling elites, even men with unblemished anti-Nazi wartime credentials such as Chancellor Konrad Adenauer, were compromised by association with men with less pristine records, such as Adenauer's right-hand man, Hans Globke. Indeed, the legal norms of the West German judicial system almost seemed designed to avoid charging any but the highest ranking Holocaust perpetrators—and to give those who must be charged a chance to slip away before indictments matured, sometimes with the active assistance of elements within the German Foreign Office, the judiciary, or the Gehlen Org. Once beyond West Germany's borders, scant efforts were made to demand extradition. Such would remain the case until the advent of Dr. Fritz Bauer as attorney general of the State of Hessen, under the powerful patronage of its SPD (Socialist Democratic Party) minister-president, George-August Zinn, in 1956, and the establishment of the Central Office for the Investigation of National Socialist Crimes in Ludwigsburg two years later.[6]

Nonetheless, Brunner was a sufficiently conspicuous Holocaust perpetrator to have cause for concern that his eventual arrest would be inevitable. He had many enemies, and any one of them might inform on him to the West Germans, the Americans, or the French. The last possibility was especially worrisome, because Brunner committed many of his crimes on French soil. In December 1953, he may have been informed that a court-martial in Marseilles sentenced him to death in absentia.[7] Bonn, where he was hiding, was too close to France. He had to move without delay.

Later, Brunner would recount an incredible story about his escape. In June 1954, according to his account, he teamed up with one Dr. Georg Fischer, a senior SS officer who worked as a liaison to the German Foreign Office.[8] During the annual carnival in Bonn, Fischer and Brunner went together to a barbershop. The two, who outwardly resembled one another, told the barber they wanted to trick their wives by exchanging their appearance. A weird practical joke, but in Bonn's carnival atmosphere even the ridiculous was possible. The barber dyed Brunner's hair and shaved his beard, so he'd resemble his comrade Fischer as much as possible. Fischer underwent a similar treatment. Then, Alois Brunner assumed not only Fischer's look, but also took his passport. Later, Fischer denied the entire story, and complained that Brunner stole his passport. Brunner, in private conversations, would also sometimes make the same admission. "He said with a grin that he found the passport outside Dr. Fischer's door," told Hermann Schaefer, one of the first journalists who exposed Brunner, ". . . and exchanged [Fischer's] picture with his own."[9]

In any case, Brunner boarded a train to Amsterdam, then a flight to Rome, armed with a forged passport under the name Georg Fischer. He received money for the trip from Rudolf Vogel, an anti-Semitic propagandist who worked in Greece during the war. After 1945, Vogel reinvented himself as a respectable conservative politician in West Germany's ruling party, the Christian Democratic Union (CDU). He might also have been blackmailed by Brunner, who knew too much about his past.[10] From Rome, Brunner traveled to Egypt. In May 1954, shortly after his escape to the Middle East, the Court of the Armed Forces in Paris approved his death sentence.[11]

Brunner entered Egypt on a tourist visa and took residence in a small apartment at Heliopolis, one of the Egyptian capital's affluent neighborhoods. Ironically enough, his landlords were Egyptian Jews whom he remembered as "very nice."[12] Established in Cairo, the fugitive hangman encountered a tangled web of German advisers, agents, intelligence peddlers, and others embroiled in the dark business of espionage and arms trafficking. He was destined to play a major role in the fights between feuding German, Western, communist, Israeli, and Arab intelligence agencies.

In spite of the high concentration of former Nazis in Cairo, Alois Brunner was unwelcome in the Egyptian capital. Cairo was already crowded with military, scientific, and technical German experts, and the Egyptian regime had no use for genocide specialists. Worse, Brunner suffered a run-in with the Egyptian Secret Service, and was forced to leave the country. With the help of Haj Amin Al Husseini, the former Mufti of Jerusalem and a major Nazi ally in the Middle East, he took a flight to yet another destination: the Syrian capital of Damascus.[13]

Former Nazis, as we have already seen, were not a rarity in 1950s Damascus. Military advisers from the Wehrmacht and the SS, including the notorious mass murderer Walter Rauff, already established a military mission in the Syrian capital in 1949. The Germans served informally as advisers, without wearing uniforms or holding command authority over troops. Other Holocaust perpetrators such as Franz Stangl, the former commandant of Treblinka, an extermination camp, lived there as fugitives without a formal position. Stangl, like Brunner, received help from the Grand Mufti of Jerusalem, that guardian angel of Nazi refugees in the Middle East.[14]

When Brunner arrived in Damascus, the German colony was already past its prime. In the late 1940s and the 1950s, Syria was rocked by frequent coups d'état and political upheavals. When one strongman was replaced by another, the new rulers did not always look with favor on the foreign advisers of their predecessors. In addition, many advisers were clearly con men, incompetent, or otherwise unqualified for their jobs. Luftwaffe fighters or NCOs with zero experience in training, for example, volunteered to oversee education programs for Syrian pilots and even infantry formation training. The West German Foreign Ministry hoped to exploit the advisers to crowd out Soviet influence in Syria, but such hopes were undermined by Bonn's reparations agreement with Israel in 1952. As a result, Syria gravitated toward the Soviet Union, and its relations with West Germany became increasingly tense.[15]

Thus, the number of German professionals in Damascus decreased with every passing year. In 1954, when Brunner arrived, there were still some German military advisers in the Syrian capital, but most would be gone in a year or two. The Germans who remained were mostly diplomats, businessmen, or war criminals on the run. Such people naturally created a tight social circle along with German-speaking Syrians who served in Nazi intelligence operations or SS units comprised of Muslim volunteers during the Third Reich.

Brunner's first patron was Karl-Heinz Späth, a corpulent businessman who managed several companies in Syria, including a pharmaceutical firm named Thameco, and Qatar Office, an import-export and real estate business. He was known in Nazi Middle Eastern circles as "the fat one." To his friends in Damascus he said that he escaped West Germany due to his past in the Gestapo or, according to another version, because he carried incriminating material on senior politicians in Bonn. In fact, he was a petty criminal. The companies of "the fat one" were a front for weapons trafficking. He procured American arms and strategic goods for the Syrian government and other Arab countries, as well as for the Soviet Union and the Eastern Bloc. Thameco, based in Vaduz, Lichtenstein, had a crucial role: to camouflage weapons, strategic items, and dual-use goods as legitimate merchandise with falsified permits from the West German authorities. As a result, the Americans barred Späth from any travel to the United States and from doing business in all NATO countries. At that point he took up spying for both the BND and the Syrian Secret Service, giving one information on Syria and the other on Germany. Obviously, the German diplomats in Damascus did not appreciate him. "A mediocre con man," reported the West German consul, "who was eager to indulge in dark talk in order to inflate his own status." In 1955, Späth hired Brunner as the executive director of his companies.[16]

Brunner, always dressed elegantly, sporting a short beard and small mustache, went under the name Dr. Georg Fischer though he had never earned an academic degree. As Späth's protégé, he quickly became known as a real estate agent, a representative of German textile companies, and an importer of luxury goods. He endeared himself to the local German community by importing first-rate beer and producing homemade sauerkraut. He also baked dark bread, and occasionally offered one of his pet rabbits to a hungry friend. And yet, always wary, he kept a certain distance from Germans who were not proven Nazis, and especially from the consulate of the Federal Republic. A German Lutheran priest who lived nearby remembered him as an unpleasant type, self-absorbed and domineering. In the street, he habitually wore dark glasses, and almost always refused to be photographed.[17]

In 1957, Brunner settled in a smart, small two-room apartment in Rue George Haddad 22, located in the affluent Abu Rummaneh district of Damascus. A British journalist who came to visit decades later wrote that it was "the sort of quiet, tree-lined thoroughfare in which pensioners prefer to end their days."[18] The Polish Embassy was nearby, as well as the serene Gardens of Sibki (Zenobia), in which Brunner used to take his morning strolls. The apartment, in fact, was government property, rented to official guests and senior government employees. Brunner was not the first Nazi to live there. In the past, it housed a succession of German fugitives, including Franz Stangl, the commandant of Treblinka extermination camp.[19]

Brunner, who did not work for the Syrian government at the time, entered as a sublessee of a stiff monocle-wearing German officer. This former cavalry captain, Curt Witzke, emigrated to Syria after 1945 and worked there as a military adviser. He retired from the Syrian army, along with many other advisers, in the mid-1950s, but remained active in Syria as a German language instructor. Like so many others, Witzke also doubled as an import-export businessman (mainly in grain) and arms merchant for anti-French rebels in North Africa, though he fared quite poorly in that business. Later he claimed he didn't know anything about the real identity of his tenant. The relations between the two were stormy from the very beginning, as Brunner habitually hosted prostitutes in the apartment, much to Witzke's chagrin.[20]

When prostitutes were not around, Brunner met with fellow Nazis in Späth's apartment for lengthy games of bridge. A frequent guest around the table was Franz Rademacher, the former director of the Foreign Ministry's Jewish Department and a wanted war criminal in his own right. He lived in Damascus under the false name Bartolomeo (Tome) Rossello and ran the import-export section of a firm managed by a nephew of the Syrian president. The leaders of the defunct neo-Nazi "Social Reich Party" (SRP), Otto Remer and Ernst-Wilhelm Springer, also came by during their visits to Damascus.[21]

At that time, Brunner always had money. Along with Späth, he smuggled restricted goods, especially weapons, from the United States to the Eastern Bloc, and from the Eastern Bloc (especially Czechoslovakia) to neo-Nazi arms merchants in Germany and onward to the Middle East.[22] Like other Nazis in the Middle East, Brunner did business with representatives of both Cold War powers and detested them both. Once, he berated a Syrian neighbor's child for wearing a shirt with the inscription "Los Angeles." The Soviet Union is bad, he said, but the USA is even worse.[23]

Unlike other Middle Eastern Nazis, Brunner never converted to Islam or mastered the Arabic language. His Arabic was broken, and mainly consisted of insults (his favorite was "humar," donkey). He even wrote to a friend, an Austrian neo-Nazi, that the New Testament, Koran, and Talmud were equally deceptive.[24] And yet, he admired the Arab states for their bitter enmity toward Israel and the Jews. Facing similar choices to that of other Middle Eastern Nazis, Brunner chose a lifelong commitment to the Arab cause. Contrary to some of his comrades, he would never sell out his new allies for Israeli dimes. Instead, he would join Wilhelm Beisner and his network in Cairo in a dark but profitable business. Through a front company named OTRACO (Orient Trading Company), both men would traffic in arms for Arab revolutionaries in the Middle East, while maintaining an uneasy cooperation with Gehlen and his colleagues in West German intelligence.[25]

· 9 ·

Orient Trading Company—
The Neo-Nazi Third World Scheme

I deal with everything, even horseshit,
if you want. It just has to bring money.
—HARTMANN LAUTERBACHER, FORMER HITLER YOUTH LEADER AND ARMS TRAFFICKER

THE OFFICE OF Ernst-Wilhelm Springer, a neo-Nazi leader from Bad Sege-berg, was not one you would expect from a follower of Adolf Hitler. An investigative journalist who visited him in the early 1960s was surprised to see an interior befitting an orientalist treasure chamber. On the table rested a cigarette case, ashtray, and matchbox holder, all engraved with Arabic letters. In front of Springer's desk "a genuine oriental prayer mat was spread out. A Damascene dagger, heavily embossed in silver, served as a letter opener, and on the bookshelves, five camels stretched their wood-carved, haughty heads." Behind the camels, the journalist observed Hitler's *Mein Kampf* and several military manuals.[1]

Along with Otto Ernst Remer, a former Wehrmacht officer who squashed the July 1944 military coup against Hitler, Springer was a leading member of the banned Social Reich Party. After his political career was cut short by that party's forced dissolution, he immersed himself in Middle Eastern conflicts. Springer was one of the neo-Nazis who truly believed that Germany had to bind its fate with the Third World and the great Arab nation. Later, when he stood trial for smuggling arms to the Middle East and North Africa, he said in his defense that "the political position of the Arabs," namely their hatred of the Jews, "and their misery moved me to act for the North African freedom movement." In 1955, he was already running back and forth between Germany, Egypt, and Syria in order to establish arms trafficking networks.[2]

Fritz Peter Krüger (alias Gerhard Krüger), another SRP activist and Springer's close partner in the arms trafficking business, also wanted to join "the common battle against the Jews."[3] Otto Remer had similar pro-Arab sentiments and a similar hatred of Israel. In addition, he hoped to use his profits in the arms-smuggling business to rebuild the Nazi movement in Germany and launch a coup against Adenauer's democratic government.[4] Springer, Krüger, and Remer were only the tip of the iceberg: the German side of a network of arms smugglers spanning across Europe, North Africa, and the Middle East.

In August 1957, Springer established in Damascus, together with Remer, Beisner, Rademacher, Späth, and a Syrian partner, Hussein Al-Husseini, a company called Orient Trading Company (OTRACO). Brunner joined the firm as well. The shares were jointly held by Springer (40%), Rademacher (25%), and Husseini (35%).[5]

This firm quickly expanded into a network based in Egypt, Syria, and West Germany. The specialty of OTRACO was trafficking arms to the Middle East and later also to non-Arab governments in Asia, Africa, South America, and the Caribbean, including Castro's Cuba. In West Germany, Springer, Remer, and Krüger managed contracts through the Brock & Schnars firm. They procured weapons and military equipment from Spain, Luxembourg, East Germany, Hungary, Bulgaria, Poland, Yugoslavia, and Czechoslovakia. Even the traditional Nazi hatred of communism was no longer that important. In the Cold War, the OTRACO leaders saw the Soviet Union as the lesser evil.[6] When the arms shipments reached Arab shores, the Middle Eastern Nazis took over from their European colleagues. In Cairo, Wilhelm Beisner was in charge and worked closely with his colleagues in Damascus.[7] The Syrian capital hosted an important branch of OTRACO, comanaged by Späth and Brunner, with Franz Rademacher's collaboration.

In Damascus, OTRACO closely collaborated with a group of Arabs who were fluent German speakers, having served the Nazi regime during the Second

World War. They now made hefty profits from the neo-Nazi arms trafficking business. In the posh Arab Club of Damascus, Nazi mercenaries and arms merchants brushed shoulders with Syrian notables of similar convictions. The club, established in 1918 as a Pan-Arab society, offered a meeting place and cultural home for Damascenes who strove for independence from French rule and the establishment of a "Greater Syria" that would include Syria, Lebanon, and Palestine. In the 1930s, the Arab Club increasingly sported Fascist and Nazi ideas, and its chairman, the dentist Sa'id Fatah Imam, worked in Berlin during the war as an SS intelligence agent and a specialist for Arab affairs, where he was notorious for his fanatic and unconditional admiration for Nazi Germany. After 1945, Imam was busy recruiting German military advisers from POW camps for the fledgling Syrian Arab Republic, with the full knowledge of the British and the French.[8]

In the shadows behind Imam lurked Colonel Mamdouh Al-Midani, yet another Nazi collaborator and now the head of the Syrian Home Ministry's Department for Political Affairs. As a lieutenant in the Waffen SS, he was a close confidant of the Mufti of Jerusalem, Haj Amin Al Husseini. After the war Al-Midani was condemned to death by the French, worked for a while as a military adviser in Saudi Arabia, and returned to Syria in the 1950s as a police commander, then a senior intelligence officer and a specialist in German affairs. Imam, Al-Midani, and other German-speaking Arabs did not limit their business circle to OTRACO, of course. They also kept contact with other neo-Nazi groups, such as Otto Skorzeny's outfit in Madrid.[9] In order to conceal their true business, ORTACO established a chain of straw companies throughout Europe. One of them, "Luxembourg Holdings," was jointly owned by Al-Midani, Remer, Springer, and the Moroccan ambassador to Bonn.[10]

• • •

IN NOVEMBER 1954, Algeria went up in flames. Considered an integral part of the French *patrie*, this North African land had been under the control of Paris for over a century. Resistance, however, was simmering as grinding poverty, economic exploitation, and heavy-handed oppression marginalized pro-French Algerians and shifted support to the secessionist *Front de Libération Nationale*

(FLN). Emboldened by the expulsion of the French from Vietnam and parallel anti-colonial uprisings in Morocco and Tunisia, the Algerian rebels launched a bloody struggle for national independence that would last eight years. In the first years of the uprising, the Algerians were ill-trained and ill-equipped. Their procurers were frantically seeking weapons, radio devices, and other military goods on the international arms market.

The original stock of the FLN was mainly comprised of WWII castoffs, inferior arms with numerous technical defects. These light weapons were of diverse types and required specialized ammunition and spare parts, creating a logistical nightmare for FLN fighters and procurers. Therefore, FLN agents looked for higher-quality hardware, especially light arms, everywhere they could, as long as a large percentage of the arms would come from identical manufacturers. After 1956, newly independent Morocco and Tunisia served as the FLN's arm depots, but the French established a system of impregnable barriers on Algeria's borders complete with dense ground, naval, and aerial patrols. The rebels in the Western provinces bordering Morocco, known as Wilaya 5, were especially starved for supplies. Algerian procurers abroad had to find smugglers who were both reliable and daring enough to sneak through the French blockade.[11]

Nasser's regime in Cairo vowed to help the FLN, but initially Egyptian capacity to supply the "Algerian brothers" was limited. As a result of Nasser's failure to stand by his promise, Europe, and especially West Germany, became an important conduit for arms smuggling. True, West German authorities severely limited exports of "weapons of war" to conflict zones such as Algeria. But in fact, transactions in light weapons (*relativwaffen*) could easily bypass this embargo because such arms could also be used for hunting and other non-military purposes. As a result, merchants had to obtain permission only from local authorities. It was very easy to evade these regulators, who often turned a blind eye, to exploit legal loopholes and camouflage heavier weapons as light ones.[12]

One of the greatest experts in such deceptive operations was Otto Schlüter, an owner of a hunting rifle business in the port city of Hamburg. Well-versed in the complex German rules and regulations, Schlüter knew to camouflage military shotguns as sporting guns, sometimes by means of slight technical modifications. For the Algerians, Schlüter was an indispensable partner, and yet he was too cautious for their taste. The Hamburg merchant was ready to bend West German law, but not break it altogether, and starkly refused to deal with bona fide military equipment such as TNT. The Algerian underground, and especially the hard-pressed Wilaya 5, needed bolder merchants and smugglers who were less legally scrupulous than Schlüter.[13] Here they turned to the BND and to the Nazi network of Beisner, Springer, Remer, and their Middle Eastern comrades.

• • •

GEHLEN AND THE BND were pulling multiple strings in the Algerian rebellion from a relatively early stage in order to push the Soviets and East Germans out of the North African sphere. Some of the assistance they gave was direct. In Tunis, a BND agent named Richard Christmann kept in close contact with members of the FLN provisional government and procured for them non-lethal military equipment such as helmets, uniforms, and medical supplies.[14]

In his reports to Bonn, Christmann drew lines between "good" pro-Westerners and "evil" communists in the Algerian ranks. Christmann's allies were the faction of Ahmed Ben Bella, who was imprisoned in France at the time. "Communists" were Ben Bella's rivals, such as Huari Boumediene, a rising leader in the FLN, and his henchmen from Wilaya 5 on the Moroccan border.[15] The BND leadership hedged its bets, as usual, and tried to exercise influence on these "communists" as well through Wilhelm Beisner and OTRACO, who were busy smuggling arms to Algeria through the Moroccan border. In the wild Moroccan theater, OTRACO was the main player.

The Algerian War was a contentious issue for the neo-Nazi movement, both in Germany and throughout the world. Parallel to the West-East debates of the late 1940s, defeated Nazis had to take a stand in a struggle that was not their own. Many of them who defaulted to traditional Eurocentric racism naturally supported "white" France against its unruly natives. Here, they joined a larger camp of pro-Western German conservatives. This support was not merely theoretical. Twenty-thousand Wehrmacht and Waffen SS veterans volunteered for the French Foreign Legion to earn money, take part in exciting adventures, and fight the "war of the white race" in Algeria.[16]

Other Nazis, however, saw the Algerian War in a very different light: a struggle of the awakening Arab world against a corrupted West and "World Judaism" led and represented by the State of Israel. For Springer, Krüger, Remer and the other leaders of OTRACO, traditional racism, with its demarcation between "white" and "colored," disappeared or receded to the background, while hatred of the United States and anti-Semitism went to the fore.

In 1955, the urgent needs of the Algerian rebels, especially Wilaya 5, the procurement difficulties, and the hesitant attitude of conservative traders such as Schlüter created a vacuum that Springer and his friends hastened to fill. On May 20, Springer wrote to Imam that "our common friends in Tangiers want to quickly purchase 10,000 units [of Astra guns from Spain] . . . I ask you, my dear Dr. Imam, to advise me as soon as possible if you can serve as the middleman. That is, if you are ready to supply us with the required import and end-use certificates . . . in such a case we will give you an approximate profit of 2 USD per unit."[17]

The letter was in German, a language in which Imam was fluent. The main item on the agenda was a long-term solution to the problems of Wilaya 5. Using the extensive connections of OTRACO, Brunner, Späth, and Springer would smuggle weapons to the Algerian rebels. From Cairo, Wilhelm Beisner, already an established arms dealer, would use his contacts and experience. Imam's role was to secure Syrian cooperation, and especially the "end-use certificates," forged documents designed to bypass the international embargo on arms trade to conflict zones such as Algeria. Should the weapon shipments be stopped by customs officials in international ports, the documents would prove that they were addressed to Syria—a legitimate, internationally recognized country. As an Arab nationalist, Imam was probably glad to help his brethren in Algeria. As a former Nazi collaborator, it was quite natural for him to work with Springer and his friends. And as a corrupt Syrian official, he looked forward to an enormous profit of 20,000 USD at the very least.[18]

The leaders of OTRACO knew well that they were not the only company in the market. The FLN used multiple agents, procurers, and smuggling routes through Germany, Switzerland, and other countries. However, Springer tried to dominate the largest possible market share and did not shy away from utilizing gangster-like threats. If you cheat me, he told another merchant, "I will not sue you in a court of law. I'll just kill you."[19]

The BND and OTRACO were not, however, operating in a vacuum. The French intelligence services were determined to halt the flow of arms into Algeria, all the more so when supplied by German Nazis, the former occupiers and tormentors of France. Just like Springer, French intelligence did not limit its efforts to legal protestations in a court of law, and the fallout from their assassination operations would endanger not only the lives of leftover Nazis with delusions of grandeur but also the reputation of the BND.

A subtle irony was at work here. Wilhelm Beisner, a very important member of OTRACO, was also an agent of Gehlen; that is, a recipient of West German taxpayer money supposed to promote West German interests. Beisner was a pawn in the larger game of the early Cold War, an actor in the Western-Soviet struggle for Arab support. Through his assistance in arms procurement to both Egyptians and Algerians, his role in Gehlen's BND was to counter Soviet influence in the Middle East.[20] That may well have been Beisner's intention. However, initially, relations with France took precedence in Soviet eyes, and Moscow did not want to sacrifice the friendship of Paris. Using OTRACO was one of many ways to secretly help the Algerians without becoming entangled in diplomatic difficulties. Obviously, it paved the way for eventual open cooperation between the Algerians and the Soviets. In other words, instead of keeping the Arabs pro-Western, Beisner and OTRACO's activity helped push them into the Soviet sphere of influence.[21] Nor was Beisner's OTRACO the only Nazi organization controlled by the Communist Bloc. The Italy-based company of Hans Sommer, another SD war criminal who worked in the BND until he was fired in 1953 due to dubious eastern connections, was in fact a Stasi decoy. Through Sommer, the Stasi planned to enhance its influence in Algeria and find more information on the BND and Nazi arms trafficking networks.[22]

Even worse, by using OTRACO in Algeria and the Arab world, Gehlen and the BND in fact undermined their country's most important interest: rapprochement with France. The BND's recklessness in supporting OTRACO and the resultant French terror campaign against it would endanger the very future of a unified European Community capable of withstanding the Soviet juggernaut.

· 10 ·

The Republic Strikes Back

You know, weapon dealers are an indispensable part of a revolution. In their own way they serve the progress of humanity.

—SI ABD-EL-HAFID BUSSUF, FLN COMMANDER OF WILAYA 5, TO A GERMAN JOURNALIST[1]

✎

UNSETTLED BY THE flow of arms shipments to Algerian insurgents, Paris decided to launch a terror campaign against the German arms merchants. A key figure in the operation was Colonel Marcel-André Mercier, SDECE's representative in West Germany. Mercier was a former fighter in the French resistance who had been jailed and tortured in German concentration camps. After the war, he established excellent "almost friendly" contacts with Reinhard Gehlen and the BND. Heinz Denko-Herre, Gehlen's closest adviser, was impressed by Mercier's cunning and political acumen ("I have the feeling that he's a sly rascal") but liked it less when the colorful Frenchman tried to dance with his wife "in a very inappropriate way."[2]

Already in January 1956, the commander of SDECE, Pierre Boursicot, established a special section inside the service, tasked with identifying and interdicting FLN procurers, intermediaries, funders, and suppliers, as well as charting the routes of this illegal arms trade. Boursicot and his successor, General Paul Grossin, then received government approval to assassinate the German arms traffickers, and assigned the mission to special squads in West Germany, aided by Colonel Mercier, whose job was to liaison with Gehlen and secure his silent assistance.

Using romantic names of fictitious terror organizations such as "The Red Hand" or "Catena" (The Chain), the Service Action, a covert ops branch of SDECE, and the organization's counterespionage department picked off the gunrunners one by one. Each victim was dispatched after approval by the prime minister in Paris and the so-called "Braintrust," a joint war room in SDECE headquarters. This campaign, led by Colonel Morlanne, the commander of Service Action, was designed to "destroy the [FLN's] ringleaders . . . annihilate their clandestine means of communication [. . . and] wipe out the traffic, transit and supply of armaments and other war materials for the benefit of the North African rebellion." Such French covert ops placed the BND in a difficult situation. On the one hand, Gehlen worked closely with Mercier and probably gave him information on some arms traffickers in line with Bonn's policy of Franco-German cooperation. In January 1957, France and West Germany signed an important treaty on armaments production and military planning, followed by understandings on nuclear collaboration. As Chancellor Adenauer recognized, it would be madness to imperil these achievements by arms trafficking to Tunisia and Morocco, let alone the FLN. On the other hand, Gehlen's own agents were deeply involved in the arms trafficking business.[3] This was a contradiction that the BND president was never able to resolve.

SDECE's first target was the relatively law-abiding Otto Schlüter. As a bomb that exploded in his office space in late 1956 failed to deter him, sterner measures were undertaken. On June 3, 1957, French agents installed a bomb under his car. The device exploded when he made a sharp turn in the parking space, killing his aged mother and wounding his daughter. It was a vicious device, with flesh-tearing little metallic balls. Schlüter himself escaped unharmed. Investigators of the Federal Police concluded almost immediately that the assassins were professionals. Schlüter did not leave the business even after his mother's death, but shifted to working through OTRACO rather than independently.[4] OTRACO's leaders, who were far less risk averse than Schlüter, saw an opportunity for the deal of a lifetime. Their involvement in the Algerian independence struggle, however, was destined to end in one of their most spectacular failures, and an international scandal for Bonn.

In 1957, shortly after the establishment of OTRACO, Fritz Peter Krüger traveled to Prague and negotiated a lucrative agreement with the Czechoslovakian government. At the time, Wilaya 5 was accumulating weapons for a planned offensive on the Moroccan-Algerian frontier, and therefore made an enormous order. Springer, Krüger, Beisner, and their fellow Nazis in the Middle East promised to supply 200 crates packed with WWII-era Wehrmacht rifles, two million rounds of ammunition, fifty machine guns, and twenty Russian bazookas. As a bonus, they added fifteen antiaircraft guns, which the Algerian rebels badly needed. The worth of the goods was around 1.6 million USD. Krüger traveled to Prague to inspect the weapons himself. He cabled back to Springer: Nothing to worry about, the goods are first grade.[5] Krüger oversaw the packing of the arms, camouflaged as "agricultural machinery." Then, along with Springer, he boarded a train to the Yugoslav port of Peroj, following the sealed freight carriages.

In Peroj, things started to go wrong. Somebody tipped off the local authorities and Yugoslav police raided the freight train. In short order they uncovered the true nature of the "agricultural machinery" and duly confiscated the weapons. Springer and Krüger were arrested and jailed in Belgrade.

While the two hapless OTRACO comrades were held in prison, Krüger's employees in Germany frantically cabled Damascus. From the Syrian capital, Imam pulled all strings he could. After a few days, Syria's foreign minister, Salah Al-Bittar, personally intervened with President Tito and secured the release of both prisoners and their cargo. The "agricultural machinery" was loaded on a ship and permitted to leave the port. Springer cabled Beisner in Cairo and asked him to fly to Damascus for a final meeting; the customers were waiting. Then, before setting sail with the weapons, Springer telegraphed the final code word: "nice time." Imam, Beisner, and the Algerians now knew that the crates were on their way.[6]

A few weeks later the entire OTRACO gang met in Damascus. Springer and Krüger were invited to a party in the luxurious New Omayyad Hotel along with Imam, Beisner, Brunner, and Rademacher. After three bottles of whiskey went dry, Imam received his commission of 20,000 USD in cash. As night was falling on Damascus, the party became so rowdy that the intoxicated guests began to break glasses and furniture. The manager of the hotel called the police, but no harm was done. The morning sun greeted a group of hungover Germans with dollar signs flashing in their bleary eyes.[7]

Krüger left Damascus immediately after the party. Springer traveled to Latakia port along with Algerian, Egyptian, and Syrian representatives in order to inspect the weapons in person. At the port, they observed a huge crowd of Syrians waving flags, greeting the festive entry of a Soviet flotilla. Amidst the hustle and bustle, the weapons merchants noticed their own freight ship docking and proceeded to examine the goods. When the crates were opened, the representatives were dumbstruck. The shipment of prime weaponry, worth 1.6 million USD for which they had worked so hard, was nothing but worthless junk. The firing pins were missing, some of the sightings and locks were forcibly removed, and much of the hardware was broken. Except for the Russian bazookas, which were in prime condition, virtually nothing was usable.

Every party blamed the other. The Czech submitted documents purportedly proving that the weapons were spotless at their end of the line. Some of OTRACO's competitors wrote Imam that "it is undoubtable that the gentlemen from Hamburg [Springer and his friends] cheated you. It just took [you] an entire year to notice that."[8] But this accusation was ridiculous. Had Springer wanted to cheat his Arab customers, it would have been sheer stupidity on his part to visit the lion's den in Damascus and to stay there when the weapons arrived. Almost certainly, sabotage was involved. French agents had meddled with the weapons during the cargo's quarantine in Yugoslavia. "That," Springer later said, "was the worst debacle of my life."[9]

The Syrians, however, needed a scapegoat, and hapless Springer was right there, ready for the slaughter. Agents of the United Arab Republic's "Second Bureau" (military intelligence) arrested him outright and leaked the affair to the press to fan the public's outrage. Instead of enjoying his new riches in Germany, the neo-Nazi leader, broke and penniless, enjoyed the hospitality of the local government in a Damascene prison. He was released after a few days. It seems Springer was able to convince his Arab partners that the real villain was Krüger. The weapons were dismantled, reassembled and given—as inferior quality arms—to pro-Syrian guerillas in the Lebanese mountains.[10]

After this debacle, known as the "Latakia Affair," the OTRACO Nazis were temporarily discredited in Algerian eyes. At the very least, the FLN wanted somebody they could rely on to manage procurement as their authorized buyer in Europe. They chose one of the most colorful figures of the arms trafficking milieu.

• • •

GEORG PUCHERT, A German of Baltic origin, was a former officer in the Third Reich navy. Strong and adventurous, he left ruined Germany for the Moroccan port of Tangier after Hitler's defeat. Tangier was an international harbor, a known haven for smugglers and adventurers of all types. However, due to Puchert's past as a German sailor, the French police refused to provide him with a residency permit. For years he lived on his boat and supported himself by fishing and cigarette smuggling. In an enterprising move, he bought a sailing license from the consul of Costa Rica and assembled a fleet of swift smuggling ships under the flag of that Central American republic.

Known as "Captain Morris" due to his favorite brand of cigarettes, Puchert deeply identified with the North African struggle for independence. He used his boats to smuggle weapons to the Moroccan, Tunisian, and then the Algerian rebels. In July 1958, he agreed to serve as the FLN's authorized buyer in Germany, under three conditions: ample monetary compensation, guarantees to support his beloved daughter, Marina, if he should die, and an Algerian citizenship. Puchert also hoped to be the future commander of the nascent Algerian Navy.[11] In Frankfurt, he worked with Helmuth Müller, a dubious Nazi who operated independently of the OTRACO network. The hard-drinking Müller was famous for keeping his mouth shut, a rare virtue among alcoholics. He was also an activist with deep ties to the German far right and used to entertain his guests with "jokes about Jews." Müller, duplicitous and sly, always presented himself as a great supporter of the Arabs. He despised his Algerian customers, but also the French, and spied for several intelligence agencies at once. His business enriched him greatly, and by 1962 he was the proud owner of a Mercedes and four apartments, each housing a different mistress.[12]

Puchert and Müller did business with OTRACO but treated it as one supplier among many. From the Algerian side, they worked with Abdelkader Yaicci (known as Abdulkader Nousairi), an important FLN procurer in Germany, and often divided the shipments into small quantities in order to hide them from prying French eyes. The life of smugglers had its glowing moments. Müller and Puchert invited their Algerian counterpart to wild parties, spoiling them with alcohol and prostitutes. They also socialized with dubious Bulgarian businessmen in Frankfurt, who were their liaisons to the cornucopia of weapons in the Communist Bloc.[13]

Notwithstanding his extravagance, Puchert was one of the rare dealers who really took his clients' interests to heart. Unlike OTRACO, which mainly relied on the Eastern Bloc, his method was to play German and other European merchants against one another and lower their bids while looking for alternative routes of supply.[14] Paradoxically, that prudence brought about his downfall. Always on the lookout for new suppliers, he signed a deal with one Hans-Joachim Seidenschnur, a greedy gourmand and connoisseur of expensive wines who lived well beyond his means and was on the lookout for easy money. This convicted con man specialized in tall tales. After being taken captive by the British as a Wehrmacht private, he promoted himself to a lieutenant and told his captors he was one of the ringleaders of the July 20, 1944 plot to kill Hitler. Then he decorated himself with faux academic titles and wormed his way into positions of authority in postwar Germany, including a short stint as a chairman of a denazification committee. After he was exposed, tried, and convicted in 1949, he remained in jail for three years. Released in 1952, he got into legal trouble almost constantly, accumulating convictions and short prison terms.

After a few years of small-time swindling and petty crime, Seidenschnur reinvented himself as an arms dealer. In fact, he hardly sold even one gun, only intermediated between other merchants and noisily created the impression that he was a leading arms trafficker in order to receive commissions and travel expenses, always in the most expensive hotels.[15] In spring 1957, he signed a contract to represent Belgian munition factories in Germany. However, when they discovered his dubious past and dealings, they severed all contact and Seidenschnur found himself in need of new sources of money.[16]

Puchert was the perfect choice. Immediately after their forced divorce from the Belgians, Seidenschnur and his pretty wife, the fashion designer Els, promised to connect Puchert with Norwegian merchants who would be able to supply him with guns and TNT at bargain prices. However, unfortunately for Puchert, his personal inclinations got mixed up with his professional duties. A single man with the adventurer's tough charm, "Captain Morris" was smitten by Seidenschnur's wife, and the two launched a stormy love affair. Furthermore, Puchert swiftly discerned there was little behind Seidenschnur's bragging and decided to sideline him and work with the Norwegian suppliers directly. Puchert, never a gentle personality, shocked his fellow arms merchant Otto Schlüter when he told him, ten minutes after visiting him for the first time, that he intended to have Seidenschnur shot or sunk in the Rhine. Bereft of both wife and commission, Seidenschnur did not stay idle. He informed on Puchert to German authorities and most probably also to French intelligence.[17]

In any case, the French were quick to spot the revitalized network and Georg Puchert was marked as a prime target for assassination. He was completely indifferent to warnings. Even an SDECE thug who threatened him at night could not deter him. Nor did the disaster that befell his ship, *Atlas*, which was blown up by French sappers in October 1958, lead him to recalculate his course. He had many reasons to worry, as French assassinations of arms smugglers to Algeria followed one another in quick succession, not only in Germany but also in other European countries and North Africa. In November 1958, Aït Ahcene, the FLN senior diplomat in Germany, was shot on the steps of the Tunisian Embassy in Bonn and succumbed to his wounds the following spring.

"I am very nervous, being followed," Puchert wrote an Algerian friend in February 1959, "must speak with you urgently." That same month, the French began a major offensive against the FLN in Algeria, and it became even more urgent to disrupt the rebels' procuring networks in Europe. Puchert, who now always carried a gun, even gave his young daughter, Marina, written control over his bank accounts, "in case something happens."[18] On March 3, 1959, Puchert felt sick, and therefore parked outside of his locked garage. An explosive device installed under his Mercedes detonated when he started the engine the next morning. "Captain Morris" was found dead in the driver's seat, smeared with blood, mouth agape. His body was pierced by shrapnel similar to those that killed Schlüter's mother. The Federal Police concluded, yet again, that the bombs were professionally designed, and probably installed by related perpetrators. Springer and other OTRACO merchants also received death threats. Mamdouh Al-Midani, called by Springer to the rescue, shared with the German police intelligence collected by the Syrian Secret Service exposing details about the assassins of Puchert. He did so with great reluctance, convinced that only German official interference could protect OTRACO's arms traffickers. The Germans, however, never dared to accuse the French publicly.[19]

But the French continued undeterred with their terror campaign. A member of Catena (The Chain), one of the SDECE front organizations, sent an anonymous note to the German authorities to take responsibility. Puchert, he charged, provided weapons to kill the European youth protecting the West in Algeria. As French and German authorities had done nothing, Catena activists took the law to their own hands. "We have no scruples anymore – terror will be answered with terror. By supplying the rebellion, Puchert has signed his own death warrant." Seidenschnur, probably in order to hide his own part in Puchert's death, notified the German police that "Captain Morris" was killed by his own Algerian comrades. Always on the lookout for easy money and devoid of any shame, he also filed a lawsuit claiming money from unpaid shipments in order to grab as much as he could from Puchert's estate.[20]

German arms traffickers and their Algerian partners were further targeted in a series of assassinations that extended all over Europe. On New Year's Day 1960, Abdelkader Yaici (aka Nousairi) was waiting for Helmuth Müller in the lobby of a luxurious Frankfurt Hotel. The two were supposed to withdraw money from the bank and proceed by air to Casablanca. Müller was late for the meeting; "overslept," he said. Suddenly, Nousairi was approached by a hotel worker—a package was waiting for him. When the Algerian opened the envelope and drew the contents, it exploded in his face. Nousairi, badly wounded, returned to North Africa.[21] Helmuth Müller, too, survived two mysterious car accidents in August and September 1960. While he was driving at high speed, the wheels of his car suddenly blew up. A Swiss arms merchant who intermediated weapon deals for the FLN was also killed in Geneva, shot by a long blowpipe equipped with a dart.[22]

The French campaign left the FLN with no option but to deal with the most daring and cutthroat adventurers they could find. In fact, French spymasters discovered that their war against the German arms dealers was akin to the arcade game known as "Whack a Mole," where the player is supposed to smack moles as they pop from the ground. Every slain German was replaced by another, and the idealistic Puchert gave way to a resurgence of Nazi arms traffickers. In 1959, only two years after the Latakia debacle, OTRACO was back in business as the main FLN supplier in Germany.[23] The Algerians, however, remembered the amateurish management of Springer, Remer, and Krüger. To remedy this, the Middle Eastern Nazis changed their leadership. Wilhelm Beisner, the former SS spy and the current business partner of Alois Brunner, was now in charge.

· 11 ·

Beisner Blown Away

I and the public know, what all schoolchildren learn.
Those to whom evil is done, do evil in return.

—W. H. AUDEN

⌣

IN APRIL 1960, Wilhelm Beisner was informed that the FLN had selected him as the chief of their purchase mission in Europe with Springer as his deputy. In fact, he had started the job unofficially already in January. Shuttling between Egypt and Europe, Beisner sought to impose order on the chaotic network. He was very hardworking, always crossing international borders, negotiating arms deals, and supervising his buyers.[1]

Beisner was horrified at the amateurish methods of Springer and Remer. They lacked any caution, dealt with unreliable suppliers, and transferred weapons in Hamburg parking lots like gangsters or petty drug dealers.[2] Admittedly, their reputation was strongly tarnished in 1960. There was the Latakia Affair three years beforehand, but also a more recent mishap. In October 1959, they tried to smuggle weapons through the Brussels airport in cookie tins. But they were inadequately packed and certainly not camouflaged. When a worker at the airport dropped a tin by mistake, its contents spilled all over the floor. One of the supervisors, a former soldier, immediately recognized the spare parts and called the police. The entire shipment, needless to say, was confiscated, an unfortunate affair preserved for posterity as the "incident of the cookie tins."

Worst of all, the Algerian secret service now strongly suspected that the Latakia Affair was not merely a debacle but a result of Springer's illicit collaboration with the French.[3]

To prevent the recurrence of such blunders, Beisner decided to concentrate all power and authority in his own hands. To Springer and Remer's great chagrin, he blocked their access to FLN bank accounts, excluded them from any further deals, and made himself the only authorized agent of the Algerian underground in Europe. Remer and Springer therefore tried to clear their name with the FLN, mainly through Colonel Midani and the Moroccan ambassador in West Germany, but the Algerians initially rebuffed them. In autumn 1960, they flew to Rabat and met a mysterious former high Nazi official who converted to Islam and worked with the FLN. This man, probably an imposter, is known to us only by the alias "Cicero." He captivated Remer and Springer with thrilling stories of a Nazi underground network in West Germany comprised of SS and SD veterans who wormed their way into leading positions in order to take the government when time was ripe. Remer, of course, was slated to become one of the leaders of that revolutionary movement. Meanwhile, Cicero ordered Remer and Springer to collect intelligence and gave them an order for several thousand guns with ammunition and ten to twenty tons of TNT.[4]

OTRACO was no longer a coherent business complex. Springer and Remer, who now believed they could renew their dealings with the FLN without Beisner's knowledge, saw it as an opportunity of a lifetime, not only for themselves but also for the neo-Nazi movement. For a while, Remer even thought of moving to Rabat, Morocco, and establishing a "German Government in Exile" with the help of "Cicero." Another idea was to use the Middle Eastern network to smuggle war criminals and Holocaust perpetrators from West Germany to safe havens in the Arab world. According to persistent rumors, Adolf Eichmann even traveled to Damascus to meet Brunner and other members of the network, and Springer tried to look into job options for him in Kuwait.[5] These rumors were false, and yet, they might explain why Simon Wiesenthal and many others believed (at least for a time) that the architect of the Holocaust was hiding in Syria, Kuwait, or other Middle Eastern countries.[6] Within a year, however, Eichmann's true whereabouts would be revealed to the world in a dramatic and unforeseen manner. At the same time, the lid was about to be blown off the carefree Nazi exile communities in the Middle East, which so far had not had to worry about public scrutiny or official attention. Their meddling in France's backyard now placed them on the radar of the SDECE, and as they were about to discover, the French had more subtle weapons than car bombs and exploding letters to apply to those who had overstepped their bounds.

Indeed, by that point the French had penetrated the networks of Remer, Springer, and Beisner. In January 1960, one of the corrupt Bulgarian collaborators of OTRACO, incensed by his marginalization, sold photographs of the German dealers to anyone willing to pay, presumably including the French.[7] SDECE had probably been on Beisner's track for quite a while, and they had their own moles inside the German arm smugglers community in Egypt and in Syria. To hunt down these Nazis, they sent to Beirut an agent named Holm (aka Said Haddad), an Alsatian who served as an SS officer during the war. When a French court sentenced him to death for war crimes in absentia, he converted to Islam and joined the Syrian Army as a military adviser. His pending sentence did not deter SDECE from recruiting him as an agent. In this capacity, Holm helped recruit German military advisers to Syria in the early 1950s. Now he began to sniff around the Nazi community in order to find more information on OTRACO.[8]

Holm's most successful agent was a German journalist named Hermann Schaefer, supposedly a publisher of a "journal for developing countries" called Afro-Asia.[9] Schaefer, a man of many faces and many masters, had a checkered past that enabled him to move in multiple circles and report to many different paymasters. Following a stint in the Hitler Youth, Schaefer had joined the Nazi party in 1935. Two years later, he enlisted in the Abwehr, the German Army's intelligence agency, but was quickly uncovered as a double agent who worked for the SD and, most probably, the Soviet secret service. Subsequently dismissed from the SD as well, he was interred for two years in a concentration camp.[10] In 1945, based on false records, Schaefer was able to pass denazification as a "victim of the Hitler Regime." In 1946, he took to journalism. As a "neutralist," he attacked Adenauer's policy of German rearmament and alliance with the West and called for closer relations with the Soviet Union. At the same time, he defended the legacy of the Nazi regime, and called for faster reintegration of former Nazis into West German society.[11] Schaefer was also involved with international neo-Nazi organizations. Gehlen Org records show that in October 1953, he met Otto Skorzeny in Madrid.[12]

The BND, BfV, the Bavarian police, and several other West German agencies suspected that Schaefer was in fact funded by East Germany as an agent of influence. In 1955, he became more critical of the Nazi regime, and his former neutralist stance increasingly tilted toward communism. In an interview with an East German radio station, Schaefer called for "reconciliation" with the East and resistance to Chancellor Adenauer's pro-Western policy, denouncing West Germany as a state led by former Nazis.[13] At the same time he published books and articles, often under pseudonyms, voicing either neo-Nazi or pro-communist opinions without any effort at ideological consistency. Eventually, his newspaper was closed when the flow of money (either from the East or other sources) died out, and he disappeared from public view under heavy suspicions of treason. The proceedings against him never matured to an indictment. Broke and destitute, Schaefer worked for the BfV for a few months in 1958, reporting on neo-Nazi and communist organizations with which he was in touch. To his great misfortune, he was dropped as unreliable in December that year.[14]

Then, in 1959, Schaefer found a new opportunity to make money. In the spring of that year, he left Germany for the Levant as a purported agent of various German firms and editor of a new journal on Middle Eastern affairs with an "anti-Jewish, anti-colonial and anti-communist" editorial line. Schaefer's activities, however, focused on gathering intelligence on the Nazi community in Damascus and Cairo, especially on Beisner, OTRACO, and the arms trafficking business.[15] As the BND wanted to conceal its own involvement in Beisner's network from the French, this was a very sensitive issue.

As we will later see, Schaefer, who was much more than an independent journalist and occasional intelligence peddler, had bigger fish to fry than OTRACO alone. However, his efforts against OTRACO were decisive enough. Publicly, Schaefer sold information, either accurate, exaggerated, or outright false, to several German newspapers, shining a public spotlight on OTRACO and its activities. Based on Schaefer's information, among other sources, the journalist Jürgen Willbrand published a series of sensational articles in the tabloid *Kristall*. They were largely designed to present the neo-Nazis as bizarre, corrupt, and despicable traitors and criminals, the equivalent of East Germany's communists. In one of these articles, Willbrand described the close connections of German right-wing extremists, including Remer and

Springer, with the community of Nazi spies and arms merchants in Damascus. In the process, he also "outed" Alois Brunner. Otto Remer, Willbrand accused, had met the mass murderer in the Syrian capital.[16] Privately, Schaefer leaked information on Beisner's illegal trade with Algeria to Hoesch, the German steel company that Beisner represented in the Middle East. Beisner's clients, who wanted no trouble with the law, severed all connections, depriving him of an important source of income. Worse for Beisner, Schaefer also acquired his address and provided it to SDECE. Beisner was oblivious to the fact that SDECE had intercepted the mail of his wife Alice.[17] Finally, in autumn 1960, the French were ready to strike.[17]

On October 14, 1960, Beisner returned to Germany from Tunis. A day later, he bought a new car from a local dealer. Very few people in the upscale Munich suburb of Schwabing even noted the former SS officer who left an apartment in Blütenstrasse on October 14, 1960. The streets were already dark. Many neighbors were home and sat around their dinner tables. Beisner was traveling so often to the Middle East and North Africa to attend his business that he was almost unknown in the neighborhood. From the windows of his Mercedes, the former SS spy was able to see his wife, Alice, who had just left the building with their two dogs. A second later, he started the engine and the car exploded.

Windows shattered throughout the neighborhood. "Glass shreds flew into our dinner table," said one astonished housewife. Soon after, rumors started to circulate that mysterious foreign agents were responsible for the explosion. The entire incident was shrouded in secrecy, and the local police had little to work with. The victim of the assassination was too badly wounded to provide testimony, and his wife Alice refused to speak with the police. She was too shocked, she said.[18]

To the wailing sound of police sirens, Beisner was evacuated to the hospital. The doctors had to amputate one of his legs and he nearly lost his eyesight. Immediately after the explosion, the newspaper *Süddeutsche Zeitung* circulated the possibility that the French "Red Hand" was behind the assassination attempt. The Bavarian criminal police noted that the method was very similar to previous French assassinations against FLN arms traffickers in Germany.[19]

The criminal police in Munich began an investigation immediately, and not an ordinary one. The BND became involved. Immediately after the explosion,

BND operatives raided the apartment of their wounded agent to remove incriminating material and the interrogation was classified as a state secret.[20] The BND had good reasons to panic, as the assassination of Beisner exposed the contradictions in their own policy. By trading in Soviet arms, Beisner abetted communist penetration of the Arab sphere. Even worse, in the late 1950s, the government in Bonn took an increasingly pro-French line.[21] While Chancellor Adenauer supported Paris, paid BND agents in the Middle East undermined this policy by arming Algerian insurgents.

Beisner and his wife, fearful of complications with both the Algerians and the BND, refused to speak to the police. A detective quoted in *Der Spiegel* said that "Beisner, who had to undergo several operations, and his wife, who went through a nervous breakdown, were very careful not to disclose information. . . . A Beisner that sings is a dead Beisner, whenever he's again out on the streets."[22]

While Beisner was recovering, it seemed that his business in North Africa got into trouble as well. His Algerian partners knew that he worked for the BND and started to suspect he did not have their best interests in mind.[23] In a letter from Tunis, Mahmoud Cherif, a senior armaments official of the Algerian Government in Exile, wrote that he had expected Beisner's arrival, but since that hadn't materialized, found himself "in a false position" and preferred to postpone the discussion until Beisner's return. "Dear friend Willi," he wrote, "tell me truthfully, must I maintain the friendships for our future affairs or can I consider them simple relationships. You understand that, after all our changes of plans, contacts and interruptions, I cannot [redacted word] them without embarrassment."[24] Ultimately, Beisner's business was taken over by Springer and Remer, who kept on shipping pistols and TNT to the FLN.[25]

The BND and police investigation of Beisner's attempted assassination concluded only on June 13, 1961. German authorities suspected that French intelligence stood behind *all* assassinations, not just that of Beisner, but did not dare say so in public. Prosecutors who insisted on investigating quickly discovered that they received no government cooperation, and their investigations reached a dead end. From Adenauer's perspective, the alliance with France was too important to shed tears over a few arms merchants, even if their assassins violated German sovereignty.[26]

• • •

THE FRENCH CAMPAIGN of assassination and intimidation influenced the course of history, but not in the way the assassins believed. Far from drying up the weapons supplies of the FLN, the terror attacks against the German arms dealers pushed the Algerians even faster into the embrace of the Communist Bloc. As French military intelligence complained in December 1960, a short while after the failed attempt on Beisner:

> State organizations have replaced the arms traffickers . . . The material is transported on Eastern-bloc cargoes that belong to state-owned companies; it is shipped from harbors situated behind the Iron Curtain . . . [although] for the time being, the transports are not executed by Soviet vessels but by satellite ships.[27]

Soon enough, Moscow itself would join the fray. The Soviet Union and Red China offered monetary assistance and free shipments to the FLN without Nazi mediation, and the French could not blow up *their* ships without risking war, nor collect intelligence or sabotage the weapons as they did with OTRACO. Thus, the French insistence of winning the war in Algeria by all means, fair or foul, further increased Soviet power in the Middle East and North Africa. At the same time, it incensed international public opinion, driving a wedge between France and its important American and European allies. Numerous international observers condemned the French struggle as criminal, desperate, and doomed.[28] That was especially true in West Germany. As the French ambassador in Bonn admitted, the assassination campaign turned dubious Nazi gunrunners into popular figures, a "type of an adventurous German . . . on the whole sympathetic, who had placed his skills and courage in the service of a good cause, in this case the fight by the Algerian insurgents for their liberty."[29]

Social-Democrat politicians, student groups, and important newspapers attacked the Adenauer government's support for France, accusing the chancellor of failure to uphold German sovereignty. The Federal Republic, wrote the *Frankfurter Allgemeine Zeitung*, "cannot remain a playground for foreign secret services." As Mathilde von Bülow writes, already in December 1959, "public agitation over the Red Hand seriously strained relations between Paris and Bonn, and that at a particularly sensitive time in the Berlin Crisis." The Soviets, always eager to exploit the weaknesses of rivals, tried to blockade

West Berlin yet again, and Bonn needed the support of Paris and Washington more than ever.[30]

Had Gehlen helped the French to intercept or undermine the arms shipments without killing the merchants, as he promised General Grossin time and again, SDECE may not have resorted to disastrous murder plots. But the president of the BND did no such thing, as the cooperation with OTRACO and the elusive attempt to crowd out the Soviets from Algeria proved too much of a temptation.[31] In the end, the obsession with Nazi arms traffickers was detrimental to both West Germany and France.

An Enemy of My Enemy— Alois Brunner's Plots

It is difficult with these evil folk to know when they are in league, and when they are cheating one another.

—J.R.R. TOLKIEN, *THE LORD OF THE RINGS*

IN FARAWAY DAMASCUS, Alois Brunner was also in trouble. Until this point, like other Nazi refugees, he had enjoyed the benefit of active West German indifference. But the advent of Fritz Bauer as attorney general of the state of Hessen in 1956 had changed the rules of the game. Enjoying the powerful and near-unconditional backing of the SPD minister-president of Hessen, George-August Zinn, the German-Jewish Bauer was determined to blow the lid off the conspiracy of indifference sheltering Nazi war criminals in West Germany and around the world. As early as 1957, he leaked the location of Adolf Eichmann, long known to West Germany's ruling circles, to the Israeli Mossad. In May 1960, Adolf Eichmann, Brunner's old superior, was kidnapped by Mossad agents from his Argentinian hideout and brought to Israel to face trial. Fugitive Nazis from all over the world, including Brunner, suspected they might be next. Moreover, the resulting public outcry and publicity both within West Germany and around the world finally gave Bauer the political teeth he needed to force the West German justice system to demand extraditions of fugitive Nazis and vigorously prosecute those who fell within its reach.

Brunner's enemies were now closing in on him as both Bauer and the BfV launched separate investigations on his whereabouts. While Bauer obviously wanted to arrest Brunner, the BfV was more interested in his connections in Germany and how he had obtained his alias of Georg Fischer.[1] The Israeli Mossad, too, knew about Brunner, and its interest in Nazi hunting was at its peak. To put the icing on the cake, Brunner had a nasty run-in with local security services, a very dangerous experience in a country such as Syria.[2]

The land itself had undergone significant changes. In 1958, Syria was united with Egypt and the two entities merged into the United Arab Republic. The union was ill-begotten from the beginning. Though President Nasser was popular in Syria, many locals resented the influx of Egyptian officers, policemen, and bureaucrats, as well as the socialist measures of the Cairo regime, inimical to the interests of many Syrian merchants.[3]

In Damascus itself, a particularly ruthless strongman sought to exploit the situation to his own advantage. Colonel Abdul Hamid Sarraj, a young man of thirty-three, was chief of the "Second Bureau," the army's intelligence service that also functioned as the country's secret police. The pro-Soviet Sarraj amassed popularity as a sworn enemy of American imperialism who had already foiled several US plots and conspiracies. According to a Syrian historian, "he had earned a reputation of being a brave and conniving man who would stop at nothing in order to achieve his ambitions."[4] An ardent supporter of Nasser, Sarraj's political clout was reinforced by unification with Egypt. Now entrenched in the powerful Interior Ministry, he imported his minions from the army into a newly minted secret police, separate from the armed forces and known as the General Investigations Directorate (GID, and in Arabic: *Mabahes*). An important commander in the new organization was Colonel Mamdouh Al-Midani, a well-known "Arab Nazi" whom we encountered earlier as an ally of OTRACO.

With more than 5,000 agents, the GID dominated Syrian life and terrorized the population like never before. According to George Chatila, a well-informed Lebanese correspondent, almost every inhabitant of Damascus had a GID file. Many agents were day laborers, porters in the market, shoeshine boys, and Palestinian refugees, all dirt-poor, dependent on the regime, and ready to inform on anybody for a few dimes. Yet another clandestine organization, the General Intelligence Agency (GIA), also known as the Special Bureau, was led by Colonel Burhan Adham and a shady type known as Captain Laham. Formally, it was controlled directly by Cairo, but in fact it was under Sarraj's supervision.[5]

In Damascus, recalled Hermann Schaefer, "nobody dared to say a political word in public . . . everyone who took a photograph was arrested." Chatila reported that rich people were abducted in exchange for ransom while political prisoners were tortured, murdered, and buried in the desert, their bodies often mutilated with acid.[6]

At the time, Brunner recalled, Syrian law enforcement agencies were looking for drug dealers. "Georg Fischer" used to pass money to his wife, Anna, and their daughter through his brother-in-law, and the frequent monetary transfers caught the eyes of the GIA. In late 1959, Captain Laham had Brunner arrested and interrogated in person. He was not convinced by his explanations. "You are under arrest until the end of the investigation," he ruled. In response, the desperate Brunner used his last card. "I have to confess," he said, "that my real name is Alois Brunner, and I was Eichmann's close colleague. I am being hunted as the enemy of the Jews." "Then," Brunner recalled, "my situation had completely changed. Laham stood up, shook my hand and said: 'Welcome to Syria. The enemies of our enemies are our friends.'"[7]

After his release, Brunner began working for Syria's intelligence services, both GID and GIA, with a monthly salary of 700 Syrian pounds, parallel to his ongoing involvement with OTRACO and arms trafficking to the FLN. Brunner and Rademacher served as advisers, instructors, and agents in the German desk of the GID. They worked with Midani and Laham, but Sa'id Fatah Imam was their direct superior. Brunner and Rademacher had to spy on Germans, Austrians, and other German-speaking foreigners in Damascus. Sometimes, they recommended the arrest, deportation, and even torture of German nationals they did not like. They were also responsible for propaganda and perhaps even espionage operations among German speakers and in German-speaking countries. To increase their penetration, they employed the Syrian translator of the West German consulate, a former Nazi collaborator called Adnan Zein, as their spy inside the German diplomatic corps. Some SRP leaders and OTRACO partners served as their eyes and ears. Brunner's activities were occasionally monitored by the CIA, who had a source inside the Damascene Nazi community. Hermann Schaefer also disclosed much information, though he tended to overstress the importance of Brunner and Rademacher.[8]

According to Schaefer's description, Brunner used to go almost daily to Midani's office in the Ministry of the Interior. Climbing stairs clogged by petitioners, he passed the heavily armed guards without difficulty on his way up. There, he, Midani, and Rademacher discussed agent reports on German issues. On one occasion, Midani read his two guests extradition requests from West Germany and asked whether Brunner and Rademacher resided in Syria. Then they formulated Midani's formal reply to the Germans: "Brunner and Rademacher are completely unknown in Damascus."[9]

· · ·

BRUNNER, HIS FELLOW Nazis, and the leaders of the Syrian security services knew very well that Hermann Schaefer was the source behind the compromising articles that gave rise to so much furor in the local Nazi community. Brunner, obsessed with conspiracy theories about Jewish power, was certain that Schaefer received 32,000 marks from the Central Committee of German Jews to hunt Nazis in Damascus. He wanted Schaefer dead. Rademacher, who was one of Schaefer's main informants, now also denounced him to the GID.[10]

Urged by Midani, the Syrian intelligence service first tried to lure Schaefer into Damascus in order to arrest him. When that failed, Midani plotted twice to kidnap Schaefer from Beirut, but the plan never took off because one of the accomplices, a German woman, betrayed the plot to Schaefer.[11] Alois Brunner also pledged to help his comrade Beisner. The latter, who felt unsafe in Germany, checked his options in Syria. Brunner wrote that he was always welcome in Damascus and that "his friends," probably the bigwigs of Syrian intelligence, would love to talk with Beisner "face to face." Brunner apologized that he could not host Beisner in his apartment because "this creature" (Witzke) was still there.[12]

Brunner was also interested in the fate of his old superior, Adolf Eichmann. "He was dear to me," he later recalled. First, Brunner contacted Robert Servatius, Eichmann's defense lawyer, and offered to meet him in Athens or Beirut to give testimony. For that, however, he had to extend his German passport, and therefore asked Rademacher to check his status in the West German consulate in Damascus. Until that day, Brunner assiduously avoided contact with the consulate, and indeed, Bonn's diplomats in Damascus were suspicious and planned to investigate his past. The consulate knew well that "Fischer" was in fact Alois Brunner, but no one could foresee how far a formal investigation would go. Brunner's attempt to secure a passport with the help of Rudolf Vogel, the politician who helped him to escape Germany in 1954, also failed. All parties came to understand that it might be better to let sleeping dogs lie. Francois Genoud, a Swiss neo-Nazi literary agent, did travel to Damascus to mediate with Brunner on Servatius's behalf, and the two met in the prestigious Umayyad Hotel, a short walk from Brunner's home. Nothing came out of the meeting. According to his later testimony, Genoud found Brunner "an unsympathetic type."[13]

Brunner now planned instead a campaign of propaganda and misinformation. In August 1960, he traveled to Cairo, probably with a Syrian passport, to attend a war council of sorts. In a conference with Nazi colleagues, including the notorious Johann von Leers and two Egyptian officials from the military intelligence and the Ministry of Information, he produced a list of "rich Jews" who collaborated with the SS during the Final Solution. They could be blackmailed to finance Nazi activity in the Middle East. Leers liked the idea, and suggested that if they refused, their names should be published for the sake of propaganda. This plan, too, came to nothing.[14]

Brunner tried to convince his friends from Syrian intelligence to intervene. In a conversation with Laham from the GIA, Brunner proposed a daring commando operation. A Syrian naval commando team would raid Israel from the sea and release Eichmann from his prison in Atlit, near Haifa. According to Brunner, Laham agreed and made some operational preparations. He even assembled a team of fighters. However, it was probably only a pipe dream. In the United Arab Republic, an operation that was so politically sensitive could have been launched only with Cairo's approval, notwithstanding Sarraj's tendency to operate independently. And even if President Nasser approved, a very remote possibility, the Syrian armed forces had no capability to launch such a complicated military action inside Israel, nor did they have precise intelligence on Eichmann's prison. The security services therefore found a polite way to discard the idea without insulting Brunner and Laham. General Ghazal, a senior intelligence officer, advised them that the Israelis had relocated Eichmann to a new impregnable prison made of reinforced concrete.[15]

And yet, Brunner would not give up, and hatched an even more audacious plan. If he and his friends were able to abduct a leader "important enough for Judaism," maybe they could swap him for Eichmann. Brunner zeroed on Dr. Nahum Goldmann, president of the World Jewish Congress. Ignorant in anything about Jews except murdering them, Brunner believed for some reason that the abduction of Goldmann, an unloved politician with little influence, would force Israel to let Eichmann go.

Brunner fundraised for the cause and was able to collect 300,000 German marks "from Arab circles." Perhaps in an attempt to mimic the Mossad's Eichmann operation, he looked for a suitable site to abduct Goldmann, whisk him onto a Tunisian or Moroccan flight, and bring him into a FLN-controlled area in Algeria. Another option was to kill him with a bomb attack in Vienna. A Lebanese friend of Brunner named Rayees who worked as a front agent of the FLN in Geneva was put in charge of the plot. He recruited a mixed gang of old Nazis and Arab adventurers and made plans to abduct Goldmann in Bonn. Indeed, in November 1960, Goldmann planned to visit the West German capital to meet with Chancellor Adenauer. The Austrian industrialist Rudolf Schneeweiss, Brunner's brother-in-law, brought Rayees in contact with two veterans of the Brandenburg Division, the elite commando unit of Nazi Germany's military intelligence.[16]

However, things started to go wrong almost from the very start. For one, the Lebanese adventurer's meetings with the two Nazi veterans went very badly. Both refused to cooperate and advised Rayees to abandon the initiative, which they saw as impractical. Rayees had to give up because it was impossible to carry out the plan without German collaborators. Moreover, unexpected developments nearly turned the aborted operation into a disaster. One of the Brandenburg veterans known only as "Dr. Z" believed that Brunner had wronged him in some business matter, and felt this was a good opportunity to take revenge. He leaked Brunner's plan to journalists, to the Nazi hunter Simon Wiesenthal, and probably also to the Austrian Secret Service. If the agents had been arrested, Brunner would have drawn unwanted attention to himself in the midst of the Eichmann trial.

Luckily for Brunner, both Wiesenthal and the Austrian Secret Service let the matter rest. The Nazi hunter even convinced the journalist who spoke with "Dr. Z" to withhold publishing the story until after Eichmann's execution so as not to give ideas to Nazi copycats around the world.[17] The atmosphere was very tense in any case. David Ben-Gurion, the Israeli prime minister, wrote in his diary that gangs of old Nazis were plotting to disrupt the Eichmann trial.[18] Isser Harel, head of the Mossad, warned the government in December 1960 that Eichmann's lawyer, Robert Servatius, was in touch with neo-Nazis and Eichmann's friends, "a very dangerous and contemptible gang of Nazis . . . of arch-murderers . . . among them some we are looking for." It was true. As we saw, Brunner and Genoud were indeed in touch with Servatius, and the Mossad was hunting for Brunner at the same time.[19]

However, the abortive plans to liberate Eichmann proved to be a mere trifle. Contrary to what Schaefer assumed, Brunner's position in Syria was not so secure. Leaving aside the rising and ebbing fortunes of Germans and Arabs alike in the Damascene game of thrones, Brunner was completely dependent on his patrons at the Home Ministry, especially the all-powerful Mamdouh Al-Midani. One of Brunner's neighbors recalled, decades later, that Al-Midani used to "hit on" Brunner's daughter, Irene, during his visits to Austria. When the mother protested, he reminded her that her husband's fate could change very quickly in Damascus. "We can do to him," Al-Midani warned, "what he did to the Jews."[20]

In the spring of 1961, Brunner could be consoled with one small victory: he was able to get rid of his troublesome flatmate, Curt Witzke, to whom he referred as "this creature." Using his newly won power in Syria, he told everybody Witzke was a "Jewish spy" and tried to frighten Syrian students who came to the house for private language lessons. Finally, Brunner reported Witzke to the authorities.

On March 28, 1961, the agents of Captain Laham, Brunner's patron from the GIA, arrested Witzke in the dead of night. Greeting him with two blows to the face, the agents covered his eyes with painfully tight dark glasses. Then he was whisked away to a police car in his pajamas and driven to one of the GIA torture facilities, an abandoned military arsenal in the suburbs of Damascus. For six weeks, he was interrogated by Laham and a translator named Talal Abdulwahab Rifa'i, whom he had known before as Brunner's pal. The two stripped him naked, tied him to a chair, and accused him of "spying for the Jews" and betraying information to Schaefer who passed it on to the Mossad (which was, in fact, true). Then, they charged him with a fraudulent arms deal in which he and Schaefer allegedly cheated both the Algerian envoy to Syria and the Moroccan consul. The consul, Rachid Al-Khatabi, was Witzke's partner in arms trafficking and a friend of Sarraj. Laham and his men beat and tortured their prisoner while drinking whiskey, intoxicated by alcohol and sadistic thrill. They asked him about his connections with Holm, the SDECE agent in Beirut, and threatened to hand him over to the Algerians for further torture.

After six weeks Witzke was released due to the German consul's energetic intervention with Colonel Sarraj. Sobbing, shaking, and crying, he told the consul about his travails and begged safe passage to West Germany. He was deported without trial after leaving all his belongings to the Syrian government and the entire apartment to Brunner.[21] From then on, Eichmann's right-hand man could host prostitutes to his heart's content. Unfortunately for him, his apartment was soon frequented by a guest with an altogether different, deadly intent.

· 13 ·

"A Punitive Attack"— Mossad Joins the Fray

As thy sword hath made women childless,
so shall thy mother be childless among women.

—1 SAMUEL 15:33. SCRIBBLED BY THE ISRAELI PRESIDENT ITZHAK BEN ZVI
ON EICHMANN'S PLEA FOR CLEMENCY

WHILE ALOIS BRUNNER was conspiring to abduct the president of the World Jewish Congress, he was all but oblivious to the eyes watching him from the shadows. His former victims, the captors of his former commander Eichmann, and the bitter enemies of his host country had him pinned on their to-do list. This was, perhaps, not as obvious as it might seem. In the 1950s, the hunt for Nazis was of relatively little interest to Israeli security services and their omnipotent chief, Isser Harel. Though the Mossad was interested in SS officers who worked in Egypt and Syria in 1952, that interest soon faded. The Israeli intelligence services had more urgent priorities.[1]

In 1959, however, a global wave of anti-Semitic attacks against Jewish institutions brought the Nazi problem to the fore again and Mossad chief Isser Harel had a change of heart. Although Mossad still had to focus predominately on enemies of the present, the priority of Nazi hunting rose. In 1959, Harel had ordered his men to hunt only Adolf Eichmann and Josef Mengele, the notoriously sadistic physician from Auschwitz. Their efforts came to fruition with the spectacular abduction of Eichmann in spring 1960, though Mengele was never caught. In July 1960, Harel ordered the establishment of a new Mossad unit called Amal (short for Amalek, the biblical archenemy of the Jewish people) designed to penetrate neo-Nazi movements, fight anti-Semitism, collect intelligence on Nazi criminals, and hunt them. Its leader was Shlomo Cohen-Abarbanel, a spy, intellectual, and accomplished artist who was also the designer of the Mossad's emblem.[2] With the Eichmann trial, the Holocaust, long suppressed, rose to the surface in Israeli public opinion and Mossad was itching for yet another success. While other Mossad agents scanned Germany, Switzerland, and South America for traces of Mengele, the agency's headquarters in Tel Aviv decided to include Brunner in the list of high priority targets.[3]

After Hermann Schaefer outed Brunner in the German press, the fugitive Nazi's notoriety skyrocketed in Germany. Schaefer had long submitted reports to the BfV, even without payment, on Nazis in the Middle East and the activity of Arab intelligence services in Germany, hoping for future employment and for the withdrawal of legal proceedings against him.[4] In addition, he reported to Fritz Bauer, who used his information to open a criminal investigation and issue an arrest warrant for Brunner. Bauer even secured the cooperation of the Lebanese prosecution (the Lebanese regime was, at that time, hostile to Syria, following the failed pro-Syrian coup of 1958). If Brunner set foot in Lebanon, the Beirut authorities promised to arrest him.[5] However, the Frankfurt prosecutor was also in touch with other enemies of Brunner, including the Israelis, who were far less legalistic than the officials of the West German government.

Bauer's clandestine relationship with the Israeli Mossad was hardly new. Frustrated by constant obstructions from German bureaucrats, many of them former Nazis, Bauer believed that Mossad might punish war criminals more efficiently. In 1957, he secretly told Mossad chief Isser Harel that Adolf Eichmann was living in Buenos Aires, thus giving the first significant lead to the famous abduction operation. He even tacitly allowed a Mossad agent to photocopy top-secret investigation documents in his office. Then, in summer 1960, Bauer contacted Mossad yet again and told the Israelis that Alois Brunner, "Eichmann's best man," was hiding in Damascus under the alias "Georg Fischer."[6]

Shortly afterward, Mossad received another clue from Peter Kubainsky, a shady neo-Nazi intelligence peddler who, in addition to working with the Mossad, was yet another accomplice of the ubiquitous Herman Schaefer (indeed, Schaefer himself communicated with the Mossad directly under the alias "Merhavia"[7]). Originally a German convert to Islam and member of various neo-Nazi organizations, Kubainsky moved to Egypt in order to establish contacts between Nazis in Europe and the Arab sphere. A drunkard and dissolute con man, he was also an informant for the CIA. In 1960, Kubainsky offered his services to the Mossad in a bid to spare himself from future Israeli vengeance. Eventually he was deemed unreliable and therefore dropped, but the intelligence he provided on Brunner was surprisingly accurate. From both Kubainsky and Bauer, the Mossad learned that Brunner lived in the Abu Rummaneh neighborhood on the third floor of an apartment building in Rue Haddad 22. They also learned about "Qatar office," one of his companies.[8]

Kubainsky told his handlers that Brunner planned to visit Europe in October 1960 to meet some of his old comrades from the war. Amal promptly decided to act. Its director, Shlomo Cohen-Abarbanel, was instructed to rely solely on the existing resources of "Junction," the Mossad unit responsible for agent recruitment in Europe. On October 14, Cohen-Abarbanel wrote Haim, Junction's director in Europe, and advised him that Brunner was about to visit Munich. He ended the letter with the ominous phrase, "good hunting." It is unclear what Cohen-Abarbanel had in mind: abduction, such as in the Eichmann operation, or assassination. In the following months, Mossad agents, with Kubainsky's help, sniffed around Munich, but nothing came of it.

As Yossi Chen, Mossad's own historian, wrote in an internal study, it was difficult to expect Brunner to imperil himself by leaving his Syrian refuge precisely when fugitive Nazis all over the world were on high alert after Eichmann's kidnapping. As we have seen, Brunner also failed in his attempt to extend his defunct German passport. Communications with the West German consulate in Damascus were too dangerous for Brunner, especially after the prosecutor's office in Frankfurt issued an arrest warrant against him.[9]

For Mossad, the best way to punish Brunner was assassination or abduction on Syrian soil. For such an operation, Kubainsky's intelligence was inadequate. Mossad updated Brunner's file with information from Holocaust survivors who had the misfortune of encountering him. Amal also received information from

Hermann Schaefer, who met Mossad agents during his trips to Athens and Istanbul. This intelligence was compared with fresh reports of two additional informants. One, codenamed "Folklore," was almost certainly Kubainsky. The second, a mysterious source in Damascus who informed on Brunner in November 1960, appears in the documents as "Swallow" (*Snunit*).[10] Some authors argued that this informant was Eli Cohen, Mossad's master spy in Syria, who entered the country in deep cover as an Argentinian-Syrian businessman. This is chronologically problematic because Swallow supplied the information in November 1960, and Cohen moved to Syria in February 1962, more than a year later.

In mid-January, 1961, the staffers of Amal believed they had obtained adequate intelligence on Brunner. Apart from his address, they had a recent photo, taken by Hermann Schaefer for the journal *Kristall*. The directors of Mossad did not consider a kidnapping operation, an extremely difficult undertaking in an enemy country, let alone a police state such as Syria. Instead, they decided to kill Brunner, or in the parlance of Mossad, to launch a "punitive attack." The mission was given to a unit codenamed *Mifratz* (Gulf) responsible for covert operations in Arab countries.

The commander of *Mifratz* was Yitzhak Shamir, a veteran of an extremist underground organization who had fought both Arabs and British with ruthless zeal before the establishment of Israel. The veterans of this defunct underground were deeply bitter about the Israeli establishment. After 1948, they were disarmed, persecuted, and often barred from government positions. And yet, realizing their clandestine skills could be useful, Isser Harel decided to recruit Shamir and several of his peers to the Mossad in 1955. There they could use their skills to fight Israel's enemies while being kept under close surveillance. Shamir, a future prime minister of Israel, was a hardened warrior and zealous Zionist for whom targeted assassinations against the nation's enemies were a matter of course.[11] Now, Shamir had to choose a suitable agent for the mission. He opted for one of his former underground comrades, a fluent Arabic speaker known to us only by his first name, Ner. This man was an experienced clandestine agent, a veteran of several operations in Arab countries.[12]

On May 21, 1961, Ner reached Beirut with a false passport and proceeded immediately to Damascus by taxi. He arrived just in time for Eid al-Adha, one of the merriest festivals in the Muslim calendar. In the Syrian capital's hustle and bustle, Ner found a room in the Abdin Hotel, took a quick shower, and proceeded immediately to Rue Hadad 22. Near the house, his sharp eyes noticed a European-looking man entering the house. But he had to be certain, so he entered a plumber's shop on the ground floor of the same building. Ner asked the plumber about Dr. Georg Fischer, Brunner's well-known alias. The plumber told him that Fischer was indeed the only European living in the building. He also said that he sometimes took packages and letters for the other residents, so if he wanted to leave a note for Fischer, he was welcome to.[13]

For such a delicate operation, Ner would need to find out the precise location of Brunner's apartment. He returned to the building the next day and climbed the stairs to the third floor. There he saw two doors. On the first was an Arab surname, and on the second, none at all. Ner knocked on the nameless door and was greeted by a European in a bathrobe. He knew immediately that he was facing Brunner, a Nazi responsible for the murder of hundreds of thousands of Jews.[14]

For Ner, killing his target there and then was out of the question. Without an escape route, an assassination in an enemy capital would be sheer madness, and he had orders to follow. His task for the moment was only to collect intelligence. Therefore, he asked Brunner for the whereabouts of a certain "Mr. Tabara." Brunner was naturally suspicious. He asked Ner why he was looking for an Arab in his apartment. Ner later said that Brunner was excited and did not speak clearly, probably fearing foul play. The memories of Eichmann's abduction were still fresh. Ner apologized, descended the stairs and wandered around for a while. He knew Brunner would follow him by eye from the window, and so feigned a search for Mr. Tabara before making a gesture of despair and leaving.[15]

Now armed with the information in Amal's study coupled with the field intelligence collected by Ner, the Mossad planners knew beyond all doubt where Brunner lived. Yitzhak Shamir visited a secret facility belonging to Aman, the IDF Intelligence Department, and signed a receipt for his weapon of choice: an explosive package.[16]

This was cutting-edge technology that Aman had received from colleagues in the French secret service. The Algerian War, combined with the deep sympathy of French civilian and military leaders to Israel's existential fight against the Arabs, facilitated close cooperation between the two countries. The French gave Israel diplomatic support and also crucial assistance with its most sensitive project: the nuclear military reactor in the Negev Desert. The two countries' intelligence agencies had also worked closely during the Algerian War and the Israelis had the benefit of learning from France's dirty war against the FLN and the German arms dealers.[17]

Nathan Rotberg, a scientist working for the Israeli intelligence services, had been taught by his French counterparts to build sophisticated explosive packages that could withstand being shuffled around in trucks and post offices. The mechanism was shock-resistant and triggered only when the contents of the package were drawn out.[18] As previously noted, the French used precisely this kind of bomb in their assassination against Nousairi, the FLN emissary in Frankfurt.

In early September 1961, Shamir met Ner in Europe and passed him the bomb concealed in a double-bottomed suitcase. On the 8th of September, the agent took a flight to Beirut and as before traveled on to Damascus by taxi. He waited near Rue Haddad 22 until he saw Brunner departing. At that point Ner remembered the plumber who took packages for the residents: maybe he could make an unwitting assassin out of him? In a later report Ner described what happened next:

> I then saw that the plumber's shop was closed. Nearby, there was a radio workshop . . . the owner told me that the plumber was out, he's been working away for more than two weeks because there's no work here. I asked him if he could take the letter [for Fischer]. 'No', he said, 'I'm leaving soon and cannot take on this errand.' I thanked him and left.[19]

"Ner made a big mistake," recalled Yossi Chen. "He should have found another way to give the package to Brunner, maybe by leaving it outside his door."[20] Instead, he went to the main post office in Rue Port Said and deposited a registered package for Georg Fischer, postal box no. 635. The woman behind the counter was suspicious. The package was too heavy. The postal clerk asked Ner about the contents, and he said, "bills." Luckily for him, that was enough. Ner paid a deposit fee, took a taxi back to Beirut, and then a flight to Frankfurt.

By the following day the package was sent to Brunner's address, but he was not at home. On September 13, the unsuspecting Austrian went to the main post office to receive his mail and the clerks handed him Ner's package. At 12:30, Brunner opened it with a long tool rather than with his hands, which probably saved his life. The Nazi lost his left eye and was wounded in his left arm, which remained partly paralyzed thereafter.[21] After a few days, Shamir and his superiors read in the international and Arab press that a "foreigner" had been wounded by an explosive package in the main post office of Damascus. A classified intelligence report from Aman specified that the wounded foreigner was German. The chief of Syrian military intelligence told an Aman source that the victim's name was Georg Fischer, and that he had a past of "activity against the Jews."[22] Shamir and the others must have known their mission had failed.

A friend from Germany who visited the wounded war criminal in Syria testified that Brunner was almost blind and completely miserable. A German physician affiliated with the consulate was able to operate on his remaining eye and save his sight, but he never regained full vision. From that day on, Brunner sported a glass eye.[23] He was not forgotten by his Syrian benefactors. Sarraj and other senior intelligence officers visited his hospital room, which was protected by a tight security detail. He was moved at least three times between hospitals, and the regime spread a rumor that he succumbed to his wounds or left for another country in an attempt to mislead assassins who might still be at large. Naturally, the authorities gave Brunner the best possible treatment available in Syria.[24]

And yet, Brunner still faced dangers from within Syria and without. In Frankfurt, Fritz Bauer's investigation and the arrest warrant against him were still in force, and the German embassy pressured the Syrian Foreign Ministry to deport Brunner from the country "for the sake of Syrian-German relations."[25]

Syria was also rocked by domestic upheavals. Though Sarraj was demoted by President Nasser in late September, the colonel's terror regime reflected badly on the Union in the mind of many Syrians. Cairo's unpopular economic policy and a general animosity against the Egyptian outsiders, aggravated by a prolonged drought, paved the way for revolutionary change. As a Japanese diplomat in Damascus observed, Nasser and his henchmen treated Syria like a colony.[26] On September 28, one day after Sarraj's downfall, a group of Syrian officers and politicians launched a coup d'état. In the early morning hours, the citizens of Damascus woke up to the sight of soldiers in battle gear occupying the city center and strategic installations. The radio declared that "the Supreme Arab Revolutionary Command" had taken power "in order to preserve the security, freedom and dignity of the country and to eliminate tyranny and corruption."[27] The new rulers declared secession from the union with Egypt, released political prisoners, and abolished the GID, Sarraj's hated intelligence apparatus. Nasser, they claimed, had made Syria "a big prison" controlled by the GID who spied on the citizenry, turned brother against brother, and destroyed the fabric of Syrian society.[28] As the united country ceased to exist, several bigwigs of the old regime were arrested in Damascus. First among them was Sarraj himself.

Propaganda outlets of the new regime accused Sarraj of establishing a "ruthless police state whose spies and torturers learned their trade from Nazi experts," and promised to publish more details in a "black book" that was soon to follow. The Lebanese newspaper *l'Orient*, almost certainly informed by Syrian government sources, told its readers that Nasser and his intelligence chief employed twenty Gestapo experts in the fields of propaganda, intelligence, investigation, and espionage. Most of these Nazi torturers were employed in Egypt, but Nasser "loaned" three of them, including Brunner, to his new Syrian province. These Nazis helped the Syrians to build a more efficient secret service and introduced sophisticated, modern, and unprecedented torture techniques to a country "renowned for its kindness, its tolerance and the goodwill of its people."[29]

As Brunner was being denounced by the Syrian government, rumors reached Germany that he would stand trial along with Sarraj and his henchmen. Fritz Bauer especially had high hopes that the new regime would extradite Brunner, though the West German embassy was not so optimistic. Bonn's ambassador warned that no Syrian regime could formally extradite a person considered to be an enemy of Israel.[30]

The ambassador, unfortunately, was proven correct. Brunner remained almost unaffected. Already in the hospital, he was interrogated by agents of the new regime on the "crimes of Sarraj" and most probably betrayed his old patron. He suspected Al-Midani was complicit in his assassination, and that might have made it easier to betray both him and Sarraj. In any case, the new regime released Serraj and his henchmen relatively quickly. Sarraj and Al-Midani were retired, but that was it. The black book, too, was never published. Most probably, a public trial would have exposed too many secrets that many in Syria preferred to bury in the dark.[31]

Dr. Sa'id Fatah Imam was quick to join the coup and became a procurement agent for the army of the newly independent Syrian Republic. He hastened to buy arms from his Nazi friends, most notably Springer and Remer.[32] Captain Laham, Brunner's friend and recruiter, miraculously survived the post-Sarraj purge and returned to military intelligence (The Second Bureau) where he was promoted to the rank of a general. Brunner accompanied him. The fact that the new regime denounced the "Nazi experts" of Sarraj obviously did not deter it from employing them as well.[33]

In 1962, after he recovered from the assassination attempt, Brunner was given his own working space, an innocent-sounding "import office" in Harika, Damascus's business quarter. There, he worked along with Talal Abdulwahab Rifa'i, the translator who helped him to torture Curt Witzke. He had quite an influence back then. The German embassy was even afraid to hire Syrian translators for their pleas of extradition, lest Brunner hear about it and take countermeasures.[34] With his new alias of "Armin Hazis," he traveled each morning to the intelligence base in Wadi Barada, a mountainous suburb of Damascus, or to the Maysalun Camp, twelve kilometers west of the city, to train officers of the dreaded military security service in counterintelligence and interrogation techniques. According to Israeli and German intelligence sources, he even served as that school's director, though this is far from certain.[35] His disciples include notorious figures in the annals of Syrian history: General Ali Haidar, the father of the Syrian special forces; Ali Duba, the much-dreaded commander of the Department of Military Counterintelligence; and even Mustafa Tlass, the future defense minister of the Assad regime.

Brunner taught his pupils German "with the charming Viennese accent."[36] The sensationalist Lebanese press described him as the mastermind of secret police terror. That was certainly exaggerated, but Brunner's influence was still malignant.[37] He certainly helped to create sophisticated torture devices, possibly even the infamous "German Chair" (*Al-kursi al-Almani*), which had no vertical support. Victims were "bent backwards until they felt like their back would break."[38] According to one account there was also "a wheel upon which prisoners could be strapped and beaten with an electric cable. Every few minutes, an automatic pump would spray water through the wheel to open a prisoner's wounds, whereupon the beatings could start again."[39] Brunner received a good salary and enjoyed other benefits, such as a chauffeur-driven car.[40] Years later, he bragged that in the early 1960s, his house was often frequented by visitors including German and Syrian businessmen, officers, and even the Israeli spy Eli Cohen.[41]

· 14 ·

Winter in Syria— The Downfall of OTRACO

Damascus is governed by weird rules.[1]

—HERMANN SCHAEFER

IN THE AFTERNOON hours of February 10, 1962, a posh Opel car stopped at the customs station of the Syrian-Lebanese border on the Beirut-Damascus highway and two men stepped out of the vehicle for customs and immigration inspection. The driver, a middle-aged Syrian aristocrat named Majid Sheikh al-Ard, introduced his younger friend to the local commander: Kamel Amin Thabet, an elegant-looking Argentinian businessman of Syrian descent. While they chatted with the station chief, an old friend of Sheikh al-Ard, the border officials completed the inspection and stamped Thabet's passport with a Syrian tourist visa for six months. They were oblivious to some odd bits and pieces of Thabet's luggage: a tiny Morse code transmitter hidden inside a double-bottomed cigarette box, powerful explosives camouflaged as Yardley soap bars, a short-wave radio, and other pieces of clandestine equipment. Thabet's real name was Eli Cohen, and he was an Israeli spy dispatched to Syria by unit 188 of Aman, IDF Military Intelligence.

With the help of Sheikh al-Ard, whom he befriended on the ship to Beirut, Cohen hoped to establish himself in Syria, cultivating the false identity of a patriot longing to return to his Arab homeland. To the growing circle of his friends and acquaintances in Damascus, "Thabet" presented himself as an import-export businessman and an agent of a European firm looking to scout the Syrian market for suitable export goods.[2] This cover was akin to that adopted by other agents in the Levant, such as our old acquaintances Wilhelm Beisner, Alois Brunner, and Hermann Schaefer.

Tel Aviv had high hopes for Eli Cohen. Maj. Gen. Meir Amit, the commander of Aman and the future head of the Mossad, wanted an agent on the ground who would report to him in real time on military and political developments in Syria after its secession from the United Arab Republic. Cohen's direct supervisors from Unit 188 advised him to rent an apartment overlooking the Syrian General Staff Headquarters. From there, he would be able to detect signs of unusual activity portending possible Syrian aggression against Israel.[3] Gradually, utilizing his social skills, connections, and an ample amount of money, Cohen cultivated friendships with Syrian higher-ups and "milked" them for information. In addition to his most crucial mission—providing early warning in case of war—he was later asked to inform Tel Aviv on Syrian attempts to divert Israeli water sources and disrupt Israeli infrastructure projects on the border.[4]

As a relatively low priority in his task list, Cohen's superiors also asked him to provide information on the Nazis in Damascus. Notwithstanding the failure of the Mossad to assassinate Brunner, the Israelis were still interested in discovering information on his whereabouts as well as on his fellow fugitive, Franz Rademacher, the former "expert for Jewish affairs" of the Nazi Foreign Office and a mass murderer in his own right.[5] In that sense, Cohen's chance meeting with Majid Sheikh al-Ard was fortunate because the latter, a fluent German speaker, was part of the circle of "Arab Nazis" in Damascus and well acquainted with the OTRACO gang.

Known as a rich playboy, the garrulous Majid Sheikh al-Ard was the scion of a family of Syrian landowners who held large tracts of land in the countryside around Damascus. In 1940, with the approval of the pro-Nazi French authorities in Syria, he left his homeland to study in Berlin and immediately became involved in espionage for Nazi Germany. After the war, Sheikh al-Ard was detained by the French as a Nazi collaborator, but was soon released. Adventurous by nature, he immediately began a second career in American service. He served in the Korean War in a civilian role, had affairs with local women, and then, in the early 1950s, returned to Syria as a spy for the CIA.[6]

For Sheikh al-Ard, the 1950s were a time of exciting adventures but also increasing frustration. Between lengthy sojourns in Damascus and Beirut, he traveled across Europe in luxurious cars, visited expensive hotels, and wined and dined in the best places, drawing on his family fortunes and a monthly salary from the CIA. As a fluent German speaker, he naturally got acquainted with the German community in Damascus, including fugitive war criminals such as Brunner and Rademacher, but also with the arms trafficking network of Wilhelm Beisner. In 1959, however, the CIA decided to "put him on ice" and stopped his monthly payments. Sheikh al-Ard, whose expenses were probably larger than his income, desperately tried to renew his contract with the Americans and passed them information pro bono in order to win their favor. Brunner suspected that he also sold information to Hermann Schaefer that allowed, in part, the French assassination attempt against Beisner.[7]

A few weeks after his arrival in Damascus, Eli Cohen rented an apartment in the Abu Rummaneh district. He picked it mainly because it overlooked the building of the Syrian General Staff, but incidentally it was also close to Brunner's abode.[8] Decades later, Brunner boasted that Cohen visited his apartment, leaving him "souvenirs" such as an ashtray. We do not have evidence that such a meeting took place, but Cohen was indeed on the lookout for Brunner. Already in June 1962, just before his first vacation in Israel, Tel Aviv cabled him and asked for more information on Eichmann's assistant and other fugitive Nazis.[9]

Brunner, however, was difficult to locate. After the assassination attempts against Beisner and Brunner, the formerly cozy Nazi social circle was broken beyond repair. Beisner, wounded and almost blind, left for Tunis and kept his distance from Syria. Brunner became intolerable, and deeply offended Rademacher by accusing him of complicity with the Mossad assassination attempt as well as the abduction of Eichmann in 1960. The former accusation, at least, was not completely undeserved. Rademacher had inadvertently provided information to Schaefer, who passed it on to Tel Aviv.[10]

At a relatively early stage, Sheikh al-Ard introduced Cohen to Ernst-Wilhelm Springer. Neo-Nazi though he was, Springer was not a war criminal and therefore of little interest to Israeli Nazi hunters. His arms deals, however, might have been of greater concern to Tel Aviv. When Cohen met Springer in one of the exclusive clubs of Damascus, the latter, along with Remer, offered the Syrians help in establishing a rocket program.

At the time, as we will see later on, the Nasser regime in Egypt was developing long-range missiles with the help of German scientists. The Syrians, whose relations with Nasser at the time were extremely tense, were jealous of their Egyptian rivals and wanted a rocket program of their own. Remer and Springer offered to connect them with a group of German scientists and to establish plants, research facilities, and experiment fields in Syria. They promised to develop rockets with remote control and navigation systems "three times stronger than those of the United States and the Soviet Union." Because Springer enjoyed great success at the time as an arms trafficker to the FLN and other Arab and Third World armies, escaping several French assassination attempts along the way, the Syrians were inclined to trust him. Along with several technical advisers, Remer and Springer traveled to Syria in November 1962 under false names on Damascus's expense. Springer was enjoying his time, spending nights out with Majid Sheikh al-Ard and other friends in the New Omayyad Hotel and the "Orient Club," and moving between Syria and Germany. Remer stayed in Damascus several months, enjoying himself while the Syrians footed the bills.

Remer was already a rowdy drunkard whose ability to distinguish between fantasy and reality was very limited. During 1962, he was observed in German bars telling anyone prepared to listen that he was hired by Franz Josef Strauss, the Federal Republic's defense minister, to lead a secret sabotage organization in East Germany. According to Springer, Remer embezzled money, failed to deliver shipments to the FLN, bought himself a Mercedes, and covered his debts with company funds. The Syrians probably did not know that Remer was under investigation for fraud in Germany and that the FLN's representative in Germany, Dr. Masoud Serghini, already threatened to shoot him dead. Springer, who increasingly contemplated getting rid of Remer, kept business ties with him mainly for public relations reasons. Remer was still very popular in Syrian and North African military circles due to his halo as a former German general, Hitler's security expert, and a "Jew eater," though he was not really involved in the Holocaust.[11]

Cohen reported to Tel Aviv on his meeting with Springer and almost certainly also on the "rocket program,"[12] but soon it was revealed as OTRACO's last swindle. The preliminary experiments flopped while Springer and Remer pocketed research money. According to an unconfirmed report of the West German embassy in Damascus, the duo, along with Brunner, was also involved in the coup of March 1963, that overthrew the relatively pro-Western government of Nazim Al-Qudsi and established a pro-Soviet dictatorship led by the Baath Party.[13] If Brunner, Remer, and Springer were indeed involved, it did not help the last two to curry favor with the new regime. In early May 1963, Springer had to admit to the Syrians that he and Remer were no rocket experts. The two were told to leave the country within twenty-four hours. When Springer returned to Germany, he was almost immediately arrested and put on trial for illegal arms trafficking. This only served to further tarnish the image of this Nazi group in the eyes of the Syrians, who now suspected that Springer too was a West German spy.[14]

With Brunner inaccessible and Springer irrelevant, there remained only one German fugitive of interest to Cohen: Franz Rademacher, the mass murderer from the Nazi Foreign Office, who was still close to Majid Sheikh al-Ard and lived in Damascus under the false name of "Rossello." One day in spring 1963, most probably in early March, Cohen was hosted by Majid on the latter's farm, where they were listening to news about the Eichmann trial.[15] Cohen used the opportunity to bring up the subject of the "German fugitives" in Damascus, especially "one of Eichmann's assistants." Cohen, probably referring to Brunner, teased Sheikh al-Ard and asked him half-mockingly whether he was still friends with that man. Sheikh al-Ard said nothing on Brunner but called Rademacher—the only OTRACO Nazi who was still available. The three men agreed to meet in Rademacher's apartment.[16]

For Cohen, visiting Rademacher was a very bad idea, as the latter was closely monitored by the Syrian secret police. Rademacher had been recruited the previous year to the BND, the West German intelligence service, through international neo-Nazi connections. In March 1962, he was approached by Hans Rechenberg and Francois Genoud, neo-Nazi literary agents who made enormous amounts of money through purchasing the copyrights of sensational Nazi memoirs and documents. At the same time, Rechenberg headed the "Arab-African Company," a front for BND spying operations in the Middle East. In doing so, he intended to down two birds with one stone: spy for West Germany, and promote his and Genoud's neo-Nazi publications.

Rademacher, in any case, was a good catch: deep inside Damascus, employed by the Syrian GID and close to elite circles, he could provide quality intelligence on Syria.[17]

Rademacher's intelligence peddling was still tolerated in Syria, but for how long? In any event, Damascus was too crowded with Western spies. The relationship between Syria and West Germany had gradually worsened, and Rademacher could be arrested following any chance crisis. True, he worked for the Syrian GID, and that had provided him with immunity so far, but there was no guarantee this would hold. The former official in the Nazi Foreign Ministry knew that the noose was tightening around his neck in West Germany as well. The proceedings against him were still pending, and in the 1960s, Fritz Bauer sought his extradition. Rademacher faced a stark choice: either stay in Damascus, which was increasingly unwelcoming and dangerous, or return home and face charges for war crimes. He was growing inclined toward the latter. After all, nothing the West Germans would do to him could equal the horrors of a Syrian prison.

In late 1962 and early 1963, Rademacher began to think about the option of repatriation. Most likely, he hoped his highly placed friends in the BND would help him avoid charges. But Hans Rechenberg, the neo-Nazi shadow man and Rademacher's handler in the BND, did not want him back in Germany. Reinhard Gehlen, too, preferred Rademacher in the Syrian shadows rather than facing a public trial in Germany that might reveal compromising details about former Nazis high up in the West German system, or worse, in the BND itself. At that time, as we will see in the next chapter, the BND was mired in serious political trouble and Gehlen was afraid for his own skin. Heinz Felfe's arrest in September 1961 convinced Chancellor Adenauer and his successor, Ludwig Erhard, that the Nazi agents of the BND were a security risk and that Gehlen was guilty of bringing them in. The federal government launched a thorough investigation of all former Nazi intelligence and security veterans in the service. In such a sensitive atmosphere, the repatriation of a vile war criminal from Syria and the exposure of his ties to the BND in a public trial was the last thing that Gehlen needed.

Rechenberg, who wanted to keep Rademacher in Syria, offered a way to fill his empty days: Rademacher should write a book about the extermination of the Jews from his own point of view. That was, of course, a corrupted ploy.

Rechenberg and his partner Genoud wanted to enrich themselves with the "help" of the forlorn BND agent in Damascus.[18]

• • •

THAT WAS THE situation when Majid Sheikh al-Ard took Eli Cohen to see Rademacher.[19] Sheikh al-Ard and Cohen parked near the Syrian Central Bank, crossed a garden, and ascended to a small and stinking apartment. Almost certainly, agents of Syrian military intelligence were lurking nearby.

The meeting with Rademacher was relatively short and he tried to receive his guests with a cheerful countenance notwithstanding his poverty. That was not the first time he saw Cohen—the two had met briefly before near the main post office of Damascus. Rademacher and Sheikh al-Ard spoke for about thirty minutes mostly in German, a language Cohen did not understand. Rademacher did tell Cohen that the "Jews and the Germans are looking for me everywhere. They are unjustly accusing me of killing Jews during the war. Fortunately, I enjoy relative peace in Damascus and can hold a respectable job." The very next day, the Israeli spy advised Tel Aviv about the whereabouts of the Nazi criminal "who works in Syrian intelligence," his precise address, and the name of his wife. He ended his cable with ominous words: "I am ready to kill Rademacher."[20]

The Mossad that just took Cohen over from Aman was cool toward the idea. Certainly they would not let their prize asset in Damascus risk himself with a reckless assassination of dubious value. Tel Aviv radioed back that "you [Cohen] should refrain at all costs from any action regarding R. [Rademacher] that may foil your main task. Maintain your interest in R. and send us more information about him."[21] According to Cohen's biographer, Samuel Segev, he was itching to do away with Rademacher and saw his discovery as one of his most important achievements in Damascus. The Mossad's enthusiasm about Brunner had cooled considerably after the failed assassination attempt in September 1961, and now, in any case, Israeli spy chiefs had more pressing concerns than Nazi hunting. After a while, Tel Aviv ordered Cohen to stay away from Rademacher: "Leave him alone and focus on your main task."[22]

In fact, Cohen's handlers in Tel Aviv made a grave mistake by not telling their agent to stay away from Nazis *in the first place*. Cohen's cover story was extremely shallow and could have been easily exposed by means of a serious background check. For example, he was supposed to have spent fifteen years in Argentina, but nobody there had known him for so long. His Spanish was also too poor for a person who had grown up in Latin America. In 1962 and 1963, the freelance Nazis in Damascus, all involved in espionage and arms trafficking, were already suspect and followed by the Syrian security services. Any contact with them was sure to bring further security screenings. For a spy such as Cohen with such a brittle cover story, the attempt to approach such people (and certainly to plot their assassination) was sheer madness.

Cohen was extremely lucky not to be caught in a wave of arrests that began in July 1963. One and a half years earlier, when he first crossed the border to Syria, the local intelligence services were still in disarray, occupied by internal fights after the downfall of the United Arab Republic.[23] But gradually, and especially after the Baath Party coup d'état on March 8, 1963, the Syrian intelligence services reorganized around the Second Bureau under the leadership of the much-dreaded Colonel Ahmad Suidani. The latter had rebuilt the oppressive security apparatus from the time of the United Arab Republic, so adroitly described by Hermann Schaefer: "Damascus is governed by weird rules . . . Every step is controlled . . . A coup is always around the corner. At any given time, somebody is expelled or arrested. Everybody conspires against everybody." In such an atmosphere, foreigners were always under strong suspicion.[24]

Encouraged by the Soviet Union, the Syrians began to collapse the networks of Western espionage in Damascus, and West Germany's agents were the first to suffer. This process was escalated by an ongoing deterioration in the relationship between Arab countries, including Syria and Egypt, and the Federal Republic of Germany. Already in late 1963, the West German ambassador in Damascus warned that formal recognition of Israel would be the death knell of German diplomacy in Syria. Local politics, he warned, is influenced by strong emotions, and relations are doomed to die in such a case, notwithstanding the generous material assistance of West Germany to the Syrian Arab Republic.[25] No longer were the Syrians ready to tolerate German intelligence peddlers such as Rademacher who worked for Gehlen and other masters. In July 1963, shortly after his meeting with Cohen, Rademacher was arrested by Syrian security officials. For more than seven months he was locked in a cell, mistreated, and tortured. Then, to his dread, he was indicted for espionage.[26] As Rademacher knew well, the punishment in Syria for such a crime was death by hanging.

The relations between the Arab world and West Germany further deteriorated in the autumn of 1964 when Bonn's secret arms deals with Israel became common knowledge.[27] In spring 1965, West Germany finally recognized Israel, and Syria promptly broke off diplomatic relations. Bonn still maintained a chargé d'affairs in the French Embassy and tried to keep in touch with Rademacher. But the Syrians did not permit the German representative to see the prisoner, nor did they heed German extradition requests. "Rossello," the Syrian Foreign Ministry declared, entered Syria with a non-German passport, and the Syrian government had no reason to assume he was a West German subject. Therefore, the Germans should not be concerned with his whereabouts.[28] A year and a half later Rademacher was finally handed over to West Germany, a thoroughly sick and broken man. He stood trial for war crimes, received a lenient sentence, and appealed it, but died in jail before his appeal could be heard.[29]

Syrian security services, egged on by the Soviets, were increasingly intolerant toward locals and expats who spied for the United States. The position of Cohen's friend Majid Sheikh al-Ard had therefore become increasingly shaky. The former CIA spy was too close to the American embassy in times of increasing Syrian-American tension.[30] The Soviets were of course happy to add fuel to the fire. In a deception operation codenamed PULYA (bullet), the KGB residency in Syria gave the local security services a heads-up on a joint CIA-BND spying scheme. The Soviet military attaché visited President Amin al-Hafez and showed him a forged BND document that he was not willing to hand over "in order to protect the sources." The attaché did allow Hafez to write down the names of suspected CIA and BND spies mentioned in the document. Subsequently, the KGB made an anonymous call to Syrian intelligence with similar information and tricked a pro-American Syrian officer into disclosing his illicit ties with the United States in a bugged conversation.[31]

In December 1964, two Syrians, one civilian and one officer, were arrested for espionage in an affair known as the "American spy ring" and a US diplomat was expelled from the country. Mamdouh Al-Midani, long fallen from grace, was interrogated on suspicion of espionage for Germany and might have fingered

Rademacher, Springer, and yet another spy, Adnan Zein, a Syrian interpreter who once served as Brunner and Rademacher's informant inside the West German consulate.[32]

Eli Cohen's turn finally came in January 1965. Agents of the Second Bureau broke into his apartment one morning while he was sitting in bed listening to the radio. An agent threw himself on the unsuspecting Israeli spy to prevent him from destroying documents or harming himself while others thoroughly searched the apartment. After a short while they found Cohen's Morse transmitter, code book, hidden explosives, and other pieces of clandestine equipment. At first Cohen insisted he was an Arab, but soon broke down. Under torture, he gave details of his acquaintances, including Majid Sheikh al-Ard, who was arrested shortly afterward.[33]

It is not clear how the Syrian authorities discovered the true identity of "Kamel Amin Thabet," as the archives in Damascus are still closed. General Dhali, Cohen's judge, wrote in his memoirs that transmissions from Cohen's radio interfered with the frequency used by the Indian Embassy, which complained to the security services.[34] In Israel, the Mossad assumed the Syrians were able to triangulate Cohen's transmissions with high-end Soviet equipment. President Amin al-Hafez later recalled that Syrian intelligence intercepted hundreds of Cohen's transmissions but could not decipher them. Hence, they resorted to methods of triangulation with the help of the Soviets.[35] Other testimonies claim Cohen was under suspicion for at least two months prior to his arrest. In an anonymous letter to the spy's family, many years after his death, a Syrian friend wrote that "Thabet" was denounced by an alert neighbor.[36]

In an interview to a Lebanese journal, the commander of the Second Bureau, Colonel Ahmad Suidani, and his minions testified Cohen was subject to surveillance "for a few months" due to his friendship with "a person known by his dubious connections," most probably Majid Sheikh al-Ard.[37] One writer even argued that Cohen's meeting with Rademacher led to his downfall. The German fugitive was already under surveillance, and anybody who meets a suspicious person becomes suspect as well.[38] However, Rademacher was arrested in July 1963, and if Cohen was already under suspicion back then, it is difficult to understand why the Syrian authorities did not arrest him outright, and even more so, why they allowed him to travel abroad several times before his final arrest in January 1965. Several things are clear: Damascus was overcrowded with Western spies and agents, and by 1963, both the Syrians and the Soviets made a concentrated effort to get rid of them, especially in light of the rising tensions between Syria and Israel, West Germany, the United States, and many Arab countries.[39] In that sense, Cohen's downfall was the logical continuation of the demise of OTRACO and Rademacher's arrest.

Colonel Salah a-Din Dhali, the president of the military tribunal that tried Cohen, Sheikh al-Ard, and other suspects, frantically attempted to connect Cohen with all other Western spies in order to project an image of a united malevolent front against Syria. Particularly, he cross-examined Sheikh al-Ard, repeatedly asking him about his ties with Nazi agents such as Springer and Rademacher. Sheikh al-Ard, the judge accused, tried to introduce Cohen to Springer and Rademacher in order to connect together all the espionage nodes in the country.

For that reason, perhaps, Sheikh al-Ard strongly denied that he ever took Cohen to Rademacher. When Sheikh al-Ard conceded to his merciless judge that he met Springer first in 1959 or 1960 and was aware of the latter's involvement in arms trafficking to the Algerian Revolution, Colonel Dhali immediately ascribed him responsibility for French assassination operations against Nazi arms traffickers. Sheikh al-Ard, he charged, was an Israeli spy already back then. He leaked information to the Israelis on arms shipments, and the Jews promptly shared their intelligence with the French. Sheikh al-Ard denied this strenuously, but nobody believed him.[40]

The results were devastating for West German intelligence. Between Rademacher's arrest and Cohen's trial, the astounded Reinhard Gehlen saw his entire network of agents in Syria collapsing. His situation in the Middle East was made no better by his close cooperation with the Israeli Mossad. After Felfe's arrest and the collapse of Gehlen's networks behind the Iron Curtain, the BND relied intensively on intelligence cooperation with the Mossad, which possessed human sources in communist countries. As a payment, Gehlen was committed to help the Israelis with their own intelligence endeavors in the Middle East.[41]

In February 1965, shortly after Eli Cohen's downfall, an Israeli-German spy named Wolfgang Lotz (on whom more later) was arrested in Egypt. Lotz's name popped up in a conversation between Israeli and BND officials as early as 1956, and the documents show that the BND supported the spy's activity in

Egypt by funding his horse farm near Cairo and, almost certainly, by helping him to obtain proper documentation. This was done to win the favor of the Israelis more than for any intelligence benefit.[42] In any case, yielding to a personal request from the head of the Mossad, Gehlen saved Lotz's neck by claiming him as a BND agent. Exerting himself, he did his best to block incriminating publications about the Israeli identity of the arrested spy, dispatched a German defense lawyer to Cairo, and used political connections to help Lotz as much as possible. The BND president suffered mightily for his close cooperation with the Israelis, yet another consequence of the Felfe debacle.[43] Cairo disgracefully expelled Gerhard Bauch, Gehlen's resident in Cairo, and began to tear down West German operations in the land of the Nile.[44] In 1965, Gehlen had nothing left in Syria and Egypt but ashes and broken dreams.

However, the old spymaster's predicament in West Germany itself was much worse. Since 1961, he had become entangled in a series of escalating crises, many of them related to the BND's complicated ties with former Nazis and skillfully manipulated by the Soviets to undermine Gehlen's position. The Third Reich skeletons Gehlen had buried in the foundations of his brainchild, the BND, clawed their way back to the surface, exposed in all their travesties to the light of day and the wrath of domestic and international public opinion.

Third Reich chickens had finally come home to roost.

· 15 ·

Nazi Skeletons Unearthed— Gehlen's Darkest Hour

Old soldiers never die. They just fade away.

—GENERAL DOUGLAS MACARTHUR, BASED ON A POPULAR ARMY BALLAD

IT ALL BEGAN with the impending exposure of Heinz Felfe, the Nazi-Soviet mole who penetrated the BND in the early 1950s. The process that ultimately led to his downfall commenced in March 1959, when Michał Goleniewski, a Polish operative who worked for the Soviets in the late 1940s and for the Americans in the late 1950s, advised Washington that the Soviets had at least two moles inside the BND.[1] According to his report, both operatives participated in a BND delegation to the United States. Heinz Felfe had indeed visited the United States in 1956 as a member of a BND delegation, and now, old suspicions against him surfaced yet again. Felfe's extravagant way of life, unusual working patterns, and incessant inquisitiveness concerning the work of other BND departments raised eyebrows among both his German and American colleagues as early as 1952. However, the CIA and the CIC, both of whom inquired into Felfe's case, failed to share their findings with one another.[2] At the same time, BND officials who expressed doubts about Felfe's true colors were brushed aside by Gehlen and his closest advisers. One of them, Ludwig Albert, was framed for espionage by the Soviets and thus driven to suicide.

In the BND, Felfe was for many years above suspicion and Gehlen employed him in a top-secret mission to penetrate the KGB compound in East Berlin. In December 1959, he even approved Felfe's request to travel to West Berlin, a dangerous frontier zone. Felfe, of course, exploited the journey to meet his KGB handlers.[3] But as CIA investigations proceeded, Gehlen uncovered the terrible truth from his own sources. In October 1960, a senior official in BND counterintelligence, Karl-Eberhard Henke, sent a detailed report to the BND president and suggested that Felfe might be a Soviet mole. This time, Gehlen took the accusations seriously.

Soon thereafter, the Americans shared their own information with Gehlen. On December 31, 1960, the CIA station chief in Frankfurt warned Gehlen that the BND was penetrated by Soviet moles, two of whom took part in the 1956 delegation to the United States. He also shared the list of the suspects. The CIA information merely confirmed Henke's report from October, and Gehlen, according to an eyewitness, read the list and immediately said that Felfe was the traitor.[4] Then he established a small investigation team, codenamed Mexico, under his personal supervision. It was clear that an enormous political scandal was likely to break out soon after Felfe's exposure.[5]

Looking forward to precisely such a scandal, the Soviets intentionally sacrificed Felfe, or at least did nothing to protect him. In a later study, CIA analysts concluded that the KGB knew of Goleniewski's treason as early as the summer of 1960, if not earlier, and permitted him to defect to the West with information on Felfe.[6] In 1993, Felfe's KGB handler Vitali Korotkov (aka Alfred) disclosed in an interview that by 1961, the KGB wanted to "put the operation on ice" because of the danger to Felfe's security, but the Politburo vetoed the decision as they wished to exploit Felfe further. "Politics won," Korotkov recalled, "and Felfe was sacrificed."[7] According to Felfe himself, Korotkov never warned him about Goleniewski's defection, though he was well aware of the associated peril.[8]

Felfe's biographer Bodo Hechelhammer notes that Felfe had already fully informed the Soviets on BND counterespionage methodology, foiled countless operations, and provided thousands of documents. He was an exhaustively exploited asset. Now was the time to sacrifice the pawn in order to provoke a public scandal and compromise the BND as much as possible.[9] Gehlen was naturally fearful of such an outcome. On November 6, 1961, shortly before Felfe's arrest, he advised State Secretary Hans Globke on the affair and implored him to try and contain negative press reports, especially about Felfe's SD past. Gehlen and Globke had much to hide. The BND employed dozens of Nazi criminals, including former Gestapo operatives, and now this practice could be associated in the public eye not only with moral perfidy but also with Soviet espionage. Gehlen, to reiterate, trusted Felfe and promoted him to high and sensitive positions. Accordingly, he could expect outrage and retaliation from Chancellor Adenauer, who had warned him already in 1958 against employing former SS and SD officials.[10]

The BND's connection with former Nazis might also prove embarrassing in the context of another incident that took place on October 14, 1960: the French assassination attempt against Wilhelm Beisner. This time, the impending scandal could endanger not only the BND's image, but also the delicate relationship between West Germany and France.[11]

Besieged by threatening exposures from all sides, Gehlen needed allies in the topmost levels of the federal government. Especially, he needed to reinforce his alliance with Hans Globke. It is telling that Gehlen did not inform Globke of Felfe's betrayal until November 6, 1961, shortly before the latter's arrest. He had only a few months to earn Globke's gratitude before the embarrassing revelations on Felfe reached the government and the press.[12]

• • •

GLOBKE NEEDED GEHLEN, now more than ever. In 1960, the state secretary's Nazi past came to haunt him from multiple quarters and he descended into fear bordering on panic. On May 23, 1960, Israeli prime minister David Ben-Gurion announced that Adolf Eichmann had been abducted by the Mossad and would face trial in Israel. Globke, who served in the Reich Ministry of the Interior and took part in the enactment of the anti-Semitic Nuremberg Laws, was afraid that Eichmann or the prosecutor might expose embarrassing details on Globke's role in the persecution of the Jews during the Third Reich. For Adenauer, Globke was an irreplaceable right-hand man, and he was accordingly prepared to go to great lengths to protect him.[13]

In order to protect Globke, Bonn vaguely threatened Jerusalem that if the trial was handled "inappropriately," West Germany might withdraw loans, cancel arms shipments, and, most importantly, postpone crucial assistance to the Israeli nuclear program.[14] In conversations with the Israelis, West German officials warned that the very existence of the Federal Republic was at stake. They expressed exaggerated fears that nobody would come to the aid of a "Nazi country" associated with Eichmann if attacked by the Soviet Union.[15] Rolf Vogel, a half-Jewish BND operative and journalist, known as a staunch supporter of Israel and mediator of arms deals, was dispatched to Jerusalem to monitor the trial and put pressure on Ben-Gurion's government. The West German efforts bore fruit, at least partially. Though the Israeli attorney general, Gideon Hausner, refused to promise Ben-Gurion that Globke would be off-limits, in practice he did not mention him during the trial. Eichmann's councilor, Robert Servatius, acquiesced to the prosecutor's request not to summon Globke as a witness "for the benefit of both sides." Nonetheless, Globke lived in constant fear that his name would be somehow dragged into the proceedings.[16]

Silencing the Israeli prosecution did nothing to neutralize Hermann Schaefer, the ubiquitous intelligence peddler who was still at large. The *Kristall* articles, besides incensing Nazi expats, thwarting secret weapon deals, and putting OTRACO in the spotlight,[17] also lit a fire under many leading figures in Bonn, Gehlen, his patron Globke, and Adenauer himself among them. All had Nazi skeletons in their closet, either due to their own wartime past, their tolerance and use of Nazi-tainted underlings and agents, or efforts to keep these skeletons under cover. Moreover, it gradually became apparent to the BND agents shadowing Schaefer during his Levantine sojourn that he was specifically digging for incriminating information on Globke.[18] Then, a new threat emerged. On November 15, 1959, Max Merten, a former official in Nazi-occupied Thessaloniki, was released from Greek custody and deported to West Germany. He blamed the federal authorities for his arrest in Greece and lusted for revenge. He particularly wished to implicate Globke in the Holocaust.

Ten days after Ben-Gurion's announcement of Eichmann's arrest, Max Merten opened a public front against Globke. On June 3, 1960, he met Fritz Bauer, the attorney general of the state of Hessen, for an informal interview in Frankfurt.[19] According to Merten's account, he [Merten] had tried to evacuate 20,000 Greek Jews to Palestine and save them from extermination and was even able to convince Eichmann to green-light the operation. Globke, however, vetoed the plan. On July 19, Merten repeated this fallacious story to a court in Berlin. Two months later, on September 17, it appeared in the *Hamburger Echo* as part of a serial on Merten's tenure in Thessaloniki. In 1961, Merten, already subject to a libel suit by Globke, hinted at the story again as part of his testimony in the Eichmann trial.[20] Fritz Bauer took the accusations very seriously. On February 15, 1961, he handed over the results of his investigation against Globke to the attorney general's office in Bonn.[21]

Simultaneously, like a bad penny sure to turn up in a trouble spot, Hermann Schaefer returned to Germany in June 1960. His eagerness to obtain information had raised too many eyebrows in both Beirut and Damascus, especially as he failed to actually pay his informants and contacts. By December 1959, the Syrian secret police advised the German general consulate in Damascus that Schaefer was lavishly paid by "Eastern" (i.e., communist) sources. When an official West German delegation was housed in the New Omayyad Hotel where Schaefer resided at the time, the German consulate asked its Syrian counterparts to evacuate Schaefer from the premises, to which the Syrians gladly obliged.[22] Soon after, Damascene security authorities deported him from the country altogether. On March 16, Syrian detectives arrested Schaefer in the popular German bar Bei Freddy where he was sipping whiskey with two friends and took him to a nearby police station. There, he was briskly told that he had two hours to leave Syria. Placed in a taxi and surrounded by security service vehicles, he was driven to the Lebanese border. When Schaefer crossed into Lebanon, he was in fact relieved. Until the border-crossing, he suspected his guards intended to kill him somewhere in the Syrian desert.[23]

Had they done so, the BND and Globke may well have been relieved, for by then they had developed genuine suspicions that Schaefer was more than a muckraking freelance journalist and intelligence peddler, but a genuine Soviet Bloc operative.[24] To be sure, the evidence for this was circumstantial rather than direct. As the expenses of Schaefer's newly founded magazine were considerable, the BND suspected that the entire operation was financed by the Stasi. The German consul in Damascus also noted that the excellent journalistic style of Schaefer's articles was inconsistent with the less eloquent style of his private letters, further corroborating the suspicion that a professional shadow writer was actually running the show. Furthermore, Schaefer provided Sa'id Fatah Imam with a recommendation letter for the East German authorities, resulting in a lavish reception for the latter in East Berlin. Thus, when the

Syrian security authorities advised their German counterparts that Schaefer was paid by "Eastern" (i.e., communist) sources in December 1959, it hardly came as a shock. The BfV noted, however, that these suspicions could never be completely proven.[25]

Upon his return to Germany, Schaefer was arrested and interrogated by the BND and testified that the entire purpose of his trip was to collect mitigating testimonies for Max Merten.[26] Indeed, during his busy schedule in Syria, Schaefer tried to secure testimonies from Brunner and Rademacher on Merten's behalf, but failed. This uncharacteristic effort, totally at odds with Schaefer's supposed anti-Nazi agenda, raised an immediate red flag in Bonn, particularly given the near-synchronized denunciation of Globke by Merten. For the BND, or so at least Gehlen presented the case to Globke, the conclusion was clear: this was a contemporary Red Orchestra directed by Soviet conductors in which Merten was offered help by Schaefer in return for incriminating one of the strongest people in West Germany, and by implication the legitimacy of the Federal Republic itself. It was Globke who had been the target all along.[27] Globke's past was, of course, a favorite pastime for communist propaganda, especially in East Germany. In 1961, Erich Mielke, East German minister of state security, incessantly fished for evidence against Globke, including anything that may link him with Eichmann and the extermination of the Jews.[28]

It is no wonder therefore that Globke was afraid of every shadow. Nor was it any wonder that Gehlen eagerly catered to his fears—for his own chickens were coming home to roost, and he knew he would need Globke's patronage to survive the upcoming crisis. The ticking time bomb that was Felfe had finally exploded, and at the most inopportune moment. Though Gehlen was forced to acknowledge Felfe's treason by October 1960, he had yet to reveal this to his superiors or publicly expose the mole. Rather, Gehlen frantically sought to delay exposure as long as possible so he could contain the fallout and buttress his position within the West German political establishment in order to survive the inevitable scandal.

Currying favor with State Secretary Hans Globke, Chancellor Konrad Adenauer's chief of staff and one of the most powerful men in the Federal Republic, seemed like the best course of action to insure Gehlen against the fallout. As the official in charge of West Germany's intelligence organizations, Globke was Gehlen's most important ally throughout the 1950s, having supported the Org and then the BND in almost all their struggles against institutional rivals in West Germany. In return, Gehlen intervened for Globke with the Americans, helping to stall legal action against his patron.[29] Now Gehlen needed Globke's support more than ever—and to secure it he was prepared to take risks that would expose both men to far stronger associations with notorious Holocaust perpetrators.[30]

In order to neutralize Merten, Gehlen cunningly stoked Globke's fears regarding the communist "propaganda campaign" against him and volunteered to muckrake his accusers, most notably Max Merten. He promised to leak condemning information against "Merten, who is controlled by East Germany" both to the press and to the Central Office for the Investigation of National Socialist Crimes in Ludwigsburg. In June 1960, one month after Eichmann's arrest, Gehlen even dispatched operatives to threaten witnesses who served in Greece during the war, lest they confirm Merten's version in court.[31]

Gehlen instructed the BND agent Hans Rechenberg, whom we encountered as Rademacher's handler, to secure funds for Eichmann's councilor in order to gain leverage on his defense strategy, i.e., make sure that Eichmann would not mention Globke during the trial. The project was canceled by the Foreign Ministry following its exposure by the press. However, Rechenberg continued collecting money for Eichmann. Parallel to his service in the BND, he was also working with Swiss Francois Genoud, a leader of a neo-Nazi network. Genoud and Rechenberg reached a deal to subsidize Eichmann's defense in return for rights on the latter's unpublished memoirs.[32] As expected, Gehlen's awkward move was about to backfire. Globke worried that Rechenberg's attempts would be ascribed to himself. He was, after all, the supervisor of the BND in the chancellor's office, and the last thing he needed was to be associated with Eichmann's defense. One of Gehlen's assistants, Kurt Weiss (aka Winterstein) told Globke there was nothing to worry about, as Rechenberg worked for the BND "only on the margins."[33] That was a lie that would put both Gehlen and Globke in a very uncomfortable position if exposed.

With Globke threatened by Merten, Schaefer, and the Eichmann trial, Gehlen came up with yet another risky scheme. He sought to convince Alois Brunner, Eichmann's assistant who found refuge in Damascus, to testify for Globke. It is unclear whether Gehlen and the BND were in touch with Brunner even before 1960. Many authors have argued that Brunner was, in fact, a bona fide BND operative, who even served as the Org's resident in Damascus. This is improbable: the documents of the German Consulate in Damascus show that Brunner feared to approach it, behavior untypical for a BND resident.[34]

There is, however, some evidence linking Brunner to the BND. We know that in 1960 and 1961, Brunner and Rademacher worked at the German desk of Syrian intelligence organizations, spied on Germans in Syria and Lebanon, and maybe even worked with agents in Germany.[35] In 1984, a BfV informant reported that as part of Brunner's work for the Syrian Secret Service, he was also in touch with "younger" BND and BfV agents who "had no Wehrmacht experience."[36]

Other records show that in late 1960, the BND negotiated with Brunner through Karl-Heinz Späth. The latter was asked, or independently came up with the idea, to bring Brunner from Syria in order to testify for Globke. Brunner, after all, was heavily involved in the deportations of the Jews of Greece. If he could refute Merten's accusations and testify that Globke had nothing do with those deportations, that would supposedly benefit Globke. On November 26, 1960, Späth's wife came to Germany and met the senior BND official codenamed 381, the very same official tasked with monitoring Schaefer, the man of many faces. Due to the sensitivity of the matter, 381 asked her not to speak with journalists or other German authorities. This 381 (and Gehlen) particularly feared that Hermann Schaefer would get wind of the operation and publish articles about the illicit connections between Globke and Brunner, "the murderer of the Jews" or "gasman Alois," as Schaefer used to call him.[37]

Soon afterward, Späth himself repatriated to Germany equipped with a letter authorizing him to negotiate with Gehlen on Brunner's behalf. However, complications almost immediately ensued. Späth was arrested upon arrival due to old charges of fraud from 1953 and 1954. There was every reason to fear that he might speak with the police, give interviews to the media, or leak Brunner's letter to Schaefer and other hostile journalists. Therefore, 381 visited Späth in jail in order to ensure the secrecy of the matter. Indeed, Späth did not say anything about the negotiations with Brunner during his police interrogation. Nobody knew, however, how long he would maintain his silence.

Then, on December 15, Brunner revoked his letter and notified Gehlen through Späth that he would not travel to Germany. The Federal Republic had become too dangerous to risk visiting due to the developments in the

Eichmann trial. He feared arrest or, even worse, abduction by the Israelis. The last thing he wanted was to be prosecuted by the ever-attentive Fritz Bauer or join Eichmann on the docks in Jerusalem. His fear was justified. Fritz Bauer had already issued an arrest warrant, and the Mossad planned to abduct or kill Brunner as soon as he arrived in Europe.[38]

Gehlen and 381 were not yet ready to give up. They rejected Späth's proposal to testify for Globke "in Brunner's name," as this was a legal impossibility. Instead, they proposed to take Brunner's testimony in Damascus. A judge would interrogate him in the West German Consulate. Brunner, however, refused again. His only contact with the consulate general was an occasional letter denouncing rivals in the local German community.[39] But if he came there and testified, in his real name, his presence in Damascus would be formally confirmed. That was too dangerous, as certified evidence for his residence in Syria could reinforce future extradition requests by Fritz Bauer or other West German prosecutors.

Gehlen's scheme was extremely perilous. Had Brunner agreed to visit the Federal Republic to give testimony, he might have been arrested to the great delight of the press. Had Brunner testified for Globke, either in Germany or in Syria, his criminal reputation would have been intermingled with that of the state secretary. Did Globke know about Gehlen's attempt to secure Brunner's testimony? We know that on November 6, 1961, when the BND advised Globke on Heinz Felfe's impending arrest, the state secretary also asked worriedly about the service's connections with Brunner. A few months later, on January 19, 1962, Weiss handed Globke a letter dated January 14, 1961, concerning Alois Brunner, but we cannot be certain whether it contained information on the negotiations that took place in late 1960 and early 1961.[40]

Ultimately, all of Gehlen's efforts came to naught. When Felfe was finally arrested on November 6, 1961, Globke was not able to help Gehlen or even to mitigate the scandal. The criticism against Gehlen in the press and in government circles was reinforced by Gehlen's own insistence to protect and promote Felfe prior to 1960.[41]

The BND policy of employing former Nazis was now attacked by Chancellor Adenauer, parliamentary leaders of all major parties, and many newspapers, not only as a moral blemish but also as a security risk. Gone were the days when former Nazi security officials were perceived as certified anti-communists.

Chancellor Adenauer was furious, particularly as he had warned Gehlen as early as 1958 not to employ former SS and SD personnel. Heinrich von Brentano, the leader of the CDU/CSU parliamentary faction and Adenauer's former foreign minister, complained to the chancellor that "three bona-fide National-Socialists . . . from the Reich Main Security Office were admitted to the BND, committing there organized treason for more than ten years . . . Personally, because of the Felfe case I can no longer trust the BND." The leaders of the FDP and SPD factions, Erich Mende and Erich Ollenhauer, wrote in almost identical terms.[42] The CIA now distrusted the BND and became reluctant to share sensitive information with its operatives. The free fall of Gehlen's credibility converged with an increasing tendency by both German and American statesmen to distrust his intelligence assessments.[43]

Gehlen, of course, sought to frame the story to cast himself in a better light, insisting that Felfe's exposure should be credited as his achievement, but few were convinced. The press attacked the BND incessantly and, as Gehlen feared, the treason of the exposed moles was immediately linked with their Nazi past.[44] On Adenauer's order, an internal commission, "Unit 85," reviewed the Nazi background of all BND employees and purged dozens of officials who had served in the SD, Gestapo, and other National Socialist security organizations.[45] On July 14, 1963, Globke promised in a press interview that the case of Felfe would not reoccur, but who could believe him? Nobody knew how many undetected moles still lurked inside the service. To quote Bodo Hechelhammer, "The BND was shocked by public criticism, and its right to exist was questioned."[46] The criticism triggered extensive demoralization throughout the ranks of the service. Heinz Denko-Herre, one of the agency's founding fathers and a close confidant of Gehlen, resigned in a move interpreted as a no-confidence vote against the BND president. Even worse, the alliance between Gehlen and Globke, the foundation of BND institutional power, was demonstrably rendered ineffective as Adenauer rejected Globke's defense of Gehlen. The state secretary could no longer serve Gehlen as a conduit to the chancellor.[47]

Suspiciously, Brunner's personal file in the BND archive was destroyed in 1994. The organization later claimed this occurred due to a "mistake," but this is difficult to believe. This decision was probably made by an official in the Information Security Department of the service who wrote to his superiors that "the BND should part from these documents." However, it is likely that if the BND destroyed the file on purpose, the goal was not to hide that Brunner was employed by Gehlen, as some had assumed. The BND connection with Brunner, as much as it existed, seems rather spotty and channeled through Syrian intelligence. Furthermore, in the 1980s it was well-known that the BND employed other Nazi war criminals. A declassified BND memo from 1988 denies that the 581-page file contained evidence of Brunner's employment by the BND, either directly or indirectly. The memo did, however, claim it contained extensive information on Brunner's business dealings, contacts, and associates in Syria and Egypt between 1957 and 1964.[48]

Based on this information, I conclude that what the organization wanted desperately to hide was Gehlen's ploy to enlist Brunner on Globke's behalf. *That* would indeed be too embarrassing to see the light of day.

• • •

FAR FROM KEEPING a low profile after the failure of his attempt to "help" Hans Globke, Reinhard Gehlen reacted to the Felfe scandal with increased recklessness. For years, the BND president enjoyed a close relationship with the news magazine *Der Spiegel*, feeding it horror stories of communist penetration of West Germany. However, Gehlen's attempts to hedge his bets by also forging a close relation with Franz Josef Strauss, the defense minister, would entangle him in a messy and exceedingly damaging conflict between the minister and the journal.[49]

On October 10, 1962, only a few days before the outbreak of the Cuban Missile Crisis, *Der Spiegel* published a critical article on Strauss and German defense policy focused on the latest NATO maneuvers. The irascible Strauss accused *Der Spiegel* of publishing state secrets, and Gehlen was trapped between the hammer and the anvil. On the 17th, Strauss notified Gehlen of impending police action against the magazine and was promised full BND cooperation. However, the BND resident in Hamburg who served as a liaison with *Der Spiegel* forewarned the editors, thus making the BND an accomplice to a crime. It was later discovered that the BND knew about the controversial publication well before October 10 but failed to inform Strauss. Called to a formal investigation in Adenauer's bureau, Gehlen was caught in awkward lies. The chancellor was close to arresting him on the spot. Brushing aside Globke's attempts to protect Gehlen, Adenauer said that "a person in such a position who does not tell the truth is unqualified for his job." In the end, Gehlen was neither arrested nor fired, but he lost his political influence. On October 2, 1963, the cabinet decided to reinforce government supervision of the BND by tying it more closely to the chancellor's office. The public trial of Hans Felfe cemented Gehlen's disgrace in the public mind. As a result, he remained a political outcast in government circles, a ghost that lingered uselessly in Pullach until his retirement in 1968.[50]

PART III

AFTERSHOCKS AND SHADOWS

The downfall of OTRACO left no organized Nazi conspiracy, however inept, active in the Middle East. At the same time, the blowup of the Globke and Gehlen affair in the Federal Republic, the efforts of Fritz Bauer, and above all the natural aging of former minions of the third Reich and the coming of age of a younger generation in Germany increasingly made Konrad Adenauer's supposed "New Germany" a reality. Yet the publicity generated by the Eichmann Trial and OTRACO's antics, the scandal engulfing Bonn, and a new generation of Israelis unprepared to maintain a wall of silence around the Holocaust left Israel, and the world at large, haunted by the shadows of the Nazi past.

It was in this context that the inept efforts of German rocket scientists in Nasser's Egypt morphed in the perception of Israel's intelligence services, media, and the public at large into nothing short of an existential threat plotted by the architects of the Final Solution to perpetrate a second genocide on the Jewish people. Like France, Israel would stop at nothing to eliminate this threat. Unlike France, Israel lacked the power, international standing, or independence of action to use brute force with impunity against West German citizens and would find, in the course of chasing the shadows of the Nazi past, that it was endangering the underpinnings of its national security in the present. The ultimate solution Israel settled on would be far less glamorous and viscerally satisfying than the vengeful slaying of the supposed German enablers of Nasser's intended genocide—but it would also prove to be far more effective.

· 16 ·

Operation Damocles—
Mossad Chasing Shadows

If you can keep your head when all about you
Are losing theirs and blaming it on you
If you can trust yourself when all men doubt you
And give allowance to their doubting too . . .

—RUDYARD KIPLING, *IF*

⌒

ON JULY 23, 1962, Revolution Day in Egypt, the Israeli public and government were riveted to the morning news. President Gamal Abdel Nasser, their fiercest enemy, was parading new long-range rockets with the ominous names Qaher (the conqueror) and Zafer (the victor) in front of cheering crowds. After a successful experiment in Wadi Natrun, a desert strip near the Cairo-Alexandria road, the Egyptian president threatened to rain death and destruction on Israeli cities ("any point south of Beirut") in the next inevitable round of hostilities.[1] These fearsome weapons had been developed by a new generation of German mercenaries in Cairo. Unlike Brunner, Beisner, and their ilk, these were not shady arms dealers but ambitious scientists who had gained valuable experience in Nazi Germany's own rocket program.

Jerusalem reacted with panic. The Israeli government that, apart from its attempt to assassinate Brunner, had hitherto ignored OTRACO altogether saw the presence of the scientists as a Nazi ploy to destroy the Jewish state. Fears of Nasser's willingness and ability to annihilate Israel's population centers were not entirely groundless, as Nasser's extensive deployment of chemical weapons against civilians during the Yemen War from June 1963 onward would show.[2] Though the Egyptian rocket program was many years away from achieving the ability to rain down conventional let alone chemical warheads on Israel's cities, this was not readily apparent to Israeli decision makers at the time. Prime Minister David Ben-Gurion, tormented by sleepless nights, began to wonder whether his Zionist movement had brought the Jews to Palestine only to lead them to a second Holocaust. Had the Jews been saved from the Nazis only to be slaughtered by Egypt's armies, now equipped with German expertise and nonconventional rockets? It was "as if the sky were falling on our heads," said Asher Ben Nathan, director general of the Defense Ministry. Isser Harel and his Mossad staffers, caught completely unaware, were also in a state of panic. Such an important development and nobody in the Mossad had predicted it.[3]

Working under the false premise that he was fighting a sinister Nazi plot, Mossad chief Isser Harel ordered a top-secret assassination and intimidation program against the German scientists in Egypt codenamed Operation Damocles (or Vitamin-C). The method that had failed to kill Brunner would be reapplied with disastrous consequences, contributing to the downfall of both Isser Harel and David Ben-Gurion, his political master. In the past, the activities of *real* former Nazis in the Cold War moved states to irrational policies: Reinhard Gehlen to swallow Gestapo fantasies along with Soviet double agents, and the SDECE to embark on assassinations that weakened their position in West Germany and pushed the Soviets deeper into the Algerian game. As the Israeli case will show, even the *false* image of Nazi activity could push states and intelligence agencies to panic, with surprising and disturbing results.

• • •

THREE YEARS EARLIER, in 1959, the German rocket scientist Wolfgang Pilz was in a gloomy mood. This veteran of the Nazi rocket program at Peenemünde, a "propulsion expert [with] deep blue eyes, the wavy silver hair of a maestro and the profile of a matinee idol," was in the lowest point of his career.[4] In truth, he had never been truly appreciated. Wernher von Braun, the famous scientific director of the Peenemünde program, had mockingly described him as one of the "lesser lights" on his team.[5] After WWII, like so many other German experts in the fields of intelligence and military science, he worked for whichever occupational power was prepared to employ him, toiling in rocket programs of first Britain and then France. With his fellow scientists Eugen Sänger, a much more talented expert in jet propulsion, and Paul Goercke, who specialized in electronics of guidance systems, he spent the early 1950s in the town of Vernon, France, working on a missile codenamed "Véronique." The political instability in France, however, made the future of the German scientists there insecure. The government in Paris decided that manned bombers, not missiles, would be the best platform for its future nuclear arms. Pilz wanted out in any case. The Normandy rains, he later said, had made him "melancholy."[6]

Not that he fared much better in West Germany. After the French program floundered, Pilz moved to Stuttgart to work, along with Sänger, in the Institute for Physics of Jet Propulsion, co-funded by the federal government and several firms. The work in this third-rate institute, however, was unsatisfying, especially due to multiple restrictions placed on the West German air industry by the Western allies.[7] As a result, Pilz was pleasantly surprised when Sänger approached him with a tempting proposal. Was he interested in joining some colleagues in an exciting new project initiated by the government of the United Arab Republic? The Egyptian leader, Gamal Abdel Nasser, was looking to rejuvenate his rocket program after the failure of several fledgling attempts in the 1950s, in which Paul Goercke also took part. Nasser needed ballistic missiles and new fighter jets to offset Israel's ground and air supremacy. Only such planes and missiles, he believed, could give him the capability to threaten the Israeli interior in case of a war. But Nasser especially needed the rockets to bolster his failing credentials in Egypt and the Arab world at large. In Cairo's imagination, German expertise was indispensable to pursuing these aims.

In 1959, Hassan Sayed Kamel, a Swiss-Egyptian businessman, and Colonel Issam a-Din Mahmoud Khalil, an old intelligence hand, established a chain of front companies in Switzerland and placed recruitment ads in West German and Austrian newspapers. Khalil, "a tall, paunchy man with receding curly hair, a walrus mustache and a smile as beguiling as Nasser's," liaised between these European companies and the government in Cairo.[8] Besides Sänger, Pilz, and

Goercke, he and Kamel recruited several other experts in aircraft engineering, air frames, guidance, and production. Heinz Krug, a former pilot who also worked in Sänger's institute, established in Munich a front company called Intra, tasked with the procurement of materials for the enterprise. Conveniently, it was located adjacent to the office of United Arab Airlines, which also served as Cairo's mail hub. Hans Kleinwächter, a friend of Paul Goercke, worked on guidance and control systems from his laboratory in the West German town of Lörrach. According to one estimate, by 1961 the Egyptians already employed 1,000 workers, a hundred of them foreign engineers and technicians mostly from Germany but also from Austria and Spain.[9]

The lives of the foreign experts in Egypt were comfortable, with a touch of the exotic. They fished in the Red Sea, played tennis in prestigious country clubs, socialized at cocktail parties, and occasionally went on horse riding expeditions to the Pyramids and the Western Desert. A reporter that visited them in Cairo later testified that "with their air-conditioned penthouses, their sports cars and their special imports of sausages and other delicacies from Hamburg, they are the inheritors of the opulence of King Farouk's days, untouched by the austerity that Nasserist socialism has imposed on Egypt."[10] For the leaders of the project, conditions were even more luxurious. Heinz Krug's children, Beate and Kaj, remembered the years they spent in Egypt as among the best of their life. The government assigned them a palatial mansion surrounded by an exotic garden, and they traveled with their father, often in a plane he piloted himself, to the pyramids, the Valley of the Kings, the Abu Simbel Temple, and other sites around the country.[11]

Professionally things were less glamorous, and the Egyptian rocket program encountered problems from the very start. First of all, with the exception of Sänger, the other scientists, including Pilz and Goercke, were third-rate experts who relocated to Egypt because they could not find a gratifying job elsewhere.[12] Then, the industrial, financial, and technical infrastructure of the country was insufficient to manage such a program in the long run and bring it to successful conclusion. Factory 333, a plant in the desert near Heliopolis where the rockets were planned and produced, was located in a former British sanatorium that lacked adequate laboratories, storage rooms, and chemical mixers, let alone sufficient stocks of specialized materials. Notwithstanding the efforts of Goercke and Kleinwächter, the rockets lacked working guidance and control systems as well, and US intelligence assumed that they could not carry sufficiently heavy warheads. In fact, when Nasser paraded the rockets before cheering Egyptian crowds in July 1962, they were far from operational. Unimpressed, the CIA defined the operation as "by and large a propaganda stunt of the kind in which Nasir [sic] excels. . . . the launchings actually have little significance in terms of any real scientific or military capability."[13] This was not, however, how things were seen in Israel.

• • •

THE ISRAELIS WERE not oblivious to the Egyptian rocket program, nor to the presence of German specialists in the land of the Nile. In fact, Israeli intelligence followed the activity of Germans in both Egypt and Syria—in 1956, Isser Harel even briefed the government about the issue—but the government took no meaningful action. Apart from the punitive interest of the Mossad in Brunner and occasional concerns that "gangs of Nazis" might disrupt the Eichmann trial, the mere presence of Germans in the Middle East did not overly perturb the military and political leaders in Jerusalem.[14] Even the early Egyptian rocket program, managed under the codename CERVA, did not seem to be much of a threat. In 1958, the Mossad penetrated the program by recruiting Rolf Engel, an SS scientist who previously managed it but did nothing beyond reporting to the government again a few months later. Engel told the Israelis "it will take years until the Egyptians may reach results, because the basic conditions of personnel and equipment in Egypt are insufficient." His words were prophetic.[15]

Israeli intelligence was more concerned with the rejuvenation of the Egyptian rocket program under the leadership of Sänger, Pilz, and Goercke, but only slightly so. Aman, the Israeli military intelligence organization, ordered its top spy in Egypt, Wolfgang Lotz, to report as much as he could on the German scientists and their work. In November 1960, Ben-Gurion was troubled enough to use his connections in Bonn to pressure the scientists to quit, and Harel traveled to Pullach to discuss the matter with Reinhard Gehlen.[16] Finally, the West German transportation minister advised Eugen Sänger that he and his scientists from the Stuttgart Institute had violated their contract with the federal government by working for the Egyptians. The federal government was worried that Western military secrets would pass to Nasser's regime and potentially also to the Soviet Bloc. As a result, Sänger left Egyptian employ on November 7. But his colleagues, Pilz and Goercke, resigned from the Stuttgart Institute and moved to Cairo, thus severing their contractual relationship with the federal government.[17] In July 1961, Israel had launched its own "Shavit II" rocket experiment, causing Nasser to urge his German scientists to step up the pace with the Qaher and Zafer programs.[18]

David Ben-Gurion and his intelligence chiefs, however, did not follow the development of the Egyptian project that closely and failed to assess the information they did possess. Possibly, as one scholar has argued, they believed nothing would come out of the project because most of the German scientists in Egypt were mediocre and none of them was an "expert of international renown."[19] "Therefore, they were dumbstruck after the rocket experiment in Wadi Natrun and the Revolution Day parade in July 1962. Oblivious to the fact that Nasser paraded the rockets prematurely to impress Egyptian and Arab crowds, Tel Aviv snapped from complacency to sheer panic. Both Isser Harel and Ben-Gurion saw the Egyptian rocket program as a harbinger of a second Holocaust. The head of the Mossad even believed that the rocket program was the first step in an eventual 'revival of Nazism.'"[20]

But why? Ben-Gurion, Harel, and other Israeli leaders detested the "old Nazis" (and in Harel's case, Germany in general), but until 1962 tended to see them as irrelevant to the problems of the present. Far from being impervious to Holocaust-related fears and traumas, however, they transferred their image of the Nazi plotting to exterminate the Jewish people to Israel's Arab enemies, especially the Egyptians, and more specifically toward Gamal Abdel Nasser, the strongest and most charismatic Arab leader. In May 1960, when Egypt and Syria were still unified under the banner of the United Arab Republic, Ben-Gurion wrote in a private letter that the "disciples of the Nazis" in Cairo and Damascus "would like to destroy Israel—this is the biggest and most eminent danger facing us." Egypt, he added, was bent on killing the Jews of Israel just like the Nazis exterminated six million of their brethren.[21] Because "new Nazis" were deemed more dangerous than "old Nazis," Ben-Gurion was ready to cooperate with West Germany, notwithstanding the conspicuous presence of former Nazis in its state apparatus.[22] Even Harel, who detested Germans, had established a close cooperation with Gehlen and the BND already in the 1950s and was largely indifferent to the presence of Nazis in the Middle East.[23] However, the parade in July 1962 created a false impression that Egypt had the capability to destroy Israel with ballistic missiles. Then, almost overnight, Nasser's dark threats, memories of the Holocaust, and the fact that the rocket scientists were German merged the images of the "old" German Nazi and the "new" Arab Nazi into an omnipotent demon.[24]

The panic about the German scientists led Israel and many of its spokesmen at home and abroad to "nazify" the German advisory corps in Egypt by over-emphasizing the presence of fugitive war criminals. Indeed, there were war criminals in Egypt, like the concentration camp physicians Aribert Heim and Hans Eisele, who gave medical services to the German scientists. There were also Nazi propagandists such as Johann von Leers (aka Omar Amin).[25] But the Cairo Nazis swelled in Israeli imagination in both numbers and importance.

The Nazi hunter Simon Wiesenthal, for example, reported again and again that 6,000-7,000 German advisers worked in Cairo, including such thugs as Leopold Gleim, "the SS commander in Poland," Heinrich Sellmann, who led the Gestapo in Ulm, and Oskar Dirlewanger, the sadistic SS general who butchered tens of thousands of civilians in Warsaw.[26] These stories, endlessly repeated after the rocket parade of July 1962, were false. Some of these people, like Gleim and Sellmann, did not exist, at least not under said names, and others, like Dirlewanger, died soon after the war and never set a foot in the Middle East.[27] Wiesenthal's fanciful information possibly came from Peter Kubainsky, a dubious neo-Nazi turned Muslim who also served as an informant of the Mossad. While he gave the Mossad accurate information on Alois Brunner's whereabouts, many of his other tips were a mix of exaggerations, inventions, and blatant lies. Another informant of Wiesenthal told him that "Cairo is seething with Germans . . . [they] have far more influence in Egypt than the Russians. They control the Secret Police. They are still training the army, their scientists are developing rockets, Western Germans are deeply committed in commerce. German cars bearing German number plates are in abundance in Cairo. But any open inquiry about the Germans is not welcome."[28]

Numerous historians and authors uncritically adopted these tall tales and reproduced the names of nonexistent Nazis, and sensationalist journalists added their own stories to the mix.[29] A French reporter wrote for example that in

July 1962, when the rockets were being paraded, the remote control expert Dr. Reinhold Strobl was "mad with joy" and yelled that "now the Jews really have to behave!"[30] The Israeli Foreign Ministry knew well that the lists of Nazis in Cairo were dubious, but did not of course share these doubts with the public.[31]

Mossad's early intelligence gathering operations only added fuel to the fire. In August, Harel presented to the government a "smoking gun," a letter of Wolfgang Pilz to his Egyptian employers that Mossad was able to intercept. In this letter, known as the "master plan," Pilz bragged of being able to produce the frightening number of 900 ballistic missiles.[32] In spite of Ben-Gurion's skepticism and the importance he placed on maintaining good relations with West Germany, Foreign Minister Golda Meir joined Harel in a demand to launch a covert war against the German scientists, whom she also saw as vicious Nazis keen to finish Hitler's job. Ben-Gurion insisted that a wholesale accusation of Germany "smacked of racism," but still green-lighted the covert operation.[33] As his biographer noted, the elderly Israeli leader made a grave mistake by taking a passive stance. Instead of leading the campaign against the German scientists himself, he delegated excessive authority to his reckless spymaster.[34]

With Ben-Gurion and Meir's agreement, Harel launched a campaign of intimidation and terror against the German scientists and their family members, codenamed Operation Vitamin-C (later Operation Damocles, already mentioned above). He collected painstaking intelligence on the project from all available sources. In Cairo, the most important of these sources was Wolfgang Lotz, nicknamed the "Champagne Spy," a case officer dispatched by Unit 188 of Aman, IDF Military Intelligence.

. . .

LOTZ, BLOND, TALL, and blue-eyed, was already mentioned in his role as an Israeli spy in Egypt. Born in 1921 in the German city of Mannheim to a Jewish theater actress and a non-Jewish father, Lotz demonstrated a considerable acting skill from a very young age. Being uncircumcised, he was also well-poised to play the role of a non-Jewish German.[35] The BND, yielding to Israeli requests, helped him to enter Egypt with proper documentation. There, he established a cover story of a Wehrmacht officer who fought in North Africa, also hinting of darker experiences in the SS. It was a wise cover. During the Second World

War, Lotz worked in the British Army as a POW interrogator in the North African theater, so he was intimately familiar with Rommel's Afrika Korps. In January 1961, he came to Egypt and established himself as a German bon vivant, leading the glamorous life of a socialite and wealthy horse breeder. With BND intelligence funds, he leased a horse farm and a riding school that were conveniently close to Egyptian military installations, including the rocket experiment site in Wadi Natrun. Lotz would ride his horse in the desert surrounding the site, noting the times and frequency of rocket launchings.[36]

As Lotz later testified, Egyptian high society was as crowded with spies as its Damascene counterpart. In numerous cocktail parties, he brushed shoulders with intelligence officers from around the world. "Cairo and even Alexandria," he later recalled, "were, and still are, like a giant intelligence bazaar. Everybody is watching everybody else—and either getting paid for it or doing it under duress. Ex-nationals, such as the German aircraft technologists and rocket builders, must at some stage have been wined and dined by the Egyptian Secret Police, by Military Intelligence, by the Israeli Secret Service, the British Secret Service and by many other intelligence organizations . . . a network of plot and counterplot, a world surrounded by eyes and ears that were impossible to hide from."[37]

One of Lotz's acquaintances from the intelligence realm was Gerhard Bauch, Gehlen's resident in Cairo, who spied for the BND since 1956 under the cover of a wealthy businessman.[38] Bauch, mockingly called by Lotz "the little bastard with the long shadow," barely tried to conceal himself. An Austrian engineer who managed the Egyptian aircraft program recalled that he had almost immediately discovered "who worked for Gehlen" and was "amused by the primitive way he spied on me." In fact, Bauch's role was similar to numerous other Gehlen agents in the Middle East, including the OTRACO Nazis: working to preserve Egypt as a pro-Western country, as well as reporting on Soviet penetration, especially about arms shipments. For security reasons, the BND tried to make sure that Lotz and Bauch would each be oblivious to the other's spying mission.[39]

Charismatic and full of charm, Lotz gained access to a large coterie of high-end clients, including Egyptian generals. At the same time, his luxurious farm and riding school were a much-beloved hub for Cairo's German community. Among others, Lotz was on friendly terms with many of the rocket scientists. In his memoirs, he described a wild drinking party in the house of the anti-Semitic propagandist Johann von Leers (aka Omar Amin), in which some of the scientists joined their host in Nazi songs. Lotz, of course, used such occasions to pick useful intelligence from the drunken conversations of the scientists and their friends. Interestingly enough, he heard the scientists complaining on the sorry state of their various projects. Waltraud, Lotz's vivacious and pretty wife, probably echoed her husband when she estimated that "even if Prof. Pilz and his company lived in Egypt for one hundred years, they would not have been able to produce, despite all of their efforts, anything of value except a glaring hole in the Egyptian defense budget." The reports of the Lotz couple, almost identical to those of cooler heads in the Israeli Defense Ministry, failed however to mitigate the panic in Tel Aviv's intelligence community.[40]

In August 1962, urgently called to Paris to receive instructions, Lotz was ordered to gather more intelligence on the German scientists, including their names and addresses. In September, he returned to Paris with the requested list, the result of painstaking efforts by him and his wife. This intelligence was juxtaposed with information from other sources, including Mossad teams who sniffed around the apartments, laboratories, and offices of the scientists in Europe. For Harel, the hunt for the German scientists, the "Nazis set to destroy Israel," in the present was far more important than parallel Mossad attempts to locate real Holocaust perpetrators of the past. In July 1962, a Mossad team led by Zvi Aharoni, a veteran of the Eichmann operation, believed it located Dr. Josef Mengele, the "death angel of Auschwitz," in an isolated farm near Sao Paulo, Brazil. This was a case of mistaken identity but there were still some indications that the fugitive criminal was hiding nearby. And yet, Harel slowed down and then postponed the Mengele hunt (Operation House Sparrow) in order to invest all available resources in the covert war against the scientists. As a result, the Israeli Secret Service might have missed an opportunity to locate, abduct, and bring to trial one of the vilest Nazi criminals on earth.[41]

• • •

IN AUTUMN 1962, Isser Harel had collected enough intelligence to launch the violent phase of Operation Damocles. In a meeting with Ben-Gurion, he received a "nod" from the prime minister. Ben-Gurion, always concerned about plausible deniability, rarely authorized covert ops in writing, doing so instead by "expressing concern" about a certain issue. A senior Mossad officer instructed his men accordingly that "we are interested in getting information from there at any price. If we can find a German who knows about the issue, we are ready to seize him by force and make him speak."[42] The first target was Wolfgang Pilz, who became the leader of the program after Sänger's resignation. In order to abduct him during his impending visit to Europe, the Mossad placed several operational squads that scouted airports and sea harbors to pinpoint his route from Egypt to Germany. According to the plan, Pilz should have been abducted somewhere along the road and brought to a luxurious French castle surrounded by gardens and converted into a Mossad safe house. However, this operation, for which no written records were preserved, ended as a farce. As Mossad historians later related, the agents traced the unsuspecting Pilz throughout central and southern Europe, but always "missed" him. In the end, they had to watch helplessly as he sailed back, unmolested, to Egypt.[43]

The furious Harel now zeroed on Heinz Krug, the administrative director of the Egyptian program and the head of Intra, its Munich front company. Krug was described by his Mossad shadows as "an unsympathetic type. In 1962 he was 42 years old, short . . . wide and plump but solid, and suffered from asthma. Fat-faced and scarred, he had a thick, typical Prussian bull neck. He did not eschew alcohol and good food, and loved the good life, especially his luxurious car... [Krug] was not involved in anti-Jewish activity during Hitler's era, but espoused typical German nationalist, anti-Semitic and pro-Nazi views."[44] The agents of the Mossad who observed Krug and learned about his weaknesses planned to trap him as numerous victims of secret services were trapped before: through his greed.

On September 10, the stout administrator traveled with his wife and a friend to an elegant restaurant for a pleasant night out. On the way, he stopped in a hotel for a short meeting with an Egyptian official who presented himself as "Qaher Salah." Upon meeting Krug, the man presented an introduction letter from Colonel Sa'id Nadim, an Egyptian intelligence officer whom Krug knew well. Sweet-talking Krug, Salah told him Nadim would like to offer him an unofficial but highly lucrative business opportunity that must be discussed in private, outside Intra premises. When Krug met Salah again the next day, he was oblivious to the real identity of his interlocutor, an Arabic-speaking Israeli operative with a dark complexion and faked Egyptian passport. Krug refused the offer of his assistant, who feared foul play, to travel with him, assuring that he was "no coward." Krug's wife also told him that "she feels bad about this dangerous meeting," but her husband was not ready to consider an escort. Naturally, he didn't want any witnesses to the "private deal."[45]

Following Harel's orders, Salah drove Krug to an affluent suburb of Munich, listening all the while to the latter's endless chatter on the amenities of his car. The two parked the vehicle on a quiet tree-lined street and went together to a secluded villa next to the river. A woman opened the door. Next to her, a male companion shook Krug's hand and pulled him inside where a third team member grabbed his neck and threw him to the ground. Salah, the door slammed in his face, later remembered that the interior of the villa was "full of smoke" and presented "an eerie sight." He never saw Heinz Krug again.[46]

After Krug regained consciousness, he was brought before a German-speaking Mossad operative. "You are a prisoner," he said, "do exactly as we say, otherwise we'll eliminate you." The terrified administrator was then taken out of the villa and pushed into a special box installed under the back seats of a car. Crossing into France, Krug and his Mossad captors hid for a while in an empty youth camp of the Jewish Agency, then boarded an Israeli Airlines plane in Marseilles. At the time, the French port city was a hub for Jewish emigrants who left North Africa for Israel. To avoid difficulties with French law, Krug was sedated and introduced to the airport officials as a "sick immigrant."[47] In his briefcase, the captors found a treasure trove of documents, including a diary with detailed lists of individuals and companies related to the Egyptian rocket program.

In Tel Aviv, the terrified German, disoriented and deprived of money and identity papers, was kept in a comfortable apartment arranged for him deep inside a Mossad facility. For a few months he was interrogated by a committee of experts who told him outright that if he spoke, he would eventually be released, but otherwise death was just around the corner. After some hesitation, Krug began to open up. As his interrogators later recalled, "he had an excellent memory, and was well-versed in all administrative and organizational details of the rocket program." He gave many details on experiments and rocket production goals, as well as the irritating failure to develop a modern guidance system. His interrogation, which lasted several months, would be crucial for Operation Damocles, first as an "encyclopedia of basic intelligence," and then because of a few details that particularly caught the ears of the Israelis. Krug said that the guidance system, without which the rockets would have no military value, was developed by Paul Goercke and Hans Kleinwächter. He also mentioned a highly secret and dangerous channel personally operated by Col. Mahmoud Khalil. The latter, he testified, used an Austrian chemist named Otto Joklik to procure materials for the production of nuclear warheads.[48]

The Mossad used this information to hunt down its next targets: Pilz, the head of the project; guidance experts Goercke and Kleinwächter; and Otto Joklik, the procurer of the nuclear materials. Krug, who was no longer useful, suffered a cruel fate. According to Ronen Bergman, Isser Harel decided that it would be too dangerous to release Krug, lest he speak about his involuntary stay in Tel Aviv. While a Mossad agent who physically resembled Krug traveled around South America in order to create false traces, the real man was taken to an abandoned spot near Tel Aviv and shot to death.[49]

While Mossad was hunting all over Europe, an incredible development materialized: the nuclear procurer Otto Joklik, one of Operation Damocles's prime targets, came to the hunters of his own free will.

· 17 ·

A Willing Quarry and Nuclear Nightmares

To hunt successfully, you must know your ground,
your pack and your quarry.

—K. J. PARKER, *DEVICES AND DESIRES*

⌒

ON OCTOBER 23, a "tall man with pig-like, protruding eyes . . . sporting an elegant suit which could barely hide his pot belly" knocked on the door of the Israeli Purchasing Mission (an unofficial legation) in Cologne, West Germany. Facing a startled Israeli official, the man introduced himself as "Prof. Otto Joklik, the senior adviser of the Egyptian government for nuclear affairs." Joklik calmly explained that he was disappointed with his work for Egypt and would therefore like to contact the Israeli government. Mysteriously, he gave the official a half-torn business card, keeping the other half as an identity mark for future clandestine meetings.[1]

The news of Joklik's appearance was quickly reported to Tel Aviv, giving rise to fierce debates inside the Mossad and the Israeli intelligence community. Who was this "walk-in?" A double agent? A hoax? Or the missing piece in Israel's quest to decipher the Egyptian nuclear program? In October and November 1962, the Cuban Missile Crisis was in full swing and people from all over the world were afraid of a nuclear holocaust. For Israel, any sign that

Arab countries were "going nuclear" was of paramount importance, and many in Tel Aviv's intelligence community believed ballistic missiles were of no real use without nonconventional warheads. Overcoming his doubts, Isser Harel gave his men permission to work with Joklik.[2]

Credible or not, Joklik made clear to his Israeli interlocutors that his decision to meet them was closely intertwined with Krug's disappearance. Mahmoud Khalil, it seems, ordered Joklik to procure radiological warheads, namely, missiles armed with Cobalt-60 capable of spreading radiation and contaminating Israeli food and water sources. He worked closely with Krug and was appalled to see (or so he said) the indifference with which the Egyptians reacted to his fate. "I think that Krug is in your hands," he told the Mossad operatives, "no one reached out to his wife . . . one cannot rely on these Egyptians." In fact, Joklik was afraid for his own skin. Khalil suspected that he was involved in Krug's abduction and ordered a security officer to investigate. That may have been the real reason for Joklik's decision to switch to the Israeli side.[3]

Then, "like a refrigerator dealer," Joklik opened his briefcase and presented documents testifying to his academic record and political connections. First, he offered to liaise between Israel and illicit dealers in nuclear materials. The Mossad was not interested in this dubious proposal, so he came with a second offer. He would tell the Israelis everything about the Egyptian nuclear program. An Israeli technical expert with whom he spoke was highly impressed with Joklik's knowledge, but warned that he was also a highly dubious type:

> Despite my rich experience with people, so far, I hadn't the honor to meet such a contemptible person. Undoubtedly, the subject [Joklik] is an international arms merchant, one of the types able to convey an outwards positive impression and disguise themselves as scientists. They try to make their riches cynically, without pangs of conscience, by selling war materials to all who are willing to pay . . . I believe that the subject is not only an international arms merchant, but also a high-level crook on an international scale.[4]

A short while later, the Austrian "walk-in" agent traveled to Tel Aviv, where he debriefed Isser Harel and his staffers on two Egyptian programs codenamed "Cleopatra" (procurement of six nuclear bombs with enriched uranium) and Ibis (production of one thousand radiological Cobalt-60 shells and rocket warheads). The technical experts of Mossad, Aman, and the Defense Ministry were divided in their assessment of Joklik. All agreed he was not a scientist but rather a dubious adventurer, and that his academic degrees were faux. One of them even said the Egyptians should have him back—better that *they* waste money on him rather than the Israelis. However, most of Joklik's interviewers were impressed, even against their will. He gave the Israelis top-secret documents from the Egyptian project, casually dropped the names of famous nuclear scientists with whom he was in touch and said much that was consistent with what the Mossad and Aman already knew from Krug and other sources. True, the devious Joklik was stealing Egyptian money and was certainly incapable of procuring enriched uranium in the United States, as he bragged. In fact, Aman concluded that the enrichment process described by Joklik was scientifically impossible. But as the Mossad historians admitted in retrospect, intelligence professionals are obsessed with secret plots, assuming that sufficiently sophisticated operations can ultimately overcome objective technical obstacles. Surely, with enough cunning, the Egyptians would somehow be able to achieve their nuclear goals.[5]

Though the analysts of Aman were generally more sanguine about the Egyptian rocket program, the organization's own technical expert, Col. Zvi Reuter, agreed with the alarmist estimates of the Mossad: Egypt was developing nuclear weapons in order to exterminate Israel once and for all.[6] The Nazi panic in Israel was so great that some even imagined that Dr. Hans Eisele, a murderous concentration camp doctor who found refuge in Egypt, was busy developing microbes for biological warheads. Eisele in fact was an ailing wreck, addicted to drugs and uninvolved in any military program, nor was he qualified to develop biological weapons.[7]

Joklik cheated *both* sides of the Israeli-Egyptian conflict. Swiss police documents show that he was a swindler, an intelligence peddler akin to Wilhelm Höttl, Heinrich Mast, Hermann Schaefer, and many others described throughout this book. From 1939 to 1945 he served in the Wehrmacht and was an officer by the end of the war. His commanders described him glowingly as brave, upright, and a good Nazi.[8] After the war, he was active for a while in a neo-Nazi party but like other intelligence peddlers, did not shy from working with the Soviets. For several years he moved between Germany, Austria, Italy, and Switzerland, collecting and selling intelligence to the KGB and other secret services, introducing himself with faked academic credentials and committing fraud virtually everywhere. Among other things, he presented himself as a professor, director of imagined companies, member of various scientific institutions, and a head of division in the Vienna Interpol Office. In the 1950s, Joklik tried his hands at journalism and took part in international arms trafficking.[9]

Joklik purported to sell scientific and nuclear secrets that were either faked or grossly exaggerated. As the Mossad wrote later, he was a "scientific fixer" who excelled in reading open-source technical material, recycling it as intriguing secrets, and lecturing about it with persuasion and self-confidence.[10] Just like Springer and Remer, who tried to sell an illusory rocket program to Damascus, Joklik milked money from Mahmoud Khalil, selling pipe dreams of nuclear prowess that Egypt was technologically incapable of achieving. "When I think of how he fooled us it brings tears to my eyes," recalled an Egyptian official. "The only thing he was an expert in was science fiction."[11] Joklik did a disservice to Israel as well. By overblowing the importance of a pathetic "nuclear program," he stoked existential fears in Israel. Haunted by the nightmare of a "second Holocaust," Isser Harel was ready to step up the Mossad's terror campaign against the German scientists, regardless of diplomatic and political consequences.[12]

More than that, the Mossad chief made the bizarre decision to not only use the crook Joklik as an informant, but also hire him as a member of the organization's operational team. Joklik's Mossad handler despised him. In later testimony, he described Joklik as a "coward and a physically dirty person. He had a dirty soul as well, in all respects. He always gave us a high expenses bill. Once, when I met him in Salzburg, he told me with great fanfare: 'This evening I invite you for dinner.' He took me to a very expensive restaurant, we ate expensive dishes, and after paying the bill, he gave me the receipt as part of his expenses. Quite a type, this Joklik."[13] Admittedly, Joklik sometimes justified his upkeep. At least in one case, he helped recruit an important agent from inside the Egyptian project who gave the Mossad access to incoming and outgoing mail.[14]

• • •

MEANWHILE, AMAN AND its ambitious commander, Maj. Gen. Meir Amit, competed with the Mossad for pride of place in dealing with the largely imaginary threat. Notwithstanding Amit's skepticism toward the threat of the Egyptian rocket program, he was not ready to let his rivals from Mossad enjoy all the glory. For quite a few years, Units 188 and 154, Aman's detachments for covert ops, had perfected the art of assassination by explosive letters and parcels. In 1956, Unit 154 killed two Egyptian officers responsible for terror attacks inside Israel with booby-trapped books that exploded once opened.[15] In the early 1960s, Nathan Rotberg, Aman's explosives expert, honed his craft with the help of French instructors. At the time, the relationship between the countries was quite intimate: Israel gave France covert assistance in the Algerian War, and France granted Israel diplomatic backing, intelligence cooperation, and secret aid in its nuclear program.[16]

The dark art of assassination was a common pursuit. Rotberg's French colleagues taught him some of their craft used in SDECE's war against German arms traffickers: explosive letters and parcels could safely be delivered via mail as they did not explode when moved and shuffled, only when opened and their contents drawn out. According to the investigative journalist Ronen Bergman, the French helped the Israelis in exchange for information supplied by Lotz on the activities of the FLN, the Algerian underground, in Egypt.[17] Alois Brunner was one of the first victims of the new technology, and now it would be applied to the German scientists. This method was admittedly controversial, even among some of Israel's most hardened assassins. One of them, Rafi Eitan, objected that "I oppose any action that I don't control. The mailman can open the envelope, a child can open the envelope. Who does things like that?"[18] Yet, Meir Amit was adamant.

Isser Harel was reluctant to support Amit, his archrival in the Israeli intelligence community, but gave him operational and intelligence support in Europe. After many attempts, Mossad agents were able to break, yet again, into the offices of United Arab Airlines and track the complicated chain through which mail was sent to German scientists in Cairo. Whenever somebody passed by, the two burglars pretended that they were a couple making out, in one case, a homosexual couple.[19] After several adventures that included car accidents, nocturnal rides, and exhausting work against a very tight schedule, Unit 188 operatives were able to bring an explosive letter and two parcel bombs camouflaged as shipments of scientific books into West Germany and then mail them to Mahmoud Khalil's office. Curiously, they mailed the letter, which contained less explosives and was hence less dangerous, to Pilz, and the two parcels to Factory 333 near Cairo.

Knowing that Pilz's secretary habitually opened his mail, the experts of Unit 188 invented a plot to spare the innocent woman. They mailed the letter purportedly from the address of the lawyer of Pilz's divorcee, assuming that the secretary would not open a letter with such personal contents, but, unfortunately, they were wrong, dead wrong—Pilz's secretary Hannelore Wende nearly ended up dead as well. As it turned out, she was also his lover and extremely interested in the contents of that specific letter. When she opened the envelope and withdrew its contents, the bomb exploded, blinding and maiming her for life.[20] Pilz, horrified but unscathed, heard immediately afterward that a parcel bomb killed several Egyptian workers in the factory while another one was discovered and neutralized. From then on, the German scientists in Egypt were escorted by security details wherever they went and all their incoming mail was X-rayed by local police. The Egyptians forbade them to travel to Germany for the holidays and hired Hermann Valentin, a bulky and scarred SS sergeant, as the security chief of the project. The latter replaced locks, assigned bodyguards, and tightened security measures in general. Life in Egypt, which seemed so comfortable in the past, became frightening. And yet, Pilz and his colleagues remained undeterred.[21]

Isser Harel was also undeterred. Wolfgang Lotz, Unit 188's spy in Egypt, notified Tel Aviv that the assassination failed and the rocket program continued unabated. Convinced more than ever that only the Mossad could stop the activity of the German scientists and save Israel from destruction, Harel now targeted Hans Kleinwächter, the guidance and control expert who worked from a laboratory in Lörrach, a quiet German town close to the Swiss and French borders. It was a highly problematic setting for either abduction or assassination. "Lörrach," write the Mossad historians, "was a quiet little town, unused to tourists. Every foreigner was conspicuous in the eyes of the locals. Access roads were limited. Eastwards, a road winded between the snowy mountains of the Black Forest, and westward, the Rhine bridges served as border stations." To add to the trouble, the security officer Hermann Valentin spent much of his time in Lörrach watching Kleinwächter in person and even accompanying him in his car.[22] For the mission, Harel chose the so-called Birds, an operational unit for covert ops, and its renowned commander, Rafi Eitan.

Operation Hedgehog, as the kidnapping action was called, did not add glory to the Mossad. In fact, it represented Harel's leadership style at its worst: noisy, domineering, and full of meaningless boisterous activity. The head of the Mossad traveled to Paris, where he supervised the operation in person. The Birds were supposed to track Kleinwächter's movement, watch him in his home, laboratory, and on the roads. Harel tyrannized the Birds and micromanaged their activity. He forced them to change hotels daily, use different border crossings in order to avoid suspicion, and report to him at every turn. The operation was extremely complicated, with far too many participants. In one of his "shopping lists" for Hedgehog, Harel ordered twelve chunks of hashish, and forged dollar bills, Egyptian postage stamps, and cyphers of a "burned" Egyptian agent of the Mossad. Retrospectively, even he failed to remember why he ordered these goods.[23]

The teams were supposed to find Kleinwächter in an isolated spot along the road when he was alone with no companions and snatch him into a Mossad car. According to the plan, he should have been brought into a James Bond–esque, if run-down, French castle owned by the Mossad that had once housed Heinz Krug: a grand chateau with dozens of rooms and large cellars surrounded by extensive gardens and forests. The custodian of the castle carved a space behind a large closet designed to serve as a prison for the abductee. The teams used the secluded forest around the chateau as training grounds.[24]

Things began to go wrong from the start. Kleinwächter, athletic, blond, and well-built, was an "introvert, stubborn and meticulous type" and eschewed social connections. Unlike Krug, who frequented restaurants and other entertainment spots, Kleinwächter returned home every day after work, apart from occasional business trips. He always carried an Egyptian military gun and was often accompanied by Valentin as bodyguard. The Birds could never find the right opportunity to abduct him. In addition, the complicated nature of the operation began to take its toll. The numerous participants, all exhausted, traveled too quickly on dark, snowy, and narrow roads, and suffered an increasing number of car accidents. The scouts, fatigued from endless shifts of surveillance and observation, were nearly overcome by the extreme cold of the European winter, sometimes twenty degrees below zero.[25]

The safehouse collapsed as well. One day, the pipes blew apart and the basements of the castle flooded, and the walls quickly grew infested with green mold. Even a plumber brought from Israel could not help, and the poor custodian had to live in horrendous conditions for months, waiting for an abductee who never came. Occasionally, Harel himself joined the surveillance teams and spent sleepless nights with them freezing in the car. In the end, his patience wearing thin, he dispatched the Birds back to Israel and brought Mossad agents who were once involved in the abduction of Eichmann, along with reinforcements from *Mifratz* (Gulf), the Mossad unit that attempted to assassinate Alois Brunner two years beforehand. Now, Harel decided that abducting Kleinwächter was too complicated. Instead, the rocket guidance expert would have to be killed.[26]

An opportunity finally presented itself on February 20, 1963. On that winter day, "the town of Lörrach was coated in snow and frost. The [assassination] team waited for Kleinwächter since the small hours of the morning. His house stood on a hill, next to some other villas. From there, there was a road passable only for one car. Along the road . . . there were waiting spots, where ascending cars could wait to let descending cars pass. The ambush was supposed to be carried out where the road crossed the lane. One of the cars waited there. The getaway car was nearby, some tens of meters in the direction of Lörrach."[27] When the team was about to leave, exhausted after fruitless hours of waiting, Kleinwächter finally appeared. Blocked by the Mossad car, he stopped. Zvi Aharoni, a native German speaker, left the car and asked Kleinwächter whether "Dr. Schlüter lives here." The German opened the window, and the assassin waiting behind Aharoni immediately squeezed the trigger.[28] "The bullet smashed the window and tore a hole through my thick woolen scarf," Kleinwächter later testified. "I grabbed the gun, turned the muzzle aside and tried to draw my own pistol from my pocket."[29]

The Gulf operative tried to shoot a second time, but his gun jammed. Aharoni yelled at everyone to flee and the assassins plowed their way through the snowy field. Kleinwächter tried to shoot back at his assailants but his gun jammed as well.[30] The team escaped, leaving forged Egyptian passports in the car to mislead the police. Soon afterward, Kleinwächter received an anonymous call. The person on the other side of the line said "those who devour Jews choke on them" and hung up.[31] The operation was a failure. Not only was

Kleinwächter, like Pilz before him, not deterred—he gave interviews to the German and international press arousing public opinion against Israeli violence in German territory. The local police began to investigate the affair, looking for the elusive assassins. Joklik called Kleinwächter at his home, and later by phone, and tried to convince him the Egyptians were behind the assassination. The angry scientist was not amused.[32]

Faced with repeated failures, Harel would not admit defeat and tried to break the impasse by once again increasing the stakes. In February 1963, while Operation Hedgehog was nearing its end, Harel ordered his men to intimidate several relatives of German scientists working in Egypt, including Heidi Goercke, the daughter of Dr. Paul Goercke, Kleinwächter's colleague in rocket guidance development. To this mission he dispatched none other than Otto Joklik, the Austrian con man and adventurer, along with a Mossad agent operating under the alias of "Joseph Ben-Gal." In December, Joklik discovered details on the whereabouts of Heidi, a young lawyer who worked in the prosecutor's office at Freiburg. The team chose the Swiss town of Basel as their operational base. When Joklik entered Switzerland with Ben-Gal, Harel should have realized that both men were taking a great risk. The Swiss authorities forbade Joklik to enter the country already in 1959 for past suspicions of fraud, arms trafficking, and espionage for foreign intelligence services.[33]

On February 19, Joklik met Heidi Goercke for the first time in the presence of her grandmother. He told her he had once worked with her father, but members of a private Israeli organization, with unlimited budget and strong political connections, threatened him to force him to quit. Now they were after her father because he helped produce biological and radiological warheads for the Egyptians. The suffering of these Jews, all former concentration camp inmates, had made them fanatical. They had already abducted Eichmann from Argentina, and now they were determined to thwart Nasser's plan to perpetrate a second genocide against the Jews.[34]

Heidi seemed positive at first. She said that if the safety of her father could be guaranteed, she might try and persuade him to leave Egypt. The two agreed to meet again. Debriefed by Joklik, Harel became increasingly optimistic, almost convinced that negotiations with Dr. Goercke himself were at hand. Two days later, Aharoni and his team tried to assassinate Kleinwächter, and the Baden Württemberg police were placed on high alert. Joklik visited Heidi again in her home, this time speaking with her in the presence of her younger brother. He told her that he could arrange a third meeting between Heidi and a "representative of the Israeli government," i.e., Joseph Ben-Gal, in the nearby Swiss town of Basel. Little did Joklik and Ben-Gal know that Heidi had set them up. She complained to the German police and they notified their Swiss counterparts. As a result, the two agents were placed under surveillance from the moment they entered Basel.[35]

On Saturday, March 2, Joklik and Ben-Gal met Heidi Goercke, along with her aunt and brother, in the lobby of the luxurious Three Kings Hotel in Basel. This place was imprinted in Israeli memory as once it served as the lodging of Theodor Herzl, the founder of Zionism, and one of the most famous photos of Herzl were taken on the bridge leading to the hotel. Upon meeting Ben-Gal, Heidi noted she was also observed by another agent who looked "typically Jewish."[36] During the meeting, Ben-Gal lectured Heidi on the horrors of the Holocaust and told her the Egyptians, with the help of her father, were determined to exterminate the Jews living in Israel. The Israeli government believed that unlike Pilz and Kleinwächter, Nazis for whom no pardon was conceivable, her father was not a committed Nazi, so they were ready to allow him leave Egypt in peace. If he promptly returned to Germany, he would not be harmed. Unwisely, Ben-Gal took responsibility for previous assassination attempts and told Heidi her family was in immediate danger. Joklik and Ben-Gal urged her to fly to Egypt at once and convince her father to leave the country. They were even ready to defray the costs. Heidi agreed to meet Ben-Gal and Joklik again in a few days in order to arrange the details.[37]

A few hours later, five Swiss policemen seized Ben-Gal. Joklik was arrested separately with a loaded gun in his pocket. He and Ben-Gal were indicted on the suspicion of espionage for a foreign country and criminal threats against the Goercke family. In addition, Joklik was also indicted for arms trafficking for Egypt and illegal entry into Switzerland.[38] The West German police suspected that they both were involved in the Kleinwächter assassination and asked for their extradition. Kleinwächter, who knew Joklik well, falsely claimed he saw the Austrian adventurer shooting at him.[39] The Swiss judicial authorities rejected the German request in the argument that the connection between Ben-Gal, Joklik, and the attempted assassination of Kleinwächter was not backed by concrete evidence.[40]

Notably influenced by pro-Israeli sentiments prevalent throughout the country, the Swiss court treated Joklik and Ben-Gal with kid gloves. Shortly before the trial, the judge secretly implied to the Swiss Justice Ministry he was not going to sentence the defendants to jail terms, and even the prosecutor could not hide his sympathy toward Ben-Gal, whom he saw as an honorable patriot. As expected, the two defendants were convicted but punished only with a slap on the wrist. Sentenced to time served, they were then deported and barred from visiting Switzerland again.[41] And yet, their arrest unsettled Isser Harel. Failed assassination, threats, intimidations—and nothing convinced the German scientists to quit Egypt. Instead, Harel's own agents were arrested, and the methods of the Mossad were exposed before the world.

Harel hastened to meet David Ben-Gurion, who was then vacationing in Tiberias, near the Sea of Galilee, and asked for his instructions. The aged prime minister, well aware of the rising tension in the relationship between Israel and West Germany, ordered Harel to remain calm, "avoid the issue of the rockets but explain [to the press] the issue of [Joklik and Ben-Gal's] arrest."[42] As usual, the head of the Mossad understood Ben-Gurion's vague words as a blank check for action. A day later, he summoned to his office a group of Israeli newspaper editors and gave them select details on the Egyptian rocket program, spiced by overblown, almost diabolical descriptions of the German scientists. To his confidant, Yaakov Karoz, Harel wrote that "we have to make sure that [the issue] will remain in the headlines and in public opinion, until we reach our goal: foiling the plots of the enemy, his German agents and their allies everywhere." In a different conversation, Harel said that "the Israeli press is our loyal and secure ally. If there is anything capable of shaking Germany and especially its government, it is the scandal in Israel that will necessarily spread, even if gradually, to other places around the world."[43]

The Israeli press that reported with hyperbole on the scientists in Egypt already in 1962 was now seething with excitement. The readers of the morning press awoke to headlines on German experts who provided their Egyptian masters with nuclear warheads capable of spreading radiation far and wide armed with poisonous gas, biological weapons, and even "death rays."[44] In its editorial, *Haaretz* related that Nasser offered prizes in millions of dollars to his German scientists, and that the reactor that they were building in Egypt was five times bigger than its Israeli counterpart.[45] Without asking for Ben-Gurion's permission, Foreign Minister Golda Meir teamed up with Harel and gave a boisterous speech in the Knesset. "The motives of this criminal gang [of German scientists]," she said, "is greed as well as Nazi inclinations to hate Israel and [wish for] the extermination of the Jews. Since Hitler's days, the strong connection between Cairo and the Nazis is well-known, and it is no secret that Cairo today serves as a refuge to the Nazi leaders." Then she laid the responsibility on the doorstep of the West German government who failed to stop the scientists. The virulently anti-German Menachem Begin, leader of the main opposition party, attacked the Germans and Ben-Gurion's conciliatory policy towards Bonn with great vehemence.[46]

The reaction in West Germany, both in the press and the parliament, became increasingly critical of Israeli rhetoric as well as of the hyperbolic and unproven claims about nonconventional weapon programs and the Mossad's violent operations in German territory.[47] Ben-Gurion was horrified. His policy, which was based on a clandestine alliance between Israel and West Germany, was threatened by Harel's press campaign and the radical rhetoric of his own foreign minister. How could Israel work with West Germany when Israeli public opinion, enflamed by the sensationalist press and a reckless secret service chief, largely considered it to be "a Nazi Reich?" The prime minister, who failed to take control over Israel's policy and was led instead by Harel and Meir, felt his foreign policy was on the verge of collapse.[48] Shimon Peres, deputy minister of defense and one of Ben-Gurion's closest advisers, was also furious with Harel. A senior West German security official who visited Israel at the time warned him and Ben-Gurion that sensitive arms deals between the two countries were now in danger.[49]

The United States also used the opportunity to take advantage of the Israelis. On March 25, 1963, the State Department declared that there was "no evidence that weapons of mass destruction are being produced or that the UAR [Egypt] has a capability to produce them."[50] Consequently, the Americans offered a deal: Nasser would give up his conventional rockets in exchange for Israel halting its nuclear program. Israel had to do a lot of diplomatic dodging to avoid such a disastrous outcome. It would have deprived Israel of nuclear weapons, its most effective strategic deterrent, in exchange for Egyptian rockets that were of little military value. Luckily for Israel, Nasser also rejected the American offer, mainly for reasons of national prestige.[51] But the entire affair shows how the panic around the German scientists harmed Israel's real security interests and its relations with both West Germany and the United States. Overblown psychological fears and hyperreaction, either in the form of diplomacy or covert operations, can have a prohibitive cost in the real world.

In Aman headquarters, Maj. Gen. Amit smelled blood. He knew that given the sensitive political situation, he should counter Harel and supply Ben-Gurion with intelligence estimates that might help to ease tensions with West Germany. Suddenly, Amit forgot his own zeal to participate in Operation Damocles and embraced Aman's in-house moderate estimates from 1962. He told Ben-Gurion that the Egyptian rocket program was, in fact, of little military value, particularly given that its planners failed to develop an effective guidance system. There was no nuclear or radiological program. Israel, he emphasized, was led astray by the crook Otto Joklik.[52]

Harel, who used to be an omnipotent force in the Israeli world of shadows, suddenly found himself isolated much like Reinhard Gehlen in Germany. On March 26, he resigned from the service. To add insult to injury, Ben-Gurion replaced him with Meir Amit, who was sworn in as the new head of the Mossad. But it was too late even for Ben-Gurion himself.[53] The public storm around the German scientists escalated into an ongoing political crisis that made his political situation increasingly precarious. In June, the government collapsed. David Ben-Gurion, the founder of Israel, found himself in a political wilderness from which he would never return. The scandal of the German scientists, fueled by existential fears of imaginary Nazi plots, helped end an era in Israeli politics.[54]

The new prime minister, Levi Eshkol, and Meir Amit, now the head of the Mossad, continued to deal with the issue of the German scientists. They did not see it, however, as a harbinger of a second Holocaust, but rather as a political problem that had to be solved.[55] In order to do so, Amit embarked upon a very unorthodox scheme: a secret alliance with one of Adolf Hitler's favorite officers.

·18·

Faustian Bargains— Nazis in the Service of the Jewish State

If Hitler invaded hell I would make at least a favorable reference to the devil in the House of Commons.

—WINSTON CHURCHILL

IN 1967, THE Polish culture minister, Kazimierz Rusinek, censured Israel in a radio broadcast for its "aggression" against the socialist and the communist world, as well as for its alliance with "imperialism" and "fascism." He called the Jews "who fought with us together on the barricades" to resist their own government. In the midst of his accusations, Rusinek also said that "it is no secret, that many Nazi criminals serve the Israeli state and live in its territory. I cannot give you a precise number, but I'm certain that more than [one] thousand professionals of the Nazi Wehrmacht serve as military advisers to the Israeli Army."[1]

Rusinek's accusations were certainly overblown, but they contained a tiny grain of truth. Faced with existential threats, the intelligence services of the besieged Jewish state did not shy away from employing former Nazis. Walter Rauff, as we saw before, was a mass murderer responsible for the extermination facilities known as the gas vans. After the war, he served the Syrian dictator Husni Z'aim as a military adviser until the overthrow of the latter in a military coup. As a result of his expulsion from Syria, Rauff sought revenge and was looking for new masters. On his way to South America, he stopped in Italy where he attempted to find employment with the CIA.[2] Eventually, he was recruited by a different agency altogether. At that time, Italy was a hub for spies of all nations, including a variety of Israeli intelligence operatives. Many Jewish soldiers served in Italy in Allied army units and the country was a major base for the smuggling of Jewish refugees past the British blockade into Mandatory Palestine. After Israel was established in May 1948, the intelligence apparatus in Italy was bequeathed to the Department of Political Research in the Israeli Foreign Ministry (Mamad), the direct predecessor of the Mossad as a foreign intelligence agency. An official in the Italian Foreign Ministry tipped off Mamad's station in Rome that a German national named "Ralif" had recently traveled to the country from Syria. His real name, so the tip went, was Walter Rauff, a high-ranking SS officer and fugitive on the run.

The director of Mamad station in Rome, Dr. Shalhevet Freier, later gained renown as one of the founding fathers of the Israeli nuclear program. Back then, his main responsibility was to gather intelligence on Arab countries. It is unclear how much Freier knew of Rauff's horrid past. In an interview with a Mossad historian, Freier claimed that he was oblivious to Rauff's role in the development of the gas vans, and merely knew that he fulfilled technical and economic functions in the Gestapo, including the production of forged money. "I didn't interrogate him too much," recalled Freier, "in my heart, I was happy that he was charged with printing [forged] money, a matter of irrelevance to the Jews."[3] In the intelligence business, ignorance is sometimes bliss.

Freier discovered Rauff was compliant and more than willing to cooperate. Though an unrepentant mass murderer and anti-Semitic to the core, Rauff was also pragmatic.[4] The SS general resented the new Syrian dictator, Sami Hinnawi, who expelled him from Damascus. Deeply embittered, he was more than willing to sell information to Israeli Jews. According to the Mossad's records, Freier met with Rauff for several intensive sessions, all the while keeping Tel Aviv in the dark. He was probably afraid the Foreign Ministry would order him to cut off contact with his loathsome agent.

Rauff debriefed Freier in great detail about Syrian conditions, and the information was later verified and proven accurate. In some cases, Rauff wrote to other German advisers and asked for more detailed information. After one week, Freier even offered Rauff a chance to serve Israel in a more permanent capacity as an agent in Egypt. The Nazi initially agreed, then changed his mind and traveled with his wife and two children to Ecuador. Only then did Freier inform Tel Aviv, but to his surprise the Foreign Ministry found nothing objectionable in Rauff's employment. Even in his new South American abode, "Ralif" toyed with the idea of serving Israel as a spy. In 1950, he asked a German émigré woman with strong connections to Egypt about emigration options to the country of the pyramids. He corresponded with Freier as late as January 1951.[5] Seven years later, in 1958, Rauff was formally hired by the BND on the recommendation of his SS comrade Wilhelm Beisner, by then a Gehlen agent. The two criminals found themselves, yet again, under the same roof. In the curriculum vitae he sent to the BND, Rauff did not mention his past in the SS, let alone Einsatzgruppe Egypt or the gas vans. Yet, the BND knew about his crimes, if not about his precise role in the extermination of the Jews ("that extremely disgusting thing," in the words of an agency official). Ostensibly, both Rauff and his employers—Israeli and German—preferred to let sleeping dogs lie.[6]

• • •

WHEN MEIR AMIT took over the Mossad in March 1963, he might have already known about the precedents of working with nefarious Nazis such as Rauff (and to a lesser extent, Rolf Engel). Certainly he decided that before committing his organization to additional covert operations, the Mossad had to receive more up-to-date intelligence on the rocket program and arrive at an accurate estimation of its state of development. Unlike Harel, who relied on emotional decision making and intuition, Meir Amit was schooled in military intelligence and insisted on cool, dispassionate analysis of facts and empirical data. But even Aman's resident agent in Cairo (possibly Wolfgang Lotz, Israel's most well-placed spy in Egypt), "could not add new information to what was already known." A Mossad official later recalled that in 1963, "the [German] scientists were very careful. They were just afraid. Namely, we did not recruit any new sources. Several sources did report, but [their information] was peripheral."[7]

To obtain enough data for a precise intelligence estimate, Meir Amit had to acquire a new source in the inner circle of the program. That was difficult not only because the German scientists were apprehensive, but due to the excellent work of the program's security officer, SS sergeant Hermann Valentin. "For a year and a half Valentin was a serious nuisance," related the organization's in-house historians, "and it was clear that we would have to deal with him sooner or later."[8] The Mossad had to somehow penetrate Valentin's security screen. Rafi Eitan, appointed by Amit as the new head of "Junction," the Mossad department responsible for the recruitment of agents in the European theater, knew that Valentin was involved with the community of Nazi fugitives, adventurers, and mercenaries. He therefore looked for a person with a high position in that community. Certainly, few of them could be more contemptible than Rauff, a major Holocaust culprit, with whom Israel had had dealings in the past.[9]

Steinbiechler, an Austrian engineer who worked in the Egyptian program while moonlighting as a Mossad source, made the first headway in proposing a solution to Valentin's problem. He told his handlers that he [Steinbiechler] was in touch with Otto Skorzeny, a famous SS commando leader and one of Hitler's favorite war heroes.[10] Skorzeny was also an authority figure to Valentin, who had served under him during the war. Given the high priority given to penetrating the German rocket scientists' security, the Mossad was prepared to think outside the box and grasp at any straw—perhaps it would be possible to recruit the famous commander in order to gain access to his former lieutenant?

Otto Skorzeny was a shady figure. He was renowned (or gained notoriety) for famous commando operations during the Second World War, including the daring raid to liberate the Italian dictator Benito Mussolini in September 1943, though he often took for himself more credit than was due. In the 1960s, he was suspected in various crimes: burning of synagogues in the Kristallnacht, killing "defeatist" German soldiers, and even experimenting with a "poison gun" on prisoners. Admittedly, much of this information originated in East German propaganda and was thus difficult to verify. In the 1960s, there were judicial proceedings against Skorzeny in Austria but nothing came out of it.[11] Tall and daunting, with a prominent dueling scar on his face, he was described by Rafi Eitan, the Mossad spy chief in Europe, as "a soldier of the first grade."[12] Robert B. Biek, US assistant air attaché in Madrid, remembered that Skorzeny was "very friendly and affable . . . not unlike being welcomed by a huge bear or engulfed by a huge Saint Bernard Dog." With a predilection for Scotch whiskey, Skorzeny loved the good life and entertained his guests well. He kept in touch, through middlemen, with the highest circles in the US administration and the Republican Party, possibly including then–Vice President Richard Nixon.[13]

However, Skorzeny's daunting record covered a more prosaic truth: after the war, he was nothing more than a mercenary businessman constantly looking for adventures to overcome his boredom. In conversations with his contacts, he regularly discussed plans to establish German legions in exile, poised to intervene in case of a war with the USSR, and other megalomaniacal schemes, most of which were far beyond his reach or skill. He tried to approach the commanders of the U.S. Army through the FBI in order to promote this plan. Skorzeny even introduced himself to one of his contacts as the "future president of Germany." As CIA analysts discovered to their chagrin, much of the information he provided on Soviet espionage in Germany was fabricated or overblown.[14]

Like many figures we have already encountered, Skorzeny was also an arms trafficker who dealt with various countries and insurgent groups. For that purpose, his company held branches in Cairo, Damascus, and Beirut. He smuggled WWII Mauser rifles and machine guns in large quantities to the Algerian FLN through Syria and Egypt. Like OTRACO, Skorzeny managed his payments through the Arab Club and its manager, Sa'id Fatah Imam, then onward to Tunisia and the eastern sector of the Algerian revolt. There is some evidence that he was at least indirectly connected to OTRACO through Beisner, who had helped him gain the ear of Egyptian government circles, but it seems most of his activity was independent.[15]

Unlike the CIA, the BND did not want anything to do with Skorzeny. In uncharacteristic prudence, Gehlen and his closest advisers shied away from Skorzeny's flamboyance and love of publicity, and generally looked down on him as a blubbering fool. Wolfgang Langkau, a confidant of Gehlen, condemned Skorzeny as a charlatan who took credit for wartime operations commanded by others, and suspected that he was, in fact, a Soviet agent. On his part, Skorzeny repeatedly tried to make himself useful to the Gehlen Org. In late September, 1951, for example, he reported with great fanfare on a communist espionage network of former SS officers with tentacles in the West German chancellor's office, the Allied High Commission, and other centers of power. Gehlen and Langkau answered briskly: they wanted nothing to do with Skorzeny.[16] But Skorzeny's tall tales held a kernel of truth: he was a hub for globe-spanning networks of Nazis and neo-Nazis, owned companies in several countries, helped recruit German advisers for Syria, and was involved in various deals with the German experts in Egypt. In 1960, Mossad chief Isser Harel briefly considered hunting him as a Nazi criminal but found that he was not responsible for crimes against Jews. Three years later, Meir Amit wanted to approach him as a source. The only question was how.[17]

The "hook" used by the Mossad was Skorzeny's beautiful wife, Countess Ilse von Finkenstein, with whom he was in an open relationship. Described by a CIA informant as a "very attractive and highly intelligent woman," the countess was seen by many as the moving force behind her famous paramour. An adventuress in her own right, Finkenstein was in touch with several intelligence services, most notably in France, invested in tourism in the Bahama Islands, and often invited rich men to parties on her horse farm.[18]

In order to approach her, the Mossad dispatched the former head of Amal, the Mossad's Nazi hunting unit, Rafi Meidan (not to be confused with Rafi Eitan). Meidan was a Jew "of German descent, known by his European looks. He was a handsome man with influence on women in a certain age."[19] Through an intermediary, Meidan introduced himself to the countess as an employee of the Israeli Defense Ministry, currently on leave, and looking for options to invest in international tourism. That was a perfect strategy: it was designed to provoke Ilse's curiosity and love of adventure without deterring her with an excessively open approach. The first meeting between the two took place in Dublin, and to Meidan's delight, the countless immediately took a liking to him. Quickly enough, the relationship developed into an intense (and according to persistent rumors, also intimate) personal bond. The countess and her Jewish brother-in-law partied with the Mossad agent in bars and clubs, drinking profusely and telling each other jokes in Yiddish and German. Finally, on October 7, 1964, the Israeli operative told Ilse that a "senior security official" from his country wanted to meet her husband regarding a matter of state of the utmost importance that had nothing to do with the colonel's Nazi past.

Flush after a night of clubbing, the countess agreed to contact her husband. Skorzeny, his curiosity aroused, informed the Israelis he was prepared to meet them immediately, preferably that same night.[20]

For the sensitive mission of negotiating with Skorzeny, Rafi Eitan, the head of "Junction" in Europe, chose Avraham Ahituv, another German-Jewish operative. A future head of the Shin Bet, Ahituv was a scion of a religious-Jewish family and intensely despised Nazis, Skorzeny included. He met Meidan and the countess in the lobby of a luxurious hotel in Madrid, and after fifteen minutes of small talk the three saw the huge hulk of Skorzeny fill the doorway. Meidan and the countess retired to a "business meeting," leaving Ahituv alone with the famous Nazi. In his report on the meeting, the Mossad operative wrote, "We remained in the hotel lobby. Our conversation took place [for two hours and fifteen minutes] until 21:00, mostly in English . . . Skorzeny was a giant, clumsy man, probably endowed with extraordinary physical power. His left cheek showed the famous scar from the pictures, extending all the way to his ear."[21]

The meeting was a difficult emotional experience for Ahituv, who hated what he was doing. Once, for example, the owner of the restaurant came, clicked his heels, and congratulated Skorzeny in German. The colonel explained to his Israeli interlocutor that he [the owner] was "one of the most important Nazis in these parts." On another occasion, Skorzeny put on his monocle, resembling "the perfect Nazi." Uncharacteristically for a secret service recruiter, Ahituv brought up the uncomfortable issue of the Holocaust right at the start of the conversation but took pains to differentiate between "criminals" and "officers" such as Skorzeny. The colonel, in turn, was not ready to apologize for anything. Instead, he emphasized (as his wife did before him) that he took no part in the Holocaust. Then, he surprised Ahituv by saying that "until their meeting, he knew little on Israel" but still liked this small, daring country, "a novelty for the Jewish people" whose inhabitants "excel in physical work." Israel, he added, is the solution to anti-Semitism, and he couldn't understand why all Jews don't emigrate there. Then, in a more anti-Semitic tone, he said he was always amazed that "Jews led all communist parties and espionage rings." Far from being insulted, Ahituv "explained the reasons for this phenomenon." Rafi Meidan, who came to check on Ahituv, found him and Skorzeny "absorbed in a conversation on the Jewish problem."[22]

In retrospect, it is amazing how quickly and naturally the conversation between Skorzeny and Ahituv flowed into recruitment. Later, Rafi Eitan surmised that Skorzeny cooperated with the Israelis because he was afraid of ending up like Adolf Eichmann, and only the Mossad could offer him "a life without fear."[23] Most probably, however, Skorzeny's recruitment was more a result of Ahituv's approach. Wisely, the Mossad operative did not try preaching to Skorzeny. When bringing up the issue of rocket scientists in Egypt, he did not adopt the common Israeli approach of "German murderers who are trying to kill us twice in a generation" and instead asked for Skorzeny's advice as a "professional intelligence operative," a colleague. The colonel, pleased by the compliment, boasted of his friendship with President Nasser and some of the leading scientists in Egypt. That was the moment Ahituv was waiting for. He asked Skorzeny whether he knew the security officer Hermann Valentin who was once his subordinate, implying that the Mossad wanted to recruit him. Skorzeny cautioned against such a direct approach and offered to recruit the security officer to a "Western intelligence service," making him a duped agent of Israel.[24]

Wisely, Ahituv played on Skorzeny's self-importance and love of adventure, allowing him to believe that he was an ally of the Jewish state's famous intelligence service rather than a hired agent. According to the Mossad's in-house report, Skorzeny did not ask for money, but only for one small favor. Hearing from Ahituv that his [Skorzeny's] memoirs appeared in Hebrew, he asked the Mossad to publicize this fact in order to counter Jewish objections to the publication of his book in West Germany. Even that small request turned out to be controversial. While Ahituv and his commander, Rafi Eitan, saw it as essential to the success of the operation, many in headquarters deemed it as whitewashing of a Nazi criminal. Mossad officials now raised again the suspicions about Skorzeny's role in the Kristallnacht. Meir Amit, the head of the Mossad, and Prime Minister Levi Eshkol also became involved. After much deliberation, they agreed to offer Skorzeny the Hebrew introduction to his translated book, but Ahituv gently convinced him not to make use of it. Such publication might expose his connection to the Israelis and discredit him in neo-Nazi circles. The colonel reluctantly agreed and promised "not to burden" his Israeli allies in the future.[25]

Rafi Meidan recalled, however, that Skorzeny also asked for another unofficial favor. Might the Mossad request that Simon Wiesenthal, the Nazi hunter from

Vienna, remove Skorzeny from his list of wanted Nazi criminals? According to
Meidan, Wiesenthal point-blank refused. For him, Skorzeny was a war criminal
involved in the burning of synagogues, and he would not let him off the hook,
even not for the benefit of the Mossad. The Mossad had a list, obtained from
Yad Vashem, of culprits of the pogrom in Vienna where Skorzeny's name, and
his alone, was marked with an X. The colonel told Meidan it proved he was
not involved in the burning of synagogues. Wiesenthal was not convinced.
Skorzeny was disappointed by the Nazi hunter's refusal, but still agreed to
cooperate with Israel.[26]

Rafi Eitan, who managed Skorzeny through Ahituv, also met with the colonel directly. His opinion of him was very positive. According to Eitan, the
colonel was a "solider of the first grade" who wanted to build a new, better Germany, nationalistic but free of Nazism. "Never did I encounter any animosity
toward Jews in our meetings," he recalled.[27] But now, Skorzeny, Eitan, and
Ahituv had to discuss the practical question of recruiting Hermann Valentin.

On October 8, Skorzeny invited Valentin to Madrid. The security officer,
surprised and greatly flattered by the attention of his former commander,
readily agreed. Then, after wining and dining Valentin, Skorzeny raised a thorny
issue. His friends in British intelligence, he said, would like to strengthen
Egypt so it would not need Russian assistance, but at the same time keep it
weak enough as not to tempt it to embark on new military adventures. Therefore, they needed precise details on Egyptian armaments. Skorzeny heard that
Valentin was working for Cairo. Would he agree to speak with the British?[28]

Valentin was apprehensive. "Aren't the Israelis involved?" he asked the colonel. "Stand in attention when you're spoken to!" Skorzeny bellowed in feigned
anger. "How dare you speak like this to your commander?" Valentin apologized.
The next day, he agreed to meet two MI6 agents, who were in fact Ahituv and
Harry Barak, an English-speaking Mossad operative with a British aristocratic
demeanor. The conversation was difficult. Valentin barely spoke any English.
Barak understood German but could speak only English and Yiddish, which
he of course could not use. The security officer repeatedly asked the "British
officials" why they had no IDs, how much they would pay him, and what
compensation he would receive if he should be fired by the Egyptians. Barak
said, through Ahituv, that "the most efficient secret service in the world does
not behave in such a way. We do not exploit a man and throw him to the

wolves. If something changes, we will take care of you for your entire life."[29] And yet, Valentin was not fully convinced. Skorzeny promised to use one last trick. He invited his former subordinate for drinks, spending time with him until the small hours of the morning.

The next morning, Valentin had to leave for Egypt, but Barak and Ahituv met him before his departure. To their surprise, the SS sergeant greeted them with a broad smile. He turned to Ahituv and said in German, "I would like you to translate my words to the major [Barak]. Yesterday I had a talk with the colonel [Skorzeny]. He told me something I didn't know. He told me that you advised him about it. It seems that I was about to become an officer, that he [Skorzeny] recommended my [promotion] to the German General Staff. They authorized it, but due to the chaos prevalent in the last days of the war . . . he never received their letter." And then he added, flush with pride, "Skorzeny is ready to give me a letter confirming that he knows about my promotion by the General Staff. I am your man!" He repeated the last phrase several times in English.[30]

As the Mossad historians wrote in their confidential study, all were surprised to see that Valentin, the much-dreaded security officer of the Egyptian rocket program, was in fact "a giant with feet of clay." In the CV he presented, Valentin introduced himself as a miserable illegitimate child, who grew up without knowing his mother, escaped from his adoptive parents at fifteen to join the French Foreign Legion, and then served in the SS. Even there he suffered discrimination, excluded from sensitive operations and never promoted above the rank of a sergeant (a weakness that, as we have seen, Skorzeny was quick to exploit). After the war, like so many others, he became an informant of the Gehlen Org before he was hired as the "security officer of Egyptian factories." After his recruitment, Valentin behaved like a purring cat, and emphasized to his employers that he admired the British all his life and would like nothing more than to become a full-fledged member of MI6. Barak told him that he would have to earn this distinction through hard work.[31]

And work hard he did. Within a few months, Valentin told his handlers almost everything they wanted to know about the Egyptian rocket program, giving up-to-date, authentic, and sometimes surprising material. He debriefed Ahituv and Barak about conversations with Kleinwächter and other scientists, the results of experiments, production goals, and the ongoing difficulties of the German experts with the Egyptians and with one another. Crucially, he told the Mossad that Kleinwächter and his team failed to develop a working guidance system for the rockets. The Egyptians, he said, were afraid to launch inaccurate rockets lest they hit Arab population centers or the Muslim holy sites in Jerusalem. This was an important calming message for the Israelis. Valentin also said that the Egyptians were disappointed with their German experts and were looking to concentrate more authority in their own hands, another sure sign of impending failure. Finally, he advised the Mossad that Mahmoud Khalil was attempting to recruit a new group of guidance experts in a desperate attempt to save the project.[32]

At this time, Khalil's own position in Egypt was on the wane. For years, he had promised President Nasser ballistic missiles, but as Waltraud Lotz predicted, delivered nothing but a glaring hole in the Egyptian defense budget. Unprepared to face the sunken costs, he doubled his bets by recruiting more and more German experts, especially in guidance, as if they would be able to compensate for Egypt's weaknesses in technology, infrastructure, and manpower. Khalil's recruiters now zeroed in on a factory named Helige in the German city of Freiburg, planning to tempt a group of laid-off engineers to move to Egypt. These were experts in guidance, skilled in building gyroscopes that could improve the accuracy of the Egyptian rockets. On October 4, 1964, the Mossad heard from another source, an Israeli politician with connections in Germany, that fifty workers had resigned from the Helige plants and signed a contract with the Egyptians.[33]

Equipped with plentiful intelligence provided by Herman Valentin, Meir Amit and his advisers discussed ways to deal with this new problem. It was clear to them that they had to prevent these scientists from moving to Egypt. In contrast to Harel's panicked and self-righteous approach, Amit admitted they did not pose an existential risk to Israel, but in Israel's sensitive position any risk was excessive.[34] Moreover, as long as the problem of the German scientists persisted, Israel would have to cope with serious domestic and international difficulties. The opposition in the Knesset did not accept Amit's prudent assessments, and Menachem Begin continued to organize inflammatory demonstrations against Israel's reconciliation with West Germany. Prime Minister Eshkol and the head of the Mossad realized that they had to solve this political problem somehow. The intelligence coup with Skorzeny and Valentin, Israel's Nazi agents, opened several courses of action. The only question was which course the Mossad would choose.

· 19 ·

Catching Flies with Honey

The affair of the German scientists leaves us unsatisfied. So much trouble, so many storms and crises, complicated, dangerous and daring operations, and we cannot conclude with certainty that the Mossad contributed anything to thwarting the danger . . .
instead, it died of itself.

—*THE AFFAIR OF THE GERMAN SCIENTISTS*—INTERNAL MOSSAD STUDY[1]

⌒

WHEN A SECRET service knows everything, even the tiniest detail, about a certain group of people, there are several ways to apply influence on them. One is intimidation. Now the master of both Mossad and Aman, Meir Amit merged the operational units of both organizations (188 and Gulf) into a new covert ops department known as Caesarea. Joseph "Yoske" Yariv, the former commander of 188, contributed his predilection for explosive letters and parcels to the unified unit he now headed. This time, however, the idea was not to kill a small number of key scientists such as Pilz or Kleinwächter. As recent experience had shown, such operations were costly, risky, and prone to failure. Linking violent means with achievable political ends, Yariv offered to dispatch letters to as many scientists as possible. Those in Egypt would receive letters with small amounts of explosives, designed to injure and frighten more than to kill, while their colleagues in Germany would receive threatening notes in the mail discouraging from relocating to Cairo. As the purpose was to deter rather than neutralize, breadth (many letters) would be prioritized over depth (well-planned assassinations of key figures). In this campaign, Hermann Valentin's intelligence was indispensable: He gave the Israelis precious details on the addresses, character, and personal life of the scientists, allowing the Mossad experts to tailor threatening messages to each and every one of them.[2] The letters were mailed in autumn 1964. A typical one reads as follows:

> *Dear Mr. Neumann,*
>
> *You will probably wonder about this anonymous letter, but by its contents you will gather that we know you very well. You are a young man, probably unaware of the long-term consequences of your work in Egypt. We assume that you are not moved by anti-Semitism. After all, at the end of World War II you were only nine years old. However, one can wonder why an alert young man such as yourself fails to understand the situation. The entire world knows that contrary to Egyptian propaganda, you and your friends are developing and producing unconventional weapons, designed only for mass destruction.[3]*

Here, the anonymous writer mentioned the names of Neumann's friends, previous jobs, and other details on his personal life. The scientist was accused of "indifference to political repercussions" and "adventurism," and finally warned of dire consequences:

> *This letter should clarify your situation . . . In any case, we see it clearly, and hope you will draw the right conclusions. Remember: even if you're innocent of the crimes committed by the German people in the past, you will not be able to avoid responsibility for your actions today. You had better consider the contents of this letter carefully, for your own future and that of your young family.[4]*

Other letters, sent to scientists, their family members, and numerous newspapers in West Germany, Switzerland, England, and France, were even more ominous. They mentioned the names of wives, children, and other relatives of experts in both Egypt and Germany, implying threats to their well-being. Meeting his commander, Joseph Yariv, in Paris, Wolfgang Lotz took three explosive letters to Cairo hidden inside Yardley soap bars and a cheese cutting board. Lotz mailed the letters from Cairo to key scientists on September 20, putting his cover story at risk. The letters were not very lethal and it was clear to everybody that the Egyptian security would intercept most if not all of them. Indeed, one of the letters failed to explode, the second injured an Egyptian postman, and the third disappeared without a trace. The idea was to deter and catch the public eye, not to kill. In November, Lotz in Cairo and Mossad operatives in Europe dispatched a second wave of letters, this time to the workers of the Helige Plant who were about to leave for Egypt. All letters were signed by the "Gideons," a fictitious guerrilla organization of Jewish partisans named after the legendary biblical judge.[5]

The Israeli government combined this intimidation with a public lobbying campaign designed to convince the West German government to recall the scientists from Egypt. These efforts were in fact going on for more than two years, but the West Germans emphasized to their Israeli counterparts there was little they could do to force the hand of their experts abroad. The Basic Law, the Federal Republic's constitution, did not authorize the government to limit the freedom of movement and employment of its citizens. True, Article 26 of the Basic Law vaguely forbade West German nationals to participate in activities undermining world peace or in aggressive wars, but it was hard to prove that this definition applied to the scientists in Egypt. Since the beginning of Harel's press campaign in March 1963, the three parties represented in the Bundestag (Christian-Democrats, Social Democrats, and Liberals) discussed legal means to limit the activity of the scientists in Egypt, but with little tangible results.

In principle, the Bundestag parties agreed there was a need to bar West German nationals from participating in "problematic" military projects abroad, but they could not agree on the precise details. How, for example, would one draw the line between military and peaceful scientific activity? The German scientists in Egypt claimed they were working on civilian projects, and it would be difficult to prove the opposite in a court of law. On December 11, 1963, the government proposed an amendment to the passport law so it could revoke travel documents from Germans who "participate in the construction of military projects." This time, the Social Democrats raised strenuous objections. Though they had so far been outspokenly pro-Israeli and championed the legislation against the scientists in Egypt, they were also afraid a future government would use such a law to forcibly recall political opponents from foreign countries. Finally, the cabinet itself rejected the draft as an unconstitutional infringement on the freedom of movement.[6]

Leaving constitutional arguments aside, the West German government also had practical considerations. First, as negotiations dragged on, the influence of the pro-Arab lobby in Bonn grew in strength. Diplomatic and commercial circles feared for the relations with the Arab world, and some were concerned that limiting employment of German experts abroad might undermine projects in non-Arab countries such as India. Chancellor Adenauer and his successor, Ludwig Erhard, were genuinely worried that if the German scientists left Egypt, Nasser would promptly replace them with East German or Soviet experts. That would, of course, undermine the Federal Republic's ongoing struggle against East German penetration of the Arab world. Besides, while working in Egypt, these scientists might gain useful experience for the future development of the German air industry.[7]

Reinhard Gehlen, who (through his resident Gerhard Bauch) used the German scientists in Egypt as a source of intelligence, tried to convince Isser Harel as early as 1961 that their repatriation would be detrimental for both Bonn and Jerusalem. Instead of non-efficient scientists whom one can monitor, West Germany and Israel would face an opaque, uncontrollable Soviet cohort likely to be much more dangerous. Importantly for Bonn, the Americans shared the same concerns.[8] This was not a theoretical danger. As we have seen, that was the exact result of the French covert action campaign against the German arms merchants in the Algerian War. Events would in fact partially confirm Gehlen's assessment—Soviet-manned Scud rocket batteries were deployed against Israel in the Yom Kippur War a decade later.

But to the Israelis, even high officials well attuned to diplomatic and international sensitivities, the German arguments rang hollow.[9] Though the Germans were of course right to claim their scientists were not involved in the development of nuclear, chemical, or biological weapons, for Israel, even a slight chance for such an outcome could not be tolerated. The real danger was indeed overblown—many security experts in Jerusalem secretly said so—but they were not ready to hear it from the Germans. "People whose relatives were murdered in gas chambers have different sensitivities than those who, knowingly or unknowingly, helped to construct these gas chambers," said an Israeli diplomat in France.[10]

As intimidation on its own did not work, and neither could formal nego-tiations, Meir Amit chose a third option: to leverage both intimidation and lobbying into informal secret talks with both the scientists and the West German government. Here, Israel cleverly used its informal connections with two key figures in West Germany: The industrialist Ludwig Bölkow, owner of several plants manufacturing helicopters, airplanes, and rockets, and Franz Josef Strauss, the former defense minister and a highly influential figure in West German politics.

The Mossad had carefully cultivated its relationship with Bölkow, prudently behaving toward him (as with Skorzeny) as if he were a political ally rather than an agent. Noting that several of the scientists in Egypt once worked in his factories, the Mossad acquired sources inside the Bölkow concern, including an official in his industrial espionage team who gave the Israelis up-to-date plans of the Egyptian rockets. In order to cultivate the relationship with Bölkow himself, the Mossad, with impressive cultural savviness, dispatched an Israeli officer of German descent, "an older gentleman with respectable and impressive demeanor, skilled in negotiating with Germans of a high social class." In early November 1964, Bölkow visited Israel with his wife as the guest of the Mossad and received VIP treatment. Amit opened business opportunities for him and treated the couple to extensive trips around the country.[11]

"In his character," his escort said, "[Bölkow] is amiable, friendly and informal . . . with impressive intellectual and philosophical inclinations . . . well-versed in international problems. He is very talkative, yet practical and resolute in his opinions . . . He is ready to give us information on the devel-opment of the Egyptian rocket program . . . and to continue working [with us] to bring scientists out of Egypt." However, Bölkow added the reservation, common in West German industrial circles, that such a course of action may not be in the best interest of Israel. After all, Egypt will eventually produce rockets with German help or without it. Better to have German scientists on whom Israel can collect intelligence than Russians, French, and British on whom the Mossad will have no influence.[12]

Franz Josef Strauss, formerly the federal defense minister, was the second key figure in the Mossad's clandestine plan. Admittedly, he was a strange broker for a deal with Israel. Deeply conservative but boisterous and colorful, he was one of the most controversial figures in West German politics, surrounded by lurid scandals and corruption allegations. His Catholic convictions, as well as past opposition to the reparations agreement with Israel, made him an unlikely partner for the Jewish state. And yet, Strauss gradually became one of Israel's best friends in the conservative establishment of West Germany. Along with Peres, with whom he kept a close personal relationship since 1957, Strauss was the architect of several confidential arms deals between the two countries. Even after his resignation in November 1962 as a result of the Spiegel Affair, Strauss still pulled strings inside the Defense Ministry and promoted military cooperation between Israel and West Germany.[13]

Strauss's alliance with Peres was based on realpolitik, but also genuine respect for the Jewish state. He saw Israel as an anti-Soviet and pro-Western bastion in the Middle East, admiring Israeli achievements in technology, agriculture, and energy as well as the Jewish state's ability to forge immigrants from more than seventy countries into one unified nation. After a visit to Israel in May 1963 he insisted—contrary to his government's position—that West Germany had to recognize Israel even if the Arab states recognized East Germany in retaliation. Strauss was not anti-Arab but believed the Federal Republic should not allow other states to dictate its foreign relations. Chancellor Adenauer, he said, had already reconciled Germany with its former enemies in Europe and America. Now, he had to crown his achievements with a reconciliation with the Jewish people.[14]

However, in 1962 Strauss was still indifferent to the problem of the German scientists. In August, he had all but ignored Peres's plea to act against them, replying that they were mediocre and posed no real danger to Israel. In any case, Strauss retired in November 1962 as a result of the Spiegel scandal, and was busy with other issues.[15] In March 1963, at the height of the anti-German press campaign in Israel, he came to visit Shimon Press. Followed by demonstrators yelling "Strauss Raus, and Peres too!" he invited his host to yet another serious conversation on the issue of the scientists in Egypt. This time, Strauss asked Peres for precise details on the production of the rockets in Egypt, and especially for evidence on their nonconventional character and the threat they posed to the Jewish state. Peres asked the Mossad but received no answer.[16] Isser Harel had become so entangled in his alarmist rhetoric, he could not use the information he did possess for meaningful negotiations.

The problem of the German scientists, as previously noted, did not really require a solution. As the historians of the Mossad admitted, it would have died of itself due to the "low technical and industrial level of Egypt, lack of local professional manpower, incompetence and inexperience in organizing and managing a large and sophisticated industrial project . . . the intimidating statue of Egyptian ambition stood on feet of clay."[17] And yet, in late 1964, both Strauss and Peres agreed this issue had to be cleared from the table in order to maintain the "special relationship" between Israel and West Germany.

That was the foundation of a unique Mossad persuasion campaign, known to posterity as Operation Employment Office. Meir Amit decided to use the furor caused by the Gideonite campaign and previous terror attacks, as well as the influence of Bölkow and Strauss, to arrange jobs for the Helige scientists in the Bölkow concern and thus prevent their departure to Egypt. At first, the scientists were reluctant to negotiate. Some of them were so upset by the threatening letters as to refuse any contact with the "Jewish partisans" or any other Israelis. One of their representatives even threatened to retaliate against the Jewish community in Freiburg. Another called the police, and Meir Amit even feared a repetition of the Heidi Goercke fiasco. As a result, the Mossad temporarily withdrew many of its operatives from Germany to Belgium.[18]

A breakthrough was achieved in early December 1964. Operating on the direct orders of Joseph Yariv, the commander of Caesarea, a Mossad agent called the representatives of the Helige Group and offered direct negotiations in Brussels. After much hesitation, the group of experts agreed to meet with the "Jewish terrorists" and sent their representatives to the Belgian capital. To avoid a run-in with the local authorities, the Mossad advised the Belgian Secret Service, which dispatched its own men to supervise the meeting.[19]

On December 7, a young girl met the German group in the airport and told them they would shortly meet official representatives of the Israeli government. The meeting was tense and stormy from the very beginning. A Caesarea operative, bulky and intimidating, sat with the Israeli negotiators, who introduced him as the "representative of the Jewish partisans." He was silent throughout the meeting, but the Germans were always afraid he would draw a gun and shoot them. At some point, one member of the Helige Group was seriously afraid of abduction. In the floor above, Meir Amit and Joseph Yariv supervised the negotiations in person.[20]

The representatives of the Helige Group demanded an enormous compensation, as well as "evidence" that the Egyptian rocket program was of military nature. Another meeting was scheduled for the evening of December 9 in a Freiburg café. The same morning, Shimon Peres traveled to Germany along with Rafi Meidan for a decisive meeting with Franz Josef Strauss. Meidan carried documents on the Egyptian rocket program, precious intelligence obtained by Skorzeny and Valentin. Strauss invited his guests for drinks while examining the documents. "We sat for six hours," recalled Peres, "God, that man could drink. Wines from all over the world, and beer. I can also drink, but quantities like that? Six hours and we didn't stop drinking."[21]

According to Ronen Bergman, "the information Peres presented to Strauss was far more detailed, cross-checked, authentic, and grave than anything that had been presented to the Germans previously . . . [Strauss] must have grasped what the leakage of this material to the international press would have meant."[22] Only two years beforehand, Strauss disregarded the importance of the Egyptian rocket program. It defies reason to believe that even the material presented by Peres, though purged from Harel's doomsday fantasies, had convinced him otherwise.[23] However, Strauss did grasp the depth of the political crisis. He called Ludwig Bölkow, who was likewise connected with the Mossad, asked for his help, and promised the German government would pay the salary of the repatriated scientists for several years. The industrialist dispatched a senior director of his company to the meeting in Freiburg in a private plane that very evening. In a subsequent conference, Bölkow called the leaders of the Helige group himself. He told them that "the government" (i.e., Strauss) offered him a large sum of money to compensate the scientists and end the affair that "compromised the good name of Germany."[24]

Meir Amit, the head of the Mossad, recalled later that this was the decisive moment. After Bölkow's call, the Helige scientists became "soft like butter." Thirteen members of the group agreed to abrogate their agreement with the Egyptians forthwith. Others who had already moved to Egypt soon harbored second thoughts. A handsome Mossad agent seduced the daughter of their leader, Werner Niemann, and the girl agreed to mediate between the Israelis and her father. In the meeting, Niemann confessed tearfully that things were going badly for the members of the group who had already emigrated. They were tyrannized by Wolfgang Pilz, languished in hotels, and the Egyptians failed to pay them. It took several additional meetings until Niemann agreed to convince the remaining members of the group to leave Egypt. Strauss and

Bölkow agreed to pay compensations and arrange jobs for all of them. As a token of appreciation, the Israeli government gave Bölkow Uzi rifles to arm the security guards in his factories.[25]

On December 29, 1964, the Israeli Foreign Ministry advised its representative in Germany that the negotiation with the Freiburg group was successful. They all canceled their contracts with Egypt and would remain in Germany.[26] That was only partly accurate. Out of the original group of thirty-four Helige experts, thirteen accepted jobs in the Bölkow concern. Twelve others resumed working for Helige, nine found other jobs, and only eight lingered in Cairo. In any case, the Egyptian project was doomed. The difficulties in Egypt, combined with job offers from Strauss and his friends in West Germany industry, tempted the other scientists to repatriate. Paul Goercke left in early 1965 to take a job at the Bölkow concern, followed in March by thirty of his colleagues. Pilz departed a few months afterward. The German government agreed to pay compensation to his former secretary and newlywed wife, Hannelore Wende, who was maimed by the Mossad letter bomb in autumn 1962.[27] In order to solve the political crisis, Strauss, Bölkow, and other West German leaders agreed to clean up after the Mossad. The clandestine ties forged by Meir Amit had paid off.

To be sure, this step was hardly unprecedented—Ben-Gurion had dispatched Isser Harel in November 1960, three years previously, to induce Bonn to entice Eugen Sänger back home. Sänger, perhaps the only first-class German rocket scientist in Nasser's employ, was offered a position in West Germany's space program, an offer he took up with alacrity. After all, his interest, and that of the other German scientists, was in sending rockets up. They didn't really care where they came down. Had Isser Harel and Ben-Gurion heeded their mothers' admonishments that it is easier to catch flies with honey than with vinegar, they may well have been able to defuse the political landmine that was the German scientists without resorting to kidnappings, botched assassinations, intimidations, arrested agents, recruiting Nazi agents of their own, and eventually derailing their own careers. On the other hand, Bonn may not have been prepared to heed Jerusalem's concerns without experiencing a preparatory dose of unpleasant vinegar and the implied threat of more to come.

Regardless, Jerusalem had to be prepared to swallow some bitter medicine of its own. We have no evidence that the issue of "Nazis" was mentioned during the meetings that led to the resolution of the scientists' crisis. However, it was also clear to all participants that Israel could not expect such cooperation from West Germany while continuing to evoke the shadows from the past. In his memoirs Strauss emphasized that "Israel gave a hand to the Germans, by recognizing the impossibility of comparing contemporary Germany with Hitler's country." Indeed, he believed West Germany would never be truly independent until it freed itself from the yoke of the past. It should not forget what Hitler did "in the name of the German people" but neither should it accept restrictions about "what we should think, say or do." In 1961, during the Eichmann trial, Strauss convinced high officials in Bonn that Ben-Gurion and his government kept their promise not to associate the Federal Republic and its leaders (for example, Hans Globke) with the Nazi regime. Therefore, he recommended, Bonn should resume arms shipments to Israel.[28] In order to preserve his cooperation, in the issue of the German scientists and beyond, Israel had to be extremely careful about this issue.

Relations with West Germany had in any case reached a very sensitive point. In November 1964, Chancellor Erhard advised Prime Minister Eshkol that secret German arms shipments to Israel, whose existence had been leaked to the press, would be replaced with financial assistance. Bonn was trapped between fears of Egypt recognizing East Germany, Jerusalem's wrath, and the expectations of the United States, because in 1964, Washington used the Federal Republic as a channel to arm Israel indirectly and at the same time expected Germany to preserve its diplomatic channels to Egypt as a Western bridgehead in the Middle East. Israel agreed to the German proposal only once it became clear that Washington would supply the weapons and Bonn would pay for them. When, in early 1965, Nasser invited Walter Ulbricht, the East German leader, for a state visit, Bonn chose to retaliate by establishing diplomatic relations with Israel. As a result, Egypt, Syria, and most other Arab states broke their own diplomatic relations with West Germany. The relations with West Germany, now formal, were still a delicate matter in Israeli public opinion. Nothing could imperil it more than continued meddling in Nazi affairs.[29] And indeed, the growing cooperation with Bonn converged with another process: the Mossad had gradually lost interest in Nazi hunting.

• • •

IN FACT, THE Mossad had begun to doubt the value of Nazi hunting operations during the height of the scientists' crisis. David Ben-Gurion, disillusioned by Harel's "Nazi obsession," told Meir Amit that such operations risked the delicate relationship between Israel and West Germany. "Ben-Gurion," recalled Amit, "was forward-looking by nature. He believed that [West] Germany was 'a different Germany,' and did not want yet another Eichmann trial or [such-like] international scandal. Therefore, it is possible that he saw the handling of Nazi criminals according to this prism."[30] Ben-Gurion remembered how Germany suspended weapons shipments during the Eichmann trial in order to guarantee Israel's "good behavior" in the various scandals surrounding Hans Globke. He was also aware of the damage that Operation Damocles caused to Israel's relations with both West Germany and the United States.

Meir Amit shared these views. While not completely disregarding the importance of Nazi hunting operations, he saw them as a diversion from the Mossad's fight against the enemies of the present. "I was against terror, abductions, international scandals and a second Eichmann trial," he said. Seeing that Levi Eshkol, Ben-Gurion's successor as prime minister, agreed with him on this crucial point, Amit gradually marginalized Amal, the department responsible for Nazi hunting, in favor of other, more important units.[31]

Admittedly, the issue was not completely off the table. On January 23, 1964, Amit convened all leaders of the Israeli intelligence community to reach a coherent decision about Nazi hunting. The mood in the meeting was hesitant, to say the least. All knew that Israel had gradually abandoned methods of coercion against the German scientists and began to phase them out in favor of secret negotiations with the authorities in Bonn. In the spirit of Ben-Gurion and Eshkol's wishes, nobody wanted another international scandal, let alone a second Eichmann trial, which likely would bring Israel onto a collision course with West Germany and other countries. To the amazement of Yehudit Nasi-yahu, who represented Amal in the meeting, the superintendent general of the Israeli police even opposed assassinations, lest they "educate our youth to murder." Yaakov Karoz, deputy head of the Mossad, countered him by saying that assassinations might deter anti-Semitic criminals in the future: "Let them think again before they lift a hand or raise a sword on a Jew."[32]

Most participants, however, agreed that in order to avoid international scandals, it was best to secure the extradition of Nazi criminals to West Germany and other relevant countries. However, they still did not rule out "silent assassinations." Then, Yehudit Nasiyahu read the names of available criminals from Amal's list. Martin Bormann, chief of the Nazi Party chancellery, and Heinrich Müller, head of the Gestapo, were missing since 1945, and no one knew whether they were even alive (in fact, both were long dead). All agreed that the Mossad had to continue the search for Josef Mengele, the sadistic "Angel of Death" of Auschwitz, and for his assistant, Horst Schumann, who was already located by the Mossad in Ghana. Alois Brunner's name was received with indifference. The low priority of the enterprise ruled out another risky operation in Damascus.[33]

When Nasiyahu, however, read the name of Herbert Cukurs, known as the "Butcher of Riga," she noticed a commotion in the room. The head of Aman, Maj. Gen. Aharon Yariv, suddenly started to sob. He hailed from Riga, and his entire family was shot by Cukurs's henchmen. Meir Amit summarized the meeting with characteristic caution. "We should not assign resources to this goal indiscriminately and without proportion. Our main task is to safeguard our existence through intelligence collection, and not to take revenge for the past . . . Abductions to Israel are out of the question. Extradition of the criminals meets our goal. Only when extradition is impossible, we should consider a terror attack, and even then, weigh every case on its own merit." Amit did not really believe that such criminals would be adequately punished in Germany and other countries, but saw extradition as a convenient way to transfer the responsibility from Israel to other governments.[34] After the approval of this decision by Prime Minister Eshkol and Foreign Minister Meir, the Mossad decided to assassinate Cukurs and Schumann, and to continue the search for Mengele. The first two operations were not risky from a diplomatic point of view. Cukurs was a Latvian Nazi, unlikely to cause much stir in West Germany, and Schumann lived in a remote jungle town in Ghana, far from the spotlight of the international press. Mengele was deemed too important to be ignored.

These decisions were then carried out. A Mossad team assassinated Cukurs on February 23, 1965, in Montevideo, Uruguay. As in the abduction operation of Heinz Krug, they lured him to an isolated villa with a tempting business proposal. But Cukurs was not taken to Tel Aviv. After a pitched struggle, one of the Mossad assassins killed him with a hammer.[35] At the same time, the Mossad gave up on Schumann's assassination due to operational difficulties, and Israel lobbied to secure his extradition instead. Schumann was indeed given over by Ghana to West Germany but declared "unfit to stand trial" due to severe illness, and died as a free man in 1983. The search for Mengele, this time not for the purpose of abduction or assassination but to secure his extradition to West Germany, continued without result. The Mossad also tried to locate the long-dead Heinrich Müller, but in vain. In November 1967, two Israeli operatives were arrested in Germany for breaking into the house of his widow.[36] However, such operations were few and far between. Despite the attempts of few enthusiasts such as Zvi Aharoni and Rafi Meidan, the word "Nazis" now evoked yawns rather than excitement in the corridors of the Mossad.

In late December 1968, head of the Mossad Zvi Zamir, Amit's successor, met Prime Minister Levi Eshkol for yet another discussion on Nazi hunting. If anything, Zamir was even more opposed to such operations than Amit. He told the prime minister that the hunt for Nazis required large-scale investment of scarce resources and advised halting it altogether. Eshkol approved. "We had enough with Eichmann," he said. "That was a symbol." He thus ordered the Mossad to collect and verify information on Nazis but stop all hunting activities and inform relevant governments on the whereabouts of fugitive criminals. The only exceptions were Bormann (who was already dead) and Mengele. In fact, even the hunt for Mengele became dormant. The Mossad placed the Nazi issue on ice, where it would remain for the next decade.[37]

· 20 ·

Fade Away

Everyone ended up finding his place in the world—
everyone except him.

—GABRIEL GARCÍA MÁRQUEZ, *THE AUTUMN OF THE PATRIARCH*[1]

⌒

OTTO SKORZENY NEVER publicized his ties with the Mossad. Openly, he boasted of his friendship with Gamal Abdel Nasser, kept in close touch with the Mufti of Jerusalem, and expressed pro-Arab and anti-Israeli views. After the Six Days War, for example, he told a sympathetic reporter that next time, the Arabs would be able to surprise and destroy Israel. Nasser would not repeat the mistakes of the past. "When the Israelis read about it in their newspapers it may be all over."[2]

However, documents released from the Mossad archives tell us that the SS colonel continued to closely cooperate with the Israeli Secret Service until the end of his life. In late December 1965, for example, he met with his handler, possibly Avraham Ahituv, for a long nocturnal conversation. The talk began in Skorzeny's office, then the two moved to a restaurant and a bar, and even continued to speak later, walking in the street. As usual with Skorzeny, they discussed world affairs from the Vietnam War to apartheid in South Africa. Sometimes the debate became quite stormy, especially when Skorzeny expressed his unabashedly racist views.[3] The SS colonel helped the Mossad get information on the dwindling community of German experts in Egypt, and later also provided secret access to political figures in Spain and elsewhere, including Arab diplomats. The efforts to approach new sources through his mediation, however, failed, and the information he gave on the Middle East was quite useless, mostly "taken from the pages of *Times Magazine*."[4]

Hermann Valentin, too, continued to work for the Mossad. In 1967, his "British" handlers offered to "give him over to the Israelis," and he readily agreed. The security officer became addicted to the money, and the Israelis, now his formal employers, spoiled him with a high salary, expense budget, and even an occasional loan to buy a new car. Like Joklik, he invited his handlers to expensive restaurants along with his wife, then handed over the bill as part of his expenses. In July 1965, Valentin had a run-in with Kleinwächter and was fired from the Egyptian program. A year later, his neo-Nazi friends suspected he was working for Israeli intelligence and ostracized him as a result. That did not deter Valentin. He went on working for the Mossad as a "private detective" and collected intelligence on Arab arms merchants and terrorists.[5]

In the late 1960s, Alois Brunner still lived in his two-room apartment in Rue George Haddad on the pension of a major in the Syrian army.[6] His work in Syria brought him no joy, and he was bitter and despondent. The gang that was once responsible for the Goldmann plot slowly dispersed. Rayees disappeared, Darwish lived in a small hotel and was almost deaf, and Windisch, another of Brunner's old pals in the weapon smuggling business, left the Middle East for Munich because he was, according to Brunner, "completely burned."[7]

Brunner himself was feeling lonely in Syrian exile. He was the sole remnant of the old network of fugitive Nazis. In Germany, he was forgotten for a while and the proceedings against him stalled.[8] And yet, Brunner did not want to be forgotten. In his correspondence with Arthur Maichanitsch, a former Nazi commando fighter who refused to take part in the Goldmann plot, he even offered a free room to visiting "comrades" from the old homeland. At that time, Maichanitsch was leading a group of young neo-Nazis who regularly met for military drills, and Brunner still hoped for an eventual Nazi revival in Germany and Austria, washing the corrupted democratic governments of the "Jew Kreisky" (in Austria) and the "Half-Jew Brandt" (in West Germany) "into the canals." Maichanitsch, he cautioned, should implant his protégés in all walks of society, and especially in the political parties, in order to prepare the leadership forces of the future.

Typically, Brunner shifted between self-pity and burning hatred. He was living from hand to mouth, he complained, and nobody was sending him any money. He continued preparing sauerkraut with the help of students and selling it to the local supermarket.[9] "Sometimes I wonder why I live, and one does not get younger," he wrote. The Jews, Brunner feared, were devouring Germany and Austria. During Golda Meir's visit to Vienna, Brunner complained in one of his more bizarre letters, Austrians were forced to wear the yellow star. Soon, Hebrew would become the official language of the land. Meanwhile, the Israelis were closing in on him in Damascus as well. Brunner asked Maichanitsch to uncover details on a visiting Nazi veteran who was, he suspected, a hired Mossad spy. "The Jews," he wrote with disdain, are now also employing former Nazis "in their dirty schemes," though such people were probably never National Socialists in the first place. Brunner's suspicions were, in fact, justified. Simon Wiesenthal had an informer in Maichanitsch's circle, probably the same Dr. Z. who gave the Nazi hunter information on the Goldmann plot. The veteran hunter was still watching Brunner, waiting for the slightest mistake.[10]

After many years of neglect, the Israelis began to shift their gaze toward Brunner yet again. In 1977, Israeli Labor Party rule finally gave way to a new right-wing government led by Menachem Begin. The new prime minister escaped from Poland shortly before the German occupation, but his entire family perished in the Holocaust, and he had always seen himself as a Holocaust survivor. In the 1950s, as a firebrand politician, he led violent crowds in spirited demonstrations against the reparations agreement with West Germany. During the crisis of the German scientists, he attacked Ben-Gurion and Eshkol's governments for their pro-German policy and poured oil on Isser Harel's inflammatory press campaign on the supposed impending "second Holocaust" planned by the German scientists with the full approval of the government in Bonn.

The memory of the Holocaust pervaded Begin's policy as prime minister, and he believed Israel was obligated to keep on hunting Nazis. Already in his first meeting with Yitzhak (Haka) Hofi, the head of the Mossad, Begin demanded to place the hunt for Nazis on the spy agency's agenda. Just like his predecessors, Hofi was reluctant to invest scarce resources in the wars of the past, while the hands of the Mossad were full with problems such as the covert war against the PLO and spying operations in Arab countries. Begin, however, was adamant, and the two men agreed to limit the new mission to the most heinous criminals still alive. On September 23, 1977, the Cabinet Committee for Security Affairs decided to "order the Mossad to renew the search for Nazi war criminals, especially Josef Mengele, in order to bring them to justice in Israel. And if that proves impossible—to assassinate them."[11]

The staffers of Amal, called back from bureaucratic oblivion, updated the list of living Nazi criminals from 1964, crossed off the names of two who died, and added a handful of new "candidates." The decision was to assassinate all of them under the cover of a "Jewish partisan organization," except for Josef Mengele, who had to be brought to Israel for trial (unbeknownst to the Mossad, Mengele died in Brazil in February 1979).[12] In March 1980, after long months of preparations, a Mossad team tried to assassinate Walter Rauff in Chile. True, he cooperated with Israel in the past, but that was overshadowed by his enormous crimes. Unfortunately, Operation Nirosta failed. Rauff's Chilean wife discovered the assassination team and started to yell. According to their instructions, the team was not allowed to kill the woman and therefore had to retreat before one of the neighbors called the police. Rauff died from lung cancer a year afterward.[13]

Alois Brunner was also on the hit list. As he lived in Syria, abducting him was out of the question, and no one believed the Syrian government would extradite him, certainly not as a result of Israeli pressure. In order to prepare for yet another assassination, the Mossad dispatched a Muslim-Bosnian agent to Damascus to collect intelligence on Brunner. This incredible man, known to us only by his alias "Stiff" (*nukshe*), was an anti-Nazi Yugoslav partisan keen to take revenge on the Germans who murdered some of his relatives during the war. He made contact with Darwish, Brunner's Bosnian friend, and visited him in Damascus, adopting a false identity of a pro-Nazi Muslim. Through Darwish, Stiff was able to call on Brunner in 1978. A few days later, he sent the Mossad astonishing amounts of material on the fugitive Nazi, including a detailed map of his apartment and its surroundings. He also advised the Israelis that there were no visible security details in or around the building.[14]

To avoid risking agents on the ground, the Mossad decided to dispatch Brunner yet again with a letter bomb. Stiff reported that Brunner was now an avid reader of an Austrian magazine on natural medicine, published by an organization named the "Friends of Medicinal Herbs." The Mossad team, based in Austria, sent Brunner a forged letter from the society, telling him that the next installment of their magazine might arrive in book form instead of the usual binder.[15] The next installment indeed arrived on July 1, 1980. When Brunner opened the package and drew the contents out, he activated the mechanism. The device exploded. Brunner survived but was badly burned and lost some of his fingers. His blood soaked to the floor of the apartment, leaving a permanent stain. The decision of the assassins to send a letter bomb instead of a parcel limited the volume of explosives and saved his life. After six weeks, Brunner was released from hospital back to Rue Haddad. From that day on, he ceased preparing and selling sauerkraut.[16] With that very limited achievement, the Mossad ceased attempts on Brunner's life.

Newly unclassified documents of the Federal Office for Constitutional Protection (BfV), West Germany's domestic intelligence service, reveal that Brunner was active even after the assassination. He kept close ties with a handful of Nazi activists, including Remer and Genoud, and even warned Remer away from an Israeli agent who penetrated Swiss neo-Nazi circles. Among other things, he tried to secure Syrian asylum for Klaus Barbie, "the Butcher of Lyon," who was then prosecuted in France, part of a far-fetched "rescue scheme" hatched by some old Nazis. But Brunner's situation was precarious. Otto Ernst Remer, whom he trusted, was in fact an informant of the BfV. The Federal Office for Constitutional Protection now collected data about Brunner, though Remer was reluctant to give precise information, and identified Brunner only as Georg, part of his well-known alias Georg Fischer. The BfV, however, quickly became convinced that Georg was Brunner and shared this information with the Israelis. Fortunately for Brunner, the German service was mainly interested in Brunner's neo-Nazi connections in Europe, and less in his extradition.[17] The Israelis were now completely passive.

Others, however, were more enthusiastic to bring the truth to light. In the early 1980s, several journalists and investigators were able to bring Brunner into the spotlight. Serge Klarsfeld, the famous French Nazi hunter, traveled to Damascus without a visa and was promptly deported, but this provocation generated international headlines. Others entered the country and were able to locate Brunner's apartment on Rue Haddad.[18] Robert Fisk, writing for *The Times Magazine*, was one of the first to witness the security precautions installed after the Mossad's second assassination attempt. The "drab, yellow painted apartment block" was blocked with a "tall, double gate of wrought iron with a list of names." Brunner's name was obviously not included. "Just opposite that undistinguished wrought iron gate," Fisk wrote, "there stands each day a tall young man with a zipped-up black leather jacket and a pistol in his belt. At opposite ends of the street there stand two more security men, one with a sub-machine gun over his right shoulder." Brunner declined Fisk's interview request, conveyed through a neighbor. "I have signed an agreement with the Syrian government," he said, "never to give interviews."[19]

And yet, Brunner could not keep silent for long. In October 1985, a reporter of the German tabloid *Bunte* called on him in his apartment. He found Brunner a bodily wreck, bald and sickly, a glaring, red hole in place of his left eye. He had ceased wearing his plastic eye, it seemed. The latest Mossad assassination attempt did not dampen Brunner's enthusiasm for a healthy lifestyle. According to the *Bunte* reporter, the only books in his library were about medicinal herbs. He kept rabbits on the roof of his mostly empty, sparingly furnished apartment. Every morning at six, the fugitive Nazi, donning a hat and dark glasses, went for a walk in the nearby Sibki (Zenobia) Garden, escorted by his security detail. There he cut some grass for his rabbits and returned home. Occasionally he visited the UAE Embassy to see some Palestinian friends who worked there, to read newspapers and "curse the Jews." Otherwise, his life seemed quite empty. He still had some Syrian friends but longed for German company. The cunning reporter offered him just that.[20]

Somehow, the reporter was able to convince the elderly Nazi to venture out of Damascus with his security guards to the beach in the resort city of Tartus. There, he not only interviewed Brunner, but was able to snatch several quick photos with a hidden camera installed in his wristwatch. "Please write what I say precisely, word by word," Brunner told the reporter, "I am ready to take responsibility before an international court, but Israel will never have me. I will not become a second Eichmann." In his breast pocket, he kept a cyanide capsule. "I have taken care of everything," he said. But apart from his empty promise to give himself over to international justice, Brunner was unrepentant. "My responsibility was to deport the Jews from the various countries" he said, "I don't have any regrets. . . . What happened to them in the East had nothing to do with me. The Federal Republic of Germany owes me a pension."[21]

The authorities in Damascus were infuriated at Brunner's interview in *Bunte*. The Assad regime, after all, had countered repeated extradition requests with stark denials. Now, the interview had awoken old demons. The Justice Ministry in Bonn demanded Brunner's extradition yet again. The Syrians still denied he had ever set foot in their country, but these denials sounded ridiculous. An embarrassed Syrian official asked the German ambassador in Damascus why they hunted Brunner for so long while ignoring Israel's foreign minister Yitzhak Shamir's past as a terrorist. This was ironic, as Shamir was the man who commanded Mossad's first attempt to assassinate Brunner.[22]

By giving interviews to the international press and justifying the Holocaust, Brunner embarrassed his Syrian hosts and presented them as liars. He was warned to keep his mouth shut. Following the interview in *Bunte*, he was also not allowed to venture alone without guards.[23] But in 1986 and 1987, he was nevertheless interviewed twice: once by an Austrian reporter who met him in a laundry shop "behind a curtain," and once on the phone by the American journalist Charles Ashman. In these interviews, he took pride in his exploits and remained unrepentant as ever. "You should thank me," he told the Austrian, "that I made your beautiful Vienna free of Jews." "I do not regret anything and would do it again," Brunner yelled at Ashman on the other side of the phone. The Jews, he said, were "all devil's agents and human garbage."[24] To an Austrian holocaust denier who met him the same year, he purported that the deportation of the Jews was a matter of self-defense. "It would be horrifying," he said, "if Hitler wouldn't have clobbered the nation guilty in two world wars and the death of six million German civilians." And yet, maybe in order to please his visitor who came to collect "evidence" for Holocaust denial, he said that he had heard about the gas chambers "only after the war."[25]

For President Assad and his advisers, Brunner became too noisy, and his disobedience could not be tolerated. Gradually Brunner's security tightened, and his movements were increasingly restricted. An ABC crew who came to Rue Haddad was chased away by armed guards. The station was warned their crews would be jailed if they repeated the attempt. Syrian policemen had reportedly beaten a British press photographer who attempted to snatch an illegal picture. In the late 1980s, Brunner's small apartment was closely guarded by a relatively large detail of twelve soldiers who worked in shifts of 24 hours. The soldiers were dressed in civilian clothes in order not to draw attention and some of them patrolled the neighborhood to intercept unwelcome visitors. The commanders of unit 300 intensified security periodically, whenever Brunner appeared in world headlines. Sometimes he was even forced to move to a cell in the basement of the Mukhabarat station in Muhajirin for a few days.[26] In late 1989, the Mossad briefly considered tricking the Syrians into arresting Brunner by framing him in espionage activity, but this idea was quickly abandoned. Given Brunner's delicate situation at the time, such a plot, if implemented, could have brought him into serious trouble.[27]

In 1987, Brunner asked a German-speaking Syrian boy who was allowed to visit him to write his "testament" in Arabic. The original document is still hidden in a Syrian archive, but the contents were given to the German author Christian Springer by the boy who typed the document, a fact separately confirmed by one of Brunner's guards. It was a lame attempt for historical justification. Brunner wrote that he never intended to kill Jews, only to help them emigrate to Madagascar, and it was the Zionist "world organization" that foiled the plan. The Zionists, not him, were responsible for the plight of the Jews.[28]

At that point, a young Syrian conscript named Muhammad Abdul Rahman Hanada had the rare opportunity to take a close look at Brunner. In 1989, he began working as a bodyguard with unit 300 (counterespionage) of the GID. He was brought to a private apartment, but instead of a Syrian dignitary, he observed a decrepit old man walking around in his underpants, a wreck of a person, his body covered with scars and burns. The man, who presented himself as "Fischer," conversed with his new guard for five minutes. When Hanada, obviously surprised and shocked, asked his commander who the person was and why he was in such terrible state, the young guard was immediately rebuffed. "Don't ask anyone questions, ever," the commander told him sternly, and then implied he might eventually be initiated into the secret. Even Brunner's false name, Fischer, should never be mentioned, especially not on radio communications. Syrian intelligence was well aware that all radio channels and phone lines might be tapped by Israeli, foreign, or Arab intelligence services. Instead, Brunner was known to his guards only as "Abu Hussein."

Hanada occasionally did errands for Brunner, including shopping for daily necessities. Brunner, who heard that his new guard grew up in the Syrian Golan Heights, often asked him to bring edible herbs from his village. "I liked the old man," recalled Hanada, "he led a very healthy lifestyle and didn't eat much except vegetables, milk, fresh cheese and once in a while also meat." Brunner, it seems, was no longer a strict vegetarian as he had once been.

Gone were the daily trips to the Sibki Park. The rabbits also vanished. Brunner spent his days listening to news and classical music and feeding pigeons with crumbs of bread. When Hanada commenced his duty as a member of Brunner's guard detail, the Nazi was only allowed short walks to the supermarket. The neighborhood was full of foreign expats, and Brunner wore dark glasses in order not to draw attention.

The fugitive criminal was still interested in world affairs. Hanada recalled that he had a special radio where he could receive reports not yet released to the public. On October 11, 1989, Brunner was one of the first to hear of the spectacular defection of the Syrian pilot, Bassam Adel, to Israel. This time, he shocked his guards. "Come quickly!" he yelled. "A Syrian pilot defected to Israel. Hafez [al-Assad] has to kill his entire family! He has to kill everyone in his village!" Hanada thought Brunner had gone insane.

Brunner was lonely. The only man allowed to visit him was a Syrian called Nabil, the son of his former chauffeur, who came with his family and brought Brunner clothes, German newspapers, and food. Then even these visits stopped. First the family was kept off-limits, then Nabil himself was told to stay out. Brunner tried to strike up conversations with the guards. Usually, he spoke about his former wife, "the love of his life," or about Saddam Hussein, whom he greatly admired. Only the Iraqi leader, Brunner said, was truly committed to destroying Israel. Brunner also criticized Assad for not expelling all Syrian Jews. One day, he even told the disgusted Hanada, who didn't know anything about the Nazis or the Holocaust before, that he killed 25,000 Jews in France. Gradually, the guards distanced themselves from Brunner, tired of his endless blabber. Sometimes he threatened them with a knife but was easily overpowered.[29]

The proceedings against him in Germany continued grinding slowly forward. In 1984, a new arrest warrant for Brunner was issued in Cologne. Every German chancellor, president, or foreign minister who visited Syria customarily asked about Brunner, only to be brusquely told that there was no such person in the Syrian Arab Republic. The German government now offered 500,000 DM for information leading to Brunner's capture.[30] Some leads crossed the line into outright absurdity. At the end of the 1980s, German investigators

looked into a claim that an elderly Austrian Jew named Alois Fischer, who
lived for decades in Australia, was actually Alois Brunner in disguise. This
investigation, of course, led nowhere, yet another dead end. Later attempts
were no more successful.[31]

In 1990, urged by Serge and Beate Klarsfeld, the East German authorities asked Syria to hand over Brunner to them, but the German Democratic
Republic collapsed shortly afterward. Unified Germany did not agree to pursue
this request as part of a general policy not to respect political and military
treaties signed by the East.[32] A year later, Serge Klarsfeld came again to Syria
in an attempt to bring Brunner yet again to the headlines. He tried to hire a
theater to organize a talk on Nazi criminals, including Brunner, knowing full
well the predictable reaction of the Syrian authorities. The next day he was
met in his hotel lobby by four Syrian policemen, two in uniform and two in
civilian clothes, and was escorted to Damascus International Airport. During
his short stay, a Syrian informant told him that "Georg Fischer" no longer
lived in the governmental apartments on Rue Haddad. He had been escorted
out by the security service in an ambulance. Now he was only a burden. "They
used him to plan their wars," recalled one the guards, "then tossed him away."[33]

In the early 1990s, rumors began to circulate that Brunner was hidden in
Slinfah, a mountainous resort in Latakia Province. A Syrian source, whom the
German embassy defined as "reliable," spotted him in the nearby port city of
Tartus in November 1990.[34] According to one of Brunner's former guards that
was a false rumor, probably circulated in order to mislead potential stalkers. In
fact, Brunner remained in Damascus, where the noose had tightened further
around his neck. Bahjat Suleiman, the director of unit 300, ordered the guards
not to let "Abu Hussein" out for whatever reason, not even to the supermarket.
Brunner, the door slammed in his face, yelled like a trapped animal and cursed
the Syrian president and the commander of his guards: "Hafez, the dog!
Bahjat, the swine!" The improper language was, of course, reported. Brunner
was thrown into a prison cell for a few days, then brought back to his apartment. The commander of unit 300 ordered the guards not to harm him, but
also not do anything to improve his health. President Assad, the guards were
told, waited for "this pig to die of natural causes so Syria can get rid of him."[35]

Finally, in 1996, French president Jacques Chirac visited Syria, and asked
yet again about Brunner. He was rebuffed, of course, but the regime used

this pretext to whisk Brunner out of his apartment into the now-familiar Mukhabarat cell in the basement of Muhajirin station, this time for good. "The door was closed," testified one of the guards, "and never reopened." Brunner spent his last years in a tiny windowless basement cell without sunlight or medical treatment. He had to subsist on military rations and choose every day between either an egg or a potato, one of the two. The guard recalled that he cursed the soldiers, yelled and cried often, but sometimes "gave them advice about their health." He developed a skin disease that covered his entire body. In 2001 he died, and his body was ritually washed and buried in the Al-Afif Cemetery in Damascus. The Muslim funeral was held secretly in the night, and apart from an imam and several guards, nobody was present. "Even an animal should not be treated like that," recalled the guard.[36] The spent criminal ended his life in far worse conditions than any Western state would have given him, and yet, far better than how his Jewish victims were murdered.

EPILOGUE

Ghosts in the Mirror— The Historical Significance of Nazi Mercenaries

*There were words that [once] . . . shook the foundations of heaven
and earth. But there came a day when these same words,
having fallen from their height, were thrown aside, and now people
wallow in them as they chat, as casually as one wallows in grass.*

—HAYIM NAHMAN BIALIK, *REVEALMENT AND CONCEALMENT IN LANGUAGE*[1]

THIS BOOK IS first and foremost about losers, the detritus of history: Nazi Germany, and the numerous individuals who served in its intelligence and security apparatus. The defeat of the Third Reich in 1945 was so decisive, even its adherents had to admit that only a few elements could be salvaged from the flotsam of its heritage. Some, like Gehlen and his associates, picked anti-communism and served the West. The fact that so many adherents of the Third Reich made the same choice explains why numerous Nazis, including nefarious war criminals, integrated into the West German democratic system without nazifying it, as so many observers had feared. But this choice was not universal. Some veterans of Nazi security organizations, like Heinz Felfe, picked anti-Westernism out of Hitler's rubbish heap and pledged secret loyalty to the

Soviet Union. For Alois Brunner, anti-Semitism, hatred of the Jews, was the most important component to adhere to. Most of the fugitive Nazis we wrote about, Höttl, Mast, Beisner, Schaefer, Rademacher, Rauff, Kubainsky, and many others, became the inheritors of the Nazi "Third Way" and saw themselves as uncommitted to any particular superpower or ideology. They spied, trafficked in arms, maneuvered between powers, and crossed boundaries in dangerous zones of the globe, such as the Middle East. In many cases, their loyalties were for sale. In different times, they served the West Germans, the East Germans, the Americans, the French, the Algerian rebels, the Syrians, the Egyptians, and in some cases, even the Israelis.

This book is also about illusions: both the illusions *of* Nazis and illusions *on* Nazis. The Nazi mercenaries dreamt of future greatness. Springer and Remer trafficked in arms and saw themselves as harbingers of Nazi-inspired revolutions across the Third World. Brunner fantasized about spectacular terror attacks, such as the abduction of Nahum Goldmann, that were nothing but wild fantasies no less illusory than his persistent belief in the revival of Nazism. Even Heinz Felfe, who served the Soviets directly, saw himself as an independent adventurer, keen to manipulate great powers to his own advantage. He was, of course, thrown to the wolves by Moscow as soon as he had outlived his usefulness. In the end, like many other "neutrals" in the Cold War, most of these Nazi adventurers were manipulated by the Soviet Union, sometimes directly, like Felfe, Clemens, Tiebel, and Sommer, and sometimes indirectly. Beisner, Brunner, Rademacher, and their fellow OTRACO arms merchants served Moscow in a more circumvented way, perhaps unknowingly. By supplying Algerian revolutionaries with Eastern European weapons, they opened the door for more direct Soviet involvement in Middle Eastern and North African affairs. Hermann Schaefer's activity in Syria was also useful for the Communist Bloc because he participated in the campaign designed to portray West Germany's leaders as former Nazis and the Federal Republic as a Fourth Reich. The word "Nazi" carried such a strong weight in collective memory that any cooperation with people deemed "Nazis" could become a potent propaganda liability in the partisan struggles of the Cold War.

The attitude of other countries and intelligence services toward Nazi fugitives and mercenaries was also based on dangerous illusions. At the beginning of the Cold War, the CIA and other American agencies believed that Hitler's former minions, with their knowledge and expertise, were indispensable in case of an eventual war with the Soviet Union. The Americans knew little about their adversaries and believed the ones most qualified to supply intelligence on the Soviets were Germans who fought them in the recent past. This persistent belief led the American intelligence community to trust dubious Nazi intelligence peddlers such as Wilhelm Höttl, but also Third Reich intelligence professionals like Hermann Baun and Reinhard Gehlen. This marriage of convenience bred the Gehlen Org that later developed into the BND, West Germany's foreign intelligence service.

Reinhard Gehlen, who truly was pro-Western, did a disservice to himself and his political masters, both Americans and West Germans, by behaving as if *all* of his former colleagues from the Nazi intelligence community, including SS, SD, and Gestapo operatives, were genuinely anti-communist and pro-Western. Though comprising only a small fraction of the Gehlen Org and the BND, these people occupied key functions in the organization and led it astray with Nazi fantasies of an omnipotent communist conspiracy. While hunting innocent people, either leftists, former anti-Nazi resistance fighters, or both, Gehlen and his advisers ignored the real source of danger: the community of Nazi intelligence veterans itself. Even those who, unlike Felfe, Clemens, Tiebel, and Sommer, did not spy directly for the Soviets, were still socially connected to former brothers-in-arms who were Soviet agents, thus contaminating the Gehlen Org like a virus infecting a computer network. Both the BND and the CIA paid dearly for these illusions with the multiple disasters caused by Heinz Felfe's treason and espionage. Felfe (along with other moles) not only provided his Soviet employers with an inside picture of Western espionage and counterespionage, he wrecked the BND after he was captured. His discovery led to a political crisis that soured the relationship between the American and West German intelligence communities, corroded Gehlen's political credibility, and contributed to his isolation and downfall.

Gehlen's reliance on National Socialist fugitives abroad, especially in the Middle East, proved no less disastrous. The BND paid dubious war criminals such as Beisner and his OTRACO partners not just to collect intelligence on the Middle East. The goal was to dominate a hefty slice of the arms trade to the Algerian FLN and other Arab states and organizations in order to crowd out the Soviets from the Middle Eastern game. Here, as in other things, Gehlen made a terrible miscalculation. By encouraging arms deliveries to the Algerians, he—along with Beisner—opened the door to more direct Soviet involvement. But at the same time, even more disastrously, he threatened the most basic premises of West German political strategy. The policy of Chancellor Adenauer constituted first and foremost in building a strong Western European alliance between West Germany and France. By comparison, West Germany's interests in the Middle East, certainly in Algeria, were of marginal importance. When Gehlen tacitly supported the arms trade of fugitive Nazis to Algeria, or at least did nothing to stop them, he pushed the French to solve the problem by assassinating these gunrunners on German soil. When the SDECE, the French secret service, almost killed Wilhelm Beisner, the BND frantically tried to silence the investigation, as it could expose the damage it had done to West German policy in Europe.

By targeting German arms merchants on Federal Republic territory, the leaders of the French secret service, Boursicot, Grossin, Mercier, Morlanne, and their colleagues, showed themselves as no less delusional than their German counterparts. As elaborated upon at length throughout this book, the removal of the German intermediaries pushed communist powers, such as the Soviets and the Chinese, even deeper into the Algerian game. Instead of dealing with merchants such as Puchert and Beisner, whose shipments the French could easily curtail, they now faced open shipments from the Soviets and the Chinese that they could do nothing against.

But in a larger sense, the irrational reaction of SDECE to the activity of the German arms merchants betrayed an even more basic truth—that operations, overt or covert, are no substitute to a coherent strategic vision. Already in December 1955, former French defense minister Pierre Koenig stated that "our continued presence or eviction from North Africa will largely depend on the failure or success of [FLN arms procurement] efforts."[2] But this brouhaha covered the fact that France did not have a viable political solution to the Algerian conflict. Instead of developing such a strategy or opting out of Algeria earlier than they did, the French used covert ops to compensate for their strategic disorientation. They achieved only further deterioration of their position in Algeria, tensions with their West German allies, and scorn throughout the international community.[3] The story of Israel's reaction to the problem of the German scientists in Egypt is yet another example of the delusional power that the word "Nazi" had on secret services, states, and governments. Initially, Israel was relatively sanguine about the presence of former Nazis in the Middle East, satisfying itself with cheap and safe covert operations against fugitive criminals such as Alois Brunner. After the rocket experiments in Egypt, however, Israeli policy makers saw the signs of an impending Holocaust. Contrary to all facts and evidence, Isser Harel believed that the presence of German scientists in Egypt—most of them uninfluenced by Nazism or other ideologies—was a sinister Nazi ploy to destroy Israel and exterminate the Jewish people. He even spoke about a revival of Nazism, a totally overblown fear. "He was not, in my opinion, quite sane," related Amos Manor, the chief of the Shin Bet (Israel's domestic security service) at the time. "It was something much more profound than an obsession. You couldn't have a rational conversation about it with him."[4]

But Harel was not alone. Many people in Israel shared his delusions, including political leaders such as Foreign Minister Golda Meir. Prime Minister Ben-Gurion, who saw the relationship with West Germany as one of the most important pillars of Israel's foreign and security policy, failed to restrain his spy chief, who threatened this relationship with reckless assassinations, intimidation operations, and a hysterical press campaign.

The secret cooperation between Israel and France and the methods of assassination once attempted on Alois Brunner were now implemented on a much larger scale. Like a car digging itself deeper in the mud, Mossad operations against the German scientists in late 1962 and early 1963 did not solve the problem but complicated it further. For example, they brought about the disastrous US "mediation" proposal to trade Israel's nuclear ambitions for the Egyptian rockets, practically exchanging gold for dross. Eventually, these complications evolved into a domestic and international crisis that removed both Harel and Ben-Gurion from power. Objectively speaking, it would have been preferable to let the scientists remain in Cairo and spend Egyptian money on useless rockets. "The non-appearance of Egypt's much-heralded secret weapon, the Al Qaher missile, is a sordid take, I regret to say," Egyptian chief of staff Sa'ad el-Shazly later wrote. "Al Qaher had been part of Egyptian folklore since word first leaked in the early 1960s that Egypt had its own short-range ballistic missiles . . . When we lost in 1967, of course, the questions started: 'Where was Al Qaher?' No answers came."[5]

Of all the intelligence and secret service chiefs we reviewed, only Meir Amit, who took over the Mossad after Harel's resignation in 1963, knew how to deal with German mercenaries, and the fears they engendered, as part of a viable political strategy. His covert ops, like the Gideons and the Employment Office, posed credible threats of violence that he skillfully coordinated with achievable political ends. Amit and his prime minister, Levi Eshkol, understood that the German scientists in Egypt, though not an existential threat in and of themselves, posed a constant irritancy to Israel's domestic stability and its relations with both the US and West Germany. The Mossad covert ops under Amit were designed to solve this essentially political problem: no more, no less.

The solution Amit finally latched onto and successfully implemented illustrates that in the secret world, clandestine connections, cultivated over a prolonged period of time, are a necessary companion to both covert ops and formal diplomacy. Indeed, the cooperation of Peres and Amit with Ludwig Bölkow and Franz Josef Strauss reflected a process of sober realistic assessment on both sides. The Israelis understood that spreading horror stories of a "second Holocaust" and accusing West Germany of being an accomplice to "new Nazis" had gotten them nowhere. Trying to force Bonn's hands to enforce legal measures that were difficult, if not impossible, was equally useless. West German influential figures such as Strauss also realized they could no longer ignore the fears of their Israeli counterparts nor the political crisis created by the presence of the scientists in Egypt. Leaving aside their prior hopes to use the mercenary scientists as a source of intelligence and as a leverage of power in the Middle East, they used informal incentives to bring them back home.

As the 1960s progressed, all sides came to understand that German fugitives and mercenaries were not as important as once believed. With Gehlen's marginalization and eventual retirement in 1968, the German intelligence community used them less and less as intelligence sources, and certainly stopped seeing them as "experts in fighting Communism" or agents of influence in the developing world. The French, too, lost interest after the end of the Algerian War. Israel stopped assigning importance to German mercenaries or Nazis in the Middle East, and gradually became tired of hunting Nazi criminals as well. True, Prime Minister Menachem Begin ordered renewed Nazi hunting in 1977, but the Mossad was unenthusiastic, and the period of renewed interest proved short-lived. Walter Rauff died of cancer, Horst Schumann passed away a free man, and Alois Brunner could languish in Damascus a few more years until he was locked away by his Syrian "hosts." In the end, the Nazi fugitives and mercenaries were not important in and of themselves. Their historical significance derived from the illusions that states, governments, and secret services harbored about them, and from the overreaction of these states, governments, and secret services to their existence. Like ghosts in the mirror, they faded into oblivion the moment mesmerized viewers turned their attention elsewhere.

ACKNOWLEDGMENTS

THROUGHOUT WRITING THIS book, I was fortunate to receive the assistance, help, and advice of numerous individuals. I am thankful to all, but especially to the incredible people mentioned below.

First, I would like to thank the witnesses who were gracious enough to grant me interviews. I was lucky to meet Rafi Eitan, the Mossad spymaster and former Israeli cabinet minister, for a fascinating conversation on covert operations shortly before his passing. Oded Gur-Arie, the son of the celebrated Israeli spy Wolfgang Lotz, gave me an interview on the clandestine career and personal life of his father. The anonymous Mossad staffer A., a silent witness to dramatic events, also met me for an illuminating interview. Yossi Chen, the Mossad in-house historian of Nazi hunting, invited me to his home and answered questions I had on his studies. I had the special honor of meeting the French Nazi hunter Serge Klarsfeld in his Paris office. Mr. Klarsfeld not only granted me an interview, but also loaned me invaluable documents from his private archive.

I was happy to gain the acquaintance of investigative journalists who offered tremendous assistance throughout my research. Similarly to historians, the trade of journalists is to create the fabric of a narrative from raw material, assess the reliability of the evidence, and tell fact from fiction. Due to their connections, acumen, and professional experience, they are often able to reach sources inaccessible to academic historians. As a result, I found collaboration with them to be extremely fruitful. Ronen Bergman from the *New York Times* and *Yedioth Ahronoth*, Israel's top investigative journalist for intelligence affairs, graciously allowed me access to materials from his private archives, including interviews with Israeli operatives and policy makers. Yossi Melman and Ofer Aderet from *Haaretz* and Iddo Epstein from *Yedioth Ahronoth* gave me useful contacts and archived articles. Liora Amir-Barmatz and Eyal Tavor, the creators of a documentary on Eli Cohen, helped me with documents and advice on the career of this incredible Israeli spy. Noam Nachman-Tepper, too, shared with me the insights of his research on Eli Cohen, as well as his interpretation of key CIA documents and transcripts from Israeli archives. David Witzthum from Israeli TV's Channel 1 clarified important points on Israeli-German relations.

From Germany, I am deeply grateful to Klaus Wiegrefe, the investigative reporter of *Der Spiegel* on contemporary history. Mr. Wiegrefe hosted me in the Hamburg headquarters of his news magazine, gave invaluable advice, and allowed me to read documents that opened new paths of research. His own articles on Nazi fugitives and intelligence history were a model of how such things are done. Christian Springer, a political comedian and astoundingly bold investigator, entered the lion's den of Damascus to follow the trail of fugitive Nazi Alois Brunner. He, too, shared interviews and information that he obtained with considerable risk. I am grateful to him and his assistant, Sina Schweikle, for their generosity during my stay in Munich. Esther Schapira and Georg Haffner, who wrote the first groundbreaking work on Brunner in German, also gave me access to their personal collection, the result of years of field investigations.

Hedi Aouidj, an investigative journalist from Bordeaux, shared the interviews he made with Brunner's Syrian bodyguards, whom he was able to locate in Jordanian refugee camps. Mr. Aouidj's original thinking, intellectual curiosity, and precious insights opened new scholarly avenues for me. Susanna Wallsten and Eric Ericson, Swedish documentary creators and two of the most charming and generous researchers I have ever met, gave me access to interviews they had made with people in Brunner's Damascus circle, including the notorious terrorist Carlos "The Jackal." Erich Schmidt-Eenboom, a top-notch investigative journalist of German intelligence, generously gave me documents from his private collection. Shraga Eilam-Sündermann advised me on the collaboration between Israeli intelligence and the Nazi fugitive criminal Walter Rauff. I am grateful to all of these journalists for long conversations by phone, as well as in their homes, apartments, and memorable restaurants and cafés. Thank you for the ambience, generosity, and fruitful exchange of information.

I am also grateful to my fellow historians who made this work possible with professional help and advice. Shlomo Shpiro, Yaacov Falkov, and Dan Diner, my colleagues from Bar Ilan University, Tel Aviv University, and the Hebrew University of Jerusalem, helped decipher the context of Israeli-German intelligence relations, Soviet Cold War operations, and West German politics, respectively. Prof. Shpiro also helped me to obtain a precious primary source from Germany. My dear friend Or Rabinowitz-Batz, also a colleague in the Hebrew University of Jerusalem, answered numerous questions on rockets and nuclear issues, her field of expertise. David Motadel, an expert on the relations between Nazi Germany and the Muslim world, generously sent me Arabic-language books and memoirs.

Again in Germany, I was fortunate to meet Gerhard Sälter for a long conversation in a Berlin beer garden. A member of the independent commission of historians of the BND (The German Federal Intelligence Service), Dr. Sälter gave me invaluable insights on the postwar careers of Nazi criminals in West German intelligence, as well as on the best ways of gaining access to German intelligence archives. Norman Ohler, a highly original and innovative historian, helped obtain a rare Syrian book that was of great help. Susanne Meinl shared her expertise on Friedrich Wilhelm Heinz, an anti-Nazi resistance fighter and one of West Germany's early and forgotten intelligence chiefs. She also helped contact Magnus Pahl from the Bundeswehr Museum in Dresden, who graciously gave me access to the papers of the German intelligence peddler Heinrich Mast. Irmtrud Wojak, the accomplished biographer of Fritz Bauer, met me several times in Germany and Israel and illuminated the career of this outstanding jurist and Nazi hunter.

Fabian Hinz, whom I met by sheer chance in the Vienna Wiesenthal Archives, shared his collection of documents and impressive research on the Egyptian rocket program in the early 1960s. Eyal Zisser and Meir Zamir, experts in Syrian and Middle Eastern politics, were generous enough to answer my questions personally and by mail, and refer me to important sources. Benjamin Carter Hett, Michael Walla, and Wolfgang Krieger, noted experts to the history of modern German intelligence, received me for conversations, answered my inquiries, and illuminated key points that were unclear to me. Ulrike Becker, an expert on German-Egyptian relations, gave me important ideas and shared rare documents. One conversation with Thomas Boghardt on the Gehlen Organization and the CIA was equivalent to three months of reading dossiers and documents. Both he and Francesco Cacciatore, important scholars of postwar American intelligence, shared insights, ideas, and sources, as well as their own studies. Yuval Ron gave me documents from the Ben-Gurion

Archives in Sde Boker, Israel. I am grateful to Thomas Riegler for sending me his work on Otto Skorzeny and the Austrian rocket experts in Egypt.

I would also like to thank my talented research assistants. My student Cher Lingord helped with interviews in Israel. Atar David combed through Arabic-language memoirs, interviews, and documents, while Sybille Duhautois and Michal Schatz—two well-informed historians of modern France—performed extremely useful research in archives throughout that country. Rebekka Windus helped decipher the difficult German handwriting of BND agents. Noam Lefler, Anna Wilson, and Alexandra Bloch-Pfister researched British and German archives when the COVID-19 pandemic prevented me from traveling. My dear friend Lina Dakheel clarified obscure points on life, society, and street geography in Damascus.

I could not have written this book but for the help of numerous staff members in archives and libraries throughout Israel, Germany, Austria, France, the United States, and other countries. I owe them all deep gratitude. Especially, I would like to thank the nameless researchers in the BND archives who guided me into their labyrinthian holdings, often exceeding their duty in their readiness to advise and assist. I owe an equally enormous debt to Shoshi Golan from the Israeli prime minister's office and to the officials in the Mossad History Department, who granted me unprecedented access to materials of Israel's foreign intelligence agency. In the Vienna archives of the Nazi hunter Simon Wiesenthal, René Bienert received me with great warmth and helped find the right documents in this enormous collection. I am also thankful to Johannes Beermann for giving me access to the archives of the Fritz Bauer Institute in Frankfurt. The Staff of the BfV (Germany's Domestic Security Service) and Stasi Archives in Berlin, the Main State Archives in Bavaria, the Ben-Gurion Archives, the IDF (Israeli Defense Forces) Archives, and the Israeli State Archives also eased my access to their collections, including documents that were previously restricted. In this respect, I am grateful to the officials of the German Federal Justice Ministry, who authorized my access to several classified files.

It is my pleasurable duty to thank the Azrieli Foundation and the Truman Institute for the Advancement of Peace at the Hebrew University of Jerusalem, as well as the university's Fund for Scientific Exchange, for their generous financial help. My wonderful agent, Andrew Lownie, played, as usual, an enormous role in the publication of this book. Without Jonathan Boxman, a masterful editor, it would never have been publishable.

And finally, as always, I would like to thank my parents, Lili and Shmuel Orbach, and my brother Gideon for their support, help, and advice. Above all, my deepest gratitude to my dear wife, Adi, for her boundless love and support. Without you, none of this could have happened.

LIST OF ABBREVIATIONS

BA-AL—Bundesarchiv—Aussenstelle Ludwigsburg

BA-K—Bundesarchiv Koblenz

BAR—Schweizerisches Bundesarchiv

BHSA—Bayerisches Hauptstaatsarchiv

BfV—Bundesamt für Verfassungsschutz (Federal Office for the Protection of the Constitution)

BStU—Bundesbeauftragter für die Unterlagen des Staatssicherheitsdienstes der ehemaligen Deutschen Demokratischen Republik

FRG—Federal Republic of Germany

GDR—German Democratic Republic

HHStA—Hessisches Hauptstaatsarchiv

NARA—National Archives and Records Administration, Washington, D.C.

PA-AA—Politisches Archiv des Auswärtigen Amts, Berlin

SAB—Staatsarchiv Bamberg

SKPA—Serge Klarsfeld Private Archive

VWA-SWA—Vienna Wiesenthal Archive, Simon Wiesenthal Archive

BIBLIOGRAPHY

ARCHIVES

Bayerisches Hauptstaatsarchiv

Ben-Gurion Archive, Ben-Gurion Institute for the Study of Israel and Zionism, Sde Boker, Israel

Bundesbeauftragter für die Unterlagen des Staatssicherheitsdienstes der ehemaligen Deutschen Demokratischen Republik (BStU, Stasi Archive)

BfV Archive, Berlin

BND Archive, Berlin

Bundesarchiv – Aussenstelle Ludwigsburg

Bundesarchiv Koblenz

CREST: 25-Year Program Archive of the Central Intelligence Agency (CIA), Name Files, https://www.cia.gov/library/readingroom/search/site/black?page=2326 (last accessed: 31.12.2020)

Albert Ludwig Name File

Beisner Wilhelm (Beissner Friedrich Wilhelm) Name File

Brunner Alois Name File

Clemens Hans Name File

Mast Heinrich Name File

Rademacher Franz Name File

Rechenberg Hans Name File

Skorzeny Otto Name File

Dayan Center Arabic Language Press Archive, Tel Aviv University

Diplomatic Archives of Japan (Gaikō Shiryōkan), Tokyo

Fritz Bauer Institute, Frankfurt

Haifa Municipal Archives, Haifa, Israel – David Even-Pinnah Papers, file 1450

Hessisches Hauptstaatsarchiv, Munich

IDF Archives, Tel ha-Shomer, Israel

Israeli State Archives, Jerusalem

Mossad Archives, Tel Aviv

National Archives and Records Administration, Washington, D.C.

Politisches Archiv des Auswärtigen Amts, Berlin

Schweizerisches Bundesarchiv, Bern

Service Historique de la Défense (SHD), Vincennes

Staatsarchiv Bamberg

Stasi Archive (see Bundesbeauftragter)

Vienna Wiesenthal Archive, Simon Wiesenthal Archive, Vienna

Yad Vashem Archives, Jerusalem

INTERVIEWS (CONDUCTED BY THE AUTHOR)

Chen, Yossi, 4.3.2018, Ramat Hasharon, Israel.

Eitan, Rafi, 19.3.2018, Tel Aviv, Israel (with the assistance of Cher Lingord).

Gur-Arie, Oded, 11.12.2020 (Zoom interview).

Klarsfeld, Serge, 3.8.2018, Paris, France.

Mossad Staffer (anonymous), 15.11.2018, a location in central Israel.

INTERVIEWS (CONDUCTED BY OTHER AUTHORS)

Abu Ra'ad, 15.10.2016, by Hedi Aouidj, courtesy of Hedi Aouidj, Hedi Aouidj Private Archive.

Abu Yaman, October 2016, by Hedi Aouidj, courtesy of Hedi Aouidj, Hedi Aouidj Private Archive.

Amit, Meir, 2006, by Ronen Bergman, courtesy of Ronen Bergman.

Eitan, Rafi, 19.2.2006, by Ronen Bergman, courtesy of Ronen Bergman.

Hanada, Abdul Rahman (recorded interview), 20.5.2020, by Susanna Wallsten and Eric Ericson, courtesy of Susanna Wallsten.

Hidscho, Mohammed, 2001, by Christian Springer, Brunner name file, Christian Springer Personal Collection.

Peres, Shimon, 19.9.2012, by Ronen Bergman, courtesy of Ronen Bergman.

PUBLISHED AND TELEVISED INTERVIEWS

Hafez, Amin, by Ahmad Mansour, "Shahed ala al-asr", 19.6.2001, *Al-Jazeera*, minutes 9:30–11:30. https://www.youtube.com/watch?v=szSPmeeEa_Q, last accessed 23.11.2020.

Halaf, Gedalia, "Be-einei ha-maf'il", by Avi Shilon and Ela Florsheim, *Tchelet*, vol. 21 (autumn 2005).

Peres, Shimon, in the documentary "Der Mossad, Die Nazis und die Racketen: Showdown am Nil" (creators: Ronen Bergman and Kersten Schüssler), min. 31–32.

Shamir, Yitzhak, *Mabat Malam*, vol. 19 (July 1998).

Suidani Ahmad and an anonymous Syrian Mukhabarat officer, by Zoheir al-Mardini, *Al Usbu'u al-Arabi*, 3.3.1965.

Vitali V. Korotkov (Alfred), *Sputnik*, 9.11.2019.

Vitali V. Korotkow [Korotkov], *Berliner Zeitung*, 3.11.1993.

NEWSPAPERS AND MAGAZINES

Al-Ba'ath (Damascus)

Allgemeine Jüdische Wochenzeitung

Al-Hayat (London)

Al-Jumhur (Damascus)

Al Usbu'u al-Arabi

Berliner Zeitung

Bunte

Chicago Sun Times

Davar

Der Blick

Der Morgen

Der Spiegel

Die Zeit

El Watan (Algeria)

Frankfurter Allgemeine Zeitung

Haaretz

Illustrierte Kristall

Journal of Commerce

L'Aurore

L'Orient (Beirut)

Le Soir (Beirut)

Neue Zürcher Zeitung

Profil (Vienna)

Saturday Evening Post

Sputnik

Süddeutsche Zeitung

Spiegel International

The Times

Wochenpresse

Yedioth Ahronot

UNPUBLISHED PRIMARY SOURCES

Ben-Gurion Diary, Ben-Gurion Archive, Ben-Gurion Institute for the Study of Israel and Zionism, Sde Boker, Israel.

Chen, Yossi, *Ha-mirdaf aharei poshe'i milhama Nazim* (internal Mossad study, declassified in 2014), 3 vols., Yad Vashem Archives.

Chen, Mossad Report: Nazi Hunting, see: Chen, Yossi, *Ha-Mirdaf.*

CIA Felfe Damage Assessment, see: "Felfe, Heinz: Damage Assessment."

Cohen Eli, Trial Transcript, Arabic original, serialized in *Al-Ba'ath* (Damascus, March 1965).

———Hebrew version of the transcript, IDF Archives, Tel ha-Shomer, Israel (courtesy of Noam Nachman-Tepper).

Deutscher Bundestag, 18. Wahlperiode, "Antwort der Bundesregierung auf die kleine Anfrage der Abgeordneten Jan Korte, Sevim Dağdelen, Ulla Jelpke, weiterer Abgeordneter und der Fraktion Die Linke," Drucksache 18/3599, 20.1.2015.

"Felfe, Heinz: Damage Assessment", RG 263, CIA Subject Files, Second Release, Box 1, National Archives and Records Administration, Washington, D.C.

Eichmann Adolf, Trial Protocol, vol.4, defense appeal to the supreme court, pp.1986, 2058, 2086, Israeli Justice Ministry, https://www.justice.gov.il/Subjects/EichmannWritten/volume/Psk_din.pdf (last accessed, 22.12.2020).

Heinrich Mast Papers, Bundeswehr Military History Museum, Dresden.

Heinz Denko-Herre Diary, 13.6.1949, pp. 8–9, James H. Critchfield Papers, Box 5, Special Collections Research Center, Swem Library, College of William & Mary.

Herre Diary (see Heinz Denko-Herre Diary).

"KGB Exploitation of Heinz Felfe: Successful KGB Penetration of a Western Intelligence Service," March 1969, National Archives and Records Administration, Washington, D.C., RG 263, CIA Subject Files, Second Release, Box 1.

KGB-Felfe Documents, James H. Critchfield Papers, Box 5, Special Collections Research Center, Swem Library, College of William & Mary.

Mitrokhin Papers (see: Papers of Vasiliy Mitrokhin).

Mossad Report: German Scientists, see: "Parashat ha-mad'anim ha-Germanim."

Papers of Vasiliy Mitrokhin (1922–2004), MITN 2/24 K24 (Near East and Middle East) Churchill College Archives, Cambridge, UK.

"Parashat ha-mad'anim ha-Germanim," internal Mossad study, Mossad Archive.

Scherer, E. W., Valentin, H. (Hermann), "Racketen, Forscher und Agenten: Anschlag auf Kleinwächter," *Die Rheinpfalz*, no. 239, 18.10.1973.

———"Racketen, Forscher und Agenten: Ein interessanter Telefonanruf," *Die Rheinpfalz*, no. 243, 18.10.1973.

"Waffenhandel: Springer-Remer Bericht," 15.9.1961, folder 101.439, BND Archive.

PRIVATE COLLECTIONS AND COMMUNICATIONS

Elam, Shraga—Collection of CIA documents on Walther Rauff.

"Farid" (alias) to Abraham Cohen (undated), courtesy of Eyal Tavor and Liora Amir-Barmatz.

Hedi Aouidj's Private Archive.

Klarsfeld, Serge, Private Archive, Paris.

Mast, Heinrich, Papers (not in the official collection)—Courtesy of Erich Schmidt-Eenboom.

Meidan, Rafi, Memoirs (unpublished—Courtesy of Ronen Bergman).

Schaefer, Hermann—Testimony on Brunner (private communication, anonymous source).

Rademacher, Franz—Testimony, "Zeugen-Vernehmung in der Untersuchung gegen Brunner Alois, Zentrale Stelle Ludwigsburg," 6.2.1968 (private communication, anonymous source).

Rademacher's testimony—Zentrale Stelle Ludwigsburg (see: Rademacher, Franz—Testimony).

Schapira-Haffner Collection, folder 1/b, Fritz Bauer Institute, Frankfurt.

Springer, Christian, Brunner Name File, Personal Collection.

"The Egyptian Project for the Development and Production of Surface-to-Surface Missiles," Mossad Document, undated, according to context—from 1964, courtesy of Ronen Bergman.

MEMOIRS AND PUBLISHED PRIMARY SOURCES

Adenauer, Konrad, *Erinnerungen: 1945–1953* (Stuttgart: Deutsche Verlags-Anstalt, 1980).

Amit, Meir, *Rosh be-Rosh: Mabat ishi al eru'im gedolim ve-parashot alumot* (Tel Aviv: Hed Artsi, 1999).

Brandner, Ferdinand, *Ein Leben zwischen Fronten: Ingenieur im Schussfeld der Weltpolitik* (München: Verlag Welsermühl, 1973).

Critchfield, James H., *Partners at the Creation: The Men Behind Postwar Germany's Defense and Intelligence Establishments* (Annapolis, Md.: Naval Institute Press, 2003).

Dhali, Salah a-Din, *Ḥaqāʾiq lam tunshar ʿan al-jāsūs al-Ṣahyūnī Īlī Kūhīn wa-qiṣṣatihi al-ḥaqīqīyah* (Damascus, 2001).

Felfe, Heinz, *Im Dienst des Gegners: 10 Jahre Moskaus Mann im BND* (Hamburg: Rasch und Röhring, 1986).

Gehlen, Reinhard, *Der Dienst: Erinnerungen, 1942–1971* (Wiesbaden: Hase & Koehler Verlag, 1971).

Harel, Isser, *Mashber Ha-madʾanim Ha-Germanin, 1962–1963* (Tel Aviv: Sifriyat Maariv, 1982).

Heikal, Mohamed Hassanein, *The Cairo Documents: The Inside Story of Nasser and his Relationship with World Leaders, Rebels and Statesmen* (New York: Doubleday & Company Inc., 1973).

Klemperer, Victor, *I Will Bear Witness: A Diary of the Nazi Years, 1942–1945*, trans. Martin Chalmers (New York: Modern Library, 2001).

Lawler, Daniel J., and Mahan, Erin R., eds., *Foreign Relations of the United States, 1961–1963* (Washington D.C.: Government Printing Office, 2010), vol. 18. Near East, 1962–1963.

Lotz, Naomi, Eliezer Karmi, *Habiti Leʾahor, Naomi: Sipura shel eshet meragel* (Tel Aviv: Boostan, 1978).

Lotz, Wolfgang, *The Champagne Spy: Israel's Master Spy Tells His Story* (London: Valentine, Mitchell & Co. LTD, 1972).

Nollau, Günther, *Das Amt: 50 Jahre Zeuge der Geschichte* (München: C. Bertelsmann Verlag, 1978).

Peres, Shimon, *Kela David* (Tel Aviv: Weidenfeld and Nicholson, 1969).

Ruffner, Kevin C., ed., *Forging an Intelligence Partnership: CIA and the Origins of the BND, 1945–1949*, (Washington, D.C.: CIA History Staff, Center for the Study of Intelligence, 1999).

Shazly, Saad, *The Crossing of the Suez* (San Francisco: American Mideast Research, 1980).

Shu'aybi, Fauzi, *Shahed min al-Mukhabarat Al-Suriya* (Beirut: Riad Al-Ris, 2018).

Soller-Krug, Beate and Krug, Kaj Rüdiger, *Am Ufer des Nils: Unser Vater 'Raketen-Krug' und der Mossad* (Stuttgart: LangenMüller, 2018).

Strauss, Franz Josef, *Die Erinnerungen* (Berlin: Sieler, 1989).

PRESS AND MAGAZINE ARTICLES

Aouidj, Hedi, and Mathieu Palain, "Die Assads und ihr Nazi: SS Hauptstrumführer Alois Brunner beriet Syriens Folterdiktatur," translation from French: Irma Wehrli, *Reportage*, vol. 33 (March 2017).

———"Le Nazi de Damas," *Revue XXI*, vol. 37, Winter 2017.

Abdessemed, Aïssa, "Georg Puchert—mort pour l'Algérie," *El Watan*, 13.7.2005.

"Ben-Gal: 'Schweizer Korrekt'," *Der Blick*, 14.6.1963.

"Bombe in der Blütenstrasse," *Der Spiegel*, 26.10.1960.

De Gramont, Sanche, "Nasser's Hired Germans," *Saturday Evening Post*, 28.7.1963.

"Der Killer," *Der Spiegel*, 25.3.1959.

"Der Prozess gegen die israelischen Agenten," *Neue Zürcher Zeitung*, 14.6.1963.

"Dr. Beisners Rolle im Krieg," *Frankfurter Algemeine Zeitung*, 21.10.1960.

"Dr. Joklik hat auf mich geschossen," *Der Blick*, no. 117, 20.5.1963.

"Eichmanns Rechte Hand: Das ist Alois Brunner, der Mörder von 125,000 Juden," *Bunte*, vol. 45, 30.10.1985.

"Ein Mann mit Namen Seidenschnur," *Die Zeit*, vol. 40 (1965).

"Er ist, was er war: Ein Feind der Juden," *Bunte* vol. 46, 7.11.1985.

"Felfe: Umarmt und geküsst," *Der Spiegel*, vol. 30 (1963).

Fisk, Robert, "Syrian Bodyguards for Torturer who was Eichmann's Assistant," *The Times*, 17.3.1983.

Freihofner, Gerald, "Eichmanns Rechte Hand," *Wochenpresse*, vol. 49, no. 25, 1988.

"Qui est Georg Fischer?", *Le Soir* (Beirut), 2.11.1961.

Riegler, Thomas, "Eine typische Landsknechtnatur—Otto Skorzeny," *Profil*, vol. 35 (2013).

Schaefer, Hermann, "Die Geisterbotschafts Heinrich Himmerls," *Afro-Asia* (November 1961).

"Sprengstoff-Attentat in Schwabing," *Süddeutsche Zeitung*, 17.10.1960.

"Springer-Prozess: Schrott in Kisten," *Der Spiegel*, 25.12.1963.

"Taube Ohren in Damascus," *Allgemeine Jüdische Wochenzeitung*, 30.1.1987.

Vasek, Thomas, "Der Mann in Damascus," *Profil*, vol. 34, no. 17 (August 1998).

Wiegrefe, Klaus, "BND Vernichtete Akten zu SS-Verbrecher Brunner," *Der Spiegel*, 20.7.2011.

———"West Germany's Efforts to influence the Eichmann Trial," *Spiegel International*, 15.4.2011.

Weitz, Yechiam, "Ben-Gurion also used the Holocaust," *Haaretz*, 30.10.2013.

Willbrand, Jürgen, "Und nichts dazu gelernt," *Illustrierte Kristall*, September 1960.

SECONDARY LITERATURE

Andrew, Christopher, *The World Was Going Our Way: The KGB and the Battle for the Third World* (New York: Basic Books, 2005).

Bar Zohar, Michael, *Phoenix: Shimon Peres and the Secret History of Israel* (New York: West 26th Street Press, 2016).

———*Ben-Gurion* (Tel Aviv: Am Oved, 1977).

———*Tseid Ha-mad'anim ha-Germanim* (Schocken: Tel Aviv, 1965).

Beevor, Anthony, *The Fall of Berlin* (New York: Penguin Group, 2003).

Ben Redjeb, Badis, "The Gehlen Organization, Nazis and the Middle East", Journal of Intelligence History, vol.18, no. 2 (June, 2019).

Bergman, Ronen, *Rise and Kill First: The Secret History of Israel's Targeted Assassinations* (New York: Random House).

Biermann, Werner, *Konrad Adenauer: Ein Jahrhundertleben* (Berlin: Rowohlt, 2017).

Boghardt, Thomas, "Dirty Work: The Use of Nazi Informants by U.S. Army Intelligence in Postwar Europe," *The Journal of Military History* 79 (April 2015).

Breyer, Wolfgang, "Dr. Max Merten—ein Militärbeamter der deutschen Wehrmacht im Spannungsfeld zwischen Legende und Wahrheit," (PhD dissertation, Mannheim University, 2003, unpublished).

Bülow, Mathilde von, "Myth or Reality? The Red Hand and French Covert Action in Federal Germany during the Algerian War, 1956–61," *Intelligence and National Security*, vol. 22, no. 6 (June 2018).

———— *West Germany, Cold-War Europe and the Algerian War* (Cambridge: Cambridge University Press, 2016).

Cacciatore, Francesco A., "Their Need was Great: Émigrés and Anglo-American Intelligence Operations in the Early Cold War," PhD thesis, University of Westminster (Submitted on March 2018, unpublished).

Chen, Chern, "Former Nazi Officers in the Near East: German Military Advisors in Syria, 1949–56," *The International History Review*, vol. 40, issue no. 4 (2018).

Cohen, Avner, *Israel and the Bomb* (New York: Columbia University Press, 1998).

Connelly, Matthew, *A Diplomatic Revolution: Algeria's Fight for Independence and the Origins of the Post-Cold War Era* (Oxford: Oxford University Press, 2003).

Cookridge, E. H., *Gehlen: Spy of the Century* (London: Hodder and Stoughton, 1971).

Cüppers, Martin, *Walther Rauff in Deutschen Diensten: vom Naziverbrecher zum BND-Spion* (Darmstadt: WBG, 2013).

Daly-Groves, Luke, "Control not Morality? Explaining the Selective Employment of Nazi War Criminals by British and American Intelligence Agencies in Occupied Germany," *Intelligence and National Security*, vol. 35, no. 3 (April 2020).

Dan, Uri, and Ben Porat, Yeshayahu, *Ha-meragel she-ba me-Israel: parashat Eli Cohen* (Ramat Gan: Masada, 1968).

Deck, Mikkel, "Crimes committed by Soviet Soldiers against German Civilians, 1944-1945: A Historiographical Analysis," *Journal of Military and Strategic Studies*, vol. 10, issue 4 (Summer 2008).

Deutschkron, Inge, *Bonn and Jerusalem: The Strange Coalition* (Philadelphia: Chilton Book Company, 1970).

Douglas, R. M., *Orderly and Humane: The Expulsion of the Germans after the Second World War* (New Haven, Conn.: Yale University Press, 2012).

Dülffer, Jost, *Geheimdienst in der Krise: Der BND in der 1960er-Jahren* (Berlin: Ch. Verlag, 2018).

Elzer, Herbert, "Deutsche Militärberater in Ägypten: Wilhelm Voss, General Fahrmbacher und die Bundesregierung 1951–1955," *Historische Mitteilungen* vol. 24 (2011).

Engelmann, Bernt, *The Weapons Merchants*, trans. Erica Detto (New York: Crown Publishers, 1968).

Faligot, Roger, and Pascal Krop, *La Piscine: The French Secret Service since 1944*, trans. W. D. Halls (Oxford: B. Blackwell, 1989).

Felstiner, Mary, "Commandant of Drancy: Alois Brunner and the Jews of France," *Holocaust and Genocide Studies* 2:1 (1987).

Franceschini, Christoph, Erich Schmidt-Eenboom, Thomas Wegener-Friis, *Spionage unter Freunden: Partnerdienstbeziehungen und Westaufklärung der Organisation Gehlen und des BND* (Berlin: Chr. Links Verlag, 2017).

Goda, Norman J. W., "The Gehlen Organization and the Heinz Felfe Case: The SD, the KGB, and West German Counterintelligence," in David A. Messenger and Katrin Paehler, eds., *A Nazi Past: Recasting German Identity in Postwar Europe* (Lexington: University Press of Kentucky, 2015).

———"Tracking the Red Orchestra: Allied Intelligence, Soviet Spies, Nazi Criminals," in Richard Breitman, Norman Goda et al., eds. *U.S. Intelligence and the Nazis* (Washington, D.C.: National Archives; New York: Cambridge University Press, 2005).

———"The Nazi Peddler: Wilhelm Höttl and Allied Intelligence," in Richard Breitman, Norman Goda et al., eds. *U.S. Intelligence and the Nazis* (Washington, D.C.: National Archives, New York: Cambridge University Press, 2005).

Guttstadt, Cory, *Turkey, the Jews and the Holocaust* (Cambridge: Cambridge University Press, 2017).

Hachmeister, Lutz, Friedemann Siering, Michael Wildt, *Die Herren Journalisten: Die Elite der deutschen Presse nach 1945* (München: Becksche Reihe, 2002).

Hafner, Georg M. and Esther Schapira, *Die Akte Alois Brunner: Warum einer der grössten Naziverbrecher noch immer auf freiem Fuss ist* (Frankfurt am Main/New York: Campus, 2000).

Hagemann, Albrecht, *Hermann Rauschning: Ein deutsches Leben zwischen NS-Ruhm und Exil* (Köln: Böhlau Verlag, 2018).

Haidinger, Martin, *Wilhelm Höttl: Spion für Hitler und die USA* (Wien: Ueberreuter, 2019).

Hechelhammer, Bodo, *Spion ohne Grenzen: Heinz Felfe—Agent in Sieben Geheimdiensten* (München: Piper, 2019).

———*Doppelagent Heinz Felfe entdeckt Amerika: Der BND, Die CIA und eine geheime Reise im Jahr 1956* (Paderborn: Ferdinand Schöningh, 2017).

———"KGB-Spione aus Dresden: Der Verratsfall Heinz Felfe," in Magnus Pahl, Gorch Pieken and Mathias Rogg, eds., *Achtung Spione! Geheimdienste in Deutschland von 1945 bis 1956* (Dresden: Sandstein Verlag, 2016).

Hechelhammer Bodo et al., eds., "Walther Rauff und der Bundesnachrichtend-ienst," in *Mitteilungen der Forschungs- und Arbeitsgruppe 'Geschichte der BND'*, no. 2 (September 2011).

Heidenreich, Ronny, Daniela Munkel, Elke Stadelmann-Wenz, *Geheimdienstkrieg in Deutschland: Die Konfrontation von DDR-Staatssicherheit und die Organisation Gehlen 1953* (Berlin: Ch. Links Verlag, 2016).

Henschke, Ekkehard, *Rosenbergs Elite und ihr Nachleben: Akademiker im Dritten Reich und nach 1945* (Köln: Böhlau Verlag, 2021).

Herman, Ora, *Ha-kivshan ve-ha-koor: me-ahorei he-kela'im shel mishpat Eichmann* (Tel Aviv: Hakibbutz Hameuchad, 2017).

Hett, Benjamin C., Michael Wala, *Otto John: Patriot oder Verräter: eine deutsche Biographie* (Hamburg: Rohwolt, 2019).

Horne, Alistair, *A Savage War of Peace: Algeria 1954–1962* (New York: New York Review Books, 2012).

Howard, Roger, *Operation Damocles: Israel's Secret War against Hitler's Scientists, 1951–1967* (New York: Pegasus Books, 2013).

Human Rights Watch, Report, "If the Dead Could Speak: Mass Deaths and Torture in Syria's Detention Facilities," (December 2015).

Jankowski, James, "The View from the Embassy: British Assessments of Egyptian Attitudes during World War II" in Israel Gershoni, ed., *Arab Responses to Fascism and Nazism: Attraction and Repulsion* (Austin, Tx.: The University of Texas Press, 2014).

Jelinek, Yeshayahu, *Israel und Deutschland, 1945–1965: Ein neurotisches Verhältnis* (München: Oldenbourg, 2004).

Jesse, Eckhard, "Biographisches Porträt: Otto Ernst Remer" in Uwe Backes and Eckhard Jesse, eds, *Jahrbuch Extermismus & Demokratie*, vol. 6 (Bonn: Bouvier Verlag, 1994).

Joffe, Josef, "Reflections on German Policy in the Middle East," in Shahram Chubin, ed., *Germany and the Middle East* (New York: St. Martin's Press, 1992).

Katz, Shmuel, *Soldier Spies: Israeli Military Intelligence* (Novato, Calif.: Presidio Press, 1992).

Krieger, Wolfgang, *Partnerdiense: Die Beziehungen des BND zu den Westlichen Geheimdiensten 1946-1958* (Berlin: Ch. Links Verlag, 2021).

Kulish, Nicholas, Souad Mekhennet, *The Eternal Nazi: From Mauthausen to Cairo, The Relentless Pursuit of SS Doctor Aribert Heim* (New York: Doubleday, 2014).

Krieger, Wolfgang, ed., *Die Auslandsaufklärung des BND: Operationen, Analysen, Netzwerke* (Berlin: Ch. Links Verlag, 2021).

Lemke, Michael, "Kampagnen gegen Bonn: die Systemkrise der DDR und die West-Propaganda der SED 1960–1963," *Vierteljahrshefte für Zeitgeschichte*, vol. 41, no. 2 (1993).

Lommatzsch, Erik, *Hans Globke (1898–1973): Beamter im Dritten Reich und Staatssekretär Adenauers* (Frankfurt am Main: Campus Verlag, 2009).

Long, Gerry, "Auftragstaktik: A Case Study: France 1940—Understanding the Mission Command in the Training of Soldiers," in Donald Vandergrif and Stephen Werber, eds., *Mission Command: The Who, What, Where, When and Why: An Anthology* (Kabul: 2017).

Marwecki, Daniel, *Germany and Israel: Whitewashing and Statebuilding* (London: C. Hurst & Co., 2020).

Mazower, Mark, *Hitler's Empire: Nazi Rule in Occupied Europe* (London: Allen Lane, Penguin Group, 2008).

Meinl, Susanne, "David gegen Goliath: Der Friedrich-Wilhelm-Heinz-Dienst und die Organisation Gehlen," in Magnus Pahl, Gorch Pieken and Mathias Rogg, ed., *Achtung Spione! Geheimdienste in Deutschland von 1945 bis 1956* (Dresden: Sandstein Verlag, 2016).

Möller, Horst, *Franz Josef Strauss: Herrscher und Rebell* (München: Piper, 2015).

Motadel, David, *Islam and Nazi Germany's War* (Cambridge, Mass.: The Belknap Press of Harvard University Press, 2014).

Moubayed, Sami M., *Damascus between Democracy and Dictatorship* (Lanham, Md.: University Press of America, 2000).

Müller, Rolf-Dieter, *Reinhard Gehlen: Geheimdienstchef im Hintergrund der Bonner Republik* (Berlin: Ch. Links Verlag, 2017), 2 vols.

Müller-Enbergs, Helmut, "Die 'Konzentrierten Schläge der DDR-Staatssicherheit gegen die Organisation Gehlen," in Magnus Pahl, Gorch Pieken and Mathias Rogg, ed., *Achtung Spione! Geheimdienste in Deutschland von 1945 bis 1956* (Dresden: Sandstein Verlag, 2016).

Murphey, David, et al., *Battleground Berlin: CIA vs. KGB in the Cold War* (New Haven, Conn.: Yale University Press, 1997).

Nachman-Tepper, Noam, *Eli Cohen: Tik Patua'h* (Tel Aviv: Efi Meltzer, 2017).

Naftali, Timothy, "The CIA and Eichmann's Associates", in Richard Breitman, Norman J. W. Goda, eds., *U.S. Intelligences and the Nazis* (Cambridge: Cambridge University Press, 2005).

Nordbruch, Götz, *Nazism in Syria and Lebanon: The Ambivalence of the German Option, 1933–1945* (London: Routledge, 2009).

Nowak, Sabrina, *Sicherheitsrisiko NS-Belastung: Personalüberprüfungen im Bundesnachrichtendienst in der 1960er Jahren* (Berlin: Ch.Verlag, 2016).

Orbach, Danny, *The Plots against Hitler* (New York: Houghton Mifflin Harcourt, 2015).

Orkaby, Asher, *Beyond the Arab Cold War: The International History of the Yemen Civil War* (New York: Oxford University Press, 2017).

Pahl, Magnus, *Fremde Heere Ost: Hitlers militärische Feindaufklärung* (Berlin: Ch. Links Verlag, 2012).

Podeh, Eli, "Demonizing the Other: Israeli Perceptions of Nasser and Nasserism", in Eli Podeh and Onn Winckler, eds., *Rethinking Nasserism: Revolution and Historical Memory in Modern Egypt* (Tampa: University Press of Florida: 2004).

Rathmell, Andrew, *Secret War in the Middle East: The Struggle for Syria, 1949–1961* (London/New York: Tauris Academic Studies, 1995).

Rass, Christoph, *Das Sozialprofil des Bundesnachrichtendienstes: Von den Anfängen bis 1968* (Berlin: Ch. Links Verlag, 2016).

Reese, Mary Ellen, *General Reinhard Gehlen: The CIA Connection* (Fairfax, Va.: George Mason University Press, 1990).

Riegler, Thomas, "Agenten, Wissenschaftler und 'Todesstrahlen': zur Rolle österreichischer Akteure in Nassers Rüstungsprogramm (1958–1969)," *JIPSS*, vol. 8, no. 2 (2014).

———"Wie eine Spinne: wie ein Netzwerk von Ex-Nazis die Gründung des VdU förderte", *Profil* 49 (2013).

———"The State as a Terrorist: France and the Red Hand," *Perspectives on Terrorism*, vol. 6, no. 6 (December, 2021), pp. 22–33.

Ritzi, Mathias, and Erich Schmidt-Eenboom, *Im Schatten des Dritten Reiches: Der BND und sein Agent Richard Christmann* (Berlin: Ch. Links Verlag, 2011).

Rubin, Barry, Wolfgang Schwanitz, *Nazis, Islamists and the Making of the Modern Middle East* (New Haven, Conn.: Yale University Press, 2014).

Ruffner, Kevin C., *Eagle and Swastika: CIA and Nazi War Criminals and Collaborators* (Washington, D.C.: History Staff, Central Intelligence Agency, 2003).

Sälter, Gerhard, *Phantome des Kalten Krieges: Die Organisation Gehlen und der Wiederbelebung des Gestapo-Feindbildes Rote Kapelle* (Berlin: Ch. Links Verlag, 2016).

Schmidt-Eenboom, Erich, *BND: Der deutsche Geheimdienst im Nahen Osten: geheime Hintergründe und Fakten* (München: Herbig, 2007).

Sereny, Gitta, *Into that Darkness: From Mercy Killing to Mass Murder* (New York: McGraw-Hill, 1974).

Segev, Samuel, *Boded be-Damesek: Hayav ve-moto shel ha-meragel ha-Israeli Eli Cohen* (Tel Aviv: Keter, expanded edition, 2012).

Segev, Tom, *Simon Wiesenthal: The Life and Legends.* trans. Ronnie Hope (New York: Schoken Books, 2010).

Shpiro, Shlomo, "Shadowy Interests: West German-Israeli Intelligence and Military Cooperation, 1957–1982," in Clive Jones and Tore Petersen, eds., *Israel's Clandestine Diplomacies* (Oxford: Hurst, Oxford University Press, 2013).

Sirrs, Owen L., *Nasser and the Missile Age in the Middle East* (London: Routledge, 2006).

Smith, Charles D., "4 February 1942: Its Causes and its Influence on Egyptian Politics and on the Future of Anglo-Egyptian Relations, 1937–1945," *International Journal of Middle Eastern Studies*, vol. 10, no. 4 (1979).

Springer, Christian, *Nazi, Komm Raus!: wie ich dem Massenmörder Alois Brunner in Syrien auf der Spur war* (München: LangenMüller, 2012).

Stangneth, Bettina, *Eichmann before Jerusalem: The Unexamined Life of a Mass Murderer.* trans.: Ruth Martin (New York: Alfred A. Knopf, 2014).

Taylor, Frederick, *Dresden: Tuesday, February 13, 1945* (New York: HarperCollins, 2004).

Walters, Guy, *Hunting Evil: The Nazi War Criminals Who Escaped and the Quest to Bring Them to Justice* (New York: Broadway Books, 2010).

Winkler, Willi, *Der Schattenmann: Von Goebbels zu Carlos: Das Mysteriöse Leben des Francois Genoud* (Berlin: Rowohlt, 2011).

Wojak, Irmtrud, *Fritz Bauer (1903–1968): The Prosecutor Who Found Eichmann and Put Auschwitz on Trial*, trans. Adam Blauhut and Karen Margolis (Munich: Buxus Edition, 2018).

Wolfe, Robert, "Coddling an Nazi Turncoat," in Richard Breitman, Norman J. W. Goda, eds., *U.S. Intelligences and the Nazis* (Cambridge: Cambridge University Press, 2005).

Wolffsohn, Michael and Ulrich Brochhagen "Hakenkreuze unter Burnus? Grossbritannien und die deutschen Militärberater in Ägypten," in Ludger Heid and Joachim H. Knoll, eds., *Deutsch-Jüdische Geschichte im 19. Und 20. Jahrhundert* (Stuttgart/Bonn: Burg Verlag, 1992).

Zamir, Meir, *The Secret Anglo-French War in the Middle East: Intelligence and Decolonization, 1940–1948* (London and New York: Routledge, 2015).

NOTES

CHAPTER 1

1 Mark Mazower, *Hitler's Empire: Nazi Rule in Occupied Europe* (London: Allen Lane, Penguin Group, 2008), 205–211.

2 R. M. Douglas, *Orderly and Humane: The Expulsion of the Germans after the Second World War* (New Haven, Conn.: Yale University Press, 2012), 1–2; Mikkel Deck, "Crimes committed by Soviet Soldiers against German Civilians, 1944–1945: A Historiogrpahical Analysis," *Journal of Military and Strategic Studies*, vol. 10, issue 4 (Summer 2008), 4–5.

3 The story of the Battle of Berlin is told in detail by Anthony Beevor, *The Fall of Berlin* (New York: Penguin Group, 2003).

4 Rolf-Dieter Müller, *Reinhard Gehlen: Geheimdienstchef im Hintergrund der Bonner Republik* (Berlin: Ch. Links Verlag, 2017), vol. 1, 376.

5 Magnus Pahl, *Fremde Heere Ost: Hitlers militärische Feindaufklärung* (Berlin: Ch. Links Verlag, 2012), 94–101.

6 Reinhard Gehlen, *Der Dienst: Erinnerungen, 1942–1971* (Wiesbaden: Hase & Koehler Verlag), 132.

7 Pahl, *Fremde Heere Ost*, 148–151, 213–214, 216–218, 327. On the July 20, 1944 plot see: Danny Orbach, *The Plots against Hitler* (New York: Houghton Mifflin Harcourt, 2015).

8 "Statement of Gerhard Wessel on Development of the German Organization (undated)," "Statement of General Winter on the History of the Organization (undated)," Maj. Gen. W. A. Burress, G-2, to Lt. Gen. Hoyt S. Vandenberg, director of Central Intelligence, 1.10.1946, reproduced in Kevin C. Ruffner, ed., *Forging an Intelligence Partnership: CIA and the Origins of the BND, 1945–1949,* (Washington, D.C.: CIA History Staff, Center for the Study of Intelligence, 1999), vol. 1, 1–3, 7, 110–111. As well as Kevin C. Ruffner, *Eagle and Swastika: CIA and Nazi War Criminals and Collaborators* (Washington, D.C.: History Staff, Central Intelligence Agency, 2003), chapter 9, 2–3.

9 Quoted in Müller, *Reinhard Gehlen*, vol. 1, 362.

10 Gehlen, *Der Dienst*, 130.

11 E. H. Cookridge, *Gehlen: Spy of the Century* (London: Hodder and Stoughton, 1971), 119; Gehlen, *Der Dienst*, 185; Müller, *Reinhard Gehlen*, vol. 1, 424; Pahl, *Fremde Heere Ost*, 319.

[12] Gehlen, *Der Dienst*, 136–137; Müller, *Reinhard Gehlen*, vol. 1, 428–429.

[13] John R. Boker Jr., "Report of Initial Contacts with General Gehlen's Organization," 1.5.1952, reproduced in Ruffner, *Forging*, vol. 1, 21–25; Ruffner, *Eagle and Swastika*, chapter 9, 3–4, 8–9; Müller, *Reinhard Gehlen*, vol. 1, 427, 478.

[14] Müller, *Reinhard Gehlen*, vol. 1, 429–431.

[15] Müller, *Reinhard Gehlen*, vol. 1, 431–433; "Debriefing of Eric Waldman on the U.S. Army's Trusteeship of the Gehlen Organization during the Years 1945–1949," 30.9.1969, Samuel Bossard to DCI, "Operation Rusty," 29.5.1947, reproduced in Ruffner, *Forging*, vol. 1, 45–46, 359. In his memoirs, Gehlen misleadingly argued he concluded a "gentlemen's agreement" with General Sibert. See: Gehlen, *Der Dienst*, 148–150.

[16] Müller, *Reinhard Gehlen*, vol. 1, 433–435, 470; Gehlen, *Der Dienst*, 142.

[17] Müller, *Reinhard Gehlen*, vol. 1, 444–445.

[18] Müller, *Reinhard Gehlen*, vol. 1, 468, 499; "Debriefing of Eric Waldman," 30.9.1969, reproduced in Ruffner, *Forging*, vol. 1, 46–47.

[19] Pahl, *Fremde Heere Ost*, 315–316.

[20] Müller, *Reinhard Gehlen*, vol. 1, 461–465; "Debriefing of Eric Waldman," 30.9.1969, reproduced in Ruffner, *Forging*, vol. 1, 46–48.

[21] Müller, *Reinhard Gehlen*, vol. 1, 454; "Debriefing of Eric Waldman," 30.9.1969, reproduced in Ruffner, *Forging*, vol. 1, 47.

[22] Wolfgang Krieger, *Partnerdienste: Die Beziehungen des BND zu den Westlichen Geheimdiensten 1946–1958* (Berlin: Ch. Links Verlag, 2021), 168.

[23] "Debriefing of Eric Waldman," 30.9.1969, reproduced in Ruffner, *Forging*, vol. 1, 46–48; Ruffner, *Eagle and Swastika*, chapter 9, 8, 24, also footnote no. 53; Müller, *Reinhard Gehlen*, vol. 1, 445, 461–463, 487, 494–497, 501.

CHAPTER 2

[1] Translation: Ralph Mandel.

[2] James H. Critchfield, *Partners at the Creation: The Men Behind Postwar Germany's Defense and Intelligence Establishments* (Annapolis, Md.: Naval Institute Press, 2003), 4–5.

[3] Critchfield, *Partners*, 68–72, 74–75.

[4] Thomas Boghardt, "Dirty Work: The Use of Nazi Informants by U.S. Army Intelligence in Postwar Europe," *The Journal of Military History* 79 (April 2015), 404.

[5] Boghardt, "Dirty Work," 401–402.

[6] Timothy Naftali, "The CIA and Eichmann's Associates," in Richard Breitman, Norman J. W. Goda, eds., *U.S. Intelligences and the Nazis* (Cambridge: Cambridge University Press, 2005), 337–366; Ruffner, *Eagle and Swastika*, chapter 4, 39–40, chapter 8, 1; Susanne Meinl, "David gegen Goliath: Der Friedrich-Wilhelm-Heinz-Dienst und die Organisation Gehlen," in Magnus Pahl, Gorch Pieken and Mathias Rogg, ed., *Achtung Spione! Geheimdienste in Deutschland von 1945 bis 1956* (Dresden: Sandstein Verlag, 2016), 98–99.

7 Boghardt, "Dirty Work," 398–399. And compare with "Draft to Deputy A: Operation Rusty," 16.10.1946, in Ruffner, *Forging*, vol. 1, 160–161.

8 See for example: [redacted] to Richard Helms, 18.3.1947, "The Bossard Report," Samuel Bossard to Donald Galloway, 5.5.1947 (hereafter cited as "Bossard Report"), reproduced in Ruffner, *Forging*, vol. 1, 215–216, 355.

9 Boghardt, "Dirty Work," 400–401; Luke Daly-Groves, "Control not Morality? Explaining the Selective Employment of Nazi War Criminals by British and American Intelligence Agencies in Occupied Germany," *Intelligence and National Security,* vol. 35, no. 3 (April 2020), 341–342.

10 Daly-Groves, "Control," 335, 342. On the Werewolves, who never constituted a serious threat, see: Mark Mazower, *Hitler's Empire: Nazi Rule in Occupied Europe* (London: Allan Lane, 2008), 546.

11 Boghardt, "Dirty Work," 395, 398; Ruffner, *Eagle and Swastika*, chapter 1, 23, chapter 3, 3–4, 9–11, chapter 9, 7.

12 SCI Department in Munich to commanding officer, OSS/X-2 Germany, 31.8.1945, quoted in Ruffner, *Eagle and Swastika,* chapter 3, 13. See also Daly-Groves, "Control," 335.

13 For the first documented evidence on this gradual shift in focus from autumn 1945 to spring 1946, see Ruffner, *Eagle and Swastika*, chapter 3, 14–20, 67. In September and October 1945, the orders did not yet mention the Soviet intelligence service explicitly, and merely ordered counterintelligence staff to watch for penetration by "all" intelligence services.

14 Critchfield, *Partners*, 119–120.

15 Francesco A. Cacciatore, "Their Need Was Great: Émigrés and Anglo-American Intelligence Operations in the Early Cold War," PhD thesis, University of Westminster (Submitted on March 2018, unpublished), 164–165, 170–171; Boghardt, "Dirty Work," 412; Ruffner, *Eagle and Swastika*, chapter 6, 3–4, chapter 7, 5.

16 Maj. Gen. W. A. Burress, G-2, to Lt. Gen. Hoyt S. Vandenberg, Director of Central Intelligence, 1.10.1946, reproduced in Ruffner, *Forging*, vol. 1, 126–127; Ruffner, *Eagle and Swastika*, chapter 3, 21, 73–74, chapter 12, 19; Cacciatore, "Their Need was Great," 69; Norman Goda, "Tracking the Red Orchestra: Allied Intelligence, Soviet Spies, Nazi Criminals," in Richard Breitman, Norman Goda et al., eds. *U.S. Intelligence and the Nazis* (Washington, D.C: National Archives, New York: Cambridge University Press, 2005), 299.

17 Naftali, "The CIA and Eichmann's Associates" in Breitman/Goda, *U.S. Intelligence and the Nazis*, 338.

18 Benjamin C. Hett, Michael Wala, *Otto John: Patriot oder Verräter: eine deutsche Biographie* (Hamburg: Rohwolt, 2019), 106.

19 Daly-Groves, "Control," 335.

20 Mark Mazower, *Hitler's Empire*, 532.

21 Bossard Report, 5.5.1947, reproduced in Ruffner, *Forging*, vol. 1, 351.

22 Hett/Wala, *Otto John*, 148–151.

23 Robert Wolfe, "Coddling an Nazi Turncoat," in Breitman/Goda, *U.S. Intelligence and the Nazis*, 330–331. Friedrich Wilhelm Heinz, the director of a short-lived West German intelligence service, began as such an entrepreneur. See: Meinl, "David gegen Goliath," in Pahl, et al., *Achtung Spione*, 98–99.

24 Guy Walters, *Hunting Evil: The Nazi War Criminals Who Escaped and the Quest to Bring Them to Justice* (New York: Broadway Books, 2010), 285–289.

25 Norman Goda, "The Nazi Peddler: Wilhelm Höttl and Allied Intelligence" in Breitman/Goda, *U.S. Intelligence and the Nazis*, 267–285; Martin Haidinger, *Wilhelm Höttl: Spion für Hitler und die USA* (Wien: Ueberreuter, 2019), 89–92, 148–177. The remark of the Austrian police, dated 3.4.1951, is cited in 168; Thomas Riegler, "Wie eine Spinne: wie ein Netzwerk von Ex-Nazis die Gründung des VdU förderte," *Profil* 49 (2013), 42–46.

26 Ruffner, *Eagle and Swastika*, chapter 3, 24; Cacciatore, "Their Need was Great," 60.

27 "Debriefing of Eric Waldman," 30.9.1969, [redacted] to Richard Helms, 18.3.1947, reproduced in Ruffner, *Forging*, vol. 1, 49–50, 215; Gerhard Sälter, *Phantome des Kalten Krieges: Die Organisation Gehlen und der Wiederbelebung des Gestapo-Feindbildes Rote Kapelle* (Berlin: Ch. Links Verlag, 2016), 216, 219; Cacciatore, "Their Need was Great," 59–63; Boghardt, "Dirty Work," 397; Naftali, "The CIA and Eichmann's Associates," in Breitman/Goda, *U.S. Intelligence and the Nazis*, 352.

28 Gerhard Sälter, *Phantome des Kalten Krieges: Die Organisation Gehlen und der Wiederbelebung des Gestapo-Feindbildes Rote Kapelle* (Berlin: Ch. Links Verlag, 2016), 156–157.

CHAPTER 3

1 Critchfield, *Partners*, 82–83.

2 Critchfield, *Partners*, 88–89. The quote is from Ruffner, *Eagle and Swastika*, chapter 3, 73.

3 Ruffner, *Eagle and Swastika*, chapter 4, 25.

4 Interview with General Edwin L. Sibert, 26.3.1970, reproduced in Ruffner, *Forging*, vol. 1, 43; Müller, *Gehlen*, vol. 1, 430.

5 DCI Hillenkoetter to Secretary of State et al., (undated), enclosing memorandum dated 6.7.1947, Brig. Gen. E. K. Wright, Memorandum for the Record, 20.7.1947, Special Operations to Karlsruhe, 27.10.1948, reproduced in Ruffner, *Forging*, vol. 1, 383, 393–394, vol. 2, 25–26; Critchfield, *Partners*, 88–89. For the evolution of the debate in Washington see: Ruffner, *Eagle and Swastika*, chapter 9, 18–30.

6 Critchfield, *Partners*, 84; Gehlen to Critchfield, 10.10.1949, reproduced in Ruffner, *Forging*, vol. 2, 301–302.

7 DCI Hillenkoetter to Maj. Gen. William E. Hall, USAF, 22.12.1948, reproduced in Ruffner, *Forging*, vol. 2, 134; Critchfield, *Partners*, 87–90; Ruffner, *Eagle and Swastika*, chapter 9, 31–33.

8   Ruffner, *Eagle and Swastika*, chapter 9, 34; Ronny Heidenreich, Daniela Münkel,
    Elke Stadelmann-Wenz, *Geheimdienstkrieg in Deutschland: Die Konfrontation von
    DDR-Staatssicherheit und die Organisation Gehlen 1953* (Berlin: Ch. Links Verlag,
    2016), 27–28; Donald Galloway, Memorandum for director CIG, 17.10.1946,
    Karlsruhe to Special Operations, 17.12.1948, James H. Critchfield to chief, Office of
    Special Operations, 17.12.1948 (hereafter cited as "Critchfield Report"), Critchfield
    to Gehlen, 15.6.1949, reproduced in Ruffner, *Forging*, vol. 1, 371–373, vol. 2, 37,
    54, 105–106, 109, 240–242.
9   Maj. Gen. W. A. Burress, G-2, to Lt. Gen. Hoyt S. Vandenberg, director of Central
    Intelligence, 1.10.1946, Reinhard Gehlen, "Reflections," 30.11.1948, in Critchfield
    Report, 17.12.1948, reproduced in Ruffner, *Forging*, vol. 1, 110–111, vol. 2, 121;
    Müller, *Gehlen*, vol. 1, 470, 556, vol. II, 1324–1325.
10 Reinhard Gehlen, "Reflections on the Further Development of this Project" 30.11.1948,
    in Critchfield Report, 17.12.1948, Gehlen to General Walsh, 9.6.1948, reproduced in
    Ruffner, *Forging*, vol. 2, 120–121, 176; " Müller, *Gehlen*, vol. 1, 557; Sälter, *Phantome*,
    55; Critchfield Report, 17.12.1948, reproduced in Ruffner, *Forging*, vol. 2, 80.
11 Reinhard Gehlen to David Even Pinnah (Theodor Eckstein), 28.2.1973, David
    Even-Pinnah Papers, file 1450, Haifa Municipal Archives, Haifa, Israel; Müller,
    Gehlen, vol. 1, 470, 556, vol. II, 1324–1325; Shlomo Shpiro, "Shadowy Interests:
    West German-Israeli Intelligence and Military Cooperation, 1957–1982," in Clive
    Jones and Tore Petersen, *Israel's Clandestine Diplomacies* (Oxford: Hurst, Oxford
    University Press, 2013) 173–175.
12 Bossard Report, 5.5.1947, CIG chief of station, Heidelberg, to FMB, 1.10.1947,
    reproduced in Ruffner, *Forging*, 352, 407; Critchfield, *Partners*, 110, 116–117;
    Sälter, *Phantome*, 41; Heidenreich et al., *Geheimdienstkrieg*, 32–39.
13 Heinz Denko-Herre Diary, 13.6.1949, 8–9, James H. Critchfield Papers, Box 5,
    Special Collections Research Center, Swem Library, College of William & Mary
    (hereafter cited as Critchfield Papers); "The Bossard Report," 5.5.1947, Maj.
    Gen. W. A. Burress, G-2, to Lt. Gen. Hoyt S. Vandenberg, Director of Central
    Intelligence, 1.10.1946, [redacted] to Richard Helms, 18.3.1947, reproduced in
    Ruffner, *Forging*, vol. 1, 146–147, 218, 344. In his report to the CIG, Samuel
    Bossard estimated the cost of American military stocks as 5,000 per month, which
    might have been well below the mark, as many of them were transferred informally
    (344). It is interesting to note that according to a memorandum submitted by
    Donald Galloway, Assistant Director for Special Operations to Director CIG,
    7.10.1946 (Ruffner, *Forging*, vol. 1, 372), the budget assigned by the US Army was
    much higher (around 208,000 USD monthly), suggesting corruption or at least
    inefficiency along the way. And see also Critchfield, *Partners*, 53–55, 90, 122, 128.
14 "Debriefing of Eric Waldman," 30.9.1969, Critchfield to Acting chief of Station,
    Karlsruhe, 7.7.1948, Gehlen to General Hall, 5.2.1949, reproduced in Ruffner,
    Forging, vol. 1, 48–49, vol. 2, 12–13, 155.

15   Gehlen to General Hall, 5.2.1949, and to Colonel Schow, 13.9.1948, Critchfield
to Chief, FBM Munich, 14.3.1949, and to chief, FMB, 18.4.1949, reproduced in
Ruffner, *Forging*, vol. 2, 156–157, 168–169, 205–206, 215.

16   Herre Diary, 20.3.1950, 140, in Critchfield Papers, box 5; Critchfield to Chief,
FBM, 18.4.1949, in Ruffner, *Forging*, vol. 2, 216–217; Müller, *Gehlen*, vol. 1, 590;
Heidenreich et al., *Geheimdienstkrieg*, 52–53; chief of CIA Station, Karlsruhe, to
chief of Foreign Division, Munich, 17.2.1950, Ludwig Albert Name file, document
no. 11, CREST; Cookridge, *Spy of the Century*, 159.

17   Herre Diary, 14.6.1949, 9, in Critchfield Papers, box 5; Critchfield to Chief, FBM,
18.4.1949, in Ruffner, *Forging*, vol. 2, 212–213, 216; Mathias Ritzi and Erich
Schmidt-Eenboom, *Im Schatten des Dritten Reiches: Der BND und sein Agent Richard
Christmann* (Berlin: Ch. Links Verlag, 2011), 121; Müller, *Gehlen*, vol. 2, 863;
Christoph Rass, *Das Sozialprofil des Bundesnachrichtendienstes: Von den Anfängen bis
1968* (Berlin: Ch. Links Verlag, 2016), 173, 297–299, 301. According to Rass, the
employment of relatives was noticeable but relatively moderate until 1955, and then
reached swaggering proportions. Between 1946 and 1948, it is assessed that at least
21.4% of Org employees had relatives in the service (301).

18   Critchfield to Acting Chief of Station, Karlsruhe, 7.7.1948, in Ruffner, *Forging*, vol. 2,
16. See also Müller, Gehlen, vol. 1, 558, Ruffner, *Eagle and Swastika*, chapter 9, 12.

19   Müller, *Gehlen*, vol. 1, 593–594; Gehlen to General Walsh, 9.6.1948, and to Critchfield,
10.10.1949, reproduced in Ruffner, *Forging*, vol. 2, 182–184, 294–298; Critchfield,
Partners, 119, 127–128. On the German doctrine of *Auftragstaktik* see Gerry Long,
"Auftragstaktik: A Case Study: France 1940–Understanding the Mission Command
in the Training of Soldiers," in Donald Vandergrif and Stephen Werber, eds., *Mission
Command: The Who, What, Where, When and Why: An Anthology* (Kabul: 2017), 69–85.

20   Müller, *Gehlen*, vol. 1, 556.

21   Herre Diary, 17.6.1949, 10, in Critchfield Papers, Box 5; Müller, *Gehlen*, vol. 1,
537–538, 576, vol. 2, 671; Gehlen to General Walsh, 9.6.1948, reproduced in
Ruffner, *Forging*, vol. 2, 176.

22   Müller, *Gehlen*, vol. 1, 537–538; Sälter, *Phantome*, 273; Critchfield, "KGB and CIC
Penetrations of the Gehlen Organization using former SD and Gestapo Members"
(undated), KGB-Felfe Documents, 135, Critchfield Papers, Box 6.

23   Samuel Bossard, "Memorandum to General Walsh," 27.6.1947, reproduced in
Ruffner, *Forging*, 399; Ruffner, *Eagle and Swastika*, chapter 9, 35–36.

24   Critchfield, *Partners*, 116–117.

25   Ruffner, *Eagle and Swastika*, chapter 10, 6–14. Critchfield was also interested in
Bolschwing's extensive connections in Romania, and among fascist Romanian exiles.
Later, the CIA helped protect Bolschwing from legal prosecution.

26   Critchfield, "KGB and CIC Penetrations of the Gehlen Organization using former
SD and Gestapo Members" (undated), KGB-Felfe Documents, 135–136, in
Critchfield Papers, Box 6; Müller, *Gehlen*, vol. 2, 670.

27 Gehlen, "Reflections," 30.11.1948, in Critchfield Report, 17.12.1948, Gehlen
    to Colonel Philps, 24.1.1949, reproduced in Ruffner, *Forging*, vol. 2, 120, 122,
    162.
28 Müller, *Gehlen*, vol. 1, 554–555; Bossard Report, 5.5.1947, reproduced in Ruffner,
    Forging, vol. 1, 351; Sälter, *Phantome*, 51–55. "Red Sex Bombs"—based on the
    memoirs of a department chief and later a vice-president of BfV. See: Günther
    Nollau, *Das Amt: 50 Jahre Zeuge der Geschichte* (München: C. Bertelsmann Verlag,
    1978), 195–197. Nollau wondered (201) whether Gehlen and his men really
    believed in the stories they told.

CHAPTER **4**

1   Critchfield Report, 17.12.1948, reproduced in Ruffner, *Forging*, vol. 2, 88; Sälter,
    Phantome, 78; Heinz Felfe, *Im Dienst des Gegners: 10 Jahre Moskaus Mann im BND*
    (Hamburg: Rasch und Röhring, 1986), 160. On the Abwehr and the German
    resistance see: Orbach, *The Plots against Hitler*, 19–32, 143–160. On the Secret Field
    Police see ibid, 148.
2   Sälter, *Phantome*, 281.
3   Critchfield Report, 17.12.1948, reproduced in Ruffner, *Forging*, vol. 2, 88–94;
    Sälter, *Phantome*, 75. For the structure of GV-L see the chart in ibid, 81; Felfe,
    Im Dienst, 161; Chief of CIA Station, Pullach (Critchfield), to Chief of Station,
    Germany, 3.8.1955 (report on conversation with Kurt Kohler, 21.7.1955), CREST,
    Ludwig Albert name file, document no. 28.
4   Sälter, *Phantome*, 60.
5   Sälter, *Phantome*, 153, 156–157, 264–266; Rass, *Sozialprofil*, 173, 177, 185. The
    name of this Nazi rapist was Fritz Fischer. See: Critchfield to Acting Chief of Station,
    Karlsruhe, 7.7.1948, reproduced in Ruffner, *Forging*, vol. 2, 12–13. For more
    information on these recruitment networks see 66th CIC Report, "Felfe, Heinz,"
    23.6.1954, NARA RG 319, Entry ZZ-5, Box 4, as well as CIA report, Chief of Base,
    Munich, to Chief EE (Eastern Europe), 19.12.1957, 7, CREST, Ludwig Albert
    name file, document no. 51.
6   For the most recent estimate of the numbers and relative proportion of Nazi
    security veterans in the Org see Rass, *Sozialprofil*, 170, 173, 177, 185, 282.
    According to Rass, a minimum number of 124 veterans of NS security and
    intelligence organizations worked in the Gehlen Org/BND between 1946 and
    1948, many of them for short periods. For Gehlen's disclosure to Adenauer in
    1963 see: Sabrina Nowak, *Sicherheitsrisiko NS-Belastung: Personalüberprüfungen
    im Bundesnachrichtendienst in der 1960er Jahren* (Berlin: Ch.Verlag, 2016), 82,
    and also Müller, *Gehlen*, vol. 1, 582–583; Sälter, *Phantome*, 273–275. For a CIA
    assessment see: Ruffner, *Eagle and Swastika*, chapter 9, 26, 36.
7   Müller, *Gehlen*, vol. 1, 606; Sälter, *Phantome*, 72–73, 83–84, 138, 264; Critchfield
    Report, 17.12.1948, reproduced in Ruffner, *Forging*, vol. 2, 88–94.

8 Sälter, *Phantome*, 271–272; Critchfield, "KGB and CIC Penetrations of the Gehlen Organization using former SD and Gestapo Members" (undated), KGB-Felfe Documents, 126–127, in Critchfield Papers, Box 6.

9 Critchfield, "KGB and CIC Penetrations of the Gehlen Organization using former SD and Gestapo Members" (undated), KGB-Felfe Documents, 126–127, 135, in Critchfield Papers, Box 6; Sälter, *Phantome*, 224–225.

10 Herre Diary, 23.3, 1.4.1950, 142, 149–150 in Critchfield Papers, box 5; Sälter, *Phantome*, 44–46, 56; Hett/Wala, *Otto John*, 92–93.

11 Sälter, *Phantome*, 47; KGB Exploitation of Heinz Felfe: Successful KGB Penetration of a Western Intelligence Service," March 1969, NARA, RG 263, CIA Subject Files, Second Release, Box 1 (hereafter cited as "KGB Exploitation, NARA"), 34.

12 Hett/Wala, *Otto John*, 100–102; Werner Biermann, *Konrad Adenauer: Ein Jahrhundertleben* (Berlin: Rowohlt, 2017), 336–339; Konrad Adenauer, *Errinerungen: 1945–1953* (Stuttgart: Deutsche Verlags-Anstalt, 1980), 346–355, 375–377; Müller, *Gehlen*, vol. 2, 664.

13 Sälter, *Phantome*, 53; Gehlen to General Walsh, 9.6.1948, reproduced in Ruffner, *Forging*, vol. 2, 184–185.

14 Sälter, *Phantome*, 47–48, 67.

15 Goda, "Tracking the Red Orchestra," in Breitman/Goda, *U.S. Intelligence and the Nazis*, 299–301; Sälter, *Phantome*, 129.

16 Sälter, *Phantome*, 102–106.

17 Sälter, *Phantome*, 209–223, 228–229, 249–251, 262, 365–366, 369–370; Chief of CIA Station, Karlsruhe to Chief, Foreign Division Munich, 17.8.1950, CREST, Ludwig Albert name file, document no.13.

18 Heidenreich, et al., *Geheimdienstkrieg*, 152.

19 Orbach, *The Plots against Hitler*, 230–231.

20 Eckhard Jesse, "Biographisches Porträt: Otto Ernst Remer" in Uwe Backes and Eckhard Jesse, eds., *Jahrbuch Extermismus & Demokratie*, vol. 6 (Bonn: Bouvier Verlag, 1994), 209–213, 216.

21 Sälter, *Phantome*, 164–170. And compare with: Hans Clemens interrogation, Security Group Koblenz, 15.1.1962, CREST, Hans Clemens name file, vol. 2, document no. 12, 190.

22 KGB Exploitation, NARA, 13.

23 Sälter, *Phantome*, 297–301.

24 BND report, "Fall Moritz," 6.6.1952, B206 51093, 236–7, BA-K; Ritzi/Eenboom, *Schatten*, 164.

CHAPTER 5

1 Translation: Robert T. Ames.

2 Frederick Taylor, *Dresden: Tuesday, February 13, 1945* (New York: HarperCollins, 2004), 448.

3 Hans Clemens interrogation, Security Group Stuttgart, 24.1.1962, CREST, Hans Clemens name file, vol. 2, document no. 2, 272–273, 277; Bodo Hechelhammer, *Spion ohne Grenzen: Heinz Felfe—Agent in Sieben Geheimdiensten* (München: Piper, 2019), 14; Mary Ellen Reese, *General Reinhard Gehlen: The CIA Connection* (Fairfax, Va.: George Mason University Press, 1990), 152; Heinz Felfe, *Im Dienst des Gegners: 10 Jahre Moskaus Mann im BND* (Hamburg: Rasch und Röhring, 1986), 129; Interview with Vitali V. Korotkov, *Sputnik*, 9.11.2019, https://sputniknews.com/europe/201911091077238391-because-moscow-sought-a-unified-germany--kgb-colonel-korotkov-on-gdr-and-agent-kurt-felfe/ (last accessed, 8.4.2020).

4 Hechelhammer, *Spion ohne Grenzen*, 65–66.

5 66th CIC Report, "Felfe, Heinz," 23.6.1954, William F. Loebel, 970th CIC, "Felfe, Heinz: Personality Report," 2.4.1948, NARA RG 319, Entry ZZ-5, Box 4; Hechelhammer, *Spion ohne Grenzen*, 45.

6 "KGB Exploitation," NARA, 15–16; Hechelhammer, *Spion ohne Grenzen*, 45–46, 153–154.

7 Hechelhammer, *Spion ohne Grenzen*, 61.

8 Hechelhammer, *Spion ohne Grenzen*, 56–57; Reese, *General Reinhard Gehlen*, 152, 168; Interview with Vasili V. Korotkov, *Sputnik*, 9.11.2019.

9 "KGB Exploitation," NARA, 16–18; 66th CIC Reports, "Felfe, Heinz," 23.6.1954, 25.10.1956, NARA RG 319, Entry ZZ-5, Box 4; Heinz Felfe Interrogation, 21.11.1961, Security Group EL II, CREST, Hans Clemens name file, vol. 2, document no. 4, 23–25; Hechelhammer, *Spion ohne Grenzen*, 62–65.

10 Hechelhammer, *Spion ohne* Grenzen, 40–41; Security Group Munich, investigation report 25.1.1962, CREST, Hans Clemens name file, vol. 2, document no. 9; Victor Klemperer, *I Will Bear Witness: A Diary of the Nazi Years, 1942–1945*, trans. Martin Chalmers (New York: Modern Library, 2001), entry 24.1.1942, 146, 221.

11 Hans Clemens interrogation, Security Group Stuttgart, 24.1.1962, CREST, Hans Clemens name file, vol. 2, document no. 2, 272–275; Bodo Hechelhammer, "KGB-Spione aus Dresden: Der Verratsfall Heinz Felfe," in Pahl, et al., *Achtung Spione*, 160–161; "Felfe: Umarmt und geküsst," *Der Spiegel*, vol. 30 (1963), 21–22; Hechelhammer, *Spion ohne Grenzen*, 83–89.

12 Protocol of the Trial of Clemens, Felfe and Tiebel, session 8.7.1963, reproduced in Chief of Base, Bonn, to Chief EE (Eastern Europe), CREST, Hans Clemens name file, vol. 3, document no. 23, 10 ;"KGB Exploitation," NARA, 19–20; Hans Clemens interrogation, Security Group Stuttgart, 24.1.1962, CREST, Hans Clemens name file, vol. 2, document no. 2, 275; Heinz Felfe Interrogation, 21.11.1961, Security Group EL II, CREST, Hans Clemens name file, vol. 2, document no. 4, 37; Hechelhammer, *Spion ohne Grenzen*, 86.

13 Reese, *General Reinhard Gehlen*, 135.

14 Reese, *General Reinhard Gehlen*, 152–153; Protocol of the Trial of Clemens, Felfe and Tiebel, 8.7.1963, excerpts reproduced in Chief of Base, Bonn, to Chief EE (Eastern Europe), CREST, Hans Clemens name file, vol. 3, document no. 23, 12.

15 Heinz Felfe Interrogation, 21.11.1961, Security Group EL II, CREST, Hans
Clemens name file, vol. 2, document no. 4, 39; CIA Felfe Damage Assessment, 1;
"KGB Exploitation," NARA, 23, 26–27; "Felfe: Umarmt und geküsst," *Der Spiegel*,
vol. 30 (1963), 23; Bodo Hechelhammer, *Doppelagent Heinz Felfe entdeckt Amerika:
Der BND, Die CIA und eine geheime Reise im Jahr 1956* (Paderborn: Ferdinand
Schöningh, 2017), 51; Hans Clemens interrogation, Security Group Koblenz,
26.2.1962, CREST, Hans Clemens name file, vol. 3, document no. 3, 153.

16 Protocol of the Trial of Clemens, Felfe and Tiebel, session 8.7.1963, reproduced in
Chief of Base, Bonn, to Chief EE (Eastern Europe), CREST, Hans Clemens name
file, vol. 3, document no. 23, 9; Heinz Felfe Interrogation, 21.11.1961, Security
Group EL II, CREST, Hans Clemens name file, vol. 2, document no. 4, 35, 42;
Hans Clemens interrogation, Security Group Koblenz, 15.1.1962, CREST, Hans
Clemens name file, vol. 2, document no. 12, 189–191; Hechelhammer, *Spion ohne
Grenzen*, 90–91.

17 Protocol of the Trial of Clemens, Felfe and Tiebel, 8.7.1963, excerpts reproduced in
Chief of Base, Bonn, to Chief EE (Eastern Europe), CREST, Hans Clemens name
file, vol. 3, document no. 23, 17–18; "KGB Exploitation," NARA, 20–22; Protocol
of the Trial of Clemens, Felfe and Tiebel, 8.7.1963, excerpts reproduced in Chief of
Base, Bonn, to Chief EE (Eastern Europe), CREST, Hans Clemens name file,
vol. 3, document no. 23, 17; Hans Clemens interrogation, Security Group Koblenz,
15.1.1962, CREST, Hans Clemens name file, vol. 2, document no. 12, 208–212.

18 Hans Clemens interrogation, Security Group Stuttgart, 24.1.1962, CREST, Hans
Clemens name file, vol. 2, document no. 2, 277.

19 "KGB Exploitation," NARA, 81–82; 66th CIC Report, "Felfe, Heinz," 10.6.1954,
NARA RG 319, Entry ZZ-5, Box 4; Critchfield, memorandum for record,
15.11.2002, in KGB-Felfe Documents, 6, in Critchfield Papers, Box 6; Hans
Clemens interrogation, Security Group Stuttgart, 24.1.1962, CREST, Hans Clemens
name file, vol. 2, document no. 2, 290.

20 CIC report from 29 October, 1955, quoted in CIA report, Chief of Base, Munich,
to Chief EE (Eastern Europe), 19.12.1957, CREST, Ludwig Albert name file,
document no. 51; Hechelhammer, *Spion ohne Grenzen*, 167.

21 Reese, *General Reinhard Gehlen*, 134–135. Many of the "Campus" documents are
available in KGB-Felfe Documents, in Critchfield Papers, Box 6.

22 Sälter, *Phantome*, 74; Critchfield, *Partners*, 168–169, 193–198; Meinl, "David gegen
Goliath," in Pahl, et al., *Achtung Spione*, 109–110; Reese, *General Reinhard Gehlen*,
150–151.

23 Hechelhammer, *Dolagent*, 49; "KGB Exploitation," NARA, 28; "Army G-2 on Felfe
Case after 1961," retrieved from disk, January 2004, KGB-Felfe Documents, 80–81,
in Critchfield Papers, box 6.

24 Hechelhammer, "KGB-Spione," in Pahl, et al., *Achtung Spione*, 162; Felfe, *Im Dienst*,
168–169.

25 Heidenreich, et al., *Geheimdienstkrieg*, 110–115, 132–133, 162–163, 166; Helmut Müller-Enbergs, "Die 'Konzentrierten Schläge der DDR-Staatssicherheit gegen die Organisation Gehlen," in Pahl, et al., *Achtung Spione*, 441.

26 Hans Clemens interrogation, Security Group Koblenz, 26.2.1962, CREST, Hans Clemens name file, vol. 3, document no. 3, 129–130; Protocol of the Trial of Clemens, Felfe and Tiebel, 8.7.1963, excerpts reproduced in Chief of Base, Bonn, to Chief EE (Eastern Europe), CREST, Hans Clemens name file, vol. 3, document no. 23, 22–23.

27 "Felfe, Heinz," CIC Report, 24.6.1954, KGB-Felfe Documents, 56, in Critchfield Papers, box 6; Sälter, *Phantome*, 84; Heidenreich, et al., *Geheimdienstkrieg*, 149–150, 176, 270; "KGB Exploitation," NARA, 29–31, 33–34.

28 Heidenreich, et al., *Geheimdienstkrieg*, 188, 192; "KGB Exploitation," NARA, 33–34; Unpublished Critchfield Draft, "Army G-2 on Felfe Case after 1961," retrieved from disk, January 2004, KGB-Felfe Documents, 79–80, in Critchfield Papers, Box 6.

CHAPTER 6

1 Chief of CIA Station, Karlsruhe, to Chief of Foreign Division, Munich, 17.2.1950, 801 to 833, 2.8.1955, CREST, Ludwig Albert Name file, documents no. 11, 27; Sälter, *Phantome*, 276–277; "KGB Exploitation," NARA, 34.

2 66th CIC Report, "Felfe, Heinz," 10.6.1954, NARA RG 319, Entry ZZ-5, Box 4; Hechelhammer, *Spion ohne Grenzen*, 124–126.

3 Heidenreich, et al., *Geheimdienstkrieg*, 145–146, 152–154, 196–197; 66th CIC Reports, "Felfe, Heinz," 10.6, 24.6, 16.11.1954, NARA RG 319, Entry ZZ-5, Box 4. Compare with Critchfield, memorandum for record, 15.11.2002, in KGB-Felfe documents, 6, in Critchfield Papers, Box 6.

4 "Felfe, Heinz: Damage Assessment," NARA, RG 263, CIA Subject Files, Second Release, Box 1 (hereafter cited as "CIA Felfe Damage Assessment"), 1.

5 "KGB Exploitation," NARA, 36–38; Hechelhammer, *Spion ohne Grenzen*, 126–130.

6 CIA document, undated, 801 to 833, 2.8.1955, Chief of Station, Germany, to Chief EE (Eastern Europe), 23.8.1953, 831, Memorandum for the Record, "The Albert-Burckhardt-Leidl Case," 25.11.1955, CREST, Ludwig Albert name file, documents no. 20, 27, 31, 34; Hechelhammer, *Spion ohne Grenzen*, 141–142.

7 CIA document, 801 to 833, 2.8.1955, Chief of CIA Station, Pullach (Critchfield), to Chief of Station, Germany (report on conversation with Kurt Kohler, 21.7.1955), 3.8.1955, Chief of Station, Germany, to Chief EE (Eastern Europe), 23.8.1953, CREST, Ludwig Albert name file, documents no. 27, 28, 31.

8 Chief of CIA Station, Pullach (Critchfield) to Chief of Station, Germany (report on conversation with Kurt Kohler, 21.7.1955), 3.8.1955, CREST, Ludwig Albert name file, document no. 28.

9 "KGB Exploitation," NARA, 39–41; Meinl, "David gegen Goliath," in Pahl, et al., *Achtung Spione*, 110–111; Critchfield, "KGB and CIC Penetrations of the Gehlen

Organization using former SD and Gestapo Members" (undated), KGB-Felfe Documents, 130, in Critchfield Papers, Box 6; Reese, *General Reinhard Gehlen*, 139–141.

10 CIA document (undated), Memo for Record, Conversation with Utility, Edinger, and Peter, 8.7.1955, 801 to 833, 2.8.1955, CREST, Ludwig Albert name file, documents no. 20, 21, 27.

11 "KGB and CIC Penetrations of the Gehlen Organization using former SD and Gestapo Members" (undated), KGB-Felfe Documents, 119, Critchfield Papers, Box 6; Norman J. W. Goda, "The Gehlen Organization and the Heinz Felfe Case: The SD, the KGB, and West German Counterintelligence," in David A. Messenger and Katrin Paehler, eds., *A Nazi Past: Recasting German Identity in Postwar Europe* (Lexington: University Press of Kentucky, 2015), 282. Mary Ellen Reese also believes that Albert spied for the East. See: Reese, *General Reinhard Gehlen*, 123, 216–217.

12 Chief of Station, Germany, to Chief EE (Eastern Europe), 23.8.1953, CREST, Ludwig Albert name file, document no. 31.

13 One of the reports found in Albert's house was in fact on Operation Balthasar, a fake operation created by the Soviets to reinforce Felfe's position. See: CIA report, "UJDRUM [Hans Clemens] interrogation report MK-3406," 8.3.1962, Ludwig Albert name file, document no. 55. In his interrogation on 8.2.1962, Felfe (Udjrowski) said the same thing, but in his usual way, tried to frame Albert by insinuation. Bodo Hechelhammer, Felfe's biographer, also believes that Albert was framed, and did not spy for the East. He notes that the KGB framed Gehlen agents who imperiled Felfe also in other cases. See: *Spion ohne Grenzen*, 142–143.

14 "KGB Exploitation," NARA, 42–49, 56–58; Protocol of the Trial of Clemens, Felfe and Tiebel, 8.7.1963, excerpts reproduced in Chief of Base, Bonn, to Chief EE (Eastern Europe), CREST, Hans Clemens name file, vol. 3, document no. 23, 40–41; Hechelhammer, *Spion ohne Grenzen*, 138–139, 144–150; Reese, *General Reinhard Gehlen*, 147–148.

15 CIA Felfe Damage Assessment (entire document), but particularly 1–2, 18–19, and conclusions and attachment (reports from CIA stations in Germany). The quote is from the attachment, 6. See also "KGB Exploitation," NARA, 43. See also: Hechelhammer, *Spion ohne Grenzen*, 173, 215–218; Nollau, *Das Amt*, 198–200; Reese, *General Reinhard Gehlen*, 150; "Regelmäsig wie ein Uhrwerk lieferte der Mann in Pullach an 'Alfred 2,' interview with Vitali V. Korotkow [Korotkov], *Berliner Zeitung*, 3.11.1993, 3.

16 Heidenreich et al., *Geheimdienstkrieg*, 181.

17 Memorandum for the Record, "Conversation with Friesen [Felfe]," 29.3.1956, CREST, Ludwig Albert name file, document no. 38; Unpublished Critchfield Draft, "The Felfe Case after 1954," retrieved from disk, January 1944, KGB-Felfe Documents, in Critchfield Papers, Box 6; Hechelhammer, *Spion ohne Grenzen*, 150–151; Reese, *General Reinhard Gehlen*, 145–149.

CHAPTER 7

1 David Motadel, *Islam and Nazi Germany's War* (Cambridge, Mass.: The Belknap Press of Harvard University Press, 2014), 15–27.

2 Mohamed Hassanein Heikal, *The Cairo Documents: The Inside Story of Nasser and His Relationship with World Leaders, Rebels and Statesmen* (New York: Doubleday & Company Inc., 1973), 320–322; Motadel, *Islam and Nazi Germany's War*, 74–75, 110–112; James Jankowski, "The View from the Embassy: British Assessments of Egyptian Attitudes during World War II" in Israel Gershoni, ed., *Arab Responses to Fascism and Nazism: Attraction and Repulsion* (Austin: The University of Texas Press, 2014), 185–186, 192–194; Charles D. Smith, "4 February 1942: Its Causes and its Influence on Egyptian Politics and on the Future of Anglo-Egyptian Relations, 1937–1945," *International Journal of Middle Eastern Studies*, vol. 10, no. 4 (1979), 453–479; Corry Guttstadt, *Turkey, the Jews and the Holocaust* (Cambridge: Cambridge University Press, 2017), 30–40. On the influence of pro-German currents in Syria and Lebanon during WWII, the best study so far is Götz Nordbruch, *Nazism in Syria and Lebanon: The Ambivalence of the German Option, 1933–1945* (London: Routledge, 2009).

3 The diary of Winterstein (Kurt Weiss), 29.8.1956, 78, N10/4 (Teil 1).OT, BND Archive. Badis Ben Redjeb, "The Gehlen Organization, Nazis and the Middle East," *Journal of Intelligence History*, vol. 18, no. 2 (June 2019), 221–222, 229–230; Michael Wolffsohn and Ulrich Brochhagen, "Hakenkreuze unter Burnus? Grossbritannien und die deutschen Militärberater in Ägypten," in Ludger Heid and Joachim H. Knoll, eds., *Deutsch-Jüdische Geschichte im 19. Und 20. Jahrhundert* (Stuttgart/Bonn: Burg Verlag, 1992), 521–522.

4 Heinrich Mast, "Erinnerungen an meine Tätigkeit als Nachrichten Offizier in den Jahren 1947–1953 bei den Nachrichten Organization 'General Gehlen' and 'Amt Blank'," 26.7.1962, Karton 15, Ma 11 (Redl/Gehlen), 2–3, BBAX 5566—BBAX 5568, Henrich Mast Papers, Bundeswehr Military History Museum, Dresden.

5 Wolffsohn and Brochhagen, "Hakenkreuze," 517–520.

6 Müller, *Gehlen*, vol. 1, 559.

7 Ben Redjeb, "The Gehlen Organization," 221–225; Krieger, *Partnerdiense*, 167; On Rauff's career during the war see Martin Cüppers's detailed study, *Walther Rauff in Deutschen Diensten: vom Naziverbrecher zum BND-Spion* (Darmstadt: WBG, 2013), 109–204.

8 BND reports, 3.10.1958, 6.3.1963, reproduced in Bodo Hechelhammer et al., eds., "Walther Rauff und der Bundesnachrichtendienst," in *Mitteilungen der Forschungs- und Arbeitsgru 'Geschichte der BND'*, no. 2 (September 2011), 9, 16–17; Müller, *Gehlen*, vol. 1, 604; Erich Schmidt-Eenboom, *BND: Der deutsche Geheimdienst im Nahen Osten: geheime Hintergründe und Fakten* (München: Herbig, 2007), 191; "Activity of former Colonel Walter Rauff in Syria," 6.11.1949, "Background information on German military experts in Syria," 23.2.1954, Chief, Foreign

Division T, to Chief of Station, 1956, Chief, PCS/ITC to Chief, CI Staff, 8.7.1977, "Walter Rauff," 30.1.1984, CIA Reports, Eilam Collection; Ben Redjeb, "The Gehlen Organization," 222–225.

9   "Namenserklärung: Heinrich Mast/Heinrich von Mast/ Heinrich Baron Mast," as well as Mast's CV, in Karton 15, Ma 1, BBAU7526-BBAU7528, Heinrich Mast Papers, Bundeswehr Military History Museum, Dresden.

10   Mast, "Erinnerungen," 2–5, 12; CIA report, 29.3.1951, Heinrich Mast name file, document no. 23. For Mast's animosity toward the resistance and service to the Nazi Party see also Mast to Schriftleitung der D. National Ztg. U. Soldaten Ztg., 22.5.1963, Karton 15, Ma 11 (Redl/Gehlen), 2–3, BBAX 5566—BBAX 5568, Meyer to Mast, 15.6.1939, K3 LOSE, BBAT5773, Mast to Dr. Peter Broucek, 8.1.1975, 3–4, K 15/3, BBAU 7569, Heinrich Mast Papers, Bundeswehr Military History Museum, Dresden.

11   Citation from Tom Segev, *Simon Wiesenthal: The Life and Legends*. Trans. Ronnie Hope (New York: Schoken Books, 2010) 102. See also: Walters, *Hunting Evil*, 285–289; Mast to Dr. Peter Broucek (undated), K 15/3, BBAU 7569, and also the rest of his correspondence with Broucek in the same folder, Mast Papers, Bundeswehr Military History Museum, Dresden. For the Israeli connection see: CIA Report, 16.11.1954, Heinrich Mast name file, document no.75, CREST.

12   See the chart of the network in "Entwurf: Mil- Pol-" and "der organisatorische Aufbau der Nebenstelle Österreich'," as well as "Personeller und organisatorischer Aufbau der neuen Italien-Linie (L606)," 17.1.1952, "Nachrichtenziele der 'Nebenstelle Österreich'," 11.1.1952, in Mast papers, courtesy of Erich Schmidt-Eenboom; Mast, "Erinnerungen," 3–5, 12.

13   Gerhard Schacht, "Die deutschen Militärberater in Syrien," 17.6.1951, 2. Nachrichtenziele der 'Nebenstelle Österreich'," 11.1.1952, in Mast Papers, courtesy of Erich Schmidt-Eenboom; Ben Redjeb, "The Gehlen Organization," 222; Mast, "Erinnerungen," 7, 13.

14   Aussenstelle München (FWHD), Nr. 1567, 3.10.1952, Höttl to Heinz, Autumn 1952 (precise date unclear), in Mast papers, courtesy of Erich Schmidt-Eenboom; Mast, "Erinnerungen," 2–5; Mast to Albert (head of XG Salzburg office), 4.11.1952, Karton 14, Ma 11 (Personliche Korrespondenz, 1951–1953) BBAZ-5558, Mast Papers, Bundeswehr Military History Museum; Gehlen Org report, 11.3.1952, CIA Report, 16.11.1954, Heinrich Mast name file, documents no. 52, 75, CREST.

15   Herbert Elzer, "Deutsche Militärberater in Ägypten: Wilhelm Voss, General Fahrmbacher und die Bundesregierung 1951–1955," *Historische Mitteilungen* vol. 24 (2011), 224–225; Heikal, *The Cairo Documents*, 320–322.

16   Elzer, "Deutsche Militärberater," 228, 235–240, 246, 250.

17   Recruiting of former German Army Officers for the Egyptian Army" (Report of Gerhard Mertens), 9.7.1951, RG 319, Entry ZZ-6, Box 6, "German Advisors for Egyptian Army," NARA; Ben Redjeb, "The Gehlen Organization," 229–231;

Elzer, "Deutsche Militärberater," 230–231; Tilman Lüdke "Die Aktivitäten von Organisation Gehlen und BND im Nahen Osten, 1946–1968" in Wolfgang Krieger, ed., *Die Auslandsaufklärung des BND: Operationen, Analysen, Netzwerke* (Berlin: Ch. Links Verlag, 2021), 435–436, 441–443.

18 Ekkehard Henschke, *Rosenbergs Elite und ihr Nachleben: Akademiker im Dritten Reich und nach 1945* (Köln: Böhlau Verlag, 2021), 156–159.

19 COS Germany to Chief of Base, Bonn, 27.1.1961, [ ] to Chief, Africa Division, (CIA report, undated, probably from around 1966), Wilhelm Beisner [Friedrich Wilhelm Beissner] name file, documents no. 64, 95, CREST; Ben Redjeb, "The Gehlen Organization," 227; Henschke, *Rosenbergs Elite*, 154. On Beisner's background see also: "Bombe in der Blütenstrasse," *Der Spiegel*, 26.10.1960.

20 "Dr. Beisners Rolle im Krieg," *Frankfurter Allgemeine Zeitung*, 21.10.1960.

21 "Biography of SS-Obersturmbahnführer Wilhelm Beissner," RG 319, Entry ZZ-5, Box 1, Beisner name file, NARA; Bernt Engelmann, *The Weapons Merchants*, trans. Erica Detto (New York: Crown Publishers, 1968), 126.

22 "UPSWING Operations in the Middle East," CIA report, 24.3.1957, CIA report, Beisner's network chart, 1961 [precise date unknown], BND to CIA, intelligence report on Beisner, 18.3.1966, Beissner name file, documents no. 54, 60, 64, 103, CREST.

23 Gehlen Org report, 22.6.1953, BND report from Damascus, 27.8.1953, Skorzeny name file, Bundesarchiv Koblenz, B 206 51093 (hereafter cited as BA-K).

24 CIA intelligence summary on Beisner, 1951–1953, CIA Report, 24.4.1953, Nachrichtenagent Willi Beisner, 9.5.1950, Chief ME to Chief of Station Frankfurt, 6.8.1953, "USPWING Operations in the Middle East," 24.3.1957, Beisner file, documents no. 5, 8, 11, 20, 23, 54 (in the title of the name file, Beisner's name is spelled "Beissner" with a double s). BND evaluation index, entry "Beisner," B206 51094, 21, BA-K.

25 "Beisner, Wilhelm," 23.11.1954, RG 319, Entry ZZ-5, Box 1, Beisner name file, NARA.

26 Mast, "Erinnerungen," 5.

27 BND report on Otto Skorzeny's activity until 1965, 10, BA-K, Skorzeny name file, B 206 51092; Deutscher Bundestag, 18. Wahlperiode, "Antwort der Bundesregierung auf die kleine Anfrage der Abgeordneten Jan Korte, Sevim Dağdelen, Ulla Jelpke, weiterer Abgeordneter und der Fraktion Die Linke," Drucksache 18/3599, 20.1.2015, 7–8; BND report, 14.6.1984, "Walter Rauff und der Bundesnachritdiesnt," in Bodo Hechelhammer et al. (eds.), *Mitteilungen der Forschungs- und Arbeitsgru 'Geschichte des BND,'* no. 2 (September 2011), 18–21; Bavarian State Criminal Police to the Public Prosecutor's Office at the State Court Munich I, 12.1.1961, Hermann Schaefer name file, 409–410, BfV Archive; Krieger, *Partnerdienste*, 168, 171; BND report, 6.9.1961, 30.212.OT, 67, BND Archive.

According to Krieger, the Americans, who initially refused to allow the Gehlen Org to operate in the Middle East, changed their mind around 1952.

CHAPTER 8

1   See the Anton Brunner trial documents in Landesgericht für Strafsachen Wien (Vg 1 g Vr 4574/45) gegen den Leiter des Amtes für judische Belange, Anton Brunner," as well as Simon Wiesenthal to Jacob Robinson, 28.1.1972, 2–3, both in Brunner name file no.1, Vienna Wiesenthal Archive: Simon Wiesenthal Archive (hereafter cited as VWI-SWA).

2   "Informationen zur Anfrage no. 1379/75 über Alois Brunner," 1.11.1976, 7, MfS HA IX/11 nr. AV 9189, 000088, *Bundesbeauftragter für die Unterlagen des Staatssicherheitsdienstes der ehemaligen Deutschen Demokratischen Republik* (hereafter cited as BStU); Chief, Munich Operations Group to Chief, COS Germany, CIA dispatch, 10.5.1961, 1, Brunner Name File, Document no. 4, CREST. As late as 1967, the Central Office for the Investigation of NS Crimes in Ludwigsburg was not yet certain whether Brunner is dead or alive. See: "Zusammenstellung" in Dr. Rückerl to Simon Wiesenthal, 23.8.1967, Egypt folder, VWI-SWA, 1–2. On the confusion between Brunner I and Brunner II see also: Mary Felstiner, "Commandant of Drancy: Alois Brunner and the Jews of France," *Holocaust and Genocide Studies* 2:1 (1987), 38.

3   Felstiner, "Commandant," 27–37, 40.

4   "Eichmanns Rechte Hand: Das ist Alois Brunner, der Mörder von 125,000 Juden," *Bunte*, vol. 45, 30.10.1985, 26–27.

5   "Er ist, was er war: Ein Feind der Juden," *Bunte* 46, 7.11.1985, 33. For a slightly different version of Skorzeny's words see: Wiesenthal to Robinson, 28.1.1972, 4, Brunner name file no.1, VWI-SWA.

6   Irmtrud Wojak, *Fritz Bauer (1903–1968): The Prosecutor Who Found Eichmann and Put Auschwitz on Trial*, trans. Adam Blauhut and Karen Margolis (Munich: Buxus Edition, 2018), 278–292, 295–297, 314–315, 363–364, 393–394; Ben Redjeb, "The Gehlen Organization," 225, 229.

7   Felstiner, "Commandant," 39.

8   On Fischer's background see: BfV report, 6.2.1961, Dr. Fischer alias Alois Brunner, file 051-P, 030243–0000, 3348–3351, 3407, BfV Archive.

9   Schaefer's testimony on Brunner, 13.5.1960, 7–8, author's private collection; Witzke's statement to the FRG Consulate in Damascus, 13.5.1961, 2, in FRG Consulate in Damascus to the Foreign Ministry, 23.5.1961, B83, Nr.417, Band 742, Politisches Archiv des Auswärtigen Amts, Berlin (hereafter cited as PA-AA).

10 Schaefer's testimony on Brunner, 13.5.1960, 8–9, author's private collection; "Er ist," *Bunte* 46, 7.11.1985, 33, "Eichmanns," *Bunte* 45, 30.10, 1985, 26–27. In a BfV interrogation, Vogel admitted that he met Brunner during the war, but denied

meeting him or helping him afterward. His testimony, however, loses credibility when one examines Brunner's letters to Vogel (see below). For Vogel's version see: BfV Conversation with Dr. Vogel, 20.1.1961, Dr. Fischer alias Alois Brunner, file 051-P, 030243–0000, 3348–3351, BfV Archive.

11   Felstiner, "Commandant," 39.

12   "Er ist," *Bunte* 46, 7.11.1985, 33.

13   "Er ist," *Bunte* 46, 7.11.1985, 34; Franz Rademacher's Testimony, "Zeugen-Vernehmung in der Untersuchung gegen Brunner Alois, Zentrale Stelle Ludwigsburg," 6.2.1968 (hereafter cited as Rademacher's testimony–Zentrale Stelle Ludwigsburg), author's private collection; Witzke's statement to the FRG Consulate in Damascus, 13.5.1961, 3, in FRG Consulate Damascus to Foreign Ministry, 23.5.1961, B83, Nr. 417, Band 742, PA-AA.

14   Gerhard Schacht, "Die deutschen Militärberater in Syrien," 17.6.1951, 2. Mast Papers, courtesy of Erich Schmidt-Eenboom; the Mufti's apartment was in Rue Sheikh Yousef. Stangl moved there only after he left the more famous address in Rue George Haddad 22. See: Gitta Sereny, *Into that Darkness: From Mercy Killing to Mass Murder* (New York: McGraw-Hill, 1974), 341.

15   Schaefer's testimony on Brunner, 13.5.1960, 23, author's private collection; Schmidt-Eenboom, *BND*, 188–197; Chern Chen, "Former Nazi Officers in the Near East: German Military Advisors in Syria, 1949–56," *The International History Review* vol. 40, issue no. 4 (2018), 736–743; Elzer, "Deutsche Militärberater," 229.

16   Fechter, FRG Consul, Damascus to the Foreign Ministry, Bonn, 13.4.1961, 5, B83, Nr. 417, Band 742, PA-AA; Schaefer's testimony on Brunner, 13.5.1960, 10–12, author's private collection; Witzke's statement to the FRG Consulate in Damascus, 23.5.1961, 3, in FRG Consulate in Damascus to the Foreign Ministry, 23.5.1961, B83, Nr. 417, Band 742, PA-AA; Of course, after he was finally arrested in Germany, Späth insisted that Thameco was an innocent pharmaceutical company, and that even Brunner's business in Damascus were completely legal. See: Karl-Heinz Späth's interrogation, 5.12.1960, 5, Abt. 361, Zug. 8/05, R3310, Hessisches Hauptstaatsarchiv (hereafter cited as HHStA). On Qatar Office (here misspelled as "Zatar Office") see also: BfV Report of conversation with an Israeli intelligence liaison, Köln, 20.7.1984, 054-P-270029–0000, BRUNNER, Alois, 7, and a BfV report, 10.2.1961, Hermann Schaefer name file, 340, BfV Archive.

17   Interrogation of Wilhelm Steinhausen, in file 9238246, "Dr. Georg Fischer alias Alois Brunner," 3510, BfV Archive; Major Richter, Hauptabteilung XX/2, "Brunner, Alois," 22.1.1976, 2, MfS HA XX Nr. 4084, 000118–119, BStU; "Er ist," *Bunte* 46, 7.11.1985, 34; Gerald Freihofner, "Eichmanns Rechte Hand," *Wochenpresse,* vol. 49, no. 25, 1988, 26; Schaefer's testimony on Brunner, 1–2, 9–10, 13.5.1960, author's private collection; Witzke's statement to the FRG Consulate in Damascus, 23.5.1961, 3, in FRG Consulate in Damascus to the Foreign Ministry, 23.5.1961,

B83, Nr. 417, Band 742, PA-AA. See also Simon Wiesenthal's report (undated, probably around 1961) based on information given by Alois Schätzl on Brunner. Much of this information is obviously false, but Wiesenthal's own note about Späth in the end of the report is useful and informative. This report can be found in Brunner Name file no. 1, VWI-SWA. About Späth's connections to the BND see also Chief, Munich Operations Group to Chief EE, 20.4.1961, Beissner name file, document no. 74, CREST.

18 Robert Fisk, "Syrian Bodyguards for Torturer who was Eichmann's Assistant," *The Times*, 17.3.1983. See also "Zweigestirn des Todes," *Der Spiegel* 49, 2.12.1996, 106. In some sources, the street address is Rue Haddad 7, but this is a mistake. The 7 is in fact the number of the apartment. This corresponds well with the Mossad information quoted by Yossi Chen, *Ha-mirdaf aharei poshe'i milhama Nazim* (internal Mossad study, declassified in 2014, Yad Vashem Archives, hereafter cited as Chen, Mossad Report: Nazi Hunting), vol. 2, 122, as well as with the CIA files, see Chief, Munich Operations Group to Chief EE, 20.4.1961, Beissner name file, document no. 74. See also Susanna Wallsten's and Eric Ericson's interview with Abdul Rahman Hanada (recorded), 20.5.2020, author's private archive, courtesy of Susanna Wallsten; BfV Note, 16.2.1961, interrogation of Wilhelm Steinhausen, file 9238246, "Dr. Georg Fischer alias Alois Brunner," 3509, BfV Archive.

19 Sereny, *Into that Darkness*, 340.

20 Fecther, FRG Consul, Damascus, to the Foreign Ministry, Bonn, 13.4.1961, 1–2, Witzke's statement to the FRG Consulate in Damascus, 23.5.1961, 4, in FRG Consulate in Damascus to the Foreign Ministry, 23.5.1961, B83, Nr. 417, Band 742, PA-AA.

21 Witzke's statement to the FRG Consulate in Damascus, 23.5.1961, 3–4, in FRG Consulate in Damascus to the Foreign Ministry, 23.5.1961, B83, Nr. 417, Band 742, PA-AA; CIA report, Director to [ ], 11.3.1958, Rademacher name file, document no. 3, CREST; Hedi Aouidj's Interview with Abu Ra'ad, 15.10.2016, author's private archive; Rademacher's testimony to the Zentrale Stelle Ludwigsburg, 16.2.1968, author's private collection; Waffenhandel: Springer-Remer Bericht," 15.9.1961, 125–127, folder 101.439, BND Archive.

22 Hermann Schaefer, statement to the Generalstaatsanwalt Frankurt a/M., 19.7.1960, Brunner name file no. 4, 97, Serge Klarsfeld Private Archive (hereafter cited as SKPA).

23 Christian Springer's interview with "Mahmoud" in Christian Springer, *Nazi, Komm Raus!: wie ich dem Massenmörder Alois Brunner in Syrien auf der Spur war* (München: LangenMüller, 2012), 154. The details in Springer's interviews are not always reliable. Often, however, they are. The witness he interviewed in Damascus knew obscure details about Brunner, such as his knowledge of Hungarian (compare with: File B162/20565, 293, Bundesarchiv—Aussenstelle Ludwigsburg, hereafter cited as BA-AL).

24 Susanna Wallsten's and Eric Ericson's interview with Abdul Rahman Hanada (recorded), 20.5.2020, author's private archive, courtesy of Susanna Wallsten; Georg Fischer (Alois Brunner) to Arthur Maichanitsch, 22.8.1969, Brunner name file no. 1, VWI-SWA.

25 "Waffenhandel: Springer-Remer Bericht," 15.9.1961, 135, folder 101.439, BND Archive; BfV Report of conversation with an Israeli intelligence liaison, Cologne, 20.7.1984, 054-P-270029–0000, BRUNNER, Alois, 7, BfV Archive.

CHAPTER 9

1 Engelmann, *The Weapons Merchants*, 112. Compare with the ruling of the Administrative Court in Schleswig-Holstein, Kamer III, Springer against the town of Bad-Segeberg, 10.2.1966, 4, Ernst-Wilhelm Springer name file, 060-P-110067–0000, 1578, BfV Archive.

2 "Springer-Prozess: Schrott in Kisten," *Der Spiegel*, 25.12.1963; Interrogation of Adolf Gerhard Gottwald, 2.4.1963, Hamburg Criminal Police, B206 51152, 103, BND report from Damascus, 27.8.1953, B 206 51092, 111, BA-K.

3 Engelmann, *The Weapons Merchants*, 125. On Krüger's past as a Nazi anti-Semitic propagandist see: BfV report, 5.1.1961, Hermann Schaefer name file, 233–234, BfV Archive.

4 "Waffenhandel: Springer-Remer Bericht," 15.9.1961, 136, 30.6.1963, 321, folder 101.439, BND Archive.

5 The primary sources on the establishment of OTRACO are scarce but can be located in various archives and juxtaposed with one another. See: "Waffenhandel: Springer-Remer Bericht," 15.9.1961, 41, 49–52, 135–136, 246, 297, 304, folder 101.439, BND Archive; BfV Report of conversation with an Israeli intelligence liaison, Cologne, 20.7.1984, 054-P-270029–0000, BRUNNER, Alois, 7, BfV Archive; BND Report (by Weisweiler), 3.12.1997, BND Archive; Ruling of the Higher Administrative Court, Schleswig-Holstein and Niedersachsen, Lüneberg, II Senat, Springer against the Town of Bad Segeberg, 16.5.1968, 2, Ernst-Wilhelm Springer name file, 060-P-010915–0000, BfV Archive.

6 BND report, 12.11.1960, Skorzeny name file, BA-K, B 206 51092; "Waffenhandel: Springer-Remer Bericht," 15.9.1961, 44, 47–52, 68–83, 97, 30.6.1962, 246, 304, 30.6.1963, 321–336, folder 101.439, BND Archive; Karl-Heinz Späth's interrogation, 5.12.1960, 10–11, Abt. 361, Zug. 8/05, R3310, HHStA; Schaefer's testimony on Brunner, 3.5.1960, 30, author's private collection. For a snippet of Beisner and Springer's deals in Syria and Algeria in 1957 and 1958, see the interrogation of Heinrich L. Kleine by the Hamburg Criminal Police, 11.2.1963, B206 51152, 53, BA-K. According to a BND report, Omnipol, the Czech company that they dealt with, was in a fact a front organization of the Czechoslovakian government. See: Lüdke "Die Aktivitäten" in Krieger, *Die Auslandsaufklärung*, 465.

7   Otto Skorzeny, BND evaluation index, entry "Wilhelm Beisner," B206 51094, 21, BA-K; BND report, 12.11.1960, Skorzeny name file, BA-K, B 206 51092.

8   Chen, "Former Nazi Officers," 735; Nordbruch, *Nazism in Syria*, 56–57, 64–65, 84, 94, 96, 108.

9   "Waffenhandel: Springer-Remer Bericht," 15.9.1961, 30.6.1963, 23–25, 30.6.1963, 322, 406–407, folder 101.439, BND Archive; BND report, 3.10.1956, Skorzeny name file, BA-K, B 206 51092; Hermann Schaefer, affidavit, 15.6.1960, an andix in LfV Niedersachsen to BfV, 15.6.1960, Horst Mahnke's affidavit, 26.5.1960, Landesgericht Hamburg, BfV Note, 16.2.1961, in file 9238246, "Dr. Georg Fischer alias Alois Brunner," 3320, 3528. Midani's role as a German collaborator during the war was so prominent as to feature in correspondence between the Syrian government and the British in 1945. See: Jabiri to Shone, 9.11.1945, reproduced in Meir Zamir, *The Secret Anglo-French War in the Middle East: Intelligence and Decolonization, 1940–1948* (London and New York: Routledge, 2015), 376–377.

10 "Waffenhandel: Springer-Remer Bericht," 15.9.1961, 53, folder 101.439, BND Archive.

11 Mathilde von Bülow, "Myth or Reality? The Red Hand and French Covert Action in Federal Germany during the Algerian War, 1956–61," *Intelligence and National Security*, vol. 22, no. 6 (June, 2018), 794, 797; Alistair Horne, *A Savage War of Peace: Algeria 1954–1962* (New York: New York Review Books, 2012), 329–332.

12 Mathilde von Bülow, *West Germany, Cold-War Europe and the Algerian War* (Cambridge: Cambridge University Press, 2016), 129–131; Bülow, "Myth or Reality," 794–795; Matthew Connelly, *A Diplomatic Revolution: Algeria's Fight for Independence and the Origins of the Post-Cold War Era* (Oxford: Oxford University Press, 2003), 78–79, 104–105, 109.

13 Interrogation of Otto Schlüter, 14.2.1963, Hamburg Criminal Police, B206 51152, 66–69, BA-K; Bülow, "Myth or Reality," 795.

14 Ritzi/Eenboom, *Im Schatten*, 162; Wolfgang Krieger, "Die BND Auslandsoperationen in Nodafrika—eine Fallstudie zu Richard Christmann in Tunesien und Algerien," in Krieger, *Die Auslandsaufklärung* 521–522.

15 Ritzi/Eenboom, *Im Schatten,* 166–167, 171.

16 Müller, *Gehlen*, vol. 2, 663.

17 Springer to Imam, 20.5.1955 (Imam documents folder), Abt. 361, Zug. 8/05, R3310, HHStA; See also the report of the Second Bureau (Intelligence Department) of the French Forces in Morocco on arms shipment from West Germany (January 1957), quoted in Bülow, *West Germany*, 142.

18 Schaefer's testimony on Brunner, 13.5.1960, 21, 29, author's private collection.

19 BND report, "Vorläufiger Bericht über Müller, Helmuth Hans," folder 100550-OT, 338, BND Archive. For an example of an alternative FLN procurement route, see interrogation of Henrich L. Kleine by the Hamburg Criminal Police, 11.2.1963, B206 51152, 52–53, BA-K. In 53, Kleine argued that in 1958, Springer was the only

German weapon trafficker he knew who was active in the Algerian market. This reflects Springer's attempts to dominate the market, but Kleine's argument is exaggerated.

20 Bavarian State Criminal Police to the Public Prosecutor's Office at the State Court Munich I, 12.1.1961, Hermann Schaefer name file, 409–410, BfV Archive. Ludwig Erhard, FRG Finance Minister and future chancellor, also shared Gehlen's hope to crowd-out Soviet influence in the Middle East through turning a blind eye to the arms trafficking. He also looked forward to "boost foreign trade, the lifeblood of West Germany's booming economy." See: Bülow, *West Germany*, 142.

21 Schaefer's testimony on Brunner, 3.5.1960, 25–26, author's private collection.

22 Ritzi/Eenboom, *Christmann*, 164–165.

CHAPTER **10**

1 Englemann, *The Weapons Merchants,* 9.

2 Müller, *Gehlen*, vol. 1, 560–561; Herre Diary, 27.9, 4,6.10.1949, 40, 44, in Critchfield Papers, box 5; See Henschke, *Rosenbergs Elite*, 247 (footnote no. 205) for references for further research in French.

3 Müller, *Gehlen*, vol. 1, 572; Bülow, "Myth or Reality," 802; Bülow, *West Germany*, 137–138, 145–146, 151–152, 319 (the quotation is from 138); Krieger, *Partnerdienste*, 307, 314.

4 Leczczynski, Bundeskriminalamt, to Breuer, director, Hamburg Kriminalamt, 12.10.1957, Abt. 544, no. 470, HHStA; Interrogation of Otto Schlüter, 14.2.1963, investigation report, 7.2.1963, interrogation of Adolf Gerhard Gottwald, 2.4.1963, Hamburg Criminal Police, B206 51152, 69–71, 97, 104. BA-K.

5 Shipment list, Intereuropa, Koper, Yugoslavia (undated), Imam documents folder, Abt. 361, Zug. 8/05, R3310, HHStA Schaefer's testimony on Brunner, 13.5.1960, 30–31, author's private collection. Engelmann, *The Weapons Merchants*, 119; Bülow, *West Germany*, 147.

6 Krüger to Imam, 26.7.1957, Beisner to Imam, 30.7.1957, Imam documents folder, Abt. 361, Zug. 8/05, R3310, HHStA ; Schaefer's testimony on Brunner, 3.5.1960, 32–35, author's private collection; Karl-Heinz Späth's interrogation, 5.12.1960, 11, Abt. 361, Zug. 8/05, R3310, HHStA; Krüger to Imam, 26.7.1957, (Imam documents folder), Abt. 361, Zug. 8/05, R3310, HHStA.

7 Schaefer's testimony on Brunner, 13.5.1960, 35, author's private collection; Karl-Heinz Späth's interrogation, 5.12.1960, 11, Abt. 361, Zug. 8/05, R3310, HHStA.

8 Nautilus S.A., (Geneva) to Imam, 12.1.1959, Imam documents folder, Abt. 361, Zug. 8/05, R3310, HHStA; Schaefer's testimony on Brunner, 35–37, 3.5.1960, author's private collection.

9 Springer-Prozess: Schrott in Kisten," *Der Spiegel*, 25.12.1963.

10 Schaefer's testimony on Brunner, 13.5.1960, 37–38, author's private collection; "Waffenhandel: Springer-Remer Bericht," 15.9.1961, 24, folder 101.439, BND Archive; *Al-Jumhur*, Damascus, 6.11.1958.

[11] Aïssa Abdessemed, "Georg Puchert—mort pour l'Algérie," *El Watan*, 13.7.2005; "Der Killer," *Der Spiegel*, 25.3.1959.

[12] "Vorläufiger Bericht über Müller, Helmuth Hans," 10,18.8.1967, 334, 354, "Waffenhandel: Springer-Remer Bericht," 15.9.1961, 41, folders 100550-OT, 101.439, BND Archive.

[13] BND report, "Vorläufiger Bericht über Müller, Helmuth Hans," folder 100550-OT, 332, BND Archive; Waffenhandel: Springer-Remer Bericht," 15.9.1961, 46, folder 101.439 BND Archive.

[14] Interrogations of Otto J. Schnitzler, 23.3.1963, Cologne Criminal Police, and Otto Schlüter, 14.2.1963, Hamburg Criminal Police, B206 51152, 15, 66, 72, BA-K.

[15] Walbaum, Bayer. LKA to Staantsanwaltschaft München I, 18.10.1962, Bayerisches Hauptstaatsarchiv (hereafter cited as BHSA), 10–11.

[16] Waffenhandel: Springer-Remer Bericht," 30.6.1962, 264, folder 101.439 BND Archive; Engelmann, *The Weapons Merchants*, 28–29, 34–38, 60–62; Peter Stähle, "Ein Mann mit Namen Seidenschnur," *Die Zeit*, vol. 40 (1965); Bayer, LKA, "Kriminalpolizelische Aufzeichnung über Hans-Joachim Seidenschnur und andere," München, 30.11.1961, 30, andix, 4–34, Pudreries Reunies de Belgique S.A. to Erwin Muermann, 30.1.1958, LKA 305, Walbaum, Bayer. LKA to Staantsanwaltschaft München I, 18.10.1962, 10–11, BHSA.

[17] Bayer. LKA, "Kriminalpolizelische Aufzeichnung über Hans-Joachim Seidenschnur und andere," München, 30.11.1961, 31–32, LKA 305, BHSA; Interrogation of Otto Schlüter, 14.2.1963, Hamburg Criminal Police, B206 51152, 72–73, BA-K; Engelmann, *The Weapons Merchants*, 34–40; Bülow, *West Germany*, 312.

[18] "Der Killer," *Der Spiegel*, 25.3.1959; Faligot and Krop, *La Piscine*, 164.

[19] Frankfurt Police Report (Detectives Galow and Neuling), 3.3.1959, Grundmeyer (regional chemist), report, 20.4.1959, Abt. 544, no. 470, 6–12, 45–48, HHStA; Generalstaatsanwaltschaft Hamburg to the Hamburg Senate, 20.5.1959, 3, B106/15783, BA-K; "Der Killer," *Der Spiegel*, 25.3.1959; BfV report on OTRACO's arm trafficking, 30.9.1959, 20, 23–24, Ernst-Wilhelm Springer name file, 060-P-110067–0000, BfV Archive. According to another version, given by a BND source, Puchert was killed by a business rival whom he kidnapped and mishandled in Madrid. See: Lüdke "Die Aktivitäten" in Krieger, *Die Auslandsaufklärung*, 465.

[20] Fischer to the Federal Minister of the Interior, 15.7.1959, translated note from Catena, B105/15783, BA-K; LKA Bericht (Kom. Scherrer), Bad Godsberg, 29.8.1961, 4, Bayer. LKA, "Kriminalpolizelische Aufzeichnung über Hans-Joachim Seidenschnur und andere," München, 30.11.1961, 2, Seidenschnur's interrogation, Bayer. LKA Munich, 10.4.1962, LKA 305, Seidenschnur's interrogation, Bayer. LKA Munich, 10.4.1962, 3–4, Walbaum, Bayer.LKA to Staatsanwaltschaft München I, 18.10.1962, 2–3, Ganz, Bayer, LKA to Staatsanwaltschaft München I, 2.4.1963, LKA 315/A, BHSA.

[21] BND reports, "Vorläufiger Bericht über Müller, Helmuth Hans," 10, 18.8.1967, folder 100550-OT, 340, 356, 358, BND Archive.

22 BND reports, "Vorläufiger Bericht über Müller, Helmuth Hans," 10, 18.8.1967, folder 100550-OT, 333, 340–341, 358–359, BND Archive; Interrogation of Otto Schlüter, 14.2.1963, Hamburg Criminal Police, B206 51152, 71, BA-K; Faligot and Krop, *La Piscine*, 166.

23 See: Waffenhandel: Springer-Remer Bericht," 30.6.1962, 191, folder 101.439 BND Archive; Note by Lenck and Krobbel, 13.2.1963, investigation report, 7.2.1963, Hamburg Criminal Police, B206 51152, 65, 97–99, BA-K. According to the aforementioned investigation report (97), One of OTRACO's suppliers, Otto Schlüter, also dealt with the OAS, the French extremist underground in Algeria, through different intermediaries.

CHAPTER 11

1 "Waffenhandel: Springer-Remer Bericht," 15.9.1961, 20–21.

2 Interrogation of Adolf Gerhard Gottwald, 2.4.1963, Hamburg Criminal Police, B206 51152, 105 104. BA-K; "Waffenhandel: Springer-Remer Bericht," 15.9.1961, 22, folder 101.439 BND Archive.

3 Waffenhandel: Springer-Remer Bericht," 15.9.1961, 32, 41, folder 101.439 BND Archive; Engelmann, *The Weapons Merchants*, 114–118.

4 Waffenhandel: Springer-Remer Bericht," 15.9.1961, 22–28, 76, 95–96, folder 101.439 BND Archive.

5 "Waffenhandel: Springer-Remer Bericht," 15.9.1961, 26–27, 95–116, 30.6.1963, 321, folder 101.439, BND Archive. Heinrich Kleine testified that Remer and Springer offered him to open a front for their arms deals in Morocco, see: interrogation of Henrich L. Kleine by the Hamburg Criminal Police, 11.2.1963, B206 51152, 54, BA-K. Kleine contradicts himself often about the nature of this company in Morocco, and vacillates about the question whether it had to do with weapons or other business. However, at one point, Springer confessed to him that he wanted to use this enterprise to facilitate weapon shipments. According to Kleine, the negotiations took place in 1961. Other witnesses (see Schlüter's interrogation, 14.2.1963, by the Hamburg Criminal Police in the same file, 80) corroborated Kleine's complicity in arms trafficking for the FLN.

6 Fechter, FRG Consul Damascus to the Foreign Ministry, Bonn, 13.4.1961, B141/528447, 22–23, BA-K; Wojak, *Bauer*, 290–292. On the false trails of Eichmann in the Middle East see also: Bettina Stangneth, *Eichmann before Jerusalem: The Unexamined Life of a Mass Murderer*. Trans.: Ruth Martin (New York: Alfred A. Knopf, 2014), 95–102.

7 BND report, "Vorläufiger Bericht über Müller, Helmuth Hans," 10.8.1967, folder 100550-OT, 343, BND Archive.

8 Karl-Heinz Späth's interrogation, Bayer.LKA, 5.12.1960, 3, Abt. 461, Zug. 8/05, R5310, HHA; Witzke's statement to the FRG Consulate in Damascus, 13.5.1961, in FRG Consulate in Damascus to the Foreign Ministry, 23.5.1961, B83, Nr. 417, Band 742, PA-AA; Schmidt-Eenboom, *BND*, 190–192; Gerhard Schacht, "Die

deutschen Militärberater in Syrien," 17.6.1951, 1. Mast papers, courtesy of Erich Schmidt-Eenboom.

9 Späth's testimony to the Bavarian Criminal Police, 12.12.1960, Hermann Schaefer name file, 290, BfV Archive.

10 BfV report, 5.1.1961, Hermann Schaefer name file, 214–215, BfV Archive.

11 BfV report, 5.1.1961, Hermann Schaefer name file, 215, BfV Archive.

12 Gehlen Org report, October 1953, Otto Skorzeny name file, B 206 51092, BA-K.

13 BfV report, 5.1.1961, Hermann Schaefer name file, 216–217, BfV Archive.

14 Kriminalpolizelische Aufzeichnung über Hans-Joachim Seidenschnur und andere," Landeskriminalamt München, 30.11.1961, 34, LKA 305, BHSA; Vortragsnotiz no.28/61 and 363/W, 15.5.1961, 30.212.OT, 137–143, BND Archiv; BfV report, 5.1.1961, Hermann Schaefer name file, 217, 222, BfV Archive. Albercht Hagemann, *Hermann Rauschning: Ein deutsches Leben zwischen NS-Ruhm und Exil* (Köln: Böhlau Verlag, 2018), 428–432, 450–465.

15 BfV Report, Dr. von Berge to II/A 4, 4.1.1961, Späth's testimony to the Bavarian State Criminal Police, 12.12.1960, Schaefer to Imam, 18.1.1960, Hermann Schaefer name file, 258, 435, BfV Archive; CIA report, 28.12.1960, Beissner name file, document no. 59, CREST.

16 Jürgen Willbrand, "Und nichts dazu gelernt," *Illustrierte Kristall*, September 1960. The editor of Kristall, Horst Mahnke, was himself a Nazi criminal, Einsatzgruppe veteran responsible for the murder of dozens of Jews in Russia. However, for complicated political reasons, the stories he published as a *Spiegel* reporter, and his editorial line in Kristall, fixated on critical exposure of certain old Nazis and neo-Nazis in West German and Austrian politics. For more information about Mahnke, see: Lutz Hachmeister, Friedemann Siering, Michael Wildt, *Die Herren Journalisten: Die Elite der deutschen Presse nach 1945* (München: Becksche Reihe, 2002), 95–118, 239.

17 Interrogation of Hans Germani, Bayer. LKA, 5.1.1961, 1–6, Abt. 461, Zug. 8/05, R5310, Karl-Heinz Späth's interrogation, 5.12.1960, 12, 17, Abt. 361, Zug. 8/05, R3310, HHStA; OSI/OCA Bonn, "Dr. Wilhelm Beisner," 10.11.1960, CIA report, 28.12.1960, COS Munich to COS Germany, 10.1.1961, Beissner name file, documents no.56,59,62 CREST.

18 "Sprengstoff-Attentat in Schwabing," *Süddeutsche Zeitung*, 17.10.1960; "Bombe in der Blütenstrasse," *Der Spiegel*, 26.10.1960; OSI/OCA Bonn, "Dr. Wilhelm Beisner," 10.11.1960, Beissner name file, document no. 56, CREST.

19 "Sprengstoff," *Süddeutsche Zeitung*, 17.10.1960; OSI/OCA Bonn, "Dr. Wilhelm Beisner," 10.11.1960, Beissner name file, document no. 56, CREST.

20 Chief, Munich liaison Office to Chief EE, 13.3.1961, Beissner name file, document no. 71, CREST. It seems that the investigation was held in such a secretive way, that even the BLKA officials were not certain where the investigation documents and the witness interrogation transcripts were located. See: Detective Pfaffenberger,

BLKA, "Ermittlungsverfahren gegen Dr. Beisner," 14.4.1961, Detective Thaler, "Ermittlungsverfahren gegen Dr. Wilhelm Beisner," 13.6.1961, Staatsanwaltschaften 27166, 11–12, BSA. According to Thaler's letter from 13.6.1961, the "state secret" classification was removed only in June 1961. This was not the first time that the BND (before 1956: Gehlen Org) took over or stopped a police investigation at will. See for example Heidenreich et al., *Geheimdienstkrieg*, 96.

21 Josef Joffe, "Reflections on German Policy in the Middle East," in Shahram Chubin, ed., *Germany and the Middle East* (New York: St. Martin's Press, 1992), 197.

22 "Bombe in der Blütenstrasse," *Der Spiegel*, 26.10.1960.

23 Note, Hermann Schaefer name file, 325, BfV Archive.

24 Cherif (Tunis) to Beisner, 17.1.1961, reproduced in Chief, Munich Liaison Office to Chief EE, 8.3.1961, Beissner name file, document no. 70, CREST.

25 Interrogation of Adolf Gerhard Gottwald, 2.4.1963, Hamburg Criminal Police, B206 51152, 108, BA-K.

26 Vernehmung des Dr. Wilhelm Beisner, 4.11.1960, BLKA, Detective Thaler to Abt. III b, 2.3.1961, Walbaum to Thaler, 21.4.1961, Staatsanwaltschaften 27166, KOI Thaler, "Ermittlungsverfahren gegen Dr. Wihlelm Beisner," 13.6.1961, 6–12, BHSA. It seems that KOI Walbaum who managed the assassination investigation tried to control access of other detectives to Beisner; Bülow, *West Germany*, 311–316.

27 Cited in Bülow, *West Germany*, 321.

28 Bülow, "Myth or Reality," 807–809; "Waffenhandel: Springer-Remer Bericht," 15.9.1961, 17, 22, folder 101.439, BND Archive.

29 Cited in Bülow, *West Germany*, 323. See also Henschke, *Rosenbergs Elite*, 48.

30 Bülow, *West Germany*, 314–315; Henschke, *Rosenbergs Elite*, 52.

31 Bülow, "Myth or Reality," 807–809; Krieger, *Partnerdienste*, 314.

CHAPTER 12

1 Bfv to the LfV, Lower Saxony and LfV Bavaria, 1.1.1961, Dr. Fischer alias Alois Brunner, file 051-P, 030243–0000, 3401–3402, BfV Archive.

2 *Der Morgen*, 5.11.1961. Hermann Schaefer's report to the BfV, 8.2.1960, Dr. Fischer alias Alois Brunner, file 051-P, 030243–0000, 3348–3351, 3313, BfV Archive.

3 Telegram, Department of State, 8.10.1961, RG 84, Entry UD 3248A, Box 37, folder 350 (Syrian Arab Republic), NARA.

4 Sami M. Moubayed, *Damascus between Democracy and Dictatorship* (Lanham, Md.: University Press of America, 2000), 151; See also: Tamura, acting Japanese ambassador in Syria, to the Foreign Minister, 29.10.1957, A-0219, A-0213, A410.9, 1181–1182, Diplomatic Archives of Japan.

5 L'Orient, 30.10.1961; Werner, FRG Consulate in Damascus to the Foreign Ministry, 16.3.1962, B83, Nr. 417, Band 742, PA-AA; Andrew Rathmell, *Secret*

War in the Middle East: The Struggle for Syria, 1949–1961 (London/New York:
Tauris Academic Studies, 1995), 146; R. B. Knight to P. E. Haring, "Syrian Region
Budget," 5.8.1961, RG 84, Entry UD 3248A, Box 38, folder 350 (UAR, 1961), Bill
Douglass to U.S. Ambassador in Damascus, "Police Organization, DEPCIRTEL
1918," 18.5.1962, RG 84, Entry UD 3248A, Box 42, folder 370.1 (Public Order
& Safety, Police, 1962), NARA. According to American and West German sources,
Sarraj's force was called "The Special Bureau" in its early phase and only later, in
winter 1959, was divided to GID and GIA. The term "Special Bureau" was still used
informally to describe the GIA. According to *L'Orient*'s George Chatila, however,
GIA's name "was synonymous with state terror in the eyes of the Syrians." Laham
and Adham's GIA was supposed to be subordinated directly to Cairo, but was
controlled in practice by Sarraj. For more information on the evolution of the Special
Bureau, see the memoirs of Fauzi Shu'aybi, *Shahed min al-Mukhabarat Al-Suriya*
(Beirut: Riad Al-Ris, 2018), 103–105.

6   Schaefer's testimony on Brunner, 13.5.1960, 19, 28, author's private collection;
    L'Orient, 30.10.1961.

7   "Er ist," *Buhne* 46, 7.11.1985, 34. In the German article, the name of the Syrian
    officer appears as "Lahan," a mistaken transliteration of "Laham." In this interview,
    Brunner dated the interrogation incorrectly to 1960. In fact it was held in late 1959.
    See: Hermann Schaefer's report to the BfV, 8.2.1960, Dr. Fischer alias Alois Brunner,
    file 051-P, 030243–0000, 3313, BfV Archive. See also: Witzke's statement to the
    FRG Consulate in Damascus, 13.5.1961, in FRG Consulate Damascus to Foreign
    Ministry, 23.5.1961, B83, Nr.417, Band 742, PA-AA. U.S. diplomatic records
    from the same period also document Syrian preoccupation with drug trafficking.
    However, informants of the U.S. Consulate strongly suspected that bigwigs in police
    and intelligence agencies, including Sarraj himself, were involved in the trafficking
    operations. In such a case, Brunner's arrest might have been an attempt to get rid of
    a competitor. See: U.S. Consulate in Aleppo to U.S. Consulate General, Damascus,
    22.5.1961, RG 84, Entry UD 3248A, Box 38, folder 370.31 (narcotics smuggling),
    NARA. See also other documents in the same folder.

8   Hermann Schaefer, "Die Geisterbotschafts Heinrich Himmerls," *Afro-Asia*
    (November 1961); Witzke's statement to the FRG Consulate in Damascus,
    13.5.1961, in FRG Consulate in Damascus to the Foreign Ministry, 23.5.1961, B83,
    Nr. 417, Band 742, PA-AA. According to Witzke, Brunner was still involved in FLN
    arms trafficking in October/November 1960. Fechter, FRG Consul, Damascus, to
    the Foreign Ministry, Bonn, 13.4.1961, B141/528447, 21, BA-K; SDECE report,
    "information from Archives, 1961," in Brunner name file no. 3, SKPA. Brunner
    is mentioned as a possible GID employee in Beisner's network chart, CIA report,
    1961 [precise date unknown], Beissner name file, as well as CIA report, 28.12.1960,
    Chief, Munich Operations Group to Chief EE, 20.4.1961, Frankfurt to Director,

17.5.1961, Mamdouh al-Midani to Wilhelm Beisner, 6.5.1961, Beissner name file, documents 59, 60, 74, 81, 82, CREST. It is clear from context that the person whose name was censored was a CIA [KUBRAK] asset, especially from the last sentence of paragraph no. 5. See also: Hermann Schaeffer to the Generalstaatsanwalt in Frankurt, 15.8.1960, First Auschwitz Trial Materials, Band 3, 497, Fond 461, No. 3768/245, HHStA; BfV Note, 16.2.1961, interrogation of Wilhelm Steinhausen, file 9238246, "Dr. Georg Fischer alias Alois Brunner," 3511, BfV Archive.

9   Schaefer's testimony on Brunner, 13.5.1960, 4–7, author's private collection.

10 Karl-Heinz Späth's interrogation, 5.12.1960, 7, Abt. 361, Zug. 8/05, R3310, HHStA; Hermann Schaefer to Oberstaatsanwalt beim Landgericht in Bamberg, 22.9.1961, Rep. K 105, Nr.1493, Staatsarchiv Bamberg (hereafter cited as SAB).

11 Mamdouh al-Midani to Wilhelm Beisner, 6.5.1961, Beissner name file, document no. 82, CREST; Willbrand, "Und nichts dazu gelernt," *Illustrierte Kristall*, September 1960; BND to BfV, 18.4.1961, Hermann Schaefer name file, 741, BfV Archive.

12 Brunner to Beisner, quoted in COS Germany to Chief EE, 3.4.1961, Beissner name file, document no. 72. Brunner appears here, and in several other documents, as Rischer, probably a typo of his pseudonym Fischer. However, his postbox, no. 635, appears as Brunner's in Mossad records. See Chen, Mossad Report: Nazi Hunting, vol. 2, 138.

13 Fechter, FRG Consul in Damascus to the Foreign Ministry, 13.4.1961, B83, Nr. 417, Band 742, PA-AA; Curt Witzke's interrogation, Staatsanwaltschaft Frankfurt, 13.6.1961, 1–2, partly reproduced and quoted in Abt. 361, Zug. 8/05, R3310, HHStA; Willi Winkler, *Der Schattenmann: Von Goebbels zu Carlos: Das Mysteriöse Leben des Francois Genoud* (Berlin: Rowohlt, 2011), 132–134.

14 Chief, Munich Operations Group to Chief, COS Germany, CIA dispatch, 10.5.1961, 1–2, Brunner name file, document no. 4, CREST. Brunner's presence in Egypt at the time is also confirmed by the Mossad files. See Chen, Mossad Report: Nazi Hunting, vol. 2, 116, as well as by Hermann Schaefer, though he was not familiar with the details. See: Hermann Schaefer, statement to the Generalstaatsanwalt Frankurt a/M., 19.7.1960, Brunner name file no. 4, SKPA, 99.

15 "Er ist," *Bunte* 46, 7.11.1985, 34.

16 For the names of the Nazi and Arab adventurers recruited by Rayees and Brunner, see: Georg Fischer (Alois Brunner) to Arthur Maichanitsch, 24.6.1972, Brunner name file no. 1, VWI-SWA. Compare with Brunner's own recollections, "Er ist," *Bunte* 46, 7.11.1985, 34. For background information on Maichanitsch, and discussion on the authenticity of the correspondence, see: Thomas Vasek, "Der Mann in Damascus," *Profil*, vol. 34, no. 17 (August 1998), 66.

17 Our information on the abortive Goldmann operation comes from three sources that largely confirm one another: Simon Wiesenthal's confidential letter to Dr. Stephen J. Roth from the World Jewish Congress from June 1962, and Brunner's interview to the German illustrated journal *Bunte* in 1985. See: Wiesenthal to Roth, 12.6.1962,

Alois Brunner Name file no.1, VWI-SWA. Compare with Brunner's recollections: "Er ist," *Bunte* 46, 7.11.1985, 34. Another version was reported to the attorney general's office in Frankfurt by Hermann Schaefer. Schaefer mistakenly said that the German police arrested some of Brunner's accomplices. See: Bundeskriminalamt, to Generalstaatsanwalt Frankfurt/Main, 11.9.1962, Brunner name file no. 4, 220, SKPA.

[18] Ben-Gurion Diary, 27.7.1960, Ben-Gurion Archive, Ben-Gurion Institute for the Study of Israel and Zionism, Sde Boker, Israel.

[19] Israeli government meeting, protocol, 4.12.1960, 23–24, Israeli State Archives; Francois Genoud to Franz Rademacher, 9.3.1962, BA-K, ALLPROZ 6/257, fol. 128.

[20] Christian Springer's interview with Muhammad Hijo in Springer, *Nazi*, 144.

[21] Georg Fischer (Brunner) to the German Consulate in Damascus, 12.11.1960, FRG Consulate in Damascus to the Foreign Ministry, 13.4, 23.5.1961, Witzke's statement to the FRG Consul in Damascus, 13.5.1961; Werner, FRG Consulate in Damascus to the Foreign Ministry, 16.3.1962, B83, Nr. 417, Band 742, PA-AA. About the Moroccan consul's relationship with Sarraj see: U.S. Consulate in Damascus to the State Department, 9.8.1961, RG 84, Entry UD 3248A, Box 38, folder 350 (UAR, 1961), NARA. For more information on Schaefer's attempts to organize fraudulent arms deals in order to penetrate the circle of arms merchants see: Karl-Heinz Späth's interrogation, 5.12.1960, 14, Abt. 361, Zug. 8/05, R3310, HHStA.

CHAPTER 13

[1] Agent report (Eduard Roditi), 2.9.1952, RG 319, Entry ZZ-6, Box 10, "Israeli Intelligence Service in Germany," NARA.

[2] Chen, Mossad Report: Nazi Hunting, vol. 1, 10–17, 20–21, vol. 3, 49–50; A Mossad staffer who worked with Cohen-Abarbanel, gave me interesting details on his personality and professional profile. Interview with an anonymous Mossad staffer, 15.11.2018. See also Ronen Bergman, *Rise and Kill First: The Secret History of Israel's Targeted Assassinations* (New York: Random House), 33.

[3] Chen, Mossad Report: Nazi Hunting, vol. 1, 21, vol. 2, 116. On the hunt for Josef Mengele, that took place in the same time, see: vol. 3, 49–84.

[4] BfV Report, Dr. von Berge to II/A 4, 4.1.1961, Hermann Schaefer name file, 209–210, BfV Archive.

[5] Mitscher to Oberstaatsanwalt Frankrurt/a.Main, 6.12.1984, B162/20564, 2, BA-AL; Schwarzmann (FRG Consulate in Beirut) to the Foreign Ministry, 1.9.1961, B83, Nr. 417, Band 742, PA-AA.

[6] Chen, Mossad Report: Nazi Hunting, vol. 2, 116.

[7] Vortragsnotiz no.28/61 an 363/W, 15.5.1961, 30.212.OT, 138, BND Archiv; BND to BfV, 18.4.1961, Hermann Schaefer name file, 741, BfV Archive. Already in summer 1960, Schaefer boasted that he will make sure to "blow up" Wilhelm Beisner.

See: Vernehmungsniederschrift Hans F. Germani, Bayerisches Landeskriminalamt, 5.1.1961, as well as Vernehmungsniederschrift, Späth, Karl-Heinz, 5.12.1960, Wiesbaden Abt. 461, Zug. 8/05, R5310, 2–6, 10, 13–15, HHStA.

8 Chen, Mossad Report: Nazi Hunting, vol. 2, 116; CIA intelligence summary on Wilhelm Beissner, 1951–1953, COS Munich to COS Germany, 10.1.1961, Beissner name file, documents no. 11, 62, CREST; "Rauff, Colonel Walter," 27.3.1953, CIA Report, Shraga Eilam Private collection; Hans Germani's interrogation, 5.1.1961, Abt. 461, Zug. 8/05, R5310, 4, HHStA. On Kubainsky's background see also: BfV report, 5.1.1961, Hermann Schaefer name file, 235–236, BfV Archive.

9 Chen, Mossad Report: Nazi Hunting, vol. 2, 118; FRG Consulate in Damascus to the Foreign Ministry, 13.4.1961, B83, Nr. 417, Band 742, PA-AA. Additional rumors on Brunner's impending European trip, allegedly planned this time for May-June 1961, had also reached the BfV, see BfV report, 17.4.1961, file 9238246, "Dr. Georg Fischer alias Alois Brunner," 3534, BfV Archive.

10 "Alois Brunner Description Table," undated, Mossad Archive, reproduced in Chen, Mossad Report: Nazi Hunting, vol. 2, 121; Hans Germani's interrogation, Bayer. LKA, 1.5.1961, 6, Abt. 461, Zug. 8/05, R5310, HHStA; BfV Report on the interrogation of Karl-Heinz Späth, 7.2.1961, Hermann Schaefer name file, 325, BfV Archive.

11 Interview with Yitzhak Shamir, Mabat Malam, vol. 19 (July 1998), 13–14; Bergman, Rise and Kill First, 37–38; Chen, Mossad Report: Nazi Hunting, 119.

12 Chen, Mossad Report: Nazi Hunting, 119–120.

13 Chen, Mossad Report: Nazi Hunting, vol. 2, 122.

14 Chen, Mossad Report: Nazi Hunting, vol. 2, 122.

15 Chen, Mossad Report: Nazi Hunting, vol. 2, 122–123.

16 Chen, Mossad Report: Nazi Hunting, vol. 2, 123.

17 Shimon Peres, Kela David (Tel Aviv: Weidenfeld and Nicholson, 1969), 31–32, 47–48; Connelly, A Diplomatic Revolution, 104; Avner Cohen, Israel and the Bomb (New York: Columbia University Press, 1998), 53–60.

18 Bergman, Rise and Kill First, 66–67, 89, 67.

19 Ner, "Operational Report—Travel to the Destination," September 1961, Mossad Archive, reproduced in Chen, Mossad Report: Nazi Hunting, vol. 2, 126.

20 Yossi Chen, interview with the author, Ramat Hasharon, Israel, 4.3.2018.

21 Wiesenthal to Robinson, 28.1.1972, 3, Brunner name file no. 1, VWI-SWA; Testimony of Brunner's guard, Muhammad Abdul Rahman Hanada (Abu Yaman), in Hedi Aouidj and Mathieu Palain, "Die Assads und ihr Nazi: SS Hauptstrumführer Alois Brunner beriet Syriens Folterdiktatur," translation from French: Irma Wehrli, Reportage 33 (March 2017).

22 IDF General Staff Intelligence Department (AMAN), Special Intelligence Brief from "S.500," 14–15.9.1961, IDF Archive, reproduced in Chen, Mossad Report: Nazi Hunting, vol. 2, 127–128; Al Hayat, 15.9.1961.

23 Wiesenthal to Robinson, 28.1.1972, 3, Brunner name file no. 1, VWI-SWA; Fechter, FRG Ambassador in Damascus, to the Foreign Ministry, 19.1.1962, B130, 5.679A, PA-AA.

24 Fechter, FRG Consulate in Damascus, to the Foreign Ministry, 10.11.1961, B83, Nr. 417, Band 742, PA-AA; Fechter to the Foreign Ministry, 16.9.1961, Hermann Schaefer's testimony to the attorney general in Frankfurt, in Fritz Bauer to the Foreign Ministry, 19.10.1961, B141/528447, 75, 84–85, BA-K; "Qui est Georg Fischer?," *Le Soir* (Beirut), 2.11.1961. The deceptive rumors spread by the Syrian government were "swallowed" by the Mossad, see Chen, Mossad Report: Nazi Hunting, vol. 2, 116. They are also reflected in the memoirs of the Syrian military judge Salah a-Din Dhali, who later investigated the connections between the Israeli spy Eli Cohen and the Nazis in Damascus. See: *Haqā'iq lam tunshar 'an al-jāsūs al-Ṣahyūnī Ilī Kūhīn wa-qiṣṣatihi al-ḥaqīqiyah* (Damascus, 2001), 197.

25 Fechter, FRG Ambassador in Damascus to the Foreign Ministry, 26.6.1962, B 130, 5.679A, PA-AA.

26 Shimada, Consul General in Damascus to the Foreign Ministry, Tokyo, 29–30.9.1961, A-0219, A-410. 17–2–2, 1026–1027, 1045, see also the statement of the new Syrian defense minister in 1097, Diplomatic Archives of Japan, Tokyo. For analysis of the revolution's economic background see also: *Journal of Commerce,* 29.9.1961.

27 "Military Coup," U.S. Consulate Report, 29, 30 September 1961, telegram, Department of State, 8.10.1961, telegram, Department of State, 16.7.1960, RG 84, Entry UD 3248A, Box 37, folder 350 (Syrian Arab Republic), Box 38, folder 350 (UAR, 1960), NARA.

28 Statement of the Revolutionary Command, 7-A, 28.9.1961, A-0219, A.410, 17–2–2, 1168, Diplomatic Archives of Japan, Tokyo.

29 *L'Orient*, 30.10.1961. For a paraphrase of this article see: U.S. Embassy Damascus, "Syrian Officials of UAR Period to be Tried," 18.10.1961, RG 84, Entry UD 3248A, Box 37, folder 350 (Syrian Arab Republic, 1961), NARA.

30 Hans Riehl to the Zentrale Stelle Ludwigsburg, 21.11.1961, B162/19723, 53, BA-AL; Fritz Bauer, Attorney General of Hessen, to the Federal Justice Minister, 8.11.1961, Fechter, FRG Ambassador in Damascus, to the Foreign Ministry, 19.1.1962, B 130, 5.679A, PA-AA.

31 Fechter, FRG Consul General in Damascus, to the Foreign Ministry, 10.11.1961, 19.1.1962, B83, Nr. 417, Band 742, and B130, 5.679A (respectively), PA-AA; Koji, Japanese Consul General in Damascus, to the Foreign Ministry, 21.12.1961, A-0219, A.410, 17–2–2, 1195–1196, Diplomatic Archives of Japan.

32 Waffenhandel: Springer-Remer Bericht," 30.6.1962, 280, Name file 101.439 BND Archive.

33 Fecther, FRG Ambassador in Damascus to the Foreign Ministry, 19.1.1962, Werner, FRG Consulate in Damascus to the Foreign Ministry, 19.1.1962, 16.3.1962, B130, 5.679A, and B83, Nr.417, Band 742 (respectively), PA-AA.

34 Foreign Ministry to the Federal Justice Minister, Bonn, 9.5.1962, B141/528448, 63, BA-K.

35 BfV report of conversation with an Israeli intelligence liaison, Cologne, 20.7.1984, Israeli intelligence report to the BfV, 19.7.1984, 054-P-270029–0000, BRUNNER, Alois, 7, 27–28, BfV Archive. According to the later report, Brunner worked as an instructor in that school at the very least during Amin al-Hafez's presidency, that is, between 1963 and 1966; Susanna Wallsten's and Eric Ericson's interview with Abdul Rahman Hanada, (recorded) 20.5.2020, author's private archive, courtesy of Susanna Wallsten.

36 "Er ist," *Bunte* 46, 7.11.1985, 34; Hedi Aouidj's interview with Abu Ra'ad, 15.10.2016, APA; Hedi Aouidj and Mathieu Palain, "Die Assads und ihr Nazis," *Reportage* 33 (March 2017).

37 *Le Soir* (Beirut), "Qui est Georg Fischer?" 2.11.1961.

38 "If the Dead Could Speak: Mass Deaths and Torture in Syria's Detention Facilities," Human Rights Watch Report, December 2015, 70. In his report (*L'Orient*, 30.10.1961), the well-informed Lebanese Correspondent George Chatila ascribed several horrifying torture techniques to Brunner and other former Nazi advisers, but not the German Chair.

39 Robert Fisk, "Syrian Bodyguards," *The Times*, 17.3.1983.

40 Hedi Aouidj's interview with Abu Ra'ad, 15.10.2016, Hedi Aouidj's private archive.

41 "Er ist," *Bunte* 46, 7.11.1985, 34.

CHAPTER 14

1 Schaefer's testimony on Brunner, 13.5.1960, 17, author's private collection.

2 Samuel Segev, *Boded be-Damesek: Hayav ve-moto shel ha-meragel ha-Israeli Eli Cohen* (Tel Aviv: Keter, expanded edition, 2012), 100–101, 130, 135, 140–144.

3 Segev, *Boded*, 126–130.

4 Segev, *Boded*, 82–87, 172, 185, 188; Avi Shilon and Ela Florsheim, "Be-einei ha-maf'il," *Tchelet*, vol. 21 (autumn 2005), 25.

5 Segev, *Boded*, 158. In his memoirs, Cohen's judge wildly exaggerated the importance of this "Nazi hunting" mission. See: Dhali, *Ḥaqā'iq*, 187–188, 193, 199.

6 Majid Sheikh Al-Ard interrogation in Eli Cohen's trial, Sessions 6 and 7, 16,17.3.1965, *Al Baath*, 18,19.3.1965; CIA report on Rademacher (undated, but after 1965), Sheikh Al-Ard's name is censored but understood from context, see: Rademacher name file, document no. 6. This is true especially when juxtaposed with Munich Operations Group to Chief EE, 20.4.1961, Beissner name file, document no. 74, CREST; Dhali, *Ḥaqā'iq*, 190, 244–246.

7 CIA report on Rademacher (undated, but after 1965), Sheikh Al-Ard's name is censored but understood from context. Rademacher name file, document no. 6, Brunner to Beisner, quoted in COS Germany to Chief EE, 3.4.1961, as well as Munich Operations Group to Chief EE, 20.4.1961, Beissner name file, documents no. 72, 74, CREST; Dhali, *Ḥaqā'iq*, 190–192, 198, 244–246.

8   Eli Cohen's interrogation, Cohen Trial Protocol, Session 2, 1.3.1965 (Hebrew version),
    19–20, IDF Archives, Tel ha-Shomer, Israel (courtesy of Noam Nachman-Tepper).

9   Majid Sheikh Al-Ard interrogation in Cohen's trial, Session 7, 17.3.1965, *Al Baath*,
    19.3.1965; Segev, *Boded*, 176.

10 Rademacher's Testimony to the Central Office for the Investigation of National-
    Socialist Crimes, Ludwigsburg, 6.2.1968, author's private collection; Curt Witzke's
    interrogation, Staatsanwaltschaft Frankfurt, 13.6.1961, 3, partly reproduced
    and quoted in Abt. 361, Zug. 8/05, R3310, HHStA; transcript of a telephone
    conversation (undated) between "the boss" (der Chef—probably a BND official)
    and Hans Rechenberg, in Chief, Munich Liaison Base to Chief, AF, Chief, NE,
    17.4.1962, Hans Rechenberg name file, vol. 2, document no. 5, conversation no. 31,
    CREST.

11 Waffenhandel: Springer-Remer Bericht," 15.9.1961, 39, 137, 30.6.1962, 191–223,
    250–256, 30.6.1963, 321, 393, 398–402, 406–407, folder 101.439, BND Archive;
    Majid Sheikh Al-Ard interrogation, Cohen Trial protocol, Session 7, 17.3.1965,
    16, IDF Archives (Arabic version in *Al Baath*, 19.3.1965, Arabic document:
    63). Compare with Kleine's testimony on Remer and Springer's unreliability,
    interrogation of Henrich L. Kleine by the Hamburg Criminal Police, 11.2.1963, as
    well as investigation report, 7.2.1963, and Interrogation of Adolf Gerhard Gottwald,
    2.4.1963, Hamburg Criminal Police, Hamburg Criminal Police, B206 51152, 56,
    99, 118, BA-K.

12 Segev, *Boded*, 158. Segev's biography of Cohen is valuable but should be read with
    caution. Due to his connections in the Mossad, Segev was able to uncover many
    interesting details of the Israeli side of the story, but his descriptions of the Nazis in
    Damascus, especially Springer, is based on mostly inaccurate Syrian accounts. Segev's
    claim that Springer spied for SDECE is actually based on a misunderstanding of the
    trial records. In the trial, Sheikh al-Ard testified that Springer was afraid of the Red
    Hand, not that he was a member of the Red Hand.

13 Kugler to the BND, 16.5.1963, B 136/50583, BA-K.

14 "Waffenhandel: Springer-Remer Bericht," 30.6.1963, 398–401, folder 101.439
    BND Archive; Majid Sheikh Al-Ard interrogation, Cohen Trial protocol, Session 7,
    17.3.1965, *Al Baath*, 19.3.1965; ruling of the Administrative Court in Schleswig-
    Holstein, Kamer III, Springer against the town of Bad-Segeberg, 10.2.1966, 6, Ernst-
    Wilhelm Springer name file, 051-P-110067–0000, 1580, BfV Archive.

15 The date of the meeting between Cohen and Rademacher is subject to some
    controversy. In the trial, Cohen gave testimony on the meeting, but neither he nor
    the judge mentioned a specific date. Authors Samuel Segev and Noam Nahman-Teper
    (*Eli Cohen: Tik Patua'h*, Tel Aviv: Efi Meltzer, 2017) believe that the meeting took
    place in December 1964, but that does not make sense, because Rademacher was
    arrested by the Syrian security services in July 1963. The correct date can be found,
    I believe, in the early hagiographic account of Uri Dan and Yeshayahu Ben Porat on

Eli Cohen. These two authors, who were close to the Mossad, quote the classified telegrams of Cohen on Rademacher. They almost certainly saw the precise date of the meeting on the telegrams. See: Uri Dan and Yeshayahu Ben Porat, *Ha-meragel she-ba me-Israel: parashat Eli Cohen* (Ramat Gan: Masada, 1968), 126. However, Cohen left for Israel in late March 1963, so the meeting must have taken place beforehand.

16 Dan and Ben Porat, *Ha-meragel*, 126, and compare with the differing version in Segev, *Boded*, 16–17 ; Cohen Trial's Protocol, session 6, 16.3.1965, *Al Baath*, 18.3.2018.

17 Chief, Munich Liaison Base, to Chief EE, 11.10.1961, Rademacher name file, document no. 5, and as document no. 6 in the same name file, and a transcript of a telephone conversation (undated) between "the boss" (der Chef—probably a BND official) and Hans Rechenberg, in Chief, Munich Liaison Base to Chief, AF, Chief, NE, 17.4.1962, Hans Rechenberg name file, vol. 2, document no. 5, conversation no. 31, CREST; Francois Genoud to Franz Rademacher, 9.3.1962, ALLPROZ 6/257, fol. 128, BA-K.

18 Winkler, *Der Schattenmann*, 138; transcript of a telephone conversation (undated) between "the boss" (der Chef—probably a BND official) and Hans Rechenberg, in Chief, Munich Liaison Base to Chief, AF, Chief, NE, 17.4.1962, Hans Rechenberg name file, vol. 2, document no. 5, conversation no. 31, CREST; Francois Genoud to Franz Rademacher, 9.3.1962, ALLPROZ 6/257, fol. 128, BA-K.

19 Cohen Trial's Protocol, session 6, 16.3.1965, *Al Baath*, 18.3.2018.

20 Eli Cohen and Majid Sheikh Al-Ard's interrogations, Cohen Trial Protocol, Session 6, 16.3.1965, 10–12, 15, Session 7, 17.3.1965, 8–12, IDF Archive (Arabic Version, *Al Baath*, 18.3.2018, Arabic document 66, 72–73); Dan and Ben Porat, *Ha-meragel*, 127.

21 Dan and Ben Porat, *Ha-meragel*, 127–128.

22 Segev, *Boded*, 18.

23 Segev, *Boded*, 124.

24 Schaefer's testimony on Brunner, 13.5.1960, 17, author's private collection.

25 Fechter to the Foreign Ministry, 24.12.1963, B36 53 PA-AA.

26 Rademacher's testimony in his trial at Bamberg, 21.2.1968, Rep. K. 105, Nr. 695, SAB, as well as his sentence: Urteil in dem Strafverfahren gegen Franz Rademacher, Das Schwurgericht bei dem Landgericht Bamberg, 2Ks 3/53, 2.5.1968, both in SAB.

27 Joffe, "Reflections," 199.

28 Pfeiffer to the Foreign Ministry, 15.6.1965, B36 204, PA-AA.

29 Urteil in dem Strafverfahren gegen Franz Rademacher, Das Schwurgericht bei dem Landgericht Bamberg, 2Ks 3/53, 2.5.1968, SAB.

30 CIA Station in Damascus to [headquarters]. 27.3.1965, Rademacher name file, document no. 8, CREST; Dhali, *Ḥaqāʾiq*, 242–243.

31 Christopher Andrew, *The World Was Going our Way: The KGB and the Battle for the Third World* (New York: Basic Books, 2005), 196. Andrew relied on KGB documents from the Mitrokhin Archive that are, for the moment, closed to other

scholars on grounds of information security (author's communication with the archive, 1.9.2021). However, in the open parts of the Mitrokhin Archive, there are descriptions of nearly identical false flag operations of the KGB from the 1970s, both in Syria and other Middle Eastern and African countries. Like PULYA, these operations were directed against the BND, and included forgery of incriminating documents sent to local counterintelligence agencies. An important goal of these operations was to tie the BND and the CIA together in the eyes of Arab and African anti-American regimes. See: The Papers of Vasiliy Mitrokhin (1922–2004), MITN 2/24 K24 (Near East and Middle East), 103, Churchill College Archives, Cambridge, UK.

32 CIA report on Rademacher (undated, but must be from 1965), Rademacher name file, document no. 7, CREST; Rauch to Referat 120, Foreign Ministry, Bonn, 24.7.1962, B36–53, PP-AA; Noam Nachman-Tepper, *Eli Cohen: Tik Patua'h* (Tel Aviv: Efi Meltzer, 2017), 134–135.

33 Zoheir al-Mardini, interview with Col. Ahmad Suidani and with the commander of the team that arrested Cohen, *Al Usbu'u al-Arabi*, 3.3.1965.

34 Dhali, *Ḥaqā'iq*, 289–291.

35 Interview with Amin al-Hafez, by Ahmad Mansour, "Shahed ala al-asr," 19.6.2001, *Al-Jazeera,* minutes 9:30–11:30, https://www.youtube.com/watch?v=szSPmeeEa_Q, last accessed 23.11.2020; Segev, *Boded*, 292–293.

36 "Farid" to Abraham Cohen (undated), author's private archive, courtesy of Eyal Tavor and Liora Amir-Barmatz.

37 Zoheir al-Mardini, interview with Col. Ahmad Suidani and with the commander of the team that arrested Cohen *Al Usbu'u al-Arabi*, 3.3.1965.

38 Nachman-Tepper, *Eli Cohen*, 136.

39 Segev, *Boded*, 248.

40 Sheikh Al-Ard's interrogation, Cohen Trial protocol, Session 8, 19.3.1965, *Al Baath*, 19.3.1965; Dhali, *Ḥaqā'iq*, 243.

41 Shlomo Shpiro, "Shadowy Interests," 173–174.

42 The diary of Winterstein.(Kurt Weiss), 29.8.1956, 78, N10/4 (Teil 1).OT, BND Archive. Much of the information here was added retrospectively, after 1965. Lotz's personal file in the BND archive is marked 31870.OT, but it contains only vague hints on BND knowledge of his operations prior to 1965, see for example BND report, 21.7.1965, 31870.OT, 113–114, K50/III to 273, 8.3.1965, 129, and the curious fact that Lotz had two BND aliases, "Löhns" (see Winterstein Diary above) and "Ludwig" (K50/III to 273/A, 15.4.1965, 31870.OT, 130). Several key documents are censored "on the grounds of state security."

43 Report to Gehlen, 27.4.1965, Gehlen to Meir Amir, 29.4.1965, BND reports, 21, 29, 30.7.1965, 31870.OT, 91, 102, 107, 113–114, 125, 137, BND Archive; Bergman, *Rise and Kill First*, 66–67, 89; Müller, *Gehlen*, vol. II, 978–979; Meir Amit, *Rosh be-Rosh: Mabat ishi al eru'im gedolim ve-parashot alumot* (Tel Aviv: Her

Artsi, 1999), 138. Gehlen followed the fate of Lotz and his wife with interest as late as the 1970s, when he was already retired. See: Gehlen to Even-Pinnah, 12.9,1973, 2, 28.11.1973, 3, Even-Pinnah Papers, file 1450, Haifa Municipal Archives.

44 BND report, 19.5.1965, 31870.OT, 115–117, BND Archive; Lüdke "Die Aktivitäten" in Krieger, *Die Auslandsaufklärung*, 470–472.

CHAPTER 15

1 David Murphey et al., *Battleground Berlin: CIA vs. KGB in the Cold War* (New Haven, Conn.: Yale University Press, 1997), 508–509 (f. 26).

2 Nowak, *Sicherheitsrisiko*, 59.

3 Hechelhammer, *Spion ohne Grenzen*, 184–185.

4 Hechelhammer, *Spion ohne Grenzen*, 192–194.

5 Nowak, *Sicherheitsrisiko*, 58–59.

6 Hechelhammer, *Spion ohne Grenzen*, 194.

7 "Regelmäsig wie ein Uhrwerk lieferte der Mann in Pullach an 'Alfred 2'," interview with Vitali V. Korotkow [Korotkov], *Berliner Zeitung*, 3.11.1993, 3.

8 Murphey, et al., *Battleground Berlin*, 435–436.

9 Hechelhammer, *Spion ohne Grenzen*, 194–195; Müller, *Reinhard Gehlen*, vol. 2, 1018–1019.

10 Hechelhammer, *Spion ohne Grenzen*, 211; Nowak, *Sicherheitsrisiko*, 59–60. According to Nowak, the public viewed the employment of former SS and SD officials in a more negative way after the Ulm Einsatzgrun trial in 1958 and Eichmann's Trial in 1961.

11 "Sprengstoff-Attentat in Schwabing," *Süddeutsche Zeitung*, 17.10.1960; "Bombe in der Blütenstrasse," *Der Spiegel*, 26.10.1960; OSI/OCA Bonn, "Dr. Wilhelm Beisner," 10.11.1960, Beisner file, document no. 56, CREST.

12 Nowak, *Sicherheitsrisiko*, 59.

13 Breyer, "Max Merten," 130.

14 Daniel Marwecki, *Germany and Israel: Whitewashing and Statebuilding* (London: C. Hurst & Co., 2020), 95–96.

15 Ora Herman, *Ha-kivshan ve-ha-koor: me-ahorei he-kela'im shel mishpat Eichmann* (Tel Aviv: Hakibbutz Hameuchad, 2017), 71, 82–107.

16 Klaus Wiegrefe, "West Germany's Efforts to Influence the Eichmann Trial," *Spiegel International*, 15.4.2011; Yeshayahu Jelinek, *Israel und Deutschland, 1945–1965: Ein neurotisches Verhältnis* (München: Oldenbourg, 2004), 391. Israeli government Meeting no. 38, 7.5.1961, 4, file: government meetings, 1961, Israeli State Archives. Only in the appeal to the Supreme Court, the defense asked to bring Globke as an "expert witness" on the Nuremberg Laws, but to little effect. See: Eichmann Trial Protocol, vol. 4, defense appeal to the supreme court, 1986, 2058, 2086, Israeli Justice Ministry, https://www.justice.gov.il/Subjects/EichmannWritten/vol. me /Psk_din.pdf (last accessed, 22.12.2020).

17 "Waffenhandel: Springer-Remer Bericht," 15.9.1961, 36–37, 93, folder 101.439

BND Archive.

[18] Vortragsnotiz no.28/61 an 363/W, 15.5.1961, 30.212.OT, 137–143, BND Archive.

[19] Wojak, *Fritz Bauer,* 291; Breyer, "Max Merten," 131.

[20] Lommatzsch, *Hans Globke,* 318–319; Max Merten's Testimony in the Eichmann Trial, Amtsgericht Tiergarten, Berlin, 29.5.1961, 3110/7-A, 18, Israeli State Archives; Breyer, "Max Merten," 93–94, 131–132.

[21] Wojak, *Bauer*, 516f.

[22] Foreign Ministy, Bonn, to the Economy Ministry, 1.6.1960, Hermann Schaefer name file, 655–656, BfV Archive.

[23] "Ein deutscher in Damaskus oder: Das Ende einer Karriere," *Aus Unseren Kreisen*, 14.4.1960, reproduced in Brunner's BfV file, Dr. Fischer alias Alois Brunner, file 051-P, 030243–0000, 3353–3354, as well as Friedrich Schack to Karl Heinz Späth (date unclear, probably 12.6.1961), BfV report, 21.4.1960, Hermann Schaefer name file, 438, 556–557, BfV Archive.

[24] As the BND notified the CIA. See: Chief, Munich Operations Group to Chief EE, 20.4.1961, Beissner name file, document no. 74, CREST.

[25] Vortragsnotiz no. 28/61 and 363/W, 15.5.1961, 30.212.OT, 137–143, BND Archiv; Vernehmungsniederschrift Hans F. Germani, Bayerisches Landeskriminalamt, 5.1.1961, Abt. 461, Zug. 8/05, R5310, 6, HHStA; Hegemann, *Rauschning*, 428; BfV Note, 16.2.1961, interrogation of Wilhelm Steinhausen, file 9238246, "Dr. Georg Fischer alias Alois Brunner," 3511, as well as FRG General Consulate in Damascus to the Foreign Ministry, 26.11.1960, Späth's testimony to the Bavarian Criminal Police, 12.12.1960, BfV report, 16.2.1961, Foreign Ministry, Bonn, to the Economy Ministry, 1.6.1960, Hermann Schaefer name file, 212–213, 281, 347, 655, BfV Archive.

[26] Hermann Schaefer's testimony to the Generalstaatsanwaltschaft Frankfurt a.M, 19.6.1960, 3, Schapira-Haffner Collection, folder 1/b, Fritz Bauer Institute, Frankfurt a./M; Vortragsnotiz no. 28/61 and 363/W, 15.5.1961, 30.212.OT, 137–143, BND Archiv; Werner von Hentig to Hans Rechenberg [undated] in Chief, Munich Liaison Base to Chief EE, 6.11.1961, Hans Rechenberg name file, document no. 21, CREST; BfV Note, 16.2.1961, interrogation of Wilhelm Steinhausen, file 9238246, "Dr. Georg Fischer alias Alois Brunner," 3508, BfV Archive. Karl-Heinz Späth's interrogation, 5.12.1960, 16–17, Abt. 361, Zug. 8/05, R3310, HHStA.

[27] Hermann Schaefer's testimony to the Generalstaatsanwaltschaft Frankfurt a.M, 19.6.1960, 3, Schapira-Haffner Collection, folder 1/b, Fritz Bauer Institute, Frankfurt a./M; Interrogation of Wilhelm Steinhausen, in file 9238246, "Dr. Georg Fischer alias Alois Brunner," 3510–3511, BfV Archive. There is no other explanation as to why Schaefer tried to help Merten, and why Merten, just at the same time, chose to pick a fight with one of the strongest people in West Germany.

[28] Ruffner, *Eagle and Swastika*, chapter 14, 11,14. Lemke, "Kampagnen," 163;

Lommatzsch, *Hans Globke*, 317–319.

29 Müller, *Gehlen*, vol. 1, 616–617, 625.

30 Müller, *Reinhard Gehlen*, vol. 2, 1328.

31 Aktennotiz, "Besprechung mit Staatssekretär Dr. Globke" [with Kurt Weiss, aka Winterstein], 15.2.1961, 1127.OT, 24–25, BND Archiv; Breyer, "Max Merten," 59.

32 Wiegrefe, "West Germany's Efforts," *Spiegel International*, 15.4.2011; Winkler, *Der Schattenmann*, 125–134. There is rich documentation of the dealings with Rechenberg and Servatius in the former's CIA name file (2 vols.), see especially vol. 1, documents no. 26 and 33, and vol. 2, transcript of a telephone conversation (undated) between "the boss" (der Chef—probably a BND official) and Hans Rechenberg, in Chief, Munich Liaison Base to Chief, AF, Chief, NE, 17.4.1962, Hans Rechenberg name file, vol. 2, document no. 5, conversation no. 31, CREST.

33 BND Report, 28.10.1960, 24056.OT, Part I, 20–21, BND Archive.

34 Fechter, FRG Consul in Damascus to the Foreign Ministry, 13.4.1961, B83, Nr. 417, Band 742, PA-AA.

35 Hermann Schaefer, "Die Geisterbotschafts Heinrich Himmerls," *Afro-Asia* (November, 1961); Witzke's statement to the FRG Consulate in Damascus, 13.5.1961, in FRG Consulate Damascus to Foreign Ministry, 23.5.1961, B83, Nr. 417, Band 742, PA AA; Fechter, FRG Consul, Damascus, to the Foreign Ministry, Bonn, 13.4.1961, B141/528447, 21, BA-K; SDECE report, "information from Archives, 1961," in Brunner folder no. 3, SKPA; Hermann Schaeffer to the Generalstaatsanwalt in Frankurt, 15.8.1960, First Auschwitz Trial Materials, Band 3, 497, Fond 461, No. 3768/245, HHStA.

36 BfV Report, 26.7.1984, addressed to Department IV, 054-P-270029–0000, BRUNNER, Alois, 16–17, BfV Archive.

37 Vortragsnotiz Nr.27/61 an 363 über 181, betr. Globus, 2.6.1961, 30.212 OT, 143–145, BND Archive.

38 Vortragsnotiz Nr.27/61 an 363 über 181, betr. Globus, 2.6.1961, 30.212 OT, 143–145, BND Archive; Vernehmungsniederschrift, Späth, Karl-Heinz, Bayerisches Landeskriminalamt, 5.12.1960, Abt. 461, Zug. 8/05, R5310, 1–19, HHStA; FRG Consulate in Damascus to the Foreign Ministry, 13.4.1961, B83, Nr. 417, Band 742, PA AA (Political Archive of the German Foreign Ministry, Berlin); Chen, Mossad Report: Nazi Hunting, vol. 2, 118.

39 Vortragsnotiz Nr.27/61 an 363 über 181, betr. Globus, 2.6.1961, 30.212 OT, 143–145, BND Archive; Georg Fischer (Brunner) to the German Consulate in Damascus, 12.11.1960, FRG Consulate in Damascus to the Foreign Ministry, 13.4, 23.5.1961, B83, Nr. 417, Band 742, PA-AA.

40 Aktennotiz, "Besprechung mit Staatssekretär Dr. Globke," 19.1.1962, 1127-OT, 39, BND Archive. The name "Alois Brunner" is written in a different font than in the rest of the document. It was probably censored by BND archivists and then

reinserted; Müller, *Reinhard Gehlen*, vol. 2, 1018.

41 Müller, *Reinhard Gehlen*, vol. 2, 1312, 1329.

42 Müller, *Reinhard Gehlen*, vol. 2, 1019–1024; Nowak, *Sicherheitsrisiko*, 60, 66–70, 79–80.

43 Jost Dülffer, *Geheimdienst in der Krise: Der BND in der 1960er- Jahren* (Berlin: Ch. Verlag, 2018), 31–32, 37–45; Christoph Franceschini. Erich, Schmidt-Eenboom, Thomas Wegener-Friis, *Spionage unter Freunden: Partnerdienstbeziehungen und Westaufklärung der Organisation Gehlen und des BND* (Berlin: Chr. Links Verlag, 2017), 297.

44 Nowak, *Sicherheitsrisiko*, 66–68; Reinhard Gehlen, *Der Dienst*, 289.

45 Müller, *Reinhard Gehlen*, vol. 2, 1018–1019, 1027; Dülffer, *Geheimdienst*, 37–45; Nowak, *Sicherheitsrisiko*, 57–58; Gehlen, *Der Dienst*, 286–288, 414–416.

46 Hechelhammer, *Spion ohne Grenzen*, 226.

47 Müller, *Reinhard Gehlen*, vol. 2, 1023, 1311; Nowak, *Sicherheitsrisiko*, 72.

48 BND report, Hagner to the President, 1.7.1988, BND Report (Weisweiler), 3.12.1997, 1127.OT, 41, 109–110, BND Archiv; Klaus Wiegrefe, "BND Vernichtete Akten zu SS-Verbrecher Brunner," *Der Spiegel*, 20.7.2011.

49 Müller, *Reinhard Gehlen*, vol. 1, 616.

50 Müller, *Reinhard Gehlen*, vol. 2, 1024–1026, 1032–1042, 1302–1304, 1323,1325, 1328–1329; Dülffer, *Geheimdienst*, 32–37; Nowak, *Sicherheitsrisiko*, 71, 83, 92.

CHAPTER 16

1 Owen L. Sirrs, *Nasser and the Missile Age in the Middle East* (London: Routledge, 2006), 48.

2 On Egyptian chemical warfare during the Yemen Civil War see: Asher Orkaby, *Beyond the Arab Cold War: The International History of the Yemen Civil War* (New York: Oxford University Press, 2017), 133–139.

3 Bergman, *Rise and Kill First*, 62.

4 Sanche de Gramont, "Nasser's Hired Germans," *Saturday Evening Post*, 28.7.1963, 61.

5 Sirrs, *Nasser*, 26.

6 Sirrs, *Nasser*, 24–33; Sanche de Gramont, "Nasser's Hired Germans," *Saturday Evening Post*, 28.7.1963, 61.

7 Inge Deutschkron, *Bonn and Jerusalem: The Strange Coalition* (Philadelphia: Chilton Book Company, 1970), 220.

8 Swiss Federal Prosecution, "Report on Mechanical Corporation AG (MECO) and Motoren-Turbinen-Und Pumpen AG (MTP) in Zürich, 2.4.1963, 3118:0, 851.5/6, Schweizerisches Bundesarchiv, Bern (hereafter cited as BAR); Sanche de Gramont, "Nasser's Hired Germans," *Saturday Evening Post*, 28.7.1963, 60; Thomas Riegler, "Agenten, Wissenschaftler und 'Todesstrahlen': zur Rolle Österreichischer Akteure in Nassers Rüstungsprogramm (1958–1969)," *JIPSS*, vol. 8, no. 2 (2014), 46.

9 Sirrs, *Nasser*, 36, 41. A Mossad document from 1964 assesses the number of

the foreign experts as 80. See: "The Egyptian Project for the Development and
Production of Surface-to-Surface Missiles," Mossad Document, undated, according
to context—written in 1964 (the document mentions that use of chemical weapons
in the Yemen War, which became known only in July 1963, and the recruitment
efforts of the Helige scientists in 1964), courtesy of Ronen Bergman.

10 Sanche de Gramont, "Nasser's Hired Germans," *Saturday Evening Post*, 28.7.1963, 60.

11 Beate Soller-Krug, Kaj Rüdiger Krug, *Am Ufer des Nils: Unser Vater 'Raketen-Krug'*
    und der Mossad (Stuttgart: LangenMüller, 2018), 63–80.

12 Deutschkron, *Bonn und Jerusalem*, 222.

13 CIA report, "UAR Rocket Launching," in Daniel J. Lawler and Erin R. Mahan, eds.,
    Foreign Relations of the United States, 1961–1963 (Washington, D.C.: Government
    Printing Office, 2010), vol. 18. Near East, 1962–1963, document no. 140 (Missile
    Potential of the United Arab Republic, UAR), 319, fn1; Sirrs, *Nasser*, 33–35, 44–49;
    Riegler, "Agenten," 65; Ferdinand Brandner, *Ein Leben zwischen Fronten: Ingenieur im*
    Schussfeld der Weltpolitik (München: Verlag Welsermühl, 1973), 332–338.

14 Isser Harel, *Mashber Ha-mad'anim Ha-Germanin, 1962–1963* (Tel Aviv: Sifriyat
    Maariv, 1982), 14–15; Israeli government meeting, protocol, 4.12.1960, 23–24,
    Israeli State Archives.

15 "Parashat ha-mad'anim ha-Germanim," internal Mossad study, Mossad Archive
    (hereafter cited as: "Mossad Report: German Scientists," 10–12.

16 Sirrs, *Nasser*, 43; Naomi Lotz, Eliezer Karmi, *Habiti Le'ahor, Naomi: Sipura shel eshet*
    meragel (Tel Aviv: Boostan, 1978), 49, 59.

17 Sirrs, *Nasser*, 43.

18 Sirrs, *Nasser*, 52; Harel, *Mashber*, 19; Lüdke "Die Aktivitäten" in Krieger, *Die*
    Auslandsaufklärung, 453–454.

19 Deutschkron, *Bonn and Jerusalem*, 222; Harel, *Mashber*, 24.

20 Harel, *Mashber*, 38, 60.

21 Ben-Gurion to Frida Sasson, cited in Yechiam Weitz, "Ben-Gurion also used the
    Holocaust," *Haaretz*, 30.10.2013; For analysis of Israeli images of Nasser as the "new
    Hitler" see Eli Podeh, "Demonizing the Other: Israeli Perceptions of Nasser and
    Nasserism," in Eli Podeh and Onn Winckler, eds., *Rethinking Nasserism: Revolution and*
    Historical Memory in Modern Egypt (Tampa: University Press of Florida: 2004), 72–94.

22 Amit, *Rosh be-Rosh*, 123.

23 Shpiro, "Shadowy Interests," 173–176.

24 Harel, *Mashber*, 11, 60.

25 Riegler, "Agenten," 46; FRG Embassy in Cairo to the Foreign Ministry, "Former
    National Socialists in the Service of the United Arab Republic," 3.10.1963, B36–10,
    PA-AA. This report mentions only Eisele and von Leers who, according to the
    author, was at that time isolated, withdrawn, and seriously ill. On Aribert Heim see
    also: Nicholas Kulish, Souad Mekhennet, *The Eternal Nazi: From Mauthausen to*

Cairo, The Relentless Pursuit of SS Doctor Aribert Heim (New York: Doubleday, 2014).

26 Simon Wiesenthal, "Flüchtige Naziverbrecher im Nahen Osten und ihre Gegenwärtige Rolle," 7.6.1967, 2, Egypt folder, VWI-SWA. Though Wiesenthal's number of resident Germans in the Middle East, 6,000 to 7,000 was probably overblown.

27 Warlo, General Staatsanwalt Frankfurt, to Dr. Artz (Zentralstelle), 20.1.1964, B162/5656, 136, see also 129, BA-AL; Lüdke "Die Aktivitäten" in Krieger, *Die Auslandsaufklärung*, 473–474.

28 Norman Barrymain, "Report on Jose Perez," February 1963, Egypt folder, VWI-SWA. Note: The date on the document is February 1953, but it is obviously a typing mistake, as events that took place in 1955 and 1956 are mentioned.

29 See for example Michael Bar Zohar, *Tseid Ha-mad'anim ha-Germanim* (Schocken: Tel Aviv, 1965), 202, Shmuel Katz, *Soldier Spies: Israeli Military Intelligence* (Novato, Calif.: Presidio Press, 1992), 157, Roger Howard, *Operation Damocles: Israel's Secret War against Hitler's Scientists, 1951–1967* (New York: Pegasus Books, 2013), 25, Barry Rubin, Wolfgang Schwanitz, *Nazis, Islamists and the Making of the Modern Middle East* (New Haven, Conn.: Yale University Press, 2014), 221, and Sanche de Gramont, "Nasser's Hired Germans," *Saturday Evening Post*, 28.7.1963, 60.

30 L'Aurore, 26.7.1963, German translation in Egypt folder, VWI-SWA.

31 Israel Meir, Information Department, New York, to Meir Padan, Foreign Ministry, "Nazis in Egypt," 8.5.1963; Y. Belsky to Padan, Foreign Ministry, 12.5.1963, ISA-mfa-Political-000krpn, Israeli State Archives.

32 Riegler, "Agenten," 49. A facsimile copy of the letter is reproduced in Mossad Report: German Scientists, 76.

33 Ben-Gurion to Hana Zemer, Davar, 2.11.1962; Harel, *Mashber*, 40.

34 Michael Bar Zohar, *Ben-Gurion* (Tel Aviv: Am Oved, 1977), 1538–1539.

35 Wolfgang Lotz, *The Champagne Spy: Israel's Master Spy Tells His Story* (London: Valentine, Mitchell & Co. LTD, 1972), 12.

36 Sirrs, *Nasser*, 45; Lotz, *The Champagne Spy*, 68–69, 71. Lotz's cooperation with the BND is documented in BND records, especially in the diary of Kurt Weiss, aka Winterstein. See: The diary of Winterstein (Kurt Weiss), 29.8.1956, 79–80, N10/4 (Teil 1).OT, BND Archive. The diary entry should, however, be read with great caution. Only the meeting talking points in the beginning are actually from 1956, and much of the rest was added later on, sometimes years later.

37 Lotz, *The Champagne Spy*, 22–23.

38 The diary of Winterstein (Kurt Weiss), 29.8.1956, 79, N10/4 (Teil 1).OT, BND Archive. Lotz, *The Champagne Spy*, 39–40, 79; Lüdke "Die Aktivitäten" in Krieger, *Die Auslandsaufklärung*, 469.

39 The diary of Winterstein (Kurt Weiss), 29.8.1956, 80, N10/4 (Teil 1).OT, BND Archive. Karmi and Lotz, *Habiti*, 49; Brandner, *Ein Leben zwischen Fronten*, 286.

40 Lotz, *The Champagne Spy*, 59–69, and compare with the description of Lotz's wife, Waltraud, in Lotz, *Habiti*, 61–62. In 1974, after Lotz's memoirs appeared in German, Leers's widow sued him for libel in a Stuttgart Court. She and her daughter claimed, among other things, that the party described by Lotz never took place. See: Ulrich K. Dreikandt to Simon Wiesenthal, 5.4.1974, Johann von Leers name file, VWI-SWA.

41 BND report to L 27/VK, 3.6.1965, 31870.OT, 126, BND Archive; Sirrs, *Nasser*, 58, 60; Chen, Mossad Report: Nazi Hunting, vol. 3, 105–112.

42 Mossad Report: German Scientists, 19; Mossad Report: Nazi Hunting, vol. 1, 8.

43 Mossad report: German Scientists, 24–30.

44 Mossad Report: German Scientists, 30–31.

45 Mossad Report: German Scientists, 31–32; Heidi Goercke's interrogation, Freiburg Police, 5.3.1963, 9, 3118:0, 851.5/6, BAR; Soller-Krug and Krug, *Am Ufer*, 38, 44, on Krug's acquaintance with Nadim see ibid, 74–75.

46 Mossad Report: German Scientists, 31–32.

47 Mossad Report: German Scientists, 34–35.

48 Mossad Report: German Scientists, 35–37.

49 Bergman, *Rise and Kill First*, 66.

CHAPTER 17

1 Mossad Report: German Scientists, 43–44. Compare with Joklik's interrogation by Canton Zürich Police, 3.3.1963, 6, 3118:0, 851.5/6, BAR.

2 Harel, *Mashber*, 43.

3 Mossad Report: German Scientists, 47; Otto Joklik to Margot Krug, 9.1.1963, reproduced in Soller-Krug and Krug, *Am Ufer*, 86–88. Joklik's claim that the Egyptians abandoned the Krug family is confirmed by the testimony of Krug's children. See ibid, 106–107.

4 Mossad Report: German Scientists, 47.

5 Mossad Report: German Scientists, 49–50. Compare with Joklik's interrogation by Canton Zürich Police, 3.3.1963, 10–11, 3118:0, 851.5/6, BAR, and see also Riegler, "Agenten," 60.

6 Mossad Report: German Scientists, 14–15, 18, 23, 26.

7 Howard, *Operation Damocles*, 205; FRG Embassy in Cairo to the Foreign Ministry, "Former National Socialists in the Service of the United Arab Republic," 3.10.1963, B36-10, PA-AA; Karmi and Lotz, *Habiti*, 61; Brandner, *Ein Leben zwischen Fronten*, 323.

8 Swiss Federal Prosecution, report on Otto Joklik, 6.4.1963, 1–2, 3118:0, 851.5/6, BAR.

9 Swiss Federal Prosecution to the Bern Police Department, 20.1.1960, Swiss Federal Prosecution, report on Otto Joklik, 6.4.1963, 2–7, Swiss Federal Police, remark on Otto Joklik, 6.6.1963, 3118:0, 851.5/6, BAR.

10 Mossad Report: German Scientists, 49; Riegler, "Agenten," 59; Harel, *Mashber*, 43.

[11] Sanche de Gramont, "Nasser's Hired Germans," *Saturday Evening Post*, 28.7.1963, 63.

[12] Bar Zohar, *Ben-Gurion*, vol. 3, 1540–1541.

[13] Mossad Report: German Scientists, 89.

[14] Mossad Report: German Scientists, 89.

[15] Bergman, *Rise and Kill First*, 50–51.

[16] Peres, *Kela David*, 31–32, 47–48; Connelly, *A Diplomatic Revolution*, 104; Avner Cohen, *Israel and the Bomb* (New York: Columbia University Press, 1998), 53–60.

[17] Bergman, *Rise and Kill First*, 67.

[18] Bergman, *Rise and Kill First*, 62. Rafi Eitan confirmed this statement in an interview with the present author, 19.3.2018.

[19] Mossad Report: German Scientists, 58–59, 120.

[20] Adv. Alfred Seidel to Prime Minister Eshkol, 23.7.1963, ISA-mfa-ReparationsGermany-000pfx1, Israeli State Archives.

[21] Mossad Report: German Scientists, 56–60; LKA Baden-Württemberg, investigation report, 4.3.1963, 4, 3118:0, 851.5/6, BAR; Soller-Krug and Krug, *Am Ufer*, 43.

[22] Mossad Report: German Scientists, 61.

[23] Mossad Report: German Scientists, 65–66.

[24] Mossad Report: German Scientists, 64.

[25] Mossad Report: German Scientists, 61–65; E. W. Scherer, H. Valentin, "Racketen, Forscher und Agenten: Anschlag auf Kleinwächter," *Die Rheinpfalz*, no. 239, 13.10.1973.

[26] Mossad Report: German Scientists, 64, 67–69.

[27] Mossad Report: German Scientists, 69.

[28] Mossad Report: German Scientists, 69–70; LKA Baden-Württemberg, investigation report, 4.3.1963, 5, 3118:0, 851.5/6, BAR.

[29] Sanche de Gramont, "Nasser's Hired Germans," *Saturday Evening Post*, 28.7.1963, 60.

[30] LKA Baden-Württemberg, investigation report, 4.3.1963, 5–6, 3118:0, 851.5/6, BAR.

[31] Sanche de Gramont, "Nasser's Hired Germans," *Saturday Evening Post*, 28.7.1963, 60.

[32] LKA Baden-Württemberg, investigation report, 4.3.1963, 6–7, 3118:0, 851.5/6, BAR; "Dr. Joklik hat auf mich geschossen," *Der Blick*, no. 117, 20.5.1963. The police transcript of the conversation between Joklik and Kleinwächter is reproduced in E. W. Scherer, H. Valentin, "Racketen, Forscher und Agenten: Ein interessanter Telefonanruf," *Die Rheinpfalz*, no. 243, 18.10.1973.

[33] Swiss Federal Department of Justice and Police, Decision concerning the appeal of Otto Joklik, 19.2.1960, 2–3, 3118:0, 851.5/6, BAR, compare with Mossad Report: German Scientists, 94.

[34] Joseph Ben-Gal's interrogation, Zürich Police, 2.3.1963, 1, Heidi Goercke's interrogation, Freiburg Police, 5.3.1963, 2–5, LKA Baden-Württemberg, investigation report, 4.3.1963, 9, Canton Zürich Police to the director of the [Swiss]

Intelligence Service, 8.3.1963, 2, 3118:0, 851.5/6, BAR.

35 Joseph Ben-Gal's interrogation, Zürich Police, 2.3.1963, 2, Heidi Goercke's interrogation, Freiburg Police, 1.3.1963, transcript of the conversation between Joklik and Heidi Goercke, 27.2.1963, 3118:0, 851.5/6, BAR.

36 Heidi Goercke's interrogation, Freiburg Police, 5.3.1963, 5, 3118:0, 851.5/6, BAR.

37 Joseph Ben-Gal's interrogation, Zürich Police, 2.3.1963, 1 Heidi Goercke's testimony, 2.3.1963, 2–7, Heidi Goercke's interrogation, Freiburg Police, 5.3.1963, 8, 3118:0, 851.5/6, 3118:0, 851.5/6, BAR.

38 LKA Baden-Württemberg, investigation report, 4.3.1963, 12, Indictment against Joseph Ben-Gal and Otto Joklik, Prosecution of Canton Basel, 25.4.1963, Zürich Police to the director of the [Swiss] Intelligence service, 8.3.1963, 3, 3118:0, 851.5/6, BAR.

39 Canton Zürich Police to the director of the [Swiss] Intelligence Service, 8.3.1963, 4, 3118:0, 851.5/6, BAR; "Dr. Joklik hat auf mich geschossen," Der Blick, no.117, 20.5.1963.

40 FRG Embassy in Bern to the Foreign Ministry, 10.4, 26.3.1963, B36–44, PA-AA.

41 Notice of the Swiss Federal Justice and Police Department, 9.5.1963, Swiss Federal Justice and Police Department, file note, 7.6.1963, 2–3, Inspector Hartmann, Police Service, Swiss Federal Prosecution to the Chief of Police, Bern, 23.6.1963, 3118:0, 851.5/6, BAR; "Ben Gal: 'Schweizer Korrekt," Der Blick, 14.6.1963. For the prosecutor's arguments and the final verdict see: "Der Prozess gegen die israelischen Agenten," Neue Zürcher Zeitung, 14.6.1963. Joklik later appealed and was acquitted of all charges, except illegal entry into Switzerland. See: Verdict of the Appeal Court, Canton Basel, 21.4.1965, 3118:0, 851.5/6, BAR.

42 Compare Harel's version in Mashber, 62–65, to Meir Amit's version in Rosh be-Rosh, 103–104.

43 Mossad Report: German Scientists, 97–99.

44 Riegler, "Agenten," 64; Amit, Rosh be-Rosh, 104–107.

45 Haaretz, 19.3.1963.

46 Foreign Minister Meir's speech in the Knesset, 20.3.1963, ISA-PMO-StateDocumentsDep-0013etd, Israeli State Archives; Harel, Mashber, 68; Jelinek, Deutschland und Israel, 418.

47 Deutschkron, Bonn and Jerusalem, 231–232; Jelinek, Deutschland und Israel, 425–426.

48 Bar Zohar, Ben-Gurion, vol. 3 1538–1539; Harel, Mashber, 68–69, 72–73, 78–79; Amit, Rosh be-Rosh, 107–108, 123.

49 Michael Bar Zohar, Phoenix: Shimon Peres and the Secret History of Israel (New York: West 26th Street Press, 2016), 281; Bar Zohar, Ben-Gurion, vol. 3, 1539; Deutschkron, Bonn and Jerusalem, 234;

50 Telegram, Department 655, State Department to U.S. Embassies in the Middle East, 27.3.1963, RG 84, Entry UD 3248A, Box 42, folder 350 (UAR 1962), NARA.

51 For a detailed description of U.S. diplomatic efforts and the reactions of Israel and

Egypt see Sirrs, *Nasser*, 102–150.

52 Harel, *Mashber*, 74–77. And compare with Amit, *Rosh be-Rosh*, 108–109, 123–124.

53 Harel to Ben-Gurion, 25.3.1963, Ben-Gurion to Amit, 26.3.1963, Subject Files, 359/60, Ben-Gurion Archives. For Harel's version see Harel, *Mashber*, 82–85

54 Bar Zohar, *Ben-Gurion*, vol. 3, 1545–1559.

55 Mossad Report: German Scientists, 105, 133; Amit, *Rosh be-Rosh*, 125; Jelinek, *Deutschland und Israel*, 425.

CHAPTER 18

1 Broadcast of Radio Warsaw (German translation), "Zeit und Menschen," 17.7.1967 (19:30), B162/5656, 55, BA-AL.

2 "Gruber, Otto," 3.2.1954, CIA Report, Eilam Collection. Compare with the BND report from 6.3.1963, in Hechelhammer et al. (eds), "Walther Rauff und der Bundesnachrichtendienst," 17; Chen, "Former Nazi Officers," 735.

3 Interview with Shalhevet Freier (undated). Interviewer: Yossi Chen. Cited in Chen, Mossad Report: Nazi Hunting, vol. 2, 165.

4 Walter Rauff to Ernie Zaugg, 8.5.1980, 3, Rauff Name file no. 2, VWI-SWA.

5 Chen, Mossad Report: Nazi Hunting, vol. 2, 161–165; Jenny Hanns to Wiesenthal, 10.2.1983, Rauff name file no. 2, VWI-SWA.

6 BND reports, 3.10.1958, 6.3.1963, 14.6.1984, as well as Rauff's CV, reproduced in Bodo Hechelhammer et al. (eds.), "Walther Rauff und der Bundesnachrichtendienst," 9, 12, 16–17, 21. Rauff was dropped by the BND on 31.10.1962, as the organization deemed his intelligence of little value (see 15).

7 Mossad Report: German Scientists, 106–109.

8 Mossad Report: German Scientists, 112.

9 Mossad Report: German Scientists, 107; Interview with Rafi Eitan, 19.2.2006, by Ronen Bergman, 2 (courtesy of Ronen Bergman).

10 Mossad Report: German Scientists, 116.

11 Kurt Forstner, Landesgerichtsrat, to Zentralle Stelle, Ludwigsburg (undated), Rückerl, Staatsanwalt, to Eugenie Kritznar, 25.4.1963, Rückerl to Generalstaatsanwalt Berlin, 6.5.1963, B162/20562, 91–98, BA-AL; Thomas Riegler, "Eine typische Landsknechtnatur—Otto Skorzeny," *Profil*, vol. 35 (2013), 1.

12 Rafi Eitan, interview with the author, 19.3.2018.

13 Major Robert B. Bieck, Assistant Air Attaché, Madrid, "SS Colonel Otto Skorzeny," CIA Report, 28.6.1951, Skorzeny name file, document no. 8, CREST; Otto Skorzeny, BND evaluation index, entry, "Carl Armfeld," B206 51094, 11, BND reports (undated and 28.12.1950), B206, 51093, 31, 54, BA-K.

14 "Colonel Otto Skorzeny, wa. Rolf Steinbauer," FBI report, 24.9.1951, "Skorzeny-Debakel: Der Geschäftemacher und Held," 3–4, Skorzeny name file, VWI-SWA;

"Future plans of Otto Skorzeny," CIA report, 27.9.1951. EE/SO to DDP, "Otto Skorzeny," 19.9.1951, CIA report. Skorzeny name file, documents no. 22, 27 CREST; BND reports (undated and 28.12.1950), B206, 51093, 31, 54, BA-K; Riegler, "Eine typische," 2.

15 Gehlen Org and BND reports, 18.10.1954, 3.10.1956, 12.11.1960, Skorzeny name file, B 206 51092, BA-K, as well as report on Skrozeny's activity until 1965 in the same file, 10, 16; Riegler, "Eine typische," 2.

16 Gehlen Org report, 26.9.1951, appendix 1, letter to department 90/III, 4.10.1951, Wolfgang Langkau, "Beurteilung Skorzeny," 5.10.1951, Langkau to 35, 9.10.1951, Gehlen Org report, "Fall Moritz," 6.6.1952, B 206 51093, 131, 138, 143–144, 151, 236–240, as well as the report on Skorzeny's career in B 206 51092, 9, BA-K.

17 "Expose of Otto Skorzeny," CIA report, 10.6.1951, Skorzeny name file, document no. 13, CREST; BND reports, 30.4.1951, 2.2.1951, Skorzeny name file, vol. I, B206 51093, 10, 56, BA-K; Mossad Report: German Scientists, 123.

18 "Skorzeny's trip in Germany," CIA report, 28.7.1951, Skorzeny name file, document no. 16, CREST.

19 Mossad Report: German Scientists, 124, 127; Mossad Report: Nazi Hunting, vol. 3, 86. At the time, Meidan served as the deputy head of "Junction" in Europe.

20 Mossad Report: German Scientists, 124, 127; Bergman, *Rise and Kill First*, 78.

21 Mossad Report, German Scientists, 125.

22 Mossad Report, German Scientists, 125–127; Rafi Meidan, Memoirs (unpublished, courtesy of Ronen Bergman), 112.

23 Interview with Rafi Eitan, 19.2.2006, by Ronen Bergman, 2 (courtesy of Ronen Bergman), quoted in Bergman, *Rise and Kill First*, 78.

24 Mossad Report: German Scientists, 126–127.

25 Mossad Report: German Scientists, 127–128.

26 Bergman, *Rise and Kill First*, 81; Wiesenthal to Ken Nelson, 18.11.1992, Skorzeny name file, VWI-SWA; Segev, *Simon Wiesenthal*, 165; Meidan Memoirs (courtesy of Ronen Bergman), 113.

27 Rafi Eitan, interview with author, 19.3.2018.

28 Mossad Report: German Scientists, 128.

29 Mossad Report: German Scientists, 128–129; Bergman, *Rise and Kill First*, 81; Meidan Memoirs (courtesy of Ronen Bergman), 113–115.

30 Mossad Report: German Scientists, 129–130.

31 Mossad Report: German Scientists, 130–131; Meidan Memoirs (courtesy of Ronen Bergman), 115.

32 Mossad Report: German Scientists, 131; Interview with Rafi Eitan, 19.2.2006, by Ronen Bergman, 3 (courtesy of Ronen Bergman); Meidan Memoirs (courtesy of Ronen Bergman), 115.

[33] Mossad Report: German Scientists, 131, 150; Meidan Memoirs (courtesy of Ronen Bergman), 115; Interview with Meir Amit, 2006, by Ronen Bergman (courtesy of Ronen Bergman).

[34] Mossad Report: German Scientists, 132–136.

CHAPTER **19**

[1] Mossad Report: German Scientists, 174.

[2] Mossad Report: German Scientists, 139.

[3] Mossad Report: German Scientists, 139–140.

[4] Mossad Report: German Scientists, 140.

[5] Mossad Report: German Scientists, 139, 155; BND report, K50 to 273, 13.8.1965, 31870.OT, 61, BND Archive; Interview with Oded Gur-Arie, 11.12.2020.

[6] Deutschkron, *Bonn and Jerusalem*, 235–240; Shenar, Cologne Israeli Office to the Foreign Ministry, Jerusalem. 30.6.1963, ISA-MFA-DirectorGeneral-000ddjf, Israeli State Archives.

[7] Leo Savir, Israel Purchasing Mission, Cologne, to Chaim Yahil, Director General of the Foreign Ministry, 23.4.1963, ISA-mfa-Political-000krpn, Israeli State Archives; Deutschkron, *Bonn and Jerusalem*, 233, 238; Jelinek, *Deutschland und Israel*, 420, 426.

[8] Sirrs, *Nasser*, 43; W. Averell Harriman, Under Secretary for Political Affairs, to Congressman Farbstein, 10.[4.].1963, ISA-mfa-Political-000krpn, Israeli State Archives; FDG Foreign Ministry, Referat I B 1, Report, 23.9.1963, B36–14, PA-AA. That was the BND's view also in September 1964. See: Lüdke "Die Aktivitäten" in Krieger, *Die Auslandsaufklärung*, 456.

[9] Foreign Minister Meir's speech in the Knesset, 20.3.1963, ISA-PMO-StateDocumentsDep-0013etd, Israeli State Archives; "Ha-memshala tadun be-peniya le-Germaniya," *Yedioth Ahronot*, 17.3.1963.

[10] Ze'ev Shack, Israeli Embassy in Paris, to the Foreign Ministry, 26.3.1963, ISA-mfa-Political-000krpn, Israeli State Archives.

[11] Mossad Report: German Scientists, 148–149.

[12] Mossad Report: German Scientists, 149–150.

[13] Bar Zohar, *Phoenix*, 197–204; Marwecki, *Germany and Israel*, 74; Franz Josef Strauss, *Die Erinnerungen* (Berlin: Sieler, 1989), 425; Jelinek, *Deutschland und Israel*, 417.

[14] Horst Möller, *Franz Josef Strauss: Herrscher und Rebell* (München: Piper, 2015), 337–338; Marwecki, *Germany and Israel*, 74–76; Jelinek, *Deutschland und Israel*, 435.

[15] Bar Zohar, *Phoenix*, 280; Jelinek, *Deutschland und Israel*, 423–424; Sirrs, *Nasser*, 60.

[16] Interview with Shimon Peres in the documentary "Der Mossad, Die Nazis und die Raketen: Showdown am Nil" (creators: Ronen Bergman and Kersten Schüssler), min. 31–32.

[17] Mossad Report: German Scientists, 174.

[18] Mossad Report: German Scientists, 155–156.

19 Mossad Report: German Scientists, 156–157.

20 Mossad Report: German Scientists, 157–159; Interview with Meir Amit, 2006, by Ronen Bergman (courtesy of Ronen Bergman).

21 Bergman, *Rise and Kill First*, 84.

22 Bergman, *Rise and Kill First*, 83; Rafi Eitan, interview with the author, 19.3.2018; Interview with Rafi Eitan, 19.2.2006, by Ronen Bergman, 3 (courtesy of Ronen Bergman). In his unpublished memoirs (Meidan Memoirs, courtesy of Ronen Bergman, 116), Meidan describes his meeting with Strauss without mentioning Peres's presence. Peres describes the meeting with Strauss in his interview with Ronen Bergman, 19.9.2012, 4–5 (courtesy of Ronen Bergman). As for the time of the meeting see Mossad Report: German Scientists, 159.

23 In the introduction to the document presented to Strauss, the Mossad authors uncommittedly wrote that the Egyptians will be able to realize their plans sometime "in the present decade." See: "The Egyptian Project for the Development and Production of Surface-to-Surface Missiles," Mossad document, undated, according to context—written in 1964 (the document mentions the use of chemical weapons in the Yemen War, that became known only in July 1963, and the recruitment efforts of the Helige scientists in 1964), courtesy of Ronen Bergman.

24 Mossad Report: German Scientists, 159–160; Interview with Rafi Eitan, 19.2.2006, by Ronen Bergman, 3 (courtesy of Ronen Bergman).

25 Mossad Report: German Scientists, 161–164.

26 Savir to Shinnar, 29.12.1964, ISA-mfa-ReparationsGermany-000pfx1, Israeli State Archives.

27 Mossad Report: German Scientists, 170; Sirrs, *Nasser*, 89–90.

28 Möller, *Franz Josef Strauss*, 338; Marwecki, *Germany and Israel*, 74–75, 96; Strauss, *Erinnerungen*, 532–534.

29 Marwecki, *Germany and Israel*, 104–107; Jelinek, *Deutschland und Israel*, 416–417, 449–461.

30 Chen, Mossad Report: Nazi Hunting, vol. 1, 31.

31 Chen, Mossad Report: Nazi Hunting, vol. 1, 31, and compare with vol. 3, 116.

32 "Summary of Discussion, Heads of Services Committee," 23.1.1964, Mossad Archive, reproduced in Chen, Mossad Report: Nazi Hunting, vol. 2, 123–125, see also discussion and a more detailed description (based on interviews with some of the participants) in 32–34.

33 Ibid.

34 Ibid. For the interview with Amit see 34–35.

35 Bergman, *Rise and Kill First*, 90–91.

36 Chen, Mossad Report: Nazi Hunting, vol. 2, 50–81, 101–107, vol. 3, 117–118, 136–150; Wojak, *Fritz Bauer*, 292–293.

37 Protocol of Meeting between Prime Minister Eshkol and Head of the Mossad Zamir, 31.12.1968, Summary for Chiefs of Departments (To "Bitzur" Department),

"Treatment of Nazis," 5.1.1969, Mossad Archive, both reproduced in Chen, Mossad
Report: Nazi Hunting, vol. 1, 134–138, vol. 3, 5. About Mengele see vol. 3, 151–
152, 155, 159.

CHAPTER 20

1   Gabriel García Márquez, *Autumn of a Patriarch*. Translation: Gregory Rabassa (New
    York: HarperPerennial, 1976), 92.
2   "Spanien: Der Mann der Mussolini Befreite arbeitet für Nasser," Skorzeny name file,
    VWI-SWA; Gehlen Org report, 30.10.1952, B206 51093, 266, BA-K.
3   Mossad Report, 1.12,1965, subject: Dr. [reducted], Skorzeny Name File, Mossad Archive.
4   Mossad Report: German Scientists, 131–132; Mossad report, [redacted] to
    [redacted], March 1966, Skorzeny Name File, Mossad Archive.
5   Mossad Report: German Scientists, 131.
6   "Er ist," *Bunte* 46, 7.11.1985, 34.
7   Fischer (Brunner) to Maichanitsch, 24.6.1972, Brunner name file no. 1, VWI-SWA.
8   Krämer, Staatsanwalt, to the Zentralle Stelle Ludwigsburg, 13.4.1972, 149–150, BA-AL.
9   See the testimony of the grocery store owner, reported in Christian Springer to
    Simon Wiesenthal, 25.4.2001, Brunner name file no. 2, VWI-SWA, as well as
    Springer's conversation with Gerda Abd-el-Qurba, in Springer, *Nazi*, 70; Chen,
    Mossad Report: Nazi Hunting, vol. 2, 137.
10 Fischer (Brunner) to Maichanitsch, 22.8.1969, 11.9.1969, 13.12.1970, 24.6.1972.
    The contact with Maichanitsch was eventually terminated due to internal neo-
    Nazi feuds. Maichanitsch suspected Brunner supported one of his rivals inside
    the movement. See: Maichanitsch to Fischer (Brunner), 25.11.1973. The entire
    correspondence is filed in Brunner name file no. 1, VWI-SWA.
11 Decision 4/2 of the Cabinet Committee for Security Affairs, 23.9.1977, Cabinet
    Secretariat, Mossad Archive, reproduced in Chen, Mossad Report: Nazi Hunting,
    vol. 1, 48, see also vol. 3, 160–161.
12 Yitzhak Hofi to unit directors, "establishment of a unit to handle Nazi criminals,"
    27.11.1977, Deputy Head of the Mossad to Director of Operations and Director of
    Masada Unit, 15.11.1977, Mossad Archive, reproduced in Chen, Mossad Report:
    Nazi Hunting, vol. 1, 52–53, about Mengele's death see vol. 3, 166–167, 173.
13 Chen, Mossad Report: Nazi Hunting, vol. 2, 175–190.
14 Chen, Mossad Report: Nazi Hunting, vol. 2, 136–138. See Stiff's detailed
    intelligence report on Brunner's building and apartment, reproduced in 316–322.
15 Josef Böhm, Verein "Freunde der Heilkräuter" to Georg Fischer, 6.6.1980 (forged
    letter), reproduced in *Bunte* 45, 30.10.1985, 21; Chen, Mossad Report: Nazi
    Hunting, vol. 2, 140–146.
16 *Bunte* 45, 30.10.1985, 25; Susanna Wallsten's and Eric Ericson's interview with
    Abdul Rahman Hanada (recorded), 20.5.2020, author's private archive, courtesy
    of Susanna Wallsten; Chen, Mossad Report: Nazi Hunting, 146–149; Springer to

Wiesenthal, 25.4.2001, Brunner name file no. 2, VWI-SWA.

17 BfV reports, Köln, 26 July, 1984 (in additional two reports from 1984 and the month and day are censored), 054-P-270029–0000, BRUNNER, Alois, 10, 16, 21, BfV Archive; Henschke, *Rosenbergs Elite*, 51.

18 Interview with Serge Klarsfeld, 3.8.2018; Abu Ra'ad's testimony as quoted in Hedi Aouidj, Mathieu Palain, "Le Nazi de Damas," *Revue XXI*, vol. 37, Winter 2017.

19 Robert Fisk, "Syrian Bodyguards for Torturer who was Eichmann's Assistant," *The Times*, 17.3.1983; Anonymous Author, "Eichmann's Rechte Hand: Das ist Alois Brunner, der Möorder von 125,000 Juden," *Bunte* 45, 30.10.1985. According to Christian Springer, who saw the house, that was Rue Haddad no. 1. See: Springer to Wiesenthal, 25.4.2001, Brunner name file no. 2, VWI-SWA.

20 *Bunte* 45, 30.10.1985, 23–24. Springer's interview with "Hisham" in Springer, *Nazi*, 60–61. For a detailed chart of Brunner's apartment (in 1980) see Mossad Report: Nazi Hunting, vol. 2, 323.

21 "Er ist," *Bunte* 46, 11.7.1985, 34; Abu Ra'ad's testimony as quoted in Hedi Aouidj, Mathieu Palain, "Le Nazi de Damas," *Revue XXI*, vol. 37, Winter 2017.

22 Hauptverwaltung A to Hauptabteilung IX, Generalmajor Fister, December 1985, MfS HA IX/11 nr. AV 9189, 000113, BStU, 2.

23 Christian Springer's interview with "Hisham," in Springer, *Nazi*, 61.

24 *Chicago Sun-Times*, 1.11.1987. See also Ashman's testimony in the German Consulate, New York, 19.4.1988, B162/40534, 331–335, BA-AL.

25 Gerd Honsik, *Freispruch für Hitler: 36 ungehörte Zeugen wider die Gaskammer* (Wien: Burgerländischer Kulturverb, 1988), 17.

26 Ashman's testimony in the German Consulate, New York, 19.4.1988, B162/40534, 334, BA-AL; Susanna Wallsten's and Eric Ericson's interview with Abdul Rahman Hanada (recorded), 20.5.2020, author's private archive, courtesy of Susanna Wallsten.

27 Mossad Report: Nazi Hunting, vol. 1, 97. This short-lived framing plot was discussed on 19.12.1989, the last meeting that the Mossad ever held on the issue of Nazi Hunting.

28 For the text of the testament see Springer, *Nazi*, 248–250. It is very similar to the version dictated by Brunner to Gerd Honsik. One of Brunner's guards, known to us only as Abu Ra'ad, confirmed the content of the testament separately to the French journalist Hedi Aouidj. See: Interview with Abu Ra'ad, 15.10.2016, in Aouidj Private Archive (hereafter cited as APA).

29 Hedi Aouidj's interview with Abu Yaman, October 2016, Hedi Aouidj's Private Archive; Hannada stopped serving in Brunner's detail in October 1990, and his information on subsequent events came from conversations with other guards. Susanna Wallsten's and Eric Ericson's interview with Abdul Rahman Hanada (recorded), 20.5.2020, author's private archive, courtesy of Susanna Wallsten.

30 B162/20565, 292–293, BA-AL. For the witness testimonies see the rest of the file;

"Taube Ohren in Damascus," *Allgemeine Jüdische Wochenzeitung*, 30.1.1987.

31 Streim, Zentralle Stelle Ludwigsburg, to R. F. Greenwood, Special Investigations Unit, Sydney, Australia, 19.5.1988, B162/20564, 206–208, BA-AL.

32 GDR government (Dr. Joseph) to the Justice Minister, Syrian Arab Republic, 12.4.1990, B162/4054, 155–157, BA-AL; Interview with Serge Klarsfeld, 6.8.2018; FRG Embassy in Damascus to the Foreign Ministry, Bonn, 13.7.1990, Internal memo, foreign ministry, Bonn, 22.2.1991, "Überleitung von Abkommen zwischen Syrien und der ehemaligen DDR," Kroneck, FRG ambassador in Damascus to the State Secretary, 17.1.1991, B83, Nr. 2439, PA-AA.

33 Interview with Serge Klarsfeld, 3.8.2018; Hedi Aouidj's interview with Abu Ra'ad and Abu Yaman, 15.10.2016, Hedi Aouidj's Private Archive.

34 FRG Embassy in Damascus to the Foreign Ministry, Bonn, 13.7.1990, 16.5.1991, B83, Nr. 2439, PA-AA. This report is based on information from the Austrians and several embassies, and it referred to 1988, in the context of President Waldheim's visit to Syria and repeated Austrian extradition requests.

35 Susanna Wallsten's and Eric Ericson's interview with Abdul Rahman Hanada (recorded), 20.5.2020, author's private archive, courtesy of Susanna Wallsten.

36 Ibid; Abu Ra'ad's testimony as quoted in Hedi Aouidj, Mathieu Palain, "Le Nazi de Damas," *Revue XXI*, vol. 37, Winter 2017; Christian Springer, research report from Damascus, 2–5.2001, Interview with Mohammed Hidscho, 2001, Brunner name file, Christian Springer personal collection; Susanna Wallsten's and Eric Ericson's interview with Abdul Rahman Hanada (recorded), 20.5.2020, author's private archive, courtesy of Susanna Wallsten.

EPILOGUE

1 Translation by Jacob Sloan, *Commentary Magazine*, February 1950.

2 Cited in Bülow, "Myth or Reality," 797.

3 Bülow, "Myth or Reality," 810–811.

4 Bergman, *Rise and Kill First*, 72.

5 Saad el-Shazly, *The Crossing of the Suez* (San Francisco: American Mideast Research, 1980), 78–79.

INDEX